INTRODUCING
ECONOMETRICS

INTRODUCING
ECONOMETRICS

William S. Brown
University of Puget Sound

West Publishing Company

St. Paul ■ New York ■ Los Angeles ■ San Francisco

Composition: Polyglot International
Copyediting and Proofreading: Lorretta Palagi
Problem Checking: Roxy Peck
Interior Design: Katharine Townes
Text Artwork: Scientific Illustrators
Cover Artwork: David Bishop
Cover Design: Kristen M. Weber

---

10 00223510

Library of Congress Cataloguing-In-Publication Data

Brown, William S. (William Stanley), 1950-
        Introducing econometrics/William S. Brown.
          p.   cm.
        Includes bibliographical references and index.
         ISBN 0-314-77062-3
        1. Econometrics.   I. Title
      HB139.B77   1991
      330'.01'5195—dc20   90-44217
                                                              CIP

For Madre

CONTENTS

■ **APPENDIX V**

STATISTICAL TABLES   409

■ **APPENDIX VI**

BIBLIOGRAPHY   417

There is no paucity of econometrics texts on the market today, and many of those texts are quite good. All take the student through simple then multiple regression, then detail the problems encountered in the real world—autocorrelated errors, multicollinearity, etc. Students can learn econometrics from these books, but too often it is quite a chore. This is unfortunate. Given the increased use of quantitative information by business and the recent development of user-friendly and powerful microcomputer software, enrollment in econometrics courses should be growing much faster than it is.

Introducing Econometrics was written with the student in mind. All ideas are illustrated using real examples with real data. Where proofs are necessary to illustrate important points, they are included—in their entirety and without skipping steps. Most often, though, proofs are relegated to chapter appendices, and intuitive arguments are given in the chapter. *Introducing Econometrics* is also modern. The standard topics are covered, of course, but so are more contemporary topics such as Hendry's concept of data generating processes, the logit model and ARIMA estimation. A unique aspect of *Introducing Econometrics* is that these ideas—as well as the rest of the book—are presented at a level appropriate for typical undergraduates. Calculus is used only in appendices and matrix algebra shows up in only one footnote.

Most of the examples in *Introducing Econometrics* were done with *Fastat*™ from Systat, Inc., an extremely friendly statistics program for the Apple Macintosh. The printouts were edited to make them appear "generic," but none of the data were cooked to make the examples work out. The problem checker, Roxy Peck, checked all of the results in Minitab™ and found them to be identical up to at least three decimal places. Occasionally the fourth decimal place was off. All of the data sets are included in Appendix 1.

The original intent was to include both MS-DOS and Macintosh software with the student workbook, but programming delays and distribution problems made this impossible. Most schools have site licenses to one or more statistics packages, so all students working through *Introducing Econometrics* should have statistics software available to them on campus. Students with their own computers who want to legally acquire sophisticated statistics software should consider *Business Mystat*. This program is available for both Macintosh and MS-DOS computers and can be obtained for just $5.00. Call Systat, Inc. at 1-708-864-5670. At this writing, *Business Mystat* does not have 2SLS (Chapter 8), ARIMA (Chapter 9), or logit (Chapter 10) capabilities but these capabilities should have been added by the time you read this.

Writing a textbook is not as hard as it is time consuming, and I found that writing an econometrics text was made even easier by the simple fact that all of my colleagues know some econometrics and were willing, if not always anxious, to provide examples and other help. Doug Goodman, my coauthor on the workbook, read the entire manuscript and offered help at most stages of the project. Two years of conversations with Wade Hands convinced me that a chapter on econometric methodology was necessary even in an undergraduate text. Bruce Mann persuaded me that a separate chapter on the logit model was a good idea and Kate Stirling helped me with the example on spousal maintenance. Two colleagues in the Politics and Government department at the University of Puget Sound, Bill Haltom and David Sousa, provided data sets and references from political science literature. The manuscript was class tested for two years, and I apologize to my students who had to put up with the innumerable typos and, occasionally, errors. One student, Dave Matsumoto, now in the Ph.D. program at the University of Colorado, found more mistakes than I would have. Dave is now studying with Bob McKnown, my thesis advisor and the person who, along with Malcolm Dowling, introduced me to econometrics. Bob and Malcolm showed me that econometrics did not have to be hard, that it could be interesting, and that it was vitally important to the profession. I hope this book reflects their teaching.

My editor at West, Bob Horan, was able to find a great group of reviewers to take apart the manuscript piece by piece. I learned from all of their reviews, and incorporated as many of their ideas as possible. The reviewers were:

Joseph Earley
Loyola Marymount University

Subhash Ray
University of Connecticut

Marcel Fulop
Kean College

Bradford Tuck
University of Alaska

Robert Gentenaar
Hope College

Michael White
St. Cloud State University

Edward Heinze
Valparaiso University

Sam Yoo
Penn State University

Jack Osman
San Francisco State University

Finally, books should be dedicated. This book, like my last, is dedicated to my Madre who encouraged all of her children to read and has been rewarded, at last count, with nine books written by the three of us. I suspect that this will be the only one she doesn't read.

INTRODUCTION

Students often ask: "But just what do economists *do*?" The understanding of marginalism and macroeconomic debates may help on exams, but does it apply in the real world? Yes. Marginalism provides an invaluable framework for thinking—not just about economics, but about *everyday* events in life. The study of theoretical debates is important not only in itself, but because it should help economists anticipate policy changes that result from new research— information useful to the business executive as well as consumers and voters. Still, classroom economics is used by "real" economists primarily as the basis for empirical models. The economic theory you have learned in the classroom so far gives largely *qualitative* answers: whether revenue will rise or fall if the price is reduced, whether profits will rise or fall if output is expanded, and so on. These are important results, but managers and other decision-makers also need *quantitative* answers. They need to know how far revenue will rise and how far profits will fall. They need forecasts of interest rates, inflation, and other variables to put into their decision-making calculations.

Econometrics provides the tools to find quantitative answers.
It is an indispensable part of the modern economist's tool kit.

1.1

WHAT IS ECONOMETRICS?

Econometrics is a set of statistical techniques used in the analysis of empirical data. In contrast, mathematical economics deals primarily with abstract representations in economic theory. The two fields are obviously closely related—econometric models require an initial mathematical specification—but the central emphasis of the two fields can differ considerably.

Many seventeenth and eighteenth century economists were trained as engineers and began studying economics as a hobby. Their efforts to apply calculus and other mathematical methods to economic questions led to the marginalist revolution of the 1870s. One of the early marginalists, William Stanley Jevons, may have best captured the spirit of these early mathematical economists when he said that because economics deals with quantities, it must be mathematical and that it "presented a close analogy to statical mechanics."[1] The mathematization of economics took a firm hold in the classroom with the publication in 1947 of Paul Samuelson's *Foundations of Economic Analysis.*[2]

Attempts to measure economic variables date back to William Petty's endeavor to develop *Political Arithmetic* (1676) and Francois Quesnay's *Tableau Economique* (1758), but little systematic progress in what is today called econometrics appeared until the late 1950s, and the first popular econometrics textbooks[3] did not appear until the early 1960s. The reason the development of econometrics took so much longer than mathematical economics was the lack of computing power. Even the simplest econometric analysis can require hundreds of calculations, something few people enjoy doing by hand. Until electronic computers became available—even the U.S. Commerce Department did not have an electronic computer until the 1950s—data analysis could not keep up with the advancement of economic theory. Once the computer revolution began, it proceeded rapidly and carried econometrics with it. By the 1960s, all major universities had computers, and

---

[1] William Stanley Jevons, *The Theory of Political Economy*, 5th ed. (New York: A. M. Kelley, 1965), p. vii.
[2] Paul Samuelson, *Foundations of Economic Analysis* (Cambridge, Mass: Harvard University Press, 1947).
[3] The two most successful, early econometrics texts were J. Johnston, *Econometric Methods* (New York: McGraw-Hill, 1963) and Arthur Goldberger, *Econometric Theory* (New York: John Wiley and Sons, 1964). The Johnston text, now in its third edition, remains one of the most popular graduate-level econometrics texts.

research economists began trying to quantify economic theory. Today, all economics graduate programs require course work in econometrics, and many undergraduate students in economics, business, and finance take econometrics as well.

1.1.1   The Role of Econometrics Today

Much of the early development of econometrics was accomplished by academic economists, but business economists saw the potential benefits of the new quantitative analysis and adopted econometric methods almost immediately. Most financial institutions and corporations now employ econometricians to develop forecasting and simulation models. The hope, of course, is that better knowledge of the present and accurate forecasts of the future can be used to gain a competitive advantage. Until recently, however, only large corporations had sufficient resources to establish econometrics divisions, so much of the econometric analysis was done by consulting firms that sold forecasting "subscriptions." One of the most popular econometric consulting firms, Data Resources Inc. (DRI), quickly made its founder, the late Harvard economist Otto Eckstein, a millionaire.

By the early 1980s, the status of econometrics and econometricians had begun to change for two reasons. First, the forecasting record of the 1970s had been, to put it politely, less than successful, and when the severe 1981–82 recession hit, corporations cut back on their econometrics divisions. A second event was more important, at least over the long term. By the mid-1980s, microcomputers had become powerful and "user-friendly" enough to allow nonspecialists to handle much of the work formerly done by econometricians. Today, most management-level professionals are computer-literate, and many econometrics software packages are friendly enough for nonspecialists to perform their own econometric studies — if they have had a semester or two of econometrics.

1.1.2   How to Study Econometrics

If you glance through the book, you will notice that it looks pretty intense. The equations and formulae are too numerous to memorize, and memorization would be the wrong way to learn econometrics anyway. To *learn* econometrics well enough to use it — to develop your own econometric studies and interpret studies done by others — you will need to *understand* econometrics; and you cannot stop there. As with all sciences, econometrics is constantly evolving, which means that you will be hopelessly out of date only a year or two after you finish this course unless you acquire enough tools to continue learning on your own. This means working through the language of econometrics — the mathematics and statistics — carefully enough to become econometrics-literate.

Few students who work through their first course in econometrics think it is easy. It is not; but neither is it as difficult as it appears. Unlike many economics courses, econometrics is pretty straightforward. For instance, at the introductory level, there are few of the theoretical debates such as those you find in macroeconomics. However, the subject matter of econometrics is very additive and technical. Thus, if you put off your studies for very long, you may find that you are too far behind to understand the new material. A good study technique is to write down *all* of the equations and formulae you encounter in your reading. If a step is unclear, you will often find an elaboration in the chapter appendix. Be sure to work the chapter exercises. Not only will this help cement the ideas in your mind, but some exercises illustrate important ideas not covered in the chapter. Finally, be prepared to go over the material several times before you retain it.

1.2

REGRESSION ANALYSIS

Econometricians use a variety of statistical techniques, but the main tool is *regression analysis*. The basic objective of regression analysis is to test hypotheses regarding the statistical relationship between two or more sets of data. While regression analysis cannot be used to prove that a causal relationship exists between the data, regression models are always constructed with the idea of causality in mind. That is, we must assume that one variable is affected ("caused") by the other variable(s). The causal variable(s) are called *independent variables* or *regressors;* the variable affected by the independent variable(s) is called the *dependent variable* or *regressand*.

1.2.1   Linear Functions

Throughout most of this book, the relationship between the variables under study is assumed to be linear. The plot of a linear relationship is a straight line. The general form of a linear equation is given in Eq. [1.1]:

$$Y = b_0 + b_1 X, \qquad\qquad [1.1]$$

where

Y = dependent variable
X = independent variable
b_0 = vertical or Y intercept
b_1 = slope, $\Delta Y / \Delta X$.

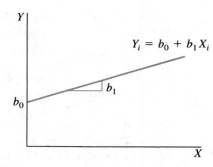

FIGURE 1.1   The linear equation.

A linear function can be completely described by two parameters, its slope (b_1) and intercept (b_0). The slope tells how much Y changes in response to a one unit change in X; the intercept gives the value of Y when $X = 0$.

Equation [1.1] is called a function because the dependent variable, Y, is "caused"[4] by the independent variable, X. The intercept of the function, b_0, gives the value of Y when $X = 0$. The slope of the function, b_1, gives the ratio of a change in Y to a change in X, denoted as $\Delta Y / \Delta X$. Linear functions can have a positive, negative or zero intercept, but they must have a constant slope. A graph of Eq. [1.1] is shown in Fig. 1.1.

The slope and intercept are the *parameters* that we attempt to estimate with regression analysis. If X and Y are linearly related, knowledge of these two parameters is sufficient to completely describe their relationship.

1.2.2   Population and Sample Regression Functions

Equation [1.1] is a mathematical function, but it is not a regression function. This is because Eq. [1.1] is *deterministic* as opposed to *probabilistic.* The distinction is important. Real-world relationships are never as precise as the graph of Eq. [1.1]. Measurement errors, omitted variables, and other factors[5] complicate the relationship between X and Y. For example, a simple theory in macroeconomics is the Keynesian consumption function. According to this

---

[4] We have enclosed the term "caused" in quotes because the issue of causality is quite complicated, especially in statistics and econometrics. We discuss causality further in this and the next three chapters, but a detailed discussion is deferred until Chapter 11.
[5] The most important of these "other factors" is probably the nonsystematic (random) component of Y that is not related to X.

theory, as family income increases, so does consumption, but by a smaller amount. However, no one would assume that an increase in income results in precisely the same increase in consumption for every family—some families would use all of their new income on additional consumption, while some would spend only a small amount of it. Still, the basic idea of the theory is correct: A study of the entire population would undoubtedly conclude that consumption does increase in response to higher income, but the increase is not exactly the same for every family. Such relationships are the norm in econometrics and explain why regression equations always contain an *error* or *disturbance term*:

$$Y_i = \beta_0 + \beta_1 X_i + \varepsilon_i, \qquad\qquad [1.2]$$

where

Y_i = dependent variable
X_i = independent variable
β_0 = true intercept
β_1 = true slope
ε_i = random error term.

If Eq. [1.2] were estimated with the benefit of the entire data set—the income and consumption for all families—it would be called a *population regression function*. The main task of regression analysis is the estimation of population regression functions. Unfortunately, econometricians are rarely able to work with the entire data set. Most often they have only a small *sample* of the data. If that sample is drawn by chance, that is, if it is a *random* sample, there are conditions when we can be confident that the estimated *sample regression function* is a good approximation of the population regression function.

We should note that the parameter estimates derived from any particular sample will differ from the population—and from other random samples. A sample is random if any particular observation has an equal chance of being selected and if each observation is drawn independently of every other observation. However, in any particular sample, for example, several high income families may be drawn and only a few low income families—even if the sample is random. Another sample might draw several low income families and only a few high income families. The hope, of course, is that the sample will be large enough to reduce the chance of either outcome, but econometricians always construct statistical confidence regions around their parameter estimates in recognition of the random nature of the data.

In econometrics, population parameters are traditionally denoted by Greek letters (β_0, β_1, and ε_i), and the equivalent roman letters (*b* and *e*) or "hats" over the Greek letters are used to indicate estimated values. Thus, the notation we will use for the sample regression function will be:

$$Y_i = \hat{\beta}_0 + \hat{\beta}_1 X_i + e_i, \qquad\qquad [1.3]$$

where

$\hat{\beta}_0$ = estimate of β_0

$\hat{\beta}_1$ = estimate of β_1

e_i = *regression residuals*, interpreted as the estimated ε_i.

We should discuss two more bits of notation before proceeding. A main task of regression analysis is to find a line consistent with theory that best "fits" the data. Points on this line are usually designated as $\hat{Y}_i$ and are found with the equation:

$$\hat{Y}_i = \hat{\beta}_0 + \hat{\beta}_1 X_i. \tag{1.4}$$

Note that the equation of the fitted line has no error term—just like the mathematical function in Eq. [1.1]. Substracting Eq. [1.4] from [1.3] reveals that

$$Y_i - \hat{Y}_i = e_i; \tag{1.5}$$

that is, the difference between the actual data points and points on the fitted line is the regression residual.

■ EXAMPLE 1.1

A TEST OF THE ACCELERATOR THEORY

As an introduction to regression analysis, consider a test of the accelerator theory of investment. The accelerator theory dates back at least as far as the 1910s when J. M. Clark noted that investment in the railroad industry— boxcar production—seemed to follow increases in railroad traffic.[6] In general terms, the implication is that investment depended on the increase in sales. Clark's original insight was based on knowledge of the railroad industry and what would today be considered rather naive statistical studies. In the 70 years since Clark formulated his ideas, the theory has been expanded to the macroeconomy. The macroeconomic accelerator holds that business fixed investment (BFI) is a positive function of the change in real GNP (DRGNP) or:

$$BFI = f(DRGNP), f' > 0. \tag{1.6}$$

The notation in Eq. [1.6] is standard and will be used throughout the book. It is read simply as "BFI is a function of DRGNP." The term $f' > 0$ indicates that there is a direct or positive relationship between the

---

[6]J. M. Clark, "Business Acceleration and the Law of Demand," *Journal of Political Economy*, March 1917, p. 217–235. An earlier discussion was in A. Aftalion, "Les Trois Notions de la Producitite et Revenus," *Revue d'Economie Politique*, 1911.

TABLE 1.1   **Real BFI and the change in real
GNP (DRGNP), 1970–87**

Year	BFI(Y)	DRGNP(X)
1970	373.3	−7.1
1971	399.7	68.6
1972	443.7	123.7
1973	480.8	135.6
1974	448.0	−14.8
1975	396.1	−34.3
1976	431.4	131.7
1977	492.2	131.9
1978	540.2	156.6
1979	560.2	77.2
1980	516.2	−5.3
1981	521.7	61.7
1982	471.8	−82.8
1983	510.4	113.1
1984	596.1	222.3
1985	628.7	106.1
1986	640.2	105.8
1987	643.0	106.3

SOURCE: *1987 Economic Report of
the President*, Table B-2. Data are
billions of 1982 dollars.

independent and dependent variables; as DRGNP increases, so does BFI. If
BFI were to decrease as DRGNP increased, the notation would be $f' < 0$.

Equation [1.6] makes a certain amount of sense—increasing sales
should serve as an incentive for increased investment, but whether or not
this is true cannot be determined without careful analysis of actual data—
and modern economists would want much more rigorous verification than
the anecdotal evidence used by Clark. This is where regression analysis and
econometrics enter.

To test the accelerator theory with regression analysis, first some data
must be collected. Annual data on real business fixed investment and real
GNP (RGNP) are available in several places including the *Economic Report
of the President*; quarterly data could be found in the *Survey of Current
Business, The Federal Reserve Bulletin*, and elsewhere. Because the
accelerator theory holds that the *change* in RGNP affects BFI, the RGNP
data have been *differenced* before being entered in the table or plotted on
Fig. 1.2. Differencing the data is simply subtracting consecutive years from
each other; i.e., $DRGNP_t = RGNP_t − RGNP_{t-1}$. Annual data covering the
years 1970–87 are presented in Table 1.1 and plotted in Fig. 1.2.

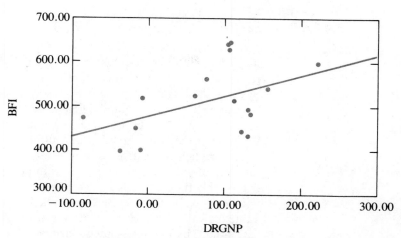

Regression Equation: BFI $= 466.04 + 0.505$DRGNP; $R^2 = 0.219$.

FIGURE 1.2   The scatter diagram.

The regression line is the straight line that fits the scatter diagram best. In this case, the intercept of the regression line, $\hat{\beta}_0$, is equal to 466.04. The slope, $\hat{\beta}_1 = 0.505$, indicates that a one unit increase in DRGNP will result in a 0.505 unit increase in BFI.

Careful inspection of the data set will allow us to determine if there is a relationship between DRGNP and BFI, but a quick glance at a plot of the data—the *scattergram*–shows the relationship between the two series to be direct; that is, as DRGNP increases, so does BFI. This is consistent with our hypothesis, but not really proof that our hypothesis is correct because a direct relationship between BFI and DRGNP could be the result of a different underlying model or merely random events. To determine whether our initial hypothesis is justified requires more detailed analysis.

How do we actually perform the regression analysis? For a small data set, the calculations may be done by hand, but they are most easily done on a computer. At the bottom of Fig. 1.2 is the regression equation—the equation of the line that best "fits" the scattergram. The estimated slope of the regression equation, $\hat{\beta}_1 = 0.505$, indicates that a one unit change in DRGNP will result in a 0.505 unit change in BFI. Because both variables are measured in billions, this means that a one billion dollar change in DRGNP will result in a \$505 million increase in BFI. Interpretation would be different had the units of measurement differed. For example, if DRGNP were measured in billions and BFI were measured in millions, a coefficient of 0.505 would mean that a one billion dollar increase in DRGNP would result in an increase in BFI of \$505,000.

The estimated intercept, $\hat{\beta}_0$, is 466.04. Assigning meaning to the intercept of regression equations is often difficult and this is no exception.

Mathematically, an intercept of 466.04 seems to imply BFI will equal 466.04 even if DRGNP is zero; however, most econometricians would reject such an interpretation. The interpretation of the intercept is discussed in more detail in later chapters, but for the time being, it is perhaps best regarded as the combined effect of omitted independent variables.

Once the regression parameters have been estimated, we must then determine how well the model fits the data. Intuitively, a good fitting model will have a tight cluster of the data points around the regression line, but the scale of the graph makes it difficult to determine whether the data points are tightly clustered or not. A much better gauge is a statistical measure of goodness of fit. The most important measure of goodness of fit is probably the *coefficient of determination*, or R^2 as it is usually called. As will be shown in Chapter 3, R^2 must lie between 0 and 1, with a higher value indicating that more of the variation of the dependent variable can be "explained" by the independent variable. For our simple test, the coefficient of determination was only 0.219—an indication that barely 22% of the variation in BFI can be "explained" by DRGNP, implying that the model could stand some improvement. We may have suspected this considering economic theory holds that interest rates, tax policy, business expectations, and other factors also affect the investment decision. To capture the effects of these variables on BFI requires multiple regression analysis, which is introduced in Chapter 4.

1.2.4 The Least-Squares Line

How do we actually find $\hat{\beta}_0$ and $\hat{\beta}_1$? With a small data set, we can find them quite simply with only the aid of a hand calculator, but as the data set increases in size, a computer becomes mandatory. Still, whether using a computer or not, a sense of the process involved in determining $\hat{\beta}_0$ and $\hat{\beta}_1$ helps to understand the philosophy and technique behind regression analysis. To find the best fitting line, $\hat{Y}_i$, we need to minimize the distance between the actual data points and those on the fitted line; that is, we need to minimize the sum of the regression residuals.

However, an infinite number of lines exist that will minimize the sum of the regression residuals,[7] so this criteria is of little help in the selection of $\hat{\beta}_0$ and $\hat{\beta}_1$. The solution is to minimize the sum of the squares of the residuals; i.e., to minimize $\sum e_i^2$. (Appendix 1.A reviews operations with summation signs.) This will result in a unique regression line that will be the line closest to the actual data points. This procedure explains why regression analysis is often called *least-squares analysis* (see Fig. 1.3).

---

[7] Exercises 5 illustrates this point.

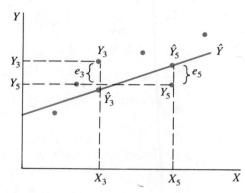

FIGURE 1.3   The least-squares line.

The least-squares line is found by minimizing the sum of the squared residuals, i.e., min Σe_i^2. Each e_i is the difference between the actual data point, Y_i, and the corresponding point on the fitted line, $\hat{Y}_i$. Note that $\Sigma e_i = 0$ since positive $e_i(e_3)$ will cancel out negative $e_i(e_5)$.

Since $e_i = Y_i - \hat{Y}_i$, minimizing the sum of the squared residuals is equivalent to minimizing $\sum(Y_i - \hat{Y}_i)^2$. The actual minimization process involves calculus and is worked in Appendix 1.B. It turns out that the formulae for $\hat{\beta}_0$ and $\hat{\beta}_1$ are:

$$\hat{\beta}_0 = \left(\frac{\sum_{i=1}^{n} Y_i}{n}\right) - \hat{\beta}_1\left(\frac{\sum_{i=1}^{n} X_i}{n}\right),$$ [1.7]

$$\hat{\beta}_1 = \frac{n\sum_{i=1}^{n} X_i Y_i - \sum_{i=1}^{n} X_i \sum_{i=1}^{n} Y_i}{n\sum_{i=1}^{n} X_i^2 - \left(\sum_{i=1}^{n} X_i\right)^2}.$$ [1.8]

These formulae are not nearly as complex as they look. The first term in parentheses on the right side of Eq. [1.7] indicates that we need to sum all of the Y values ($\sum Y$) and then divide by n, the number of observations on Y. This is simply the average or *mean* of Y. The second term in parentheses is the mean of X. It too is found by adding together all of the X values ($\sum X$) and dividing by n. Letting $\bar{Y}$ stand for the mean of Y and $\bar{X}$ represent the mean of X, Eq. [1.7] can be written as:

$$\hat{\beta}_0 = \bar{Y} - \hat{\beta}_1\bar{X},$$ [1.9]

which is a little less intimidating.

The formula for $\hat{\beta}_1$ can be simplified by introducing one more bit of notation. Standard notation in econometric literature uses upper case letters to denote the actual data points and lower case letters to indicate their *deviations from the mean.* In general notation, the deviations of Y and X are:

$$y_i = Y_i - \bar{Y},$$

$$x_i = X_i - \bar{X}. \tag{1.10}$$

As an example, the mean of the BFI ($= \bar{Y}$) data in Table 1.1 is about 505.21. The first observation, Y_1, is 373.3. Given that $\bar{Y} = 505.21$, the deviation of the first observation, y_1, is equal to $373.3 - 505.21 = -131.91$. Because the mean of the DRGNP ($= \bar{X}$) series is 77.57, and $X_1 = -7.1$, $x_1 = -7.1 - 77.57 = -84.67$.

Equation [1.8] looks much less intimidating when written in deviation form:

$$\hat{\beta}_1 = \frac{\sum_{i=1}^{n} x_i y_i}{\sum_{i=1}^{n} x_i^2}. \tag{1.11}$$

As shown in Appendix 1.B some substitution and a bit of algebra were all that was necessary to convert Eq. [1.8] into Eq. [1.11].

Before we go on, we need to point out a result that will be important later: When the data are converted into deviation form, the slope of the regression equation does not change, but the intercept becomes zero. This can be shown quite easily. Because $y_i = Y_i - \bar{Y}$ and $x_i = X_i - \bar{X}$, we can substitute $y_i + \bar{Y}$ for Y_i and $x_i + \bar{X}$ for X_i into the regression equation:

$$y_i + \bar{Y} = \hat{\beta}_0 + \hat{\beta}_1(x_1 + \bar{X}) + e_i. \tag{1.12}$$

Now, use Eq. [1.9] to substitute for $\hat{\beta}_0$:

$$y_i + \bar{Y} = (\bar{Y} - \hat{\beta}_1 X_i) + \hat{\beta}_1(x_i + \bar{X}) + e_i. \tag{1.13}$$

The $\bar{Y}$'s vanish, and after distributing the $\hat{\beta}_1$, we have:

$$y_i = -\hat{\beta}_1 X_i + \hat{\beta}_1 x_i + \hat{\beta}_1 X_i + e_i = \hat{\beta}_1 x_i + e_i; \tag{1.14}$$

that is, the regression equation in deviation form is simply $y_i = \hat{\beta}_1 x_i + e_i$. Because the intercept rarely has economic content, and Eq. [1.11] is so much easier to work with than Eq. [1.8], we will usually work in deviation form. Figure 1.4 illustrates both regression equations.

The procedure to calculate $\hat{\beta}_0$ and $\hat{\beta}_1$ using Eqs. [1.9] and [1.11] and the information in Tables 1.1 and 1.2 is simple. The slope of the regression line, $\hat{\beta}_1$, is found by taking the ratio of $\sum x_i y_i$ to $\sum x_i^2$. The use of sums from the bottom of Table 1.2 gives $\hat{\beta}_1 = 52211.724/103403.018 = 0.505$, as expected. For $\hat{\beta}_0$, the calculations are $\hat{\beta}_0 = 505.21 - (0.505)(77.57) = 466.04$. We will not calculate the other important piece of information shown in Fig. 1.2, the coefficient of determination, R^2, until later.

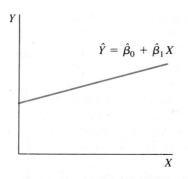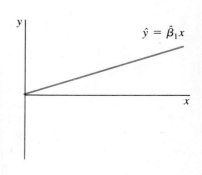

FIGURE 1.4   Deviation form versus intercept form.

When converted into deviation form, the regression line passes through the origin. The slope does not change.

T A B L E 1.2   **Regression Calculations**

BFI(Y)	DRGNP(X)	y	x	x^2	xy
373.3	-7.1	-131.91	-84.67	7169.009	11168.820
399.7	68.6	-105.51	-8.97	80.461	946.425
443.7	123.7	-61.51	46.13	2127.977	-2837.456
480.8	135.6	-24.41	58.03	3367.481	-1416.512
448.0	-14.8	-57.21	-92.37	8532.217	5284.488
396.1	-34.3	-109.11	-111.87	12514.897	12206.136
431.4	131.7	-73.81	54.13	2930.057	-3995.335
492.2	131.9	-13.01	54.33	2951.749	-706.833
540.2	156.6	34.99	79.03	6245.741	2765.260
560.2	77.2	54.99	-0.37	0.137	-20.346
516.2	-5.3	10.99	-82.87	6867.437	-910.741
521.7	61.7	16.49	-15.87	251.857	-261.696
471.8	-82.8	-33.41	-160.37	25718.537	5357.962
510.4	113.1	5.19	35.53	1262.381	184.401
596.1	222.3	90.89	144.73	20946.773	13154.510
628.7	106.1	123.49	28.53	813.961	3523.170
640.2	105.8	134.99	28.23	796.933	3810.768
643.0	106.3	137.79	28.73	825.413	3958.707

Summary Statistics: $\bar{X} = 77.57$, $\bar{Y} = 505.21$, $\sum x_i^2 = 103403.018$,
$$\sum x_i y_i = 52211.724$$

1.1.4 Using the Regression Equation

Once we have found $\hat{\beta}_0$ and $\hat{\beta}_1$, what do we do with them? As noted earlier, there is rarely very much economic significance attached to $\hat{\beta}_0$, the estimated intercept. At most it is a *locus* parameter that tells us where the regression line is located. The estimated slope parameter, $\hat{\beta}_1$, however, is often the most important piece of information we need. It gives a measure of the dependence of Y on X. This is important information in several contexts. In forecasting, for example, if you suspect that DRGNP will increase 200 next year, your forecast would be for BFI to increase about $101 = 0.505(200)$. Of course, any error made in the estimation of X would affect the forecast.

Don't get carried away just yet. Few econometricians would stop here because there are several reasons not to trust the equation we have just estimated. For example, to illustrate the computations, we restricted our data to only 18 observations. This means that we have ignored quite a bit of data—data that could change the parameter estimates considerably. Also, a more reasonable model would have to include several other independent variables, and would very likely be nonlinear, not linear as we have supposed. Finally, most economists would suggest that the accelerator theory of investment, even one developed with multiple regression, is really only one of a much larger macroeconomic equation system. As we will discover in Chapter 8, when we try to estimate single equations that are really part of a larger simultaneous equation system, we run into potentially serious problems.   ◆ ◆ ◆

LOOKING AHEAD

This chapter was intended to provide you with an idea of the kind of issues of concern to econometricians and to illustrate the basic approach to econometric modeling. We have purposely left out many of the details that will be covered in subsequent chapters. The remainder of Part I, Chapters 2, 3, 4, and 5, reviews important statistical concepts, looks at both simple and multiple regression models in more detail, and discusses methods for specifying regression models. Part II, Chapters 6, 7, and 8, explores the problems encountered when the data are not as well behaved as we would like them to be, and suggests solutions to these problems. Part III, Chapters 9, 10, and 11 covers additional topics—simultaneous equations, time series analysis, qualitative dependent variables, and econometric methodology.

CONCEPTS FOR REVIEW

This chapter is meant to be a brief introduction to the kind of problems dealt with by econometricians. Don't worry if it went by a bit too quickly, because everything will be covered in more detail in later chapters. However, now is the right time to make sure you:

- know why regression analysis is sometimes called least-squares analysis;
- can work with summation signs as covered in Appendix 1.A:
- know the difference between x_i, X_i, and $\bar{X}$, and between y_i, Y_i, and $\bar{Y}$;
- can define and use the following terms in context.

KEY TERMS

causality
dependent variable
deviation form
econometrics
endogenous variable
error term
exogenous variable
independent variable
intercept
least-squares analysis
mathematical economics
mean
multiple regression

parameter
population regression function
R^2, coefficient of determination
regressand
regression analysis
regression residual
regressor
sample regression function
simple regression
slope

EXERCISES

1.1   The following data are percentage changes in $M2$ and the GNP deflator (P):

Year	M2	P	Year	M2	P
1975	12.6	9.8	1981	9.9	9.7
1976	13.7	6.4	1982	8.8	6.4
1977	10.6	6.7	1983	11.8	3.9
1978	8.0	7.3	1984	8.4	3.7
1979	8.0	8.9	1985	8.5	3.2
1980	8.9	9.0			

    a. Using the 1975–84 data, estimate the regression line. Let P be the dependent variable and $M2$ the independent variable.

    b. Use your results to forecast the inflation rate for 1985. Are you satisfied with your forecast?

    c. Plot the data points and sketch in the regression line. Does the plot indicate a good fit?

1.2   Under what conditions is the following true?:

$$\hat{\beta}_1 = \frac{\sum x_i y_i}{\sum x_i^2} = \frac{\sum X_i Y_i}{\sum X_i^2}.$$

1.3   Many students contend that econometrics and mathematical economics are more difficult than "literary economics." Many, perhaps most, economists would disagree. Why?

1.4   An economics major collected the following data while watching the sunset in his backyard:

Temperature:	73	86	77	81	92	88
Cricket chirps per hour:	21	33	32	33	41	35

How could regression analysis be used to determine if cricket chirping is a response to the heat, or if cricket chirping—caused by the friction of the cricket rubbing its legs together—raises the backyard temperature?

1.5   In Sec. 1.2.3, we noted that minimization of $\sum e_i$ instead of $\sum e_i^2$ will result in several regression lines, not the unique one we desire. Prove this statement. (*Hint:* This does *not* require calculus.)

1.6   The BFI/DRGNP study was conducted again but the last two observations were omitted. The revised regression equation was:

$$\text{BFI} = 456.48 + 0.428\text{DRGNP}, R^2 = 0.237$$

Are these results better than the first results? Why or why not? Do you consider the differences significant?

1.7   An interesting rule of thumb in macroeconomics is Okun's Law, a relationship between the quarterly unemployment rate (U) and the unemployment gap (GAP), defined as the difference between rate of potential real GNP growth and the actual rate of real GNP growth. In "Potential GNP: Its Measurement and Significance," from *The Political Economy of Prosperity* (Washington, D.C.: Brookings Institute, 1970), Okun estimated the following equation for the 1953–60 period. The average rate of growth of real potential GNP is estimated at about 3.5%:

$$U = 3.72 + 0.36\text{GAP}, R^2 = 0.87.$$

a. Interpret these results.

b. Suppose that actual real GNP growth fell to 2.0%. What would happen to the unemployment rate?

c. Suppose that actual real GNP growth accelerated to 8.0%. What does Okun's Law say will happen to the unemployment rate? Do you think this is reasonable? Why or why not?

APPENDIX 1.A

PROPERTIES OF THE SUMMATION OPERATOR

We will be dealing with sums and summation signs frequently throughout the text, so a review of the properties of sums is in order.

Notations and Definitions

Given the data set $X = \{X_1, X_2, X_3, \ldots, X_n\}$, the sum of X is indicated with the capital Greek letter sigma, $\sum$:

$$\sum_{i=1}^{n} X_i = X_1 + X_2 + X_3 + \cdots + X_n. \qquad \text{[A.1]}$$

The subscripts are called *indices* and indicate specific observations on the data. As written, this expression indicates to add together all of the n pieces of data. For convenience, indices on the summation sign are frequently omitted when the intent is to sum all of the observations. We will follow that convention in later chapters to eliminate some of the clutter. Alternatively, some authors simply place an i beneath the summation sign to indicate that the entire series is to be summed. Thus, the following notations are equivalent:

$$\sum_{i=1}^{n} X_i = \sum_{i} X_i = \sum X_i. \qquad \text{[A.2]}$$

The sum does not have to include all of the observations. In fact, we will occasionally begin the sum with the second observation in the series; i.e.,

$$\sum_{i=2}^{n} X_i = X_2 + X_3 + \cdots + X_n. \qquad \text{[A.3]}$$

For a specific example, suppose that there are only five observations on $X = \{2, 4, 5, 6, 7\}$. Then the "sum over all X" or simply $\sum X_i$ would be:

$$\sum_{i=1}^{n} X_i = 2 + 4 + 5 + 6 + 7 = 24.$$

Properties of Summations

Summations are often used in algebraic operations. Several properties are worth remembering:

PROPERTY 1

If a is a constant and X is a variable, then,

$$\sum_{i=1}^{n} aX_i = aX_1 + aX_2 + \cdots + aX_n \qquad [A.4]$$

$$= a(X_1 + X_2 + \cdots + X_n) = a \sum_{i=1}^{n} X_i;$$

that is, constants can be taken outside the summation sign.

PROPERTY 2

The summation of a constant over n observations is n times the constant:

$$\sum_{i=1}^{n} a = a + a + \cdots + a = na. \qquad [A.5]$$

Properties 1 and 2 make it clear why it is so important to index the variables to be summed, even if the index is left off of the summation sign.

PROPERTY 3

The summation of the sum of two series is the sum of the summations:

$$\sum_{i=1}^{n} (X_i + Y_i) = \sum_{i=1}^{n} X_i + \sum_{i=1}^{n} Y_i. \qquad [A.6]$$

Property 3 can be illustrated with a simple example. Let the series X be defined as above and let Y have the following values: $Y = \{1, 2, 3, 4, 5\}$. Then,

$$\sum (X_i + Y_i) = (2 + 1) + (4 + 2) + (5 + 3) + (6 + 4) + (7 + 5) = 39$$

$$\sum X_i + \sum Y_i = 24 + (1 + 2 + 3 + 4 + 5) = 39.$$

The rules for working with summations are similar to standand algebra, but just different enough to get you into trouble occasionally. Many potential problems crop up when using double summations and sums involving joint distributions, topics we discuss in Chapter 2.

PROPERTY 4

The double summation of a product is the product of two single summations:

$$\sum_{i=1}^{n} \sum_{j=1}^{m} X_i Y_j = \sum_{i=1}^{n} X_i \sum_{j=1}^{m} Y_j. \qquad \text{[A.7]}$$

As an example, suppose that X is defined as $X = \{1, 3, 4\}$ and Y is defined as $Y = \{1, 2\}$. Thus the i index on X goes from $i = 1, 2, 3$, while the j index on Y goes from $j = 1, 2$. The calculations for the double sum are:

$$\sum_{i=1}^{n} \sum_{j=1}^{m} X_i Y_j = 1(1) + 1(2) + 3(1) + 3(2) + 4(1) + 4(2) = 24.$$

The benefit of Property 4 is that it allows us to calculate the same double sum as:

$$\sum_{i=1}^{n} X_i \sum_{j=1}^{m} Y_j = [1 + 3 + 4][1 + 2] = 24$$

Be careful not to extend Property 4 to the single summation of a product or quotient. ◆ ◆ ◆

The summation of a product is *not* equal to the product of two single summations:

$$\sum_{i=1}^{n} X_i Y_i \neq \sum_{i=1}^{n} X_i \sum_{i=1}^{n} Y_i \qquad \text{[A.8]}$$

For example, let X be defined as $\{1, 2, 3\}$ and Y as $\{2, 3, 4\}$. Then,

$$\sum_{i=1}^{n} X_i Y_i = 1(2) + 2(3) + 3(4) = 20$$

However,

$$\sum_{i=1}^{n} X_i \sum_{i=1}^{n} Y_i = (1 + 2 + 3)(2 + 3 + 4) = 54.$$

Neither is the quotient of two sums equal to the sum of a quotient:

$$\frac{\sum_{i=1}^{n} X_i}{\sum_{i=1}^{n} Y_i} \neq \sum_{i=1}^{n} \frac{X_i}{Y_i} \qquad \text{[A.9]}$$

Again defining X as $\{1, 2, 3\}$ and Y as $\{2, 3, 4\}$, we have:

$$\sum_{i=1}^{n} X_i = 1 + 2 + 3 = 6 \qquad \sum_{i=1}^{n} Y_i = 2 + 3 + 4 = 9,$$

$$\frac{\sum_{i=1}^{n} X_i}{\sum_{i=1}^{n} Y_i} = \frac{6}{9} \neq \sum_{i=1}^{n} \frac{X_i}{Y_i} = \frac{1}{2} + \frac{2}{3} + \frac{3}{4} = \frac{23}{12}.$$

A Result: $\sum(X_i - \bar{X}) = 0$

These summation properties can be used to illustrate some important ideas we will use again and again. Recall that $\bar{X}$, the estimated mean of X, is found by adding all of the observations and dividing by n, the number of observations. Thus, we could write:

$$\bar{X} = \frac{1}{n} \sum_{i=1}^{n} X_i.$$ [A.10]

The *deviation* of X is defined as the difference between individual observations and the mean. Econometricians usually denote the deviation with lower case letters and the actual observations with upper case letters:

$$x_i = X_i - \bar{X}.$$ [A.11]

The properties we have just developed can be used to show that $\sum(X_i - \bar{X}) = 0$. First, use Property 3 to distribute the summation sign:

$$\sum_{i=1}^{n} (X_i - \bar{X}) = \sum_{i=1}^{n} X_i - \sum_{i=1}^{n} \bar{X}.$$ [A.12]

Now, because $\bar{X}$ is a constant, we can use Property 2 to eliminate the second summation sign on the right side:

$$\sum_{i=1}^{n} (X_i - \bar{X}) = \sum_{i=1}^{n} X_i - n\bar{X}.$$ [A.13]

The definition of $\bar{X}$ allows us to set the right side equal to zero:

$$\bar{X} = \frac{1}{n} \sum_{i=1}^{n} X_i \text{ so } n\bar{X} = \sum_{i=1}^{n} X_i$$ [A.14]

Thus,

$$\sum_{i=1}^{n} (X_i - \bar{X}) = \sum_{i=1}^{n} X_i - \sum_{i=1}^{n} X_i = 0.$$ [A.15]

Finally, because $x_i = X_i - \bar{X}$, $\sum x_i = 0$ as well.

Exercises

A.1 Let $y_i = Y_i - \bar{Y}$. Show that:

$$\sum_{i=1}^{n} y_i = 0.$$

A.2 Show that:

$$\frac{1}{n} \sum_{i=1}^{n} (X_i - \bar{X})^2 = \frac{1}{n} \sum_{i=1}^{n} X_i^2 - \bar{X}^2.$$

A.3 Suppose that X is defined as $X = \{1, 2, 3, 4\}$ and Y is defined as $Y = \{0, 1, 4, 5\}$. Find:

$$\sum_{i=1}^{n} \sum_{j=1}^{n} X_i Y_j - \bar{X}\bar{Y}.$$

A.4 Show that, in general,

$$\sum X_i^2 \neq \left(\sum X_i\right)^2.$$

A.5 Show that, in general,

$$\sum x_i^2 \neq 0,$$

where x is measured in deviation form.

APPENDIX 1.B

DERIVATION OF $\hat{\beta}_0$ AND $\hat{\beta}_1$

The procedure for finding the estimated intercept, $\hat{\beta}_0$, and the estimated slope, $\hat{\beta}_1$, is to minimize the sum of squared residuals, $\sum e_i^2$. This is done by summing and then partially differentiating Eq. [1.8] with respect to $\hat{\beta}_0$ and $\hat{\beta}_1$. Setting these partial derivatives to zero will minimize the functions. The two resulting equations are then solved simultaneously to yield the formulae for $\hat{\beta}_0$ and $\hat{\beta}_1$.

The equation of the regression model is written as:

$$Y_i = \hat{\beta}_0 + \hat{\beta}_1 X_i + e_i. \qquad\qquad \text{[B.1]}$$

Because the fitted line is assumed to be:

$$\hat{Y}_i = \hat{\beta}_0 + \hat{\beta}_1 X_i, \qquad\qquad \text{[B.2]}$$

it follows that:

$$e_i = Y_i - \hat{Y}_i, \qquad\qquad \text{[B.3]}$$

where e_i is the regression residual.

Now, the best line through the data minimizes the sum of the distances between Y_i and $\hat{Y}_i$:

$$\min \sum_{i=1}^{n} (Y_i - \hat{Y}_i) = \min \sum_{i=1}^{n} e_i. \qquad\qquad \text{[B.4]}$$

However, there are an infinite number of lines that will minimize the sum of the regression residuals, so this criteria is of little help in the selection of $\hat{\beta}_0$ and $\hat{\beta}_1$. The solution is to minimize the sum of the squares of the residuals; i.e., to minimize $\sum e_i^2$:

$$\min \sum_{i=1}^{n} e_i^2 = \min \sum_{i=1}^{n} (Y_i - \hat{Y}_i)^2 \qquad\qquad \text{[B.5]}$$

If we substitute for $\hat{Y}_i$, the sum on the right side of Eq. [B.5] can be written as:

$$\sum_{i=1}^{n} (Y_i - \hat{Y}_i)^2 = \sum_{i=1}^{n} (Y_i - \hat{\beta}_0 - \hat{\beta}_1 X_i)^2. \qquad\qquad \text{[B.6]}$$

We need to partially differentiate Eq. [B.6] twice, first with respect to $\hat{\beta}_0$ and then with respect to $\hat{\beta}_1$. Differentiation with respect to $\hat{\beta}_0$ and applying the chain rule gives:

$$\frac{\partial \sum e_i^2}{\partial \hat{\beta}_0} = \frac{\partial}{\partial \hat{\beta}_0} \left(\sum_{i=1}^{n} (Y_i - \hat{\beta}_0 - \hat{\beta}_1 X_i)^2 \right)$$

$$= -2 \sum_{i=1}^{n} (Y_i - \hat{\beta}_0 - \hat{\beta}_1 X_i). \qquad\qquad \text{[B.7]}$$

To minimize, we set this to zero. After dividing by -2, we have:

$$\sum_{i=1}^{n} (Y_i - \hat{\beta}_0 - \hat{\beta}_1 X_i) = 0 \qquad\qquad \text{[B.8]}$$

which can be simplified quite easily. First, distribute the summation sign and solve for $\sum Y_i$:

$$\sum_{i=1}^{n} Y_i = \sum_{i=1}^{n} \hat{\beta}_0 + \sum_{i=1}^{n} \hat{\beta}_1 X_i. \qquad\qquad \text{[B.9]}$$

Noting that $\sum \hat{\beta}_0 = n\beta_0$ and $\sum \hat{\beta}_1 X_i = \hat{\beta}_1 \sum X_i$, we have:

$$\sum_{i=1}^{n} Y_i = n\hat{\beta}_0 + \hat{\beta}_1 \sum_{i=1}^{n} X_i. \qquad\qquad \text{[B.10]}$$

Now, divide each side of Eq. [B.10] by n to get Eq. [B.11], which is the same as Eq. [1.9]:

$$\hat{\beta}_0 = \bar{Y} - \bar{\beta}_1 \bar{X}. \qquad\qquad \text{[B.11]}$$

Equations [B.8] through [B.11] are different formulations of the *first normal equation*, one of the two equations used to solve for $\hat{\beta}_0$ and $\hat{\beta}_1$.

Partial differentiation with respect to $\hat{\beta}_1$ also requires use of the chain rule:

$$\frac{\partial \sum e_i^2}{\partial \hat{\beta}_1} = \frac{\partial}{\partial \hat{\beta}_1} \left(\sum_{i=1}^{n} (Y_i - \hat{\beta}_0 - \hat{\beta}_1 X_i)^2 \right)$$

$$= -2 \sum_{i=1}^{n} X_i(Y_i - \hat{\beta}_0 - \hat{\beta}_1 X_i). \qquad\qquad \text{[B.12]}$$

Again, setting the sum on the right to zero and dividing by -2 gives:

$$\sum_{i=1}^{n} X_i(Y_i - \hat{\beta}_0 - \hat{\beta}_1 X_i) = 0. \qquad\qquad \text{[B.13]}$$

Distributing the summation sign, moving the constants outside the sums, and solving for $\sum X_i Y_i$ yields:

$$\sum_{i=1}^{n} X_i Y_i = \hat{\beta}_0 \sum_{i=1}^{n} X_i + \hat{\beta}_1 \sum_{i=1}^{n} X_i^2. \qquad\qquad \text{[B.14]}$$

Equations [B.13] and [B.14] are different forms of the *second normal equation*.

The formulae for $\hat{\beta}_0$ and $\hat{\beta}_1$ can be found by solving the two normal equations simultaneously. First, substitute Eq. [B.11] for $\hat{\beta}_0$ in Eq. [B.14]:

$$\sum_{i=1}^{n} X_i Y_i = (\bar{Y} - \hat{\beta}_1 \bar{X}) \sum_{i=1}^{n} X_i + \hat{\beta}_1 \sum_{i=1}^{n} X_i^2. \qquad\qquad \text{[B.15]}$$

This gives us one equation with one unknown, $\hat{\beta}_1$. Expanding the right side gives:

$$\sum_{i=1}^{n} X_i Y_i = \bar{Y} \sum_{i=1}^{n} X_i - \hat{\beta}_1 \bar{X} \sum_{i=1}^{n} X_i + \hat{\beta}_1 \sum_{i=1}^{n} X_i^2. \qquad \text{[B.16]}$$

Factoring out $\hat{\beta}_1$ and moving $\bar{Y} \sum X_i$ to the other side gives[8]:

$$\sum_{i=1}^{n} X_i Y_i - \bar{Y} \sum_{i=1}^{n} X_i = \hat{\beta}_1 \left(\sum_{i=1}^{n} X_i^2 - \bar{X} \sum_{i=1}^{n} X_i \right) \qquad \text{[B.17]}$$

It is a simple matter now to isolate $\hat{\beta}_1$. If we substitute $x_i + \bar{X}$ for X_i and $y_i + \bar{Y}$ for Y_i and divide by the term in parentheses on the left side, we have:

$$\hat{\beta}_1 = \frac{\sum_{i=1}^{n} (x_i + \bar{X})(y_i + \bar{Y}) - \bar{Y} \sum_{i=1}^{n} (x_i + \bar{X})}{\sum_{i=1}^{n} (x_i + \bar{X})^2 - \bar{X} \sum_{i=1}^{n} (x_i + \bar{X})}. \qquad \text{[B.18]}$$

When we multiply the terms in parentheses and distribute the summation signs, we get:

$$\hat{\beta}_1 = \frac{\sum_{i=1}^{n} x_i y_i + \bar{X} \sum_{i=1}^{n} y_i + \bar{Y} \sum_{i=1}^{n} x_i + n\bar{X}\bar{Y} - \bar{Y} \sum_{i=1}^{n} x_i - n\bar{Y}\bar{X}}{\sum_{i=1}^{n} x_i^2 + 2\bar{X} \sum_{i=1}^{n} x_i + n\bar{X}^2 - \bar{X} \sum_{i=1}^{n} x_i - n\bar{X}^2}. \qquad \text{[B.19]}$$

Two things allow us to simplify Eq. [B.19] immensely. First, note that the $\bar{X}\bar{Y}$ terms in the numerators and the $\bar{X}^2$ terms in the denominator cancel. This leaves us with something a bit more tractable:

$$\hat{\beta}_1 = \frac{\sum_{i=1}^{n} x_i y_i + \bar{X} \sum_{i=1}^{n} y_i + \bar{Y} \sum_{i=1}^{n} x_i - \bar{Y} \sum_{i=1}^{n} x_i}{\sum_{i=1}^{n} x_i^2 + 2\bar{X} \sum_{i=1}^{n} x_i - \bar{X} \sum_{i=1}^{n} x_i}. \qquad \text{[B.20]}$$

We can also eliminate all of the terms involving $\sum x_i$ and $\sum y_i$ because they equal zero. To see this, sum $x_i = X_i - \bar{X}$; that is:

$$\sum_{i=1}^{n} x_i = \sum_{i=1}^{n} X_i - \sum_{i=1}^{n} \bar{X}. \qquad \text{[B.21]}$$

---

[8]Be careful. As shown in Appendix 1. A, in general, $\sum X \sum X \neq \sum X^2$ and $\sum Y \sum X \neq \sum XY$.

The sum of a constant, however, is just n times that constant so $\sum \bar{X} = n\bar{X}$, and by the definition of the mean of X, $\sum X_i = n\bar{X}$. Thus,

$$\sum_{i=1}^{n} x_i = n\bar{X} - n\bar{X} = 0. \qquad\qquad \text{[B.22]}$$

We are thus left with the definition of $\hat{\beta}_1$ that we have been looking for:

$$\hat{\beta}_1 = \frac{\sum_{i=1}^{n} x_i y_i}{\sum_{i=1}^{n} x_i^2}. \qquad\qquad \text{[B.23]}$$

CHAPTER TWO

REQUISITE STATISTICS: A REVIEW

Econometric statements are probabilistic; that is, econometricians always qualify their predictions with statements such as "GNP growth will be 3% next year, plus or minus 1%." These statements are not merely safeguards against error, they are also methodologically correct. Whenever regression analysis is performed on economic data, the resulting estimates are true only in the probabilistic sense. For example, the 0.505 slope estimate we obtained in the accelerator model from Chapter 1 may be correct, but it is far more likely that the true slope is between about 0.1 and 0.9. In fact, the true slope may be zero—meaning that DRGNP has no effect on BFI—despite the 0.505 figure that was calculated. Construction of intervals around regression estimates and evaluation of the reliability of these intervals requires familiarity with basic statistics.

2.1

RANDOM VARIABLES AND PROBABILITY DISTRIBUTIONS

A *random variable* takes on values by chance. For example, suppose we toss a coin and assign a value of 1 for heads and 0 for tails. Because the possible outcomes are determined by chance, the values 1 and 0 are random events. If we define $X = 1$ for heads, and $X = 0$ for tails, then X is said to be a random variable. The long run behavior of the coin toss experiment is called a *probability density function* or PDF. The PDF connects the act of tossing the coin to the outcomes. The coin toss PDF is said to be *discrete* because the number of possible outcomes can be counted. In this case, 1 and 0 are the only two possible outcomes, but a PDF is considered discrete whenever the number of permissible values is finite. *Continuous* random variables can take on an infinite number of values. For example, a PDF that could generate any number between 0 and 1 (i.e., 0.1, 0.11, 0.111, etc.) would be continuous.

A PDF must fulfill two requirements. First, the probability of observing any particular outcome must be between 0 and 1. Letting p_i represent the probability assigned to outcome i, this can be written as:

$$0 \le p_i \le 1. \tag{2.1}$$

Second, the sum of all probabilities must equal one:

$$\sum_{i=1}^{n} p_i = 1. \tag{2.2}$$

In the coin toss example, the probability of tossing a head or a tail is 0.5. This fulfills the first requirement. Because these are the only two possible outcomes, the sum of all probabilities is $0.5 + 0.5 = 1$, so the second criteria is satisfied as well. It is often useful to present PDFs graphically, as is done in Fig. 2.1.

Before continuing, we need to emphasize again the difference between the population and the sample. Generally, we have access to only a small sample of the population so we cannot observe the actual PDF. In the case of the coin toss, it is possible—though not likely—that a sample of ten tosses would result in ten heads.[1] However, if the sample is large and random, we can generate a reasonable estimate of the population PDF. In fact, the main goal of regression analysis and statistical inference is the estimation of the population characteristics from a sample of the population.

---

[1] How likely? If the coin is fair, the chance of the first toss being a head is 0.5. The chance of the first two tosses being heads is $0.5(0.5) = 0.25$; the chance of the first three being heads is $0.5^3 = 0.125$; and the chance of getting ten heads in a row is $0.5^{10} = 0.0009765625$!

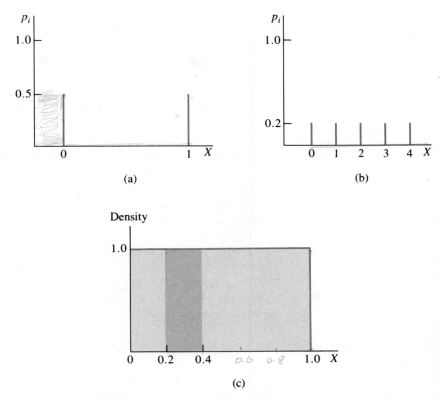

FIGURE 2.1   Discrete and continuous PDFs.

(a) Illustration of the coin toss PDF, a discrete random variable. In this case, there are two outcomes, heads and tails (1 and 0), and each has a probability of 0.5. The sum of all probabilities must equal 1 and each outcome must have a probability between 0 and 1. (b) Illustration of a discrete random variable that can take on the values { 0, 1, 2, 3, 4 }. If each outcome is equally likely, the probability of observing each outcome will be 0.2. (c) Illustration of a continuous probability distribution, the uniform distribution. In this case, X can take on all values between 0 and 1 and each outcome is equally likely as indicated by the constant height Because the number of outcomes is infinite, the probability of observing any *particular* value is zero. However, the probability of the random variable falling within a certain region (say between 0.2 and 0.4) can be calculated. The area under the entire PDF is 1, and the probability of X falling within any region is a fraction less than 1. Because one-fifth of the observations between 0 and 1 fall between 0.2 and 0.4, the probability of an observation falling within this region is 0.2. In order for the area between 0.2 and 0.4 to equal 0.2, the vertical measure of the PDF rectangle must equal 1.

TABLE 2.1   **A probability density function**

X_i	1	2	3	4	5
p_i	0.1	0.3	0.2	0.1	0.3

2.1.1   Population Parameters: The Mean and Variance

We can usually describe a random variable and its PDF by means of summary parameters. The two most important summary parameters are the *mean* and the *variance*.

The mean of a random variable is merely the arithmetic average. For example, suppose that the discrete random variable X can take on the values 1, 2, 3, 4, or 5, and that the probability of observing each value is as given in Table 2.1.

The mean of X, denoted μ_X (μ is the lower case Greek letter mu), is found by multiplying each outcome by the respective probabilities; that is, by applying the formula in Eq. [2.3]:

$$\mu_X \equiv \sum_{i=1}^{n} p_i X_i, \tag{2.3}$$

where the triple equals sign ($\equiv$) indicates an identity and reads "is defined as." For the PDF in Table 2.1, the calculations are:

$$\mu_X = 0.1(1) + 0.3(2) + 0.2(3) + 0.1(4) + 0.3(5) = 3.2.$$

The population variance of a random variable, denoted var(X) or σ_X^2 (σ is the lower case Greek letter sigma), is a measure of dispersion. The variance tells how individual observations are distributed around the mean. The formula for the population variance is:

$$\text{var}(X) \equiv \sigma_X^2 \equiv \sum_{i=1}^{n} p_i(X_i - \mu_X)^2. \tag{2.4}$$

The variance for the PDF of Table 2.1 is:

$$0.1(1 - 3.2)^2 + 0.3(2 - 3.2)^2 + 0.2(3 - 3.2)^2 + 0.1(4 - 3.2)^2 + 0.3(5 - 3.2)^2$$
$$= 0.1(4.84) + 0.3(1.44) + 0.2(0.04) + 0.1(0.64) + 0.3(3.24) = 1.96.$$

Variance calculations can be simplified considerably by expanding Eq. [2.4]. Expanding the term in parentheses gives:

$$\text{var}(X) = \sum_{i=1}^{n} p_i(X_i^2 - 2X_i\mu_X + \mu_X^2) \tag{2.5}$$

Now, distribute the p_i and take the constants (2 and μ_X) outside the sum to obtain:

$$\text{var}(X) = \sum_{i=1}^{n} p_i X_i^2 - 2\mu_X \sum_{i=1}^{n} p_i X_i + \mu_X^2 \sum_{i=1}^{n} p_i. \qquad [2.6]$$

Because $\sum p_i X_i = \mu_X$ and $\sum p_i = 1$, this simplifies to:

$$\text{var}(X) = \sum_{i=1}^{n} p_i X_i^2 - \mu_X^2. \qquad [2.7]$$

Equation [2.7] is almost always easier to use than Eq. [2.4] when calculating the variance by hand. Using Eq. [2.7], the calculations for Table 2.1 are:

$$0.1(1)^2 + 0.3(2)^2 + 0.2(3)^2 + 0.1(4)^2 + 0.3(5)^2 - (3.2)^2$$
$$= 0.1 + 1.2 + 1.8 + 1.6 + 7.5 - 10.24 = 1.96.$$

The positive square root of the variance is known as the *standard deviation*. The usual notation for the standard deviation of X is σ_X. The standard deviation is especially important in hypothesis testing and the construction of confidence intervals, a subject we will discuss shortly.

2.1.2   Linear Functions of a Random Variable

We will frequently need to work with linear functions of random variables. Three rules are worth remembering. If X is a random variable and Y is a linear function of X such that $Y = a + bX$, then:

$$\mu_Y = a + b\mu_X \qquad [2.8]$$

$$\text{var}(Y) = b^2 \text{var}(X) \qquad [2.9]$$

$$\sigma_Y = |b|\sigma_X \qquad [2.10]$$

These results can be verified quite easily. The rule of Eq. [2.8] can be illustrated by example. (Remember, however, that a single example does not constitute proof that the equation is universally true.) Define X as in Table 2.1 and Y as $Y = 10 + 0.5X$. This gives the PDF illustrated in Table 2.2. The

T A B L E 2.2   **Linear function of a random variable**

Y_i	10.5	11	11.5	12	12.5
p_i	0.1	0.3	0.2	0.1	0.3

calculations for μ_Y are:

$$\mu_Y = 0.1(10.5) + 0.3(11) + 0.2(11.5) + 0.1(12) + 0.3(12.5) = 11.6.$$

The same result could have been deduced from an application of Eq. [2.7]. Because $\mu_X = 3.2$, we have $\mu_Y = 10 + 0.5(3.2) = 11.6$.

Equation [2.9], the rule for linear functions of the variance, could also be verified by example, but a general solution is almost as easy. First, write the variance of Y as:

$$\text{var}(Y) = \sum_{i=1}^{n} p_i Y_i^2 - \mu_Y^2. \qquad [2.11]$$

Now substitute for Y:

$$\text{var}(Y) = \sum_{i=1}^{n} p_i(a + bX_i)^2 - (a + b\mu_X)^2 \qquad [2.12]$$

and expand the terms in parentheses:

$$\text{var}(Y) = \sum_{i=1}^{n} p_i(a^2 + 2abX_i + b^2X_i^2) - (a^2 + 2ab\mu_X + b^2\mu_X^2). \qquad [2.13]$$

Distribute the summation signs and take the constants outside to obtain:

$$\text{var}(Y) = a^2 \sum_{i=1}^{n} p_i + 2ab \sum_{i=1}^{n} p_iX_i + b^2 \sum_{i=1}^{n} p_iX_i^2 - a^2 - 2ab\mu_X - b^2\mu_X^2. \qquad [2.14]$$

Now, because $\sum p_i = 1$ and $\sum p_iX_i = \mu_X$, we can write:

$$\text{var}(Y) = a^2 + 2ab\mu_X + b^2 \sum_{i=1}^{n} p_iX_i^2 - a^2 - 2ab\mu_X - b^2\mu_X^2. \qquad [2.15]$$

Cancelling terms gives:

$$\text{var}(Y) = b^2 \sum_{i=1}^{n} p_iX_i^2 - b^2\mu_X^2. \qquad [2.16]$$

After factoring out the b^2 we get:

$$\text{var}(Y) = b^2\left(\sum_{i=1}^{n} p_iX_i^2 - \mu_X^2\right) = b^2\text{var}(X), \qquad [2.17]$$

which is what we have been trying to find. What happened to the constant a? The variance of a constant is 0, so constants have no affect on the variance of linear functions.

2.2

THE EXPECTED VALUE OPERATOR

Many of the analytical results we will need later can be developed more easily with the *expected value operator* than by manipulating summation signs. The expected value of the random variable X is a weighted average of all possible values of the random variable. The weights attached to the values are the probabilities that the random variable will have these values. For a discrete random variable, expected value, $E(X)$, is merely the mean:

$$E(X) \equiv \mu_X \equiv \sum_{i=1}^{n} p_i X_i. \qquad [2.18]$$

Notice, that $E(X)$ may be a value that cannot actually be obtained from the experiment. For example, in the coin toss example, the expected value is:

$$E(X) = \sum_{i=1}^{2} p_i X_i = \sum_{i=1}^{2} [0.5(0) + 0.5(0.1)] = 0.5.$$

This result means simply that there is an equal chance of observing a head ($=1$) or tail ($=0$), not that we expect the coin to land on edge!

The expected value operator can also be applied to functions of a random variable. For example, the expected value of X^2 is:

$$E(X^2) = \sum_{i=1}^{n} p_i(X_i^2). \qquad [2.19]$$

Because the expectations operator is merely a shortcut to express probability sums, the expected value operator has properties similar to the summation properties we developed in Appendix 1.A. We introduce three such properties now and save two additional properties for Sec. 2.6.

PROPERTY 1

The expected value of a constant is the constant itself:

$$E(a) = a. \qquad [2.20]$$

Note that this differs from the sum of a constant, which is equal to n times the constant.

PROPERTY 2

The expected value of a linear function of a random variable is the linear function times the random variable:

$$E(bX) = bE(X). \qquad [2.21]$$

PROPERTY 3

The expected value operator is distributive over addition. That is, if $g(X)$ and $h(X)$ are functions of X, we can show that:

$$E[g(X) + h(X)] = E[g(X)] + E[h(X)].$$ [2.22]

Property 3 may not be intuitive at first. As an example, suppose that X can take on three values, $X = \{1, 2, 3\}$, with each outcome equally likely so that $E(X) = 2$. If $g(X) = X + 7$, and $h(X) = 2X$, then:

$$E[g(X) + h(X)] = E[(X + 7) + 2X] = 7 + E(3X) = 7 + 3E(X) = 13.$$

Property 3 holds since:

$$E[g(X)] = E(X + 7) = E(X) + 7 = 9$$

and

$$E[h(X)] = E(2X) = 2E(X) = 4.$$

The distributive property will frequently come in handy when deriving regression formulae and manipulating expressions.

We can use these properties to develop an expected value formulation for the variance. The expected value operator allows us to write the variance of X as:

$$\text{var}(X) = \sum_{i=1}^{n} p_i(X_i - \mu_X)^2 = E[X - E(X)]^2.$$ [2.23]

To simplify Eq. [2.23], expand the square on the right side to obtain:

$$\text{var}(X) = E\{X^2 - 2XE(X) + [E(X)]^2\}.$$ [2.24]

Because $E(X)$ is a constant, applying the expectations operator to each term gives[2]:

$$\text{var}(X) = E(X^2) - 2E(X)E(X) + [E(X)]^2.$$ [2.25]

After combining the last two terms we have:

$$\text{var}(X) = E(X^2) - [E(X)]^2,$$ [2.26]

which is analogous to Eq. [2.7].

---

[2] Be careful with the notation. In general, $E(X^2) \neq [E(X)]^2$. The term on the left should be read "the expected value of x-squared." The term on the right is "the square of expected value of x."

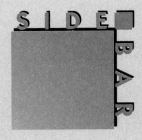

AVOIDING CONFUSION BETWEEN *E* AND Σ

STUDENTS OFTEN have difficulty working with summation signs, and when the expected value operator is introduced, this difficulty is often multiplied. The two concepts are related, but they are definitely not the same. As we pointed out in Appendix 1.A, the summation sign ($\sum$) indicates the algebraic operation of adding together all of the subscripted terms, i.e.,

$$\sum_{i=1}^{n} X_i = X_1 + X_2 + \cdots + X_n.$$

We have just defined the expected value operator (*E*) as the weighted average of a random variable. For a discrete random variable, the expected value is found by summing the product of the individual terms. That is:

$$\sum_{i=1}^{n} p_i X_i = p_1 X_1 + p_2 X_2 + \cdots + p_n X_n \equiv \mu_X.$$

Some of the confusion between the two concepts probably arises because the properties associated with the concepts are similar—but just different enough to cause trouble. For example, the sum of a constant is *n* times the constant:

$$\sum_{i=1}^{n} a = a + a + \cdots + a = na,$$

but the expected value of a constant is the constant itself:

$$E(a) = a.$$

On the other hand, the sum of a constant times an indexed random variable is the constant times the sum:

$$\sum_{i=1}^{n} a X_i = a \sum_{i=1}^{n} X_i;$$

continued on page 36

and the expected value of a constant times a random variable is the constant times the expected value:

$$E(aX) = aE(X).$$

To help you avoid making these kinds of common mistakes, remember these three comments: First, avoid messy work; a poorly hand-written "E" can look quite a bit like a "$\sum$." Second, *always* remember to write the subscript in indexed variables inside of summation signs, even if you choose to omit the index notation on the summation sign itself. Finally, make sure you are comfortable with the properties of summations and expected values.

2.3

ESTIMATION

The formulae for mean and variance developed thus far assume that we have all of the data from the population with which to work. In fact, this is rarely the case. The usual situation is to work with a small sample of the entire population and to use a statistical *estimator* to derive *sample estimates* of the important summary statistics. Whether we can trust these estimates depends on the sample that is selected. The sample must be random and large enough to capture the important characteristics of the population. If these criteria are met, sample parameter estimates should be reliable. However, any particular sample estimate will probably miss the population parameter because sample estimates are themselves random variables with PDFs. A key to inferential statistics—and econometrics—is to make deductions about the population from sample distributions.

2.3.1   The Sample Mean and Variance

The formulae for sample mean and variance differ slightly from the formulae for population mean and variance. The sample mean, $\bar{X}$, is found by taking a random sample from the population, summing it, and dividing by n, the sample size. Equation [2.27] presents the formula for the sample mean:

$$\bar{X} = \frac{1}{n} \sum_{i=1}^{n} X_i.$$

[2.27]

Because $\bar{X}$ is an estimate of μ_X, a logical assumption might be to estimate the sample variance as $(1/n)\sum(X_i - \bar{X})^2$; however, we show in Appendix 2.A that this potential estimator is inferior to the estimator in the following equation[3]:

$$\widehat{\mathrm{var}}(X) = s_X^2 = \hat{\sigma}_X^2 = \frac{1}{n-1}\sum_{i=1}^{n}(X_i - \bar{X})^2. \qquad [2.28]$$

We will also frequently speak of the variance of the sample mean, $\mathrm{var}(\bar{X})$. The formula for $\mathrm{var}(\bar{X})$ is:

$$\mathrm{var}(\bar{X}) = \sigma_{\bar{X}}^2 = \frac{\mathrm{var}(X)}{n}, \qquad [2.29]$$

where $\mathrm{var}(\bar{X})$ is a measure of the dispersion of the sample mean around the true mean. This dispersion decreases as the sample size increases.[4]

The formula in Eq. [2.29] is appropriate only if the variance of X is known; and because it rarely is, we will normally have to estimate the variance of the sample mean. The estimated variance of the sample mean is found by dividing the estimated variance of X by n.

$$\widehat{\mathrm{var}}(\bar{X}) = s_{\bar{X}}^2 = \frac{s_X^2}{n}. \qquad [2.30]$$

2.3.2 Desirable Properties of Estimates

The estimators for mean and variance were chosen because they fulfill the two most desirable properties of estimators.

LACK OF BIAS Good estimators result in estimates that are unbiased. In other words, the sample estimate is, on average, equal to the true population parameter. Strictly speaking, this means that if 1,000 estimates of the mean were calculated using Eq. [2.27], the distribution of these estimates would be centered around the true mean. Why do we need 1,000 estimates of the mean? Bias refers to the *distribution* of the sample estimates. Any particular estimate may be too high or too low, but if a large number of random samples are taken, most of the sample estimates will be clustered around the true

---

[3]With regard to the notation, standards for econometric literature indicate true parameter values with Greek letters—μ for mean, σ for standard deviation, etc. Estimated values are noted in one of two ways: Either by placing a hat ($\hat{\ }$) over a variable, or by using the English letters that correspond to the Greek. Lower case "s" is the common notation for estimated standard deviation, but to prove every rule has its exception, $\bar{X}$ is used instead of m for estimated mean.

[4]Exercise 2.5 asks you to derive $\mathrm{var}(\bar{X})$. Simply apply the rule $\mathrm{var}(aX) = a^2\mathrm{var}(X)$.

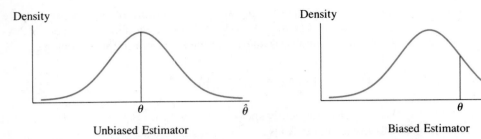

FIGURE 2.2   Biased and unbiased estimates.

If the estimator is unbiased, the distribution of the sample estimates (θ)
will be centered around the true population parameter (θ) as illustrated
by the figure on the left. If the estimator is biased, the distribution of the
sample estimates will be centered away from the true parameter, as
illustrated by the figure on the right.

population parameter if the estimator is unbiased. Figure 2.2 illustrates biased
and unbiased estimators.

How do we know that $\bar{X}$ is unbiased? An estimator is unbiased if its
expected value equals the true parameter; that is, $\bar{X}$ is unbiased if

$$E(\bar{X}) = \mu_X, \qquad [2.31]$$

which can be demonstrated quite easily. First, take the expected value of the
formula for $\bar{X}$:

$$E(\bar{X}) = E\left(\frac{1}{n} \sum_{i=1}^{n} X_i\right). \qquad [2.32]$$

Now, because $1/n$ is a constant, it can be taken outside the expectations
operator:

$$E(\bar{X}) = \frac{1}{n} E\left(\sum_{i=1}^{n} X_i\right). \qquad [2.33]$$

Expectations Property 2 allows us to treat the expected value of the sum of X_i
as the sum of the expected values, i.e.,

$$E(\bar{X}) = \frac{1}{n} \sum_{i=1}^{n} E(X_i). \qquad [2.34]$$

However, the expected value of any particular observation on X is μ_X, which is
a constant, and the sum of a constant is n times the constant. This allows us to
write:

$$E(\bar{X}) = \frac{1}{n} n\mu_X = \mu_X, \qquad [2.35]$$

which is what we wanted to show.

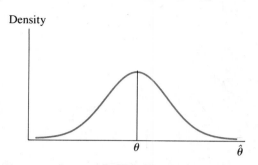
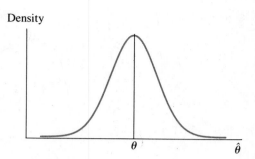

FIGURE 2.3   Efficient and inefficient estimators.

Because the variance of the distribution in (a) is greater than the variance of (b), the estimator behind the distribution of (b) is more efficient than the estimator used to generate the values of (a).

Strictly speaking, bias is a small sample property. The properties of some estimators differ as the sample size increases. In fact, some of the estimators we develop in later chapters are biased in small samples but unbiased as the sample size increases. Such estimators are said to be biased but *consistent*.

EFFICIENCY   A second desirable property of estimators is efficiency. An efficient estimator has a small variance relative to other estimators; the *best estimator* has the smallest possible variance. When it is impossible or too difficult to find the best estimator, statisticians look for the estimator that is most efficient relative to other parameter estimates. This is known as *relative efficiency*. Figure 2.3 illustrates efficient and inefficient estimators.

Efficient estimators are important because they allow us to make stronger statistical statements about parameter estimates. In the limiting case of $\text{var}(\hat{\theta}) = 0$, we could state with certainty that our estimate was correct if we also knew that it was unbiased. As $\text{var}(\hat{\theta})$ increases, our confidence in the estimate decreases. Both $\bar{X}$ and s_X^2 are efficient, but demonstrating this can be tedious. The interested reader is referred to Kmenta (1986) or Judge, et. al., (1980).

MEAN SQUARE ERROR   At times it is impossible to find an estimator that is both unbiased and efficient. In these cases, we may need to make a trade-off; we may need to trade a bit of bias for some efficiency. We can do this by minimizing the *mean square error*. The mean square error (MSE) is defined as:

$$\text{MSE}(\hat{\theta}) = E(\hat{\theta} - \theta)^2,$$

[2.36]

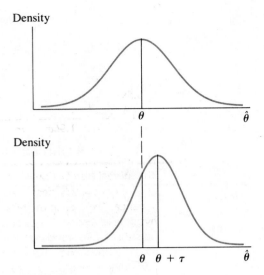

FIGURE 2.4   Mean square error.

The top diagram is unbiased [$E(\hat{\theta}) = \theta$], but has a large variance. The
bottom diagram is biased [$E(\hat{\theta}) \neq \theta$], but has a smaller variance.
Minimizing MSE might result in the selection of the estimator
represented in the bottom diagram.

where $E(\hat{\theta}) \neq \theta$. It can be shown that the MSE criterion is equivalent to the
bias squared plus the variance.[5] Figure 2.4 illustrates MSE.

2.4

THE NORMAL DISTRIBUTION AND HYPOTHESIS TESTING

Most econometric modeling involves *hypothesis testing* of one sort or another.
That is, the goal is to determine whether a specific conjecture is supported or
rejected by the data. Real data are rarely definitive, so most often we can only
assign a probability to the acceptance or rejection of the hypothesis. In this
section, we review the normal distribution and simple concepts of hypothesis
testing. In Sec. 2.5, we will look at hypothesis testing with the *t*-distribution.

---

[5] Exercise 2.7 verifies this result.

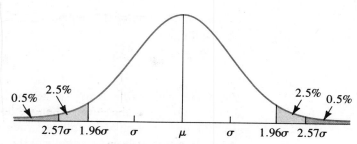

FIGURE 2.5   The normal distribution.

The normal distribution is smooth, symmetrical, and bell shaped, and can be completely described by two parameters, the mean and variance. The area in the tails of the normal curve is important in hypothesis testing. The probability that a random observation will fall outside of 1.96 standard deviations from the mean is approximately 5%. The probability that a random observation will fall outside of 2.57 standard deviations from the mean is approximately 1%.

2.4.1   The Normal Distribution

The basis for most inferential procedures is the normal distribution. The normal distribution is the smooth, bell-shaped distribution shown in Fig. 2.5. It can be completely described with two parameters, the mean and variance. Thus, if the random variable X is normally distributed, writing simply $X \sim \mathcal{N}(\mu_X, \sigma_X^2)$ would be a sufficient description of the entire curve. This notation is standard. The symbol "$\sim$" is read "is distributed as" and the $\mathcal{N}$ indicates a normal distribution.

2.4.2   The Central Limit Theorem

One of the reasons the normal distribution is so important is its association with the *central limit theorem*, one of the most powerful theorems in inferential statistics.[6] For our purposes, the most important result of the central limit theorem is this: The distribution of the sample mean ($\bar{X}$), taken from a large random sample of a distribution with a finite variance, will follow a normal distribution regardless of the distribution of the parent population. Because we already know that the mean of $\bar{X}$ is μ_X, and that $\text{var}(\bar{X}) = \sigma_X^2/n$, when n

---

[6]Several versions of the central limit theorem exist. We will rely on only one of the most simple versions.

is large, application of the central limit theorem allows us to write:

$$\bar{X} \sim \mathcal{N}\left(\mu_X, \frac{\sigma_X^2}{n}\right).$$ [2.37]

This result will enable us to use the normal distribution to make inferences about random variables even when we do not know what kind of distribution the parent population follows when the sample is large. For example, income is not distributed normally in the United States. However, if we took large samples and calculated the sample mean, they would be normally distributed—because of the central limit theorem. Additionally, there will be times when we will have to *assume* that something follows a normal distribution. Such an assumption is warranted by appeal to the central limit theorem.

2.4.3 Using the Normal Table

Because the normal distribution is a continuous probability distribution, the area under the entire curve is equal to one. The probability that any outcome will fall within a certain region is necessarily less than one, and can be found by finding the area under a portion of the curve. For example, if $\mu_X = 10$, the probability that X_i will be between 11 and 12 is found by calculating the area under the normal curve between 11 and 12. Whether this area is "large" or "small" depends on the shape of the particular normal curve. For example, both of the curves in Fig. 2.6 are normal and both have a mean of 10, but the chance of observing X_i between 11 and 12 on the wider curve is obviously greater than on the narrow curve.

Calculating the area under the curve can be done with some rather tedious calculus,[7] but is much easier with the aid of a normal table. The normal table (located in Appendix 5) contains the area under the standard normal or the Z-distribution. To use the table, you must first convert the X-distribution into the Z-distribution, which is accomplished by subtracting the mean from each X_i

---

[7]You would need to integrate the normal curve between 11 and 12. Unfortunately, the normal curve is defined as:

$$f(x) = \frac{1}{\sqrt{2\pi\sigma^2}} \exp -\frac{1}{2}\left(\frac{X - \mu}{\sigma}\right)^2,$$

so learning how to use the tables is easier.

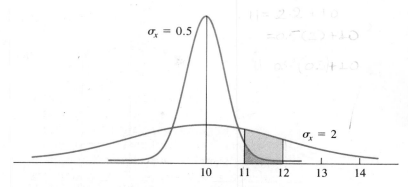

FIGURE 2.6   Estimating the area under the normal curve.

Both normal curves have the same mean, but the chance of an observation falling between 11 and 12 is higher when $\sigma_x = 2$ than when $\sigma_x = 0.5$. To find the area under either curve requires conversion to the standard normal distribution, $Z = (X - \mu_x)/\sigma_x$.

and dividing by the standard deviation:

$$Z = \frac{X_i - \mu_X}{\sigma_X}.$$ [2.38]

The Z-distribution has a zero mean and unit variance,[8] $Z \sim \mathcal{N}(0, 1)$.

Now we can answer the question we posed a moment ago. What is the probability of observing $11 \leq X_i \leq 12$ if $\mu_X = 10$? The solution requires us to find the area under the Z-distribution that corresponds to the area between 11 and 12 under the X-distribution. For the wide curve with $\sigma_X = 2$, the z-values are:

$$z_1 = \frac{11 - 10}{2} = 0.5, \qquad z_2 = \frac{12 - 10}{2} = 1$$

These values represent, in standard deviations, the distance that the points 11 and 12 are from the mean of X. The table entry for $z_2 = 1$ is 0.1587. This is the area that is one standard deviation to the right on a normal curve. The table entry for $z_1 = 0.5$ (one-half standard deviation to the right of the mean) is 0.3085. The area between $z_1 = 0.5$ and $z_2 = 1.0$ (and hence between 11 and 12

---

[8]This can be shown by taking the expected value and variance of Z. This proof is left as Exercise 2.7.

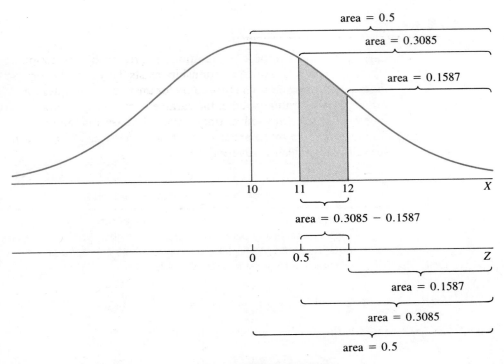

FIGURE 2.7   **Correspondence between *X*- and *Z*-distributions.**

The area under the normal curve, $X \sim N(10, 4)$ between 11 and 12 is the same as the area under the standard normal curve, $Z \sim N(0, 1)$ between 0.5 and 1.

on the *X*-distribution) is found by subtraction: $0.3085 - 0.1587 = 0.1498$. Our conclusion: If $X \sim \mathcal{N}(10, 4)$, the chance of a random observation falling between 11 and 12 is about 15%. Remember, the notation $X \sim \mathcal{N}(10, 4)$ says "*X* is distributed normally with a mean of 10 and a *variance* of 4." Calculating probabilities requires the use of the square root of the variance, i.e., the standard deviation. This correspondence between the *X*- and *Z*-distributions is illustrated in Fig. 2.7.

For the narrow curve, $X \sim \mathcal{N}(10, 0.25)$, the calculations are $z_1 = 2$ and $z_2 = 4$. The table entry for $z_1 = 2$ is 0.0228. There is no table entry for $z_2 = 4$ because the chance of an observation lying four standard deviations from the mean is extremely small—not significantly different from zero. Thus, the probability of a random observation falling between 11 and 12 if $\mu_X = 10$ and $\sigma_X = 0.5$ is only 0.0228.

2.4.4 Hypothesis Testing

One of the most important questions addressed by regression analysis is whether or not a linear relationship exists between the dependent and independent variables. The procedure for answering this question, *hypothesis testing*, is to determine whether the parameter estimates fall into one of the two tails of the standardized normal curve. Because the standardized normal distribution has a mean of zero, any parameter estimate that falls into one of the tails is significantly different from zero.

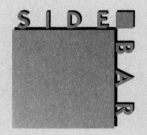

READING THE NORMAL TABLE

READING A normal table is straight forward—if you know what you are doing and you pay attention to the notes at the bottom of the table. Normal tables are presented in one of two ways: The entries in the table represent either the probability that $Z_i \geq z_i$, or the probability that $Z_i \leq z_i$. The normal table in Appendix 5 at the back of this book uses the first method. The entries in the table represent the probability that a random observation will exceed the calculated z_i; thus it presents the area in one tail of the normal distribution.

Inspection of a few entries in the normal table is instructive. Notice that the entry corresponding to $z_i = 0.0$ is 0.5000. This should be expected because if $z_i = 0.0$, then $X_i = \mu_X$ and the probability of a random observation greater than the mean is 0.5. Likewise, the probability that a random observation will fall below the mean is 0.5.

To find the entry corresponding to $z_i = 1.96$, move down the left column to 1.9 and move across the top to 0.06. The table entry is 0.025, an indication that the probability a random observation on X will have a z-value equal to or greater than 1.96 is 2.5%. Since $2(0.025) = 0.05$, the probability that X will have a z-value greater than 1.96 or less than -1.96 is 5%.

Knowledge of the area in the tails keeps us from having to refer to the normal table all the time. Two statements are worth remembering:

$$\Pr(\mu_X - 1.96\sigma_X < X_i < \mu_X + 1.96\sigma_X) \approx 0.95, \qquad [2.39]$$

$$\Pr(\mu_X - 2.57\sigma_X < X_i < \mu_X + 2.57\sigma_X) \approx 0.99. \qquad [2.40]$$

Equation [2.39] says that the probability of a random observation on X falling within 1.96 standard deviations on either side of the mean is 95%; thus the probability that a random observation will fall more than 1.96 standard deviations away from the mean is 5%. Equation [2.40] says that 99% of all observations will be within 2.57 standard deviations; only 1% will be more than 2.57 standard deviations away from the mean. The z-values 1.96 and 2.57 are the *critical values* that determine whether to reject the statistical hypotheses. The critical values were illustrated in Fig. 2.5.

For example, suppose that as quality control officer of a manufacturing plant, you need to test whether the average number of product defects is equal to a specific value, say μ_0. This can be determined by constructing a *null hypothesis*, H_0, where $\mu = \mu_0$, and testing this hypothesis against the *alternate hypothesis*, H_a, where $\mu \neq \mu_0$. The procedure is to collect a sample mean, calculate the standard deviation from the variance, and construct a standardized z-statistic. If the null hypothesis is correct, the sample mean should lie "close" to the hypothesized mean. If the sample mean is "far" from the hypothesized mean, the calculated z-value will be greater in absolute value than the critical value, and we would reject the null hypothesis.

How far from the hypothesized mean does the z-value have to be before we can reject the null hypothesis? That depends on the *statistical significance* of the test. Generally, econometricians prefer to use a 5 or 1% significance level. Rejection at the 5% level requires that the absolute value of z-value be greater than $1.96 \approx 2$. A z-value of 2.0 indicates that the sample mean is two standard deviations away from the hypothesized mean, not a likely occurrence if the null hypothesis were correct. Rejection at the 1% level requires an absolute value of z greater than 2.57.

■ **EXAMPLE 2.1**

USING THE NORMAL DISTRIBUTION TO TEST FOR THE MEAN

Suppose that to test the null hypothesis $H_0: \mu = 0$, versus $H_a: \mu \neq 0$, we take a sample of size $n = 64$ and calculate $\bar{X} = 3$. Suppose further that we know the population standard deviation to be 6. According to the central limit theorem, $\bar{X}$ is distributed normally with a standard deviation of $\sigma/\sqrt{n} = 6/8$. Thus, the z-value corresponding to the sample mean of 3 is[9]:

$$z = \frac{\bar{X} - \mu}{\frac{\sigma}{\sqrt{n}}} = \frac{3 - 0}{\frac{6}{8}} = 4.$$

Because 4 is greater than 2.57—the critical value at a 1% significance level—the null hypothesis would be rejected at both the 5 and the 1% significance level. *2.01*

The previous example is a *two-tailed test* because we would have rejected the null hypothesis had we found a sample mean that was either too high or too low. However, it is often more appropriate to conduct a *one-tailed test*. One-tailed tests are used when the investigator has an idea of the sign of the parameter in question. For example, economic theory requires that demand curves be downward sloping. Thus, a statistical test of the average slope of a demand curve might be $H_0: \mu = 0$ versus $H_a: \mu < 0$. In this case, the null hypothesis would be rejected only if the z-value were too low; that is, only if the sample statistic were located in the left tail of the z-distribution. For an upward sloping supply curve, the appropriate one-tailed test would be $H_0: \mu_0 = 0$ versus $H_a: \mu_0 > 0$, and the null hypothesis would be rejected if the sample mean fell in the right tail. Since all of the rejection region lies in one tail, the critical z-values for one-tailed tests are smaller than those for two-tailed tests. For a one-tailed, 95% test, the critical z-value is 1.64; for a 99% test, it is 2.33. Exercise 2.9 provides an example of a one-tailed test.

2.4.5 Type I and Type II Errors

Because hypothesis testing is probabilistic, the possibility for error always exists. In fact, at the 5% significance level, we will incorrectly reject the null hypothesis 5% of the time. This is known as a *Type I* error. Type I errors can be reduced by increasing the level of significance; however, this increases the possibility of incorrectly accepting a false null hypothesis. Accepting a false

---

[9] When testing hypotheses about the mean, the confidence intervals in Eqs. [2.39] and [2.40] become:

$$\Pr(\mu_X - 1.96\sigma_X/n < \bar{X} < \mu_X + 1.96\sigma_X/n) \approx 0.95, \qquad \textbf{[2.39']}$$

$$\Pr(\mu_X - 2.57\sigma_X/n < \bar{X} < \mu_X + 2.57\sigma_X/n) \approx 0.99 \qquad \textbf{[2.40']}$$

Density   True Distribution = Hypothesized Distribution

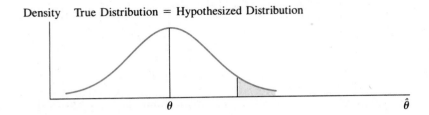

θ $\hat\theta$

Density

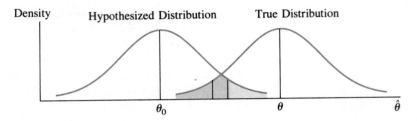

Hypothesized Distribution   True Distribution

θ_0 θ $\hat\theta$

Density

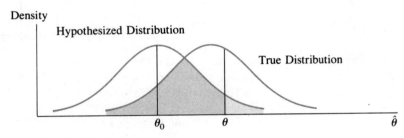

Hypothesized Distribution

True Distribution

θ_0 θ $\hat\theta$

FIGURE 2.8   Type I and type II errors.

If the null hypothesis is correct, the chance of making a Type I error is equal to the rejection region. For a one-tailed test, this is the shaded area in the tail of the top figure. A Type II error occurs when a false null hypothesis is incorrectly accepted. If the hypothesized parameter is far from the true parameter value, the probability of making a Type II error is small; if the hypothesized value is close to the true value, the chance of making a Type II error is large. The dark shading in the middle and bottom diagrams represents the probability of making a Type II error.

null hypothesis is known as a *Type II* error. Ironically, the risk of a Type II error is greatest when the null hypothesis is false, but just barely. For example, suppose that the true marginal propensity to consume is 0.9. The probability of a Type II error would be much greater if the null hypothesis H_0: MPC = 0.89 than if it is H_0: MPC = 0. Both types of error can be reduced by increasing the sample size. Figure 2.8 illustrates Type I and Type II errors.

HYPOTHESIS TESTING WITH THE NORMAL DISTRIBUTION

Hypothesis testing with the normal distribution is appropriate only if there is a large (30 or greater) sample and the population variance is known. These tests are usually designed to determine whether the mean of a distribution is equal to, greater than, or less than zero.

1. Two-Tailed Tests: Standard Hypotheses: $H_0: \mu = 0$; $H_a: \mu \neq 0$.

   • Construct the test statistic:

   $$z = \frac{\bar{X}}{\frac{\sigma_X}{\sqrt{n}}}.$$

   • If $|z| > 1.96$, reject the null hypothesis at the 5% significance level.
   If $|z| > 2.57$, reject the null hypothesis at the 1% significance level.

   • Rejection of the null hypothesis indicates that, if H_0 is true, the sample mean $\bar{X}$ would occur only 5% (or 1%) of the time.

2. One-Tailed test: Standard Hypotheses: $H_0: \mu = 0$; $H_a: \mu > 0$.

   • Construct the test statistic:

   $$z = \frac{\bar{X}}{\frac{\sigma_X}{\sqrt{n}}}.$$

   • If $z > 1.64$, reject the null hypothesis at the 5% significance level.
   If $z > 2.33$, reject the null hypothesis at the 1% significance level.

   • Rejection of the null hypothesis indicates that the sample mean is so large that it is very unlikely to occur if H_0 is true.

   • If the alternative hypothesis is $H_a: \mu < 0$, the null hypothesis is rejected only if $\bar{X}$ is too low; i.e., if $z < -1.64$ or $z < -2.33$.

2.5
OTHER PROBABILITY DISTRIBUTIONS:
t, χ^2, AND F

The example we used to illustrate hypothesis testing was contrived: How often do you think you would really know the variance and standard deviation of a distribution but not the mean? Rarely. Most often we need to estimate both the mean and the variance and, unfortunately, when we must estimate the variance, we can no longer use the normal distribution or the normal tables. The appropriate distribution is the t-distribution. Two other probability distributions, the χ^2- (the lowercase Greek letter chi) and F-distributions also play important roles in econometric analysis.

2.5.1   The t-Distribution

The t-distribution is used in hypothesis testing when the variance must be estimated and/or when the sample size is small (under 30). As with the normal distribution, the t-distribution can be completely described by the mean and variance. However, the t-distribution has wider tails than the normal distribution for small samples. As the sample size approaches 30, the t-distribution approaches the normal distribution, and can be approximated with the normal table. The t-distribution is shown in Fig. 2.9.

FIGURE 2.9   The t-distribution.

With small sample size, the t-distribution is spread out with wide tails. As the sample size approaches 30, the t-distribution approaches the normal distribution, and t-values can be approximated from the normal table.

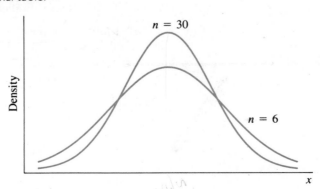

To use the t-distribution, first we need to calculate the *degrees of freedom*. Degrees of freedom is a difficult concept, but it generally refers to the number of pieces of data used in the calculation of the test statistic minus the number of constraints. For a t-test of the sample mean, the number of degrees of freedom is $n - 1$, which means that we have n pieces of data and one constraint—the constraint that $\sum X_i / n = \bar{X}$. Once the degrees of freedom are determined, we decide the significance level of the test, generally 5 or 1%. Then we simply read down the first column on the t-table to find the degrees of freedom and read across the top to find the area in the tail(s) consistent with the chosen level of significance. The corresponding entry in the table gives us the critical t-value used to accept or reject hypotheses.

Many hypothesis tests in econometrics involve construction of a *t-ratio*. When the null hypothesis is that the test statistic is zero, the t-ratio is formed by dividing the sample estimate by its estimated standard deviation. If the

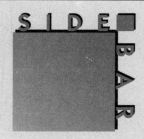

READING THE t-TABLE

READING A t-table is no more difficult than reading a normal table. Most t-tables, including the t-table in Appendix 5, plot the degrees of freedom (df) down the left column and label different probabilities across the top. As with the normal table, it is important to read the note at the bottom of the page: The entries in Appendix 5 represent the critical t-values associated with the area in both tails of the t-distribution; some tables give the critical t-value for the area in only one tail. The t-table in Appendix 5 is appropriate for two-tailed tests, but for a one-tailed test, you need only divide each probability in half.

To get a feel for the t-distribution, examine a few entries. First, notice that when df $= \infty$, the corresponding entries (i.e., 1.96 under $P = 0.05$, 2.576 under $P = 0.01$) are exactly the same as those for a normal distribution. This is to be expected because we mentioned that the t-distribution degenerates to the standard normal as the sample size gets large. More importantly, notice that when df $\rightarrow 25$, the table entries approach the normal values. This explains the use of the critical value of 2.0 as a convenient and accurate rule of thumb.

absolute value of this ratio is greater than the critical t-value found in the t-table, the null hypothesis is rejected. For example, suppose we want to test the null hypothesis H_0: $\mu = 0$ versus the alternate, H_a: $\mu \neq 0$. As in hypothesis testing with the normal distribution, the first step is to standardize the distribution: Subtract the hypothesized mean from the sample mean and divide by the standard deviation of the sample mean:

$$t = \frac{\bar{X} - \mu_0}{\frac{s}{\sqrt{n}}}. \qquad\qquad [2.41]$$

Now, if the null hypothesis is correct, i.e., if $\mu_X = 0$, this ratio becomes simply:

$$t = \frac{\bar{X}}{\frac{s.}{\sqrt{n}}}. \qquad\qquad [2.42]$$

Equation [2.42] is the t-ratio. If this ratio is greater than the critical value in the t-table, then the sample mean is too many standard deviations away from the hypothesized mean, and the null hypothesis must be rejected. On the other hand, if this ratio is less than the critical value, we cannot reject the null hypothesis because the sample mean is sufficiently close to the hypothesized mean.

■ EXAMPLE 2.2

A t-TEST OF THE MEAN

Suppose that we wish to test the hypothesis that the mean of a particular random variable is zero. To test the null hypothesis, H_0: $\mu = 0$ versus the alternative, H_a: $\mu \neq 0$, we take a sample of 16 observations and calculate a sample mean of 1 and a sample variance of 4. Because the sample size is small (< 30) and we had to estimate the variance, we must use the t-distribution in this test. The t-ratio resulting from the sample is:

$$t = \frac{\bar{X} - \mu_0}{\frac{s}{\sqrt{n}}} = \frac{1 - 0}{\frac{2}{4}} = 2. \qquad\qquad [2.43]$$

This value must be compared to the critical value in the t-table. Because $n = 16$, we have 15 degrees of freedom. The critical t-value for a 5% confidence interval is 2.131. Since our t-ratio is less than the critical value, we would fail to reject the null hypothesis of a zero mean at the 5% significance level. Note, however, that had we chosen a 10% significance level, we would have rejected the null hypothesis.

2.5.2　The χ^2- and F-distributions

In addition to the normal and t-distributions, we will need to use the χ^2- and F-distributions on occasion.

THE χ^2-DISTRIBUTION　The sum of the squares of n independent [10] standard normal distributions follows a χ^2-distribution with n degrees of freedom. The χ^2-distribution has several uses in econometrics—especially in relation to hypothesis tests regarding the variance—but our initial, primary use will be as it relates to the F-distribution. In Chapters 9 and 10, the χ^2-distribution will be used to assess the fit of ARIMA and logit models.

THE F-DISTRIBUTION　The ratio of two independent χ^2-random variables divided by their respective degrees of freedom follows an F-distribution. The chief use of the F-distribution is to conduct tests of the significance of the regression equation and to test joint hypotheses in multiple regression. The F-distribution is discussed in more detail in later chapters.

2.6

JOINT DISTRIBUTIONS: COVARIANCE, CORRELATION, AND STATISTICAL INDEPENDENCE

Econometricians are most often interested in the relationship between two or more variables. Does one of the variables affect the other? Or are the two variables completely unrelated? Answering these questions requires analysis of their *joint distribution*.

2.6.1　Joint Distributions of Random Variables

Suppose the random variables X and Y are related in the manner as shown in Table 2.3. This table represents the joint distribution on X and Y. The random variable X can take on the values down the left side of the table—1, 2, 3—while Y can take on the values across the top of 0, 1, and 2. The fractions in the box represent the probability of observing the joint occurrence of X and Y. For example, the probability of observing $X = 3$ at the same time $Y = 2$ is 0; the probability of observing $(X = 2, Y = 2)$ is 0.1, etc. This table fulfills the two requirements of a probability distribution since each individual probability is between 0 and 1 and the sum of all joint probabilities is 1.

---

[10] The term "independence" is defined in Sec. 2.6.3

TABLE 2.3   **A joint distribution**

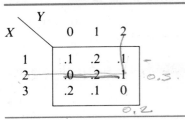

Table entries are interpreted as follows: The joint probability of observing $X = 1$ and $Y = 0$ is 0.1. The joint probability of observing $X = 2$ and $Y = 1$ is 0.2.

We can calculate the mean and variance of each of the random variables. The mean of X is defined as before—$\mu_X = \sum p_i X_i$—but be careful to include the calculations for each value of X and each Y. The calculations would be:

$$\mu_X = 1(0.1) + 1(0.2) + 1(0.1) + 2(0) + 2(0.2) + 2(0.1) + 3(0.2)$$
$$+ 3(0.1) + 3(0) = 1.9.$$

This can be simplified somewhat by use of the *marginal distribution*. The marginal distribution of X is found by summing across the probabilities to find the probability of observing X_i regardless of the value of Y. The marginal distribution on X is:

$$p(X = 1) = p(X = 1, Y = 0) + p(X = 1, Y = 1) + p(X = 1, Y = 2)$$
$$= 0.1 + 0.2 + 0.1 = 0.4$$

$$p(X = 2) = p(X = 2, Y = 0) + p(X = 2, Y = 1) + p(X = 2, Y = 2)$$
$$= 0.0 + 0.2 + 0.1 = 0.3$$

$$p(X = 3) = p(X = 3, Y = 0) + p(X = 3, Y = 1) + p(X = 3, Y = 2)$$
$$= 0.2 + 0.1 + 0.0 = 0.3$$

Note that the marginal distribution sums to one and that each outcome has a probability between 0 and 1. Thus, marginal distributions fulfill the requirements of a PDF. If we call $m(X)$ the marginal distribution of X, the mean of X can be found by:

$$\mu_X = \sum_{i=1}^{n} X_i m(X), \qquad\qquad [2.44]$$

or, simplified,

$$\mu_X = 1(0.4) + 2(0.3) + 3(0.3) = 1.9.$$

The marginal distribution is also useful in the calculation of the variance of X. Simply substitute $m(X)$ for p_i in Eq. [2.7]:

$$\text{var}(X) = \sum_{i=1}^{n} m(X)X_i^2 - \mu_X^2.$$

[2.45]

Similar calculations can be done for μ_Y and var(Y).

2.6.2 Covariance and Correlation

A concept related specifically to joint distributions is the *covariance*. The covariance is a measure of the linear relationship between X and Y. The covariance between X and Y is defined as:

$$\text{cov}(X, Y) = \sum_{i=1}^{n} \sum_{j=1}^{m} p_{ij}(X_i - \mu_X)(Y_j - \mu_Y),$$

[2.46]

where the p_{ij} refers to the probability of observing the i'th X and the j'th Y. For example, using the data in Table 2.3, when $X_i = 1$ and $Y_j = 0$, $p_{ij} = 0.1$; when $X_i = 2$ and $Y_j = 1$, $p_{ij} = 0.2$.

Working with double summations can get complicated, but they are only necessary when there is a different number of X and Y observations. Fortunately, this is usually not the case in econometrics so double summations usually can be avoided. Notice that when $n = m$, there are $nm = m^2$ individual probabilities. If we then relabel each of the ij joint probabilities with the index i, the definition in Equation [2.45] can be written as:

$$\text{cov}(X, Y) = \sum_{i=1}^{nm} p_i(X_i - \mu_X)(Y_i - \mu_Y)$$

Since $n = m = 3$, the single sum would be indexed from 1 to 9. Using double summations, the entry in the upper right corner of Table 2.3 is written $p_{11}(X_i = 1, Y_j = 0) = 0.1$; using a single summation, this entry is $p_1(X_i = 1, Y_i = 0) = 0.1$. The second entry in the first row would be designated $p_{12}(X_i = 1, Y_j = 1) = 0.2$ with double summations or $p_2(X_i = 1, Y_i = 1) = 0.2$ with a single summation.

When plotted in (X, Y)-space, a distribution with a negative covariance will have a negative slope. One example of negative covariance is the Phillips curve, which posits an inverse relationship between inflation and the unemployment rate. A simple version of the Phillips curve is estimated in Chapter 5. A positive covariance will have a positive slope. The upward slope of the Keynesian consumption function implies that the covariance between consumption and disposable income is positive. Positive and negative covariances are illustrated in Fig. 2.10.

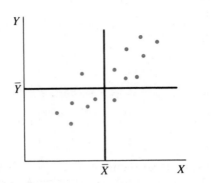

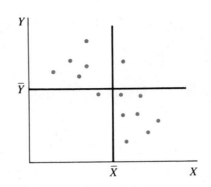

Positive Covariance   Negative Covariance

FIGURE 2.10   Covariance.

The diagram on the left illustrates positive covariance because most points where $X_i > \bar{X}$ correspond to points where $Y_i > \bar{Y}$. The diagram on the right illustrates negative covariance—most points where $X_i > \bar{X}$ correspond to points where $Y_i < \bar{Y}$ and vice-versa.

Defined in terms of expectations, the covariance between X and Y is:

$$\text{cov}(X, Y) = E\{[X - E(X)][Y - E(Y)]\}. \tag{2.47}$$

A little manipulation will allow us to make Eq. [2.47] more manageable before we find the covariance of the joint distribution with which we have been working. First, expand the terms in braces:

$$\text{cov}(X, Y) = E\{XY - XE(Y) - YE(X) + E(X)E(Y)\}. \tag{2.48}$$

Now distribute the expectations operator:

$$\text{cov}(X, Y) = E(XY) - E(X)E(Y) - E(Y)E(X) + E(X)E(Y). \tag{2.49}$$

Cancelling the last two terms gives:

$$\text{cov}(X, Y) = E(XY) - E(X)E(Y). \tag{2.50}$$

When this is converted to summation notation, we have[11]:

$$\text{cov}(X, Y) = \sum_{i=1}^{n} \sum_{j=1}^{n} p_{ij} X_i Y_j - \mu_X \mu_Y \tag{2.51}$$

---

[11] To understand this, expand and simplify Eq. [2.45], and note that $\sum_i \sum_j p_{ij} X_i = \mu_X$.

or, if $i = j$, as is usually the case in regression analysis,

$$\text{cov}(X, Y) = \sum_{i=1}^{nm} p_i X_i Y_i - \mu_X \mu_Y, \qquad [2.52]$$

which is *much* easier to work with than Eq. [2.46]. The calculations are:

$$\text{cov}(X, Y) = 0.1(1)(0) + 0.2(1)(1) + 0.1(1)(2) + 0(2)(0) + 0.2(2)(1) + 0.1(2)(2)$$
$$+ 0.2(3)(0) + 0.1(3)(1) + 0(3)(2) - (1.9)(0.9) = -0.21.$$

Thus, a negative linear relationship exists between X and Y.

As with the mean and variance, we have to estimate the covariance while working with only a sample of the data. The formula for the estimated covariance is:

$$\hat{\sigma}_{XY} = s_{XY} = \frac{1}{n-1} \sum_{i=1}^{n} (X_i - \bar{X})(Y_i - \bar{Y}) = \frac{1}{n-1} \sum_{i=1}^{n} X_i Y_i - n\bar{X}\bar{Y}.$$
$$[2.53]$$

Closely related to the covariance is the *simple correlation coefficient*. The simple correlation coefficient is defined as the covariance divided by the product of the standard deviations of X and Y:

$$\text{corr}(X, Y) = \rho_{XY} = \frac{\text{cov}(X, Y)}{\sigma_X \sigma_Y} = \frac{\text{cov}(X, Y)}{\sqrt{\text{var}(X)\text{var}(Y)}}, \qquad [2.54]$$

where ρ is the lowercase Greek letter rho.

Because standard deviations are always positive, the correlation coefficient will have the same sign as the covariance. The correlation coefficient is often a more useful summary statistic than the covariance because it can indicate how strongly X and Y are related. The simple correlation coefficient is always between -1 and $+1$. Thus, a coefficient close to $+1$ indicates a strong positive relationship between the two random variables, while a coefficient close to -1 indicates a strong negative relationship. A correlation coefficient close to zero indicates little linear relationship between the two random variables. Calculation of the simple correlation coefficient is left as a chapter exercise.

The sample correlation coefficient, r_{XY}, is the sample covariance divided by the product of the estimated standard deviations of X and Y:

$$\widehat{\text{corr}}(X, Y) = r_{XY} = \frac{\hat{\sigma}_{XY}}{s_X s_Y}. \qquad [2.55]$$

2.6.3 Statistical Independence

Generally speaking, when we are concerned with joint distributions, we are dealing with random variables that are statistically dependent. That is, the outcome on Y is influenced by the outcome on X. For example, in Table 2.3, the probability that $Y = 1$ is 0.5. However, the probability that $Y = 1$ *given* that $X = 2$ is 0.67. Thus, X obviously has an influence on Y. This can be stated more generally. If X and Y are independent, then the probability of observing the pair $X_i Y_j$ is equal to the probability of observing X_i times the probability of observing Y_j. This can be stated more formally as:

$$\text{If } X \perp Y, \text{ then } p(X_i, Y_j) = p(X_i)p(Y_j) \qquad \forall \ X_i, Y_j, \qquad [2.56]$$

where the symbol $\perp$ is read "is independent to" and the symbol "$\forall$" means "for all." Further, the covariance between X and Y will be zero if they are independent. However, the converse to this last statement does not necessarily hold: X and Y may be *nonlinearly* dependent yet still have a zero covariance.

Can we use Eq. [2.56] to test whether the random variables in Table 2.3 are independent? The probability that $X = 2$ and $Y = 2$ is 0.1. From the marginal distributions, the probability that $X = 2$ is 0.3 and the probability that $Y = 2$ is 0.2. The product $0.3(0.2) \neq 0.1$ so X and Y are not independent.

2.6.4   More Properties of the Expectations Operator

Two properties of the expectations operator are related to joint distributions that we will find useful later.

PROPERTY 4

The expected value of the sum of two random variables is the sum of the expected values:

$$E(X + Y) = E(X) + E(Y). \qquad [2.57]$$

This follows directly from the definition of summations and expectations.

PROPERTY 5

The variance of the sum of two random variables equals the sum of the variances plus twice the covariance:

$$\text{var}(X + Y) = \text{var}(X) + \text{var}(Y) + 2\text{cov}(X, Y). \qquad [2.58]$$

Property 5 is not obvious at first, but can be proved by writing $\text{var}(X + Y)$ as $E\{(X + Y) - [E(X + Y)]\}^2 = E\{[X - E(X)] + [Y - E(Y)]\}^2$, etc. This proof is provided in Appendix 2.A.

CONCEPTS FOR REVIEW

This chapter was meant to be a quick review of the basic statistics that will be needed in the chapters that follow. The discussion has necessarily been very brief, so if some of it seems vague, talk to your professor and/or get out your statistics book. Before going on, make sure you:

- can work with summations and the expected value operator;
- know the definition and two characteristics of a probability density function;
- can calculate the mean and variance of discrete probability density functions;
- are able to read and use the normal and *t*-tables;
- can conduct simple hypothesis tests using the normal and *t*-distributions;
- understand the relationship between covariance, correlation, and statistical independence;
- can define and use the following terms and concepts in context:

KEY TERMS

alternative hypothesis	MSE
best estimate	normal distribution
bias	null hypothesis
central limit theorem	probability density function (PDF)
confidence level	
consistency	random variable
correlation	standard deviation
covariance	standard (*z*) normal distribution
degrees of freedom	
efficiency	statistical independence
estimation	*t*-ratio
expected value	type I error
joint distribution	type II error
marginal distribution	variance
mean	

EXERCISES

2.1 Verify that the values in Table 2.1 constitute a PDF.

2.2 Prove Eq. [2.8] by using the definition of μ_X.

2.3 Show that $\text{var}(a + bX) = b^2\text{var}(X)$ using the expected value operator.

2.4 The mean of X was defined as $\mu_X = \sum p_i X_i$, where the p_i represented probabilities. Why doesn't the formula for the sample mean, $\bar{X} = 1/n \sum X_i$ include the term p_i?

2.5 Show that $\operatorname{var}(\bar{X}) = \operatorname{var}(X)/n$. (*Hint:* Unless you substitute for $\bar{X}$ right away, this proof will get complicated.)

2.6 Show that

$$ s_{XY} = \frac{1}{n-1} \sum_{i=1}^{n} (X_i - \bar{X})(Y_i - \bar{Y}) = \frac{1}{n-1} \sum_{i=1}^{n} X_i Y_i - n\bar{X}\bar{Y}. $$

EXTRA CREDIT: Show that this is unbiased.

2.7 Show that MSE $=$ bias^2 $+$ variance. [*Hint:* The presence of bias means that $E(\hat{\theta}) \neq \theta$.]

2.8 Let $Z = (X - \mu_X)/\sigma_X$. Show that $E(Z) = 0$ and $\operatorname{var}(Z) = 1$.

2.9 Suppose you hypothesize that the mean of a certain distribution is 12. To test this hypothesis, collect a sample, $n = 49$, and complete the following calculations: $\bar{X} = 10$, $s_X^2 = 9$.

    a. Set up a two-tailed test to test your hypothesis at the 5% significance level. Draw a graph to illustrate your test.

    b. Now suppose that the alternative hypothesis is that $\mu_X > 12$. Set up a one-tailed test with a 5% significance level. Draw a graph to illustrate your test.

2.10 Suppose that you collect 16 observations on X and find the following:

$$ \sum X_i = 408, \quad \sum X_i^2 = 15{,}080. $$

    a. Calculate $\bar{X}$.

    b. Find s_X^2 and $s_{\bar{X}}^2$. (*Hint:* Expand the right side of Eq. [2.26].)

    c. Test the hypothesis $H_0: \mu = 20$ versus $H_a: \mu \neq 20$.

2.11 Calculate σ_X, σ_Y, and ρ_{XY} from the data in Table 2.3.

2.12 Given the joint distribution on X and Y with each outcome equally probable as follows:

X	9	4	1	0	1	4	9
Y	3	2	1	0	-1	-2	-3

    a. Plot the data. Does it look like $X \perp Y$?

    b. Calculate the covariance between X and Y and determine if they are linearly independent.

2.13 Estimation of the sample covariance involves dividing by $n - 1$, the degrees of freedom. Since both $\bar{X}$ and $\bar{Y}$ must be calculated, why don't you divide by $n - 2$?

2.14 Show that $\text{var}(X - Y) = \text{var}(X) + \text{var}(Y) - 2\text{cov}(X, Y)$.

2.15 Let $E(X) = 2$, $\text{var}(X) = 8$, $E(Y) = 1$, $\text{var}(Y) = 3$, and $\text{corr}(X, Y) = 0.25$. Find:

   a. $\text{var}(X + Y)$.

   b. $\text{cov}(X, Y)$.

   c. $\text{cov}(X, X + Y)$.

2.16 Suppose $X \sim \mathcal{N}(5, 2)$. What is the probability that:

   a. $4 \leq X_i \leq 4.2$?

   b. $4.5 \leq X_i \leq 5.5$?

   c. $X_i = 4$?

APPENDIX 2.A

PROOFS

We have delayed two of the more tedious derivations until now. Working through these derivations will give you important practice with summation signs and the expected value operator and should help you work through the chapter exercises and exam questions.

Var(X) is unbiased

We need to show that:

$$s_X^2 = \frac{1}{n-1} \sum_{i=1}^{n} (X_i - \bar{X})^2 \qquad [A.1]$$

is unbiased. An estimator is unbiased if its expected value equals the true parameter. Thus, if we can show that

$$E(s_X^2) = \sigma_X^2, \qquad [A.2]$$

we will know that the estimator is unbiased.

Intuitively, the $n-1$ shows up because we lost a degree of freedom when we calculated $\bar{X}$. However, intuition is not always correct, so a formal demonstration of unbiasedness is necessary. We can simplify the proof by just working with part of the expression, $\sum (X_i - \bar{X})^2$. Our first step is a trick often used in statistical derivations—add and subtract the same number—μ_X in this case. This does not affect the value of the expression, but it does introduce a term that will be useful as the demonstration progresses. Write:

$$\sum_{i=1}^{n} (X_i - \bar{X})^2 = \sum_{i=1}^{n} [(X_i - \mu_X) - (\bar{X} - \mu_X)]^2. \qquad [A.3]$$

Expanding the term in brackets and distributing the summation sign gives:

$$\sum_{i=1}^{n} (X_i - \mu_X)^2 - 2(\bar{X} - \mu_X) \sum_{i=1}^{n} (X_i - \mu_X) + n(\bar{X} - \mu_X)^2. \qquad [A.4]$$

Now, the middle summation is actually:

$$\sum_{i=1}^{n} (X_i - \mu_X) = \sum_{i=1}^{n} X_i - n\mu_X = n\bar{X} - n\mu_X = n(\bar{X} - \mu_X). \qquad [A.5]$$

Substituting allows us to simplify Eq. [A.3] considerably:

$$\sum_{i=1}^{n} (X_i - \bar{X})^2 = \sum_{i=1}^{n} (X_i - \mu_X)^2 - n(\bar{X} - \mu_X)^2. \qquad [A.6]$$

Take the expected value of Eq. [A.6]:

$$E\left[\sum_{i=1}^{n}(X_i - \bar{X})^2\right] = \sum_{i=1}^{n} E[(X_i - \mu_X)^2] - nE[(\bar{X} - \mu_X)^2]. \qquad \text{[A.7]}$$

Because $E[(X_i - \mu_X)^2] = \text{var}(X)$ and $E[(\bar{X} - \mu_X)^2] = \text{var}(\bar{X})$, we can write:

$$E\left[\sum_{i=1}^{n}(X_i - \bar{X})^2\right] = n\sigma_X^2 - n\left(\frac{\sigma_X^2}{n}\right) = (n-1)\sigma_X^2. \qquad \text{[A.8]}$$

Substituting this into Eq. [A.7] to show that our estimator is unbiased is a simple matter:

$$E(s_X^2) = \frac{1}{n-1} E\left[\sum_{i=1}^{n}(X_i - \bar{X})^2\right] = \frac{1}{n-1}[(n-1)\sigma_X^2] = \sigma_X^2. \qquad \text{[A.9]}$$

A similar demonstration can be used to show that the formula for the sample covariance is unbiased.

Var(X + Y) = Var(X) + Var(Y) + 2Cov(X, Y)

Unless begun correctly, this derivation can also be quite cumbersome. Start by writing var($X + Y$) in expectation form:

$$\text{var}(X + Y) = E[(X + Y)^2] - [E(X + Y)]^2. \qquad \text{[A.10]}$$

Expand the square in the first term on the right and express the second term on the right as a product:

$$\text{var}(X + Y) = E[X^2 + Y^2 + 2XY] - [E(X + Y)E(X + Y)]. \qquad \text{[A.11]}$$

Apply the expectation operator term by term:

$$\text{var}(X + Y) = E(X^2) + E(Y^2) + 2E(XY) \\ - [E(X) + E(Y)][E(X) + E(Y)]. \qquad \text{[A.12]}$$

and multiply out the second term on the right side:

$$\text{var}(X + Y) = E(X^2) + E(Y^2) + 2E(XY) \\ - E(X)^2 - E(Y)^2 - 2E(Y)E(X). \qquad \text{[A.13]}$$

Rearranging, we have:

$$\text{var}(X + Y) = [E(X^2) - E(X)^2] + [E(Y^2) - E(Y)^2] \\ + 2[E(XY) - E(Y)E(X)]. \qquad \text{[A.14]}$$

The first term in brackets on the right is simply var(X), the second term in brackets is var(Y), and the last term is twice cov(X, Y), which is what we wanted to show:

$$\text{var}(X + Y) = \text{var}(X) + \text{var}(Y) + 2\text{cov}(X, Y). \qquad \text{[A.15]}$$

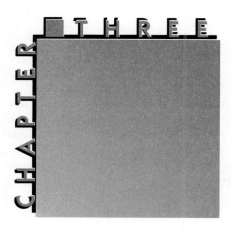

CHAPTER THREE

THE SIMPLE REGRESSION MODEL

Despite the seemingly good results we obtained when we estimated the accelerator model in Chapter 1, our data and the interpretation of results were less than perfect: To make the calculations tractable by hand, the data set was limited to only 18 annual observations. Most econometricians would recommend using a much larger sample to increase the chance that the sample accurately reflects the population. Second, we should not have interpreted $\hat{\beta}_0$ and $\hat{\beta}_1$ as being exact. The values we obtained for $\hat{\beta}_0$ and $\hat{\beta}_1$ are really estimates of the means of probability distributions that we can only hope are unbiased. In this chapter we will remedy those and other problems by combining the statistical hypothesis testing of Chapter 2 with the line-fitting mathematics of Chapter 1.

3.1

BEST LINEAR UNBIASED ESTIMATES

Several points would have to hold before we could be confident of the ordinary least-squares (OLS) results we obtained in Chapter 1. First, we would have to be certain that the data we used were accurate, and, second, that the data set of 18 observations contained all of the relevant information necessary to understand the relationship between fixed investment and the change in real GNP. Neither point holds. A measurement error could have occurred in either of the data series, but this might be safely dismissed as long as we had no reason to believe that observations were consistently too high or too low. More important is the fact that we were dealing with only a small sample of the data set. The fact that we had only a *sample* of the larger population means that any parameter estimates are just that—estimates. Thus, we need to construct confidence intervals around these estimates instead of accepting them as point estimates. In addition to these requirements, several more assumptions must hold before we can be sure that our regression estimates are *BLUE*, an acronym for *best linear unbiased estimates*.

3.1.1 The Gauss–Markov Theorem

One of the most important theorems in statistics, the Gauss-Markov theorem, holds that if certain criteria are met, least-squares parameter estimates are BLUE. These criteria can be stated as a series of assumptions, only the first five of which are relevant to the simple, two-variable regression model:

ASSUMPTION 1 (A1)

The true model is linear and correctly specified by the regression equation.

Linear regression analysis applies to linear functions of the form we illustrated in Chapter 1; i.e.,

$$Y_i = \beta_0 + \beta_1 X_i + \varepsilon_i. \tag{3.1}$$

In order for regression analysis to generate BLUE parameter estimates, the true model must be of this form. In particular, correct specification requires that all relevant independent variables be included in the estimated model. In the case of simple regression, only one independent variable can affect the dependent variable. In multiple regression analysis, A1 requires that all relevant variables be included in the tested model. Omission of relevant independent variables results in biased parameter estimates.

The meaning of the term "linear" may not be as obvious as it appears at first. As we will find out in Chapter 5, the model needs to be *linear in the parameters*, not necessarily *linear in the variables*. For example, the equation $Y = \beta_0 + \beta_1 X^2$ is linear in the parameters because β_0 and β_1 are raised to only the first power. However, even though the equation is not linear in the variable X, it is possible to test this equation with regression analysis. Testing this equation requires only that X^2 be redefined as $Z = X^2$ and the equation be rewritten as $Y = \beta_0 + \beta_1 Z$. On the other hand, the equation $Y = \beta_0 + \beta_1^2 X$ is nonlinear in the parameter β_1. Estimation of this model is possible, but advanced methods are required. Chapter 5 discusses techniques that can be used to estimate certain nonlinear equations with linear regression analysis.

ASSUMPTION 2 (A2)

The independent variables are nonstochastic. [FIXED]

"Nonstochastic" means nonrandom. Thus, A2 requires that we assume X to be "fixed in repeated samples." In the case of the accelerator model from Chapter 1, the application of A2 means that the DRGNP series does not change each time the model is tested—in short, the independent variable, X, must be known to the investigator.[1] In fact, the assumption that X is non-random is unrealistic—remember that we are usually dealing with a random sample—but it does fit the spirit of econometric investigation in that the X observations can be controlled by the investigator as necessary.

An important corollary to A2 is that the error term and the independent variable are noncorrelated:

$$\rho(X, \varepsilon) = 0 \qquad\qquad [3.2]$$

If this corollary does not hold, $\hat{\beta}_0$ and $\hat{\beta}_1$ will be biased. Exercise 3.5 asks you to prove Eq. [3.2], but a little intuition is almost as good: If X is fixed but ε is a random variable, how can they "vary together"? They cannot.

ASSUMPTION 3 (A3)

The error term has a zero mean.

This assumption can be written succinctly as:

$$E(\varepsilon) = 0. \qquad\qquad [3.3]$$

If this assumption is violated, $\hat{\beta}_0$ will be biased.

---

[1]This assumption is not required in order for the Gauss-Markov theorem to hold, though derivation of least-squares results gets complicated with a more general assumption. Gauss-Markov does require that X be independent of the error term.

We also usually assume that the error terms follow a normal distribution,[2] but we really cannot determine if this is correct because the true errors cannot be observed. The best we can do is perform statistical tests on the regression residuals and take solace in knowing that we can trust the estimated slope parameters even if the error has a nonzero mean[3]; and with a large enough sample size, the errors will usually approach a normal distribution.

ASSUMPTION 4 (A4)

The error terms are noncorrelated.

The correlation between error terms must be zero. This can be written as[4]:

$$\rho(\varepsilon_i, \varepsilon_j) = 0, \qquad \forall \, i \neq j. \tag{3.4}$$

This assumption implies that the errors are truly random and that knowing ε_i will not help us predict ε_j.

When A4 is violated, the error terms are said to be *autocorrelated* or *serially correlated*. Autocorrelation is a common problem in time series studies and is treated in depth in Chapter 6. Tests exist to determine whether the errors exhibit autocorrelation but the presence of autocorrelation can sometimes be detected by examination of the regression residuals. Figure 3.1 illustrates well-behaved as well as autocorrelated errors. Careful analysis of the regression residuals often provides vital information.

ASSUMPTION 5 (A5)

The error terms have a constant variance.

If this assumption holds, the errors are said to be *homoscedastic*. When A5 is violated, the error terms are said to exhibit *heteroscedasticity*, the main topic of Chapter 7. Heteroscedasticity is most common in cross-sectional data. A5 can be written mathematically as:

$$\sigma_i^2 = \sigma_j^2, \qquad \forall \, i, j. \tag{3.5}$$

---

[2] The normality assumption is not a requirement of the Gauss-Markov theorem and is thus not necessary for BLUE parameter estimates. We make this assumption only to simplify the construction and interpretation of confidence intervals around the parameter estimates.

[3] This point is made in Exercise 3.4.

[4] Recall from Chapter 2 that the symbol "$\forall$" means "for all" and that the Greek letter ρ represents the correlation coefficient.

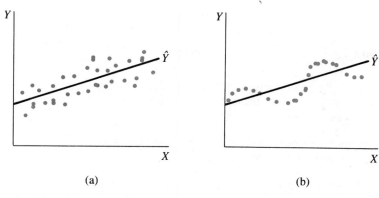

FIGURE 3.1   Well-behaved and autocorrelated errors.

(a) Illustration of well-behaved errors because there is no pattern among the regression residuals. (b) Positive autocorrelation. Notice that consecutive errors usually have the same sign; i.e., if $e_i > 0$, so is e_{i+1}. (c) Negative autocorrelation; if $e_i > 0$, then $e_{i+1} < 0$ most of the time.

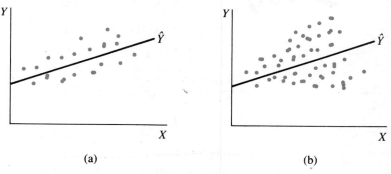

FIGURE 3.2   Homo- and heteroscedastic residuals.

(a) Illustration of homoscedastic errors; notice that residuals associated with both high and low values of X are approximately equal. (b) Heteroscedastic errors; the errors associated with high X's are larger than those associated with low X's.

The statistical tests for heteroscedasticity are not as powerful as those for autocorrelation, so examination of the regression residuals often becomes especially important. Figure 3.2 illustrates homo- and heteroscedastic residuals. Figure 3.2(b) indicates heteroscedasticity because the dispersion of the residuals around the regression line increases as X increases.

THE FIVE ASSUMPTIONS OF ORDINARY LEAST SQUARES (OLS)

The assumptions are so important they are worth repeating: Ordinary least-squares parameter estimates will be *best linear unbiased estimates* (BLUE) if five key assumptions hold:

A1. The model is linear and correctly specified by the equation: $Y_i = \beta_0 + \beta_1 X_i + \varepsilon_i$

  - *If A1 is violated, parameter estimates will be biased or inefficient.*

A2. The independent variables are nonstochastic and thus noncorrelated with the random error term: $\rho(X, \varepsilon) = 0$.

  - *If A2 is violated, parameter estimates will be biased.*

A3. The error term has a zero mean: $E(\varepsilon) = 0$.

  - *If A3 is violated, $\hat{\beta}_0$ will be biased. We usually also assume the errors follow a normal distribution to facilitate hypothesis testing.*

A4. Error terms are noncorrelated: $\rho(\varepsilon_i, \varepsilon_j) = 0$.

  - *If A4 is violated, the errors terms are said to be autocorrelated and parameter estimates will be inefficient.*

A5. The errors have a constant variance: $\sigma_i^2 = \sigma_j^2 \; \forall \; i, j$.

  - *If A5 is violated, the errors terms are said to be heteroscedastic and parameter estimates will be inefficient.*

3.2

HYPOTHESIS TESTS ON $\hat{\beta}_0$ AND $\hat{\beta}_1$

Now that we have discussed the necessary assumptions, we are ready to perform regression analysis and analyze the results more carefully than we did in the simple line-fitting exercise of Chapter 1. The example we will use is the Keynesian consumption function, a concept you probably discussed in your first economics class. According to Keynes's psychological law of consumption, as disposable personal income (DPI) increases, so does con-

TABLE 3.1 Regression results

```
Dep var:CONS  N: 28  R-squared: .997  SER: 25.78

Variable  Coefficient  Std Error      T  P(2 tail)

CONSTANT    -33.38        19.85     -1.68   0.10
    DPI       0.93         0.01     89.46   0.00
```

sumption (CONS), but by a smaller amount. Mathematically, Keynes's theory is usually expressed as a linear function with a positive intercept and a slope that is between 0 and 1:

$$\text{CONS} = \beta_0 + \beta_1 \text{DPI}; \qquad \beta_0 > 0, \qquad 0 < \beta_1 < 1.$$

We can determine whether this theory is consistent with real-world data by means of regression analysis. The data used for this test were annual and covered the period 1960–87, as provided in Data Set 1 in Appendix 1. The initial regression results are shown in Table 3.1. Interpretation of this information requires that we back up a bit.

The main difference between the analysis in this chapter and the curve-fitting exercise of Chapter 1 is that we will be performing statistical tests on the estimated regression parameters, $\hat{\beta}_0$ and $\hat{\beta}_1$. These tests generally check whether the population parameters, β_0 and β_1, are significantly different from zero. As we discovered in Chapter 2, this kind of hypothesis test takes the form:

$$H_0: \mu = 0 \quad \text{versus} \quad H_a: \mu \neq 0,$$

and we reject or fail to reject the null hypothesis by examining the t-ratio:

$$t_{n-1} = \frac{\bar{X} - 0}{\frac{s}{\sqrt{n}}} = \frac{\bar{X}}{\frac{s}{\sqrt{n}}}. \qquad [3.6]$$

If this ratio is greater than the critical value in the t-table, we can reject the null hypothesis in favor of the alternative.

In regression analysis, similar t-tests allow us to determine whether the slope and intercept are statistically different from zero. That is, the standard hypothesis test in regression analysis involves replacing μ with β_0 or β_1 then forming a t-ratio by dividing $\hat{\beta}_0$ and $\hat{\beta}_1$ by their respective standard deviations. If the resulting t-ratio is greater than the critical t-value, the null hypothesis is rejected. However, before we are ready to perform hypothesis tests on $\hat{\beta}_0$ and $\hat{\beta}_1$, we need to make sure they are unbiased and define their variances.

3.2.1 $\hat{\beta}_1$ is Unbiased

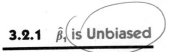

We found out in Chapter 1 that the estimated slope of a regression line is:

$$\hat{\beta}_1 = \frac{\sum x_i y_i}{\sum x_i^2}.$$ [3.7]

Because $\hat{\beta}_1$ is a linear combination of Y_i, and Y is a random variable, $\hat{\beta}_1$ is a random variable as well. Our first order of business, then, is to establish that the estimator in Eq. [3.7] is unbiased. The proof is somewhat tedious, but it is important not only in its own right but because it introduces techniques that will be used frequently throughout this text.

Once we know that $\hat{\beta}_1$ is unbiased, we only need to find its standard deviation; then we can conduct the t-tests to determine its statistical significance.

PROOF: $\hat{\beta}_1$ IS UNBIASED The parameter $\hat{\beta}_1$ is unbiased if $E(\hat{\beta}_1) = \beta_1$. To show this, take the expected value of Eq. [3.7]:

$$E(\hat{\beta}_1) = E\left(\frac{\sum x_i y_i}{\sum x_i^2}\right).$$ [3.8]

Substitute $y_i = \beta_1 x_i + \varepsilon_i$ and expand the numerator:

$$E\left(\frac{\sum x_i(\beta_1 x_i + \varepsilon_i)}{\sum x_i^2}\right) = E\left(\frac{\sum(\beta_1 x_i^2 + x_i \varepsilon_i)}{\sum x_i^2}\right).$$ [3.9]

Because β_1 is a constant,[5] we can take it outside the summation sign. After distributing the summation sign, we have:

$$E\left(\frac{\beta_1 \sum x_i^2 + \sum x_i \varepsilon_i}{\sum x_i^2}\right) = E\left(\beta_1 \frac{\sum x_i^2}{\sum x_i^2} + \frac{\sum x_i \varepsilon_i}{\sum x_i^2}\right).$$ [3.10]

Apply the expected value operator term by term and we obtain:

$$E\left(\beta_1 \frac{\sum x_i^2}{\sum x_i^2}\right) + E\left(\frac{\sum x_i \varepsilon_i}{\sum x_i^2}\right) = \beta_1.$$ [3.11]

The first term on the left side obviously simplifies to β_1, which means that $\hat{\beta}_1$ is unbiased only if the second term on the left side goes to zero, which it does. The proof is in Appendix 3.A, but the intuition used in A2 gives the same result: Because both the error term and x_i have a zero mean, the term $E(\sum x_i \varepsilon_i)$ is actually $n - 1$ times the covariance between x_i and ε_i. However, from A2, we know that X and ε are noncorrelated, so their covariance is zero.

---

[5]The *true* slope is a constant; the estimated slope is a random variable.

3.2.2   The Variance of $\hat{\beta}_1$

We need to define the variance of $\hat{\beta}_1$ before we are ready for hypothesis testing. As shown in Appendix 3A, the true variance of $\hat{\beta}_1$ is:

$$\text{var}(\hat{\beta}_1) \equiv \frac{\sigma^2}{\sum x_i^2}.$$

[3.12]

Notice that the variance of X and the variance of $\hat{\beta}_1$ are inversely related. Why? Because $x_i = X_i - \bar{X}$, the denominator of $\text{var}(\hat{\beta}_1)$ is actually $n - 1$ times the sample variance of X.

The true error variance cannot be observed and must be estimated from the regression residuals. As we pointed out in Chapter 1, the regression residuals, e_i, are the difference between the actual observations on Y_i and the fitted values, $\hat{Y}_i$. The sample variance of e_i is found by summing the square of the difference between e_i and its mean, and then dividing by the degrees of freedom. However, by construction of the OLS line, the mean of e is zero, so the variance is simply the sum of the e_i^2 divided by $n - 2$:

$$s^2 = \hat{\sigma}^2 = \frac{\sum e_i^2}{n - 2} = \frac{\sum (Y_i - \beta_0 - \beta_1 X_i)^2}{n - 2}.$$

[3.13]

Why do we divide by $n - 2$ instead of $n - 1$? To calculate e_i, we had to first calculate $\hat{Y}_i$. That process required estimation of $\hat{\beta}_0$ and $\hat{\beta}_1$—and consequently the loss of two degrees of freedom.

As might be expected, the estimated variance of $\hat{\beta}_1$ is found by substituting s^2 for σ^2 in Eq. [3.12]:

$$\widehat{\text{var}}(\hat{\beta}_1) = \frac{s^2}{\sum x_i^2}.$$

[3.14]

Finally, the estimated standard error of $\hat{\beta}_1$, $\text{se}(\hat{\beta}_1)$, is found by taking the positive square root of Eq. [3.14].

Where do we find s^2? Table 3.1 does not give s^2, but it does give its square root, the *standard error of the regression* or SER. Notation for the SER is not standard—other acronyms for the SER include SE and SEE—and not all regression programs even print it. All programs do, however, provide the information necessary to calculate the SER by hand. It can always be calculated from information provided in an ANOVA table, a topic we discuss in Sec. 3.3.3.

3.2.3   Testing the Significance of $\hat{\beta}_1$

We can now conduct hypothesis tests on $\hat{\beta}_1$. The most common null hypothesis is that β_1 equals zero. If we have no *a priori* reason to suspect that β_1 will be positive or negative, the test would be two tailed, resulting in the following null and alternate hypotheses:

$$H_0: \beta_1 = 0 \quad \text{versus} \quad H_a: \beta_1 \neq 0.$$

These hypotheses are tested by comparing the critical t-value to the t-ratio:

$$t_{n-2} = \frac{\hat{\beta}_1 - 0}{\text{se}(\hat{\beta}_1)} = \frac{\hat{\beta}_1}{\text{se}(\hat{\beta}_1)}. \qquad [3.15]$$

If this ratio is greater than the critical t-value from the table, we would reject the null hypothesis of a zero slope. In essence, the independent variable "caused" the dependent variable. Remember, however, that regression analysis cannot prove causality. A statistically significant slope parameter means only that the data are consistent with our *a priori assumptions* concerning causality.

Now, consider Table 3.1 again. The coefficient on DPI (= 0.93) is the estimated slope parameter, $\hat{\beta}_1$. Dividing 0.93 by its standard error [se($\hat{\beta}_1$) = 0.01] gives[6] a t-ratio (T) of 89.46. At the 5% significance level, the critical t-value for 26 degrees of freedom is 2.056. Because 89.46 > 2.056, we can reject the null hypothesis and conclude that DPI does have an effect on CONS. How confident can we be in rejecting the null hypothesis? The column in Table 3.1 labeled "P(2 tail)" gives the area in the two tails of the t-distribution, assuming that the null hypothesis ($H_0: \beta_1 = 0$) is correct. The entry in the DPI row of this column, 0.00, means that, rounded to two decimal places, there is a 0% chance that the null hypothesis is correct. This should make sense because the t-ratio of 89.46 indicates that $\hat{\beta}_1$ is 89.46 standard deviations away from the hypothesized value of $\beta_1 = 0$. Since about 95% of the observations fall within ± 2 standard deviations of the mean, the probability of randomly drawing an observation almost 90 standard deviations away from the mean is *very* small.

The slope of the consumption function is called the *marginal propensity to consume*, which, as we mentioned earlier, is hypothesized to be positive. This suggests that the appropriate test on $\hat{\beta}_1$ is actually a one-tailed test:

$$H_0: \beta_1 = 0 \quad \text{versus} \quad H_a: \beta_1 > 0.$$

A one-tailed test also allows us to reject the null hypothesis. The critical t-value decreases from 2.056 to 1.706 because 5% of the distribution is now in the left tail.

One-tailed tests are probably more common in econometric analyses than two-tailed tests because the signs of regression coefficients are usually hypoth-

---

[6] Rounding error accounts for the discrepancy. Carried to five decimal places, $\hat{\beta}_1 = 0.92516$ and se($\hat{\beta}_1$) = 0.01034.

esized *a priori.* Most regression programs calculate two-tailed probabilities, but one-tailed probabilities can be calculated simply by dividing the two-tailed probability by two. Note, however, that the null hypothesis can be rejected only if the estimated coefficient has the same sign as the alternate hypothesis

3.2.4   Testing the Significance of $\hat{\beta}_0$

The same methods are used to test for the statistical significance of the intercept. Like $\hat{\beta}_1$, $\hat{\beta}_0$ is unbiased,[7] and its variance is given by:

$$\text{var}(\hat{\beta}_0) = \sigma^2 \frac{\sum X_i^2}{n \sum (X_i - \bar{X})^2}.$$ [3.16]

The estimated variance of $\hat{\beta}_0$ is again found by substituting s^2 for σ^2:

$$\widehat{\text{var}}(\hat{\beta}_0) = s^2 \frac{\sum X_i^2}{n \sum (X_i - \bar{X})^2}.$$ [3.17]

The expression in Eq. [3.17] is complex, but fortunately, the calculations are usually done on a computer. Whether or not you use a computer, it is important to understand just what this formula means: Like $\widehat{\text{var}}(\hat{\beta}_1)$, $\text{var}(\hat{\beta}_0)$ varies directly with s^2 and indirectly with $\text{var}(X)$. Also, $\text{se}(\hat{\beta}_0)$ is formed by taking the positive square root of $\text{var}(\hat{\beta}_0)$.

Looking again at Table 3.1, the t-ratio on the estimated intercept, -1.68, seems to suggest that the intercept is significant at the 12 or 15% level because the critical t-value is 1.706 at 10%. However, this interpretation leaves us with two problems. First, most econometricians prefer to use a 5% significance level. More importantly, the sign of the intercept does not make economic sense: Is it reasonable to assume consumption will be negative when income is zero? Certainly not. A one-tailed test of the intercept would not permit rejection of the null hypothesis at any level of significance, which suggests that there may be a problem with the Keynesian theory of consumption,[8] or that there has been a violation of one of the five assumptions. We will have more to say about this later.

---

[7] Curious students can prove that $\hat{\beta}_0$ is unbiased. Refer to the second proof in Appendix 3.A for help.

[8] Many macroeconomists would argue that it is just as unreasonable to think that there is a positive intercept as we initially hypothesized. How is it possible to have positive consumption when income is zero? It's not possible in the long run; it may be possible in the short run.

HYPOTHESIS TESTING IN SIMPLE REGRESSION

1. Hypothesis testing on the regression coefficients involves determining whether the estimate is statistically different from a hypothesized value, usually zero. Most common in econometrics are one-tailed tests, whereby the alternate hypothesis suggests the expected sign of the population parameter. The usual null and alternate hypotheses are:

$$H_0: \beta_j = 0 \quad \text{versus} \quad H_a: \beta_j < 0 \text{ or } H_a: \beta_j > 0.$$

For two-tailed tests, the null and alternate hypotheses are:

$$H_0: \beta_j = 0 \quad \text{versus} \quad H_a: \beta_j \neq 0.$$

2. To test the null hypothesis, form the *t*-ratio:

$$t_{n-2} = \frac{\hat{\beta}_j}{\text{se}(\hat{\beta}_j)}.$$

If this *t*-ratio is greater than the critical *t*-value, approximately 2.00 for a large sample, the null hypothesis is rejected in favor of the alternate. In the case of one-tailed tests, the estimated coefficient must also have the same sign as hypothesized in the alternate hypothesis before the null hypothesis can be rejected.

3.3

REGRESSION, CORRELATION, AND THE COEFFICIENT OF DETERMINATION

Table 3.1 also presents the coefficient of determination, R^2. As we mentioned in Chapter 1, R^2 gives the ratio of "explained" variation in Y to the total variation in Y. Before we can demonstrate why, we need to discuss the relationship between regression analysis and correlation.

3.3.1 Regression and Correlation

As mentioned, regression analysis cannot be used to prove causality; the most it can do is show that the data are consistent with a given hypothesis. Still, most regression analysis is *interpreted* as implying causality between the dependent and independent variables, even though what has been demonstrated is little more than glorified correlation analysis. In fact, we can easily show that $\hat{\beta}_1$ is very closely related to the correlation coefficient between X and Y.

First, recall from Chapter 2 that the simple correlation coefficient between X and Y is defined as:

$$\rho(X, Y) = \frac{\text{cov}(X, Y)}{\sigma_x \sigma_y},$$

[3.18]

while $\hat{\beta}_1$ is defined as:

$$\hat{\beta}_1 = \frac{\sum x_i y_i}{\sum x_i^2},$$

[3.19]

where x_i and y_i are in deviation form. The numerator of Eq. [3.19] is $n - 1$ times the sample covariance between X and Y. By the same reasoning, the denominator of Eq. [3.19] is $n - 1$ times the sample variance of X. Also, because var(X) is the square of σ_x, we could write $\hat{\beta}_1$ as:

$$\hat{\beta}_1 = \frac{(n - 1)\text{cov}(X, Y)}{(n - 1)\sigma_X^2} = \frac{\text{cov}(X, Y)}{\sigma_X \sigma_X}.$$

[3.20]

Comparing Eqs. [3.20] and [3.18] reveals that the only difference between $\hat{\beta}_1$ and $\rho(X, Y)$ is the presence of the standard deviation of Y in the denominator of Eq. [3.18].

One final observation. When the regression model is initially specified, a distinction must be made between the dependent and independent variables. How we make this distinction will affect the estimated slope parameter, but it will not affect the correlation coefficient. For example, consider two regression specifications:

$$Y_i = \beta_0 + \beta_1 X_i + \varepsilon_i,$$

[3.21]

and

$$X_i = \theta_0 + \theta_1 Y_i + v_i$$

[3.22]

The estimated slope parameter for Eq. [3.21] would be the same as Eq. [3.19]. For Eq. [3.22], it would be:

$$\hat{\theta}_1 = \frac{\sum x_i y_i}{\sum y_i^2}.$$

[3.23]

Note, however, that the correlation coefficient between X and Y would be the same for both models. Thus, correlation analysis makes no distinction between independent and dependent variables, while regression analysis does.

3.3.2   The Coefficient of Determination

Many people would argue that the single most important piece of information from a regression analysis printout is the coefficient of determination, or R^2. While there are many reasons to question this assertion, R^2 is indeed very important so we will discuss it in detail.

Recall that the regression residual, e_i, is the difference between the actual data points, Y_i, and the fitted line, $\hat{Y}_i$; that is:

$$e_i = Y_i - \hat{Y}_i. \qquad [3.24]$$

Adding $\hat{Y}_i$ to each side of Eq. [3.24] gives:

$$Y_i = \hat{Y}_i + e_i \qquad [3.25]$$

Subtract $\bar{Y}$, which is the mean of Y, from each side of Eq. [3.25] and substitute Eq. [3.24] for e_i:

$$Y_i - \bar{Y} = (\hat{Y}_i - \bar{Y}) + (Y_i - \hat{Y}_i). \qquad [3.26]$$

Finally, square and sum each side of Eq. [3.26]:

$$\sum(Y_i - \bar{Y})^2 = \sum(\hat{Y}_i - \bar{Y})^2 + \sum(Y_i - \hat{Y}_i)^2 + 2\sum(\hat{Y}_i - \bar{Y})(Y_i - \hat{Y}_i). \qquad [3.27]$$

Equation [3.27] is the key to understanding R^2. The term on the left side tells how Y varies about its mean. This is the total variation in Y, or the _total sum of squares_ (TSS). The first term on the right side measures how the fitted regression line varies about the mean of Y. This is known as the explained variation in Y, or the _regression sum of squares_ (RSS). The middle term on the right side is called the _error sum of squares_ (ESS) because it is a measure of the unexplained variation in Y—the amount of variation in Y that is left to the residual. We can dismiss the final term on the right side because it becomes zero, a proposition we prove in Appendix 3.A.

For simplicity, we will rewrite Eq. [3.27] as:

$$\text{TSS} = \text{RSS} + \text{ESS}. \qquad [3.28]$$

Now, divide each side by TSS,

$$1 = \frac{\text{RSS}}{\text{TSS}} + \frac{\text{ESS}}{\text{TSS}}, \qquad [3.29]$$

and we are done: The coefficient of determination, R^2, is defined as the first term on the right side of Eq. [3.29]—the ratio of the explained variation in Y to the total variation in Y. Rearranging reveals that R^2 is also equal to 1 minus

TABLE 3.2 **Analysis of variance**

Analysis of Variance					
Source	Sum-of-Squares	DF	Mean-Square	F-Ratio	P
Regression	5320775.80	1	5320775.80	8003.41	0.00
Residual	17285.16	26	664.81		

the second term on the right side of Eq. [3.29]:

$$R^2 \equiv \frac{\text{RSS}}{\text{TSS}} \equiv 1 - \frac{\text{ESS}}{\text{TSS}}.$$

[3.30]

Finally, because all of the terms in Eq. [3.29] are squares, a quick inspection reveals that R^2 must be between 0 and 1. The closer it is to 1, the greater the amount of variation "explained" by the regression equation.

3.3.3 Analysis of Variance

The R^2 calculated in Table 3.1 exceeds 0.99, an apparent indication that our simple model has explained more than 99% of the total variation in consumption expenditures. Whether it does, of course, depends on whether all of our assumptions are fulfilled (we will see momentarily that they are not), but the immediate question is whether we should trust our estimated coefficient of determination even if the assumptions are satisfied. The reliability of the coefficient of determination and the regression equation is done with a technique called *analysis of variance* or ANOVA. Table 3.2 presents an ANOVA table that accompanies the other regression statistics.

While various statistical packages present slight differences in ANOVA tables, they all provide the same sort of information. The entries in the "Sum-of-Squares" column are RSS and ESS, respectfully. Thus, R^2 could be found by taking the ratio of $5320775.80/(5320775.80 + 17285.16) = 0.99+$.

The information in the "DF" and "Mean-Square" columns is used in the construction of the *F-statistic*, a test to determine the overall significance of the regression equation. The basis for the F-test is the idea that the ratio of the explained variation to the unexplained variation should be high if the tested model is a reasonable approximation of the true model. Just how high this ratio needs to be is determined by calculating an F-statistic and comparing it to the critical value in the F-table.

As we mentioned briefly in Chapter 2, the F-distribution is the ratio of two χ^2-distributions divided by their respective degrees of freedom. Now, dividing RSS and ESS by their degrees of freedom will convert them from variations to variances. Further, if A3 holds (i.e., the error terms are normally distributed with a zero mean), the sample variances will follow a χ^2-distribution. The ratio of these distributions, divided by their respective degrees of freedom, is the F-statistic we need. However, we need to calculate the degrees of freedom. The F-test for a simple regression model has 1 degree of freedom in the numerator and $n - 2$ degrees of freedom in the denominator. How do we know? TSS has $n - 1$ degrees of freedom because 1 degree of freedom was used to calculate $\bar{Y}$. We know that TSS = RSS + ESS, and the number of degrees of freedom on the right side must equal the number on the left side, $n - 1$. To estimate ESS, we must use two degrees of freedom—one to estimate $\hat{\beta}_0$ and one to estimate β_1—meaning that ESS has $n - 2$ degrees of freedom. Only 1 degree of freedom is left for RSS. The formula for the F-statistic in simple regression is:

$$F_{1, n-2} = \frac{\text{explained variance}}{\text{unexplained variance}} = \frac{\text{RSS}/1}{\text{ESS}/n - 2}. \qquad [3.31]$$

We can use this information in the same manner in which we use the information for a t-test.[9] If the calculated F-value is larger than the critical value in the table, we reject the null hypothesis of no significant linear relationship between X and Y. Rejection of the null hypothesis is an indication that X and Y are linearly related. If the calculated F-value is smaller than the table value, we fail to reject the null hypothesis and conclude that there is no significant linear relationship between X and Y. In simple regression, a model with low t-scores and a low R^2 will also have a low F-value. This is usually the case in multiple regression as well.

Referring to Table 3.2, the F-value has been calculated as the ratio of the two entries in the "Mean-Square" column. Note that the "Mean-Square" column is merely the "Sum-of-Squares" column divided by the degrees of freedom—one for the numerator (RSS) and 26 for the denominator (ESS). Reading the F-table is straightforward. First, choose either a 1 or 5% significance level because these are the only entries in most F-tables. Next find the table entry corresponding to the numbers closest to the degrees of freedom in the numerator (across the top) and the denominator (down the left column). This is the critical F-value that must be compared to the calculated F-statistic. In this case, we use the entry for $F_{1,26}$. At the 5% significance level, the critical F-value is 4.23. Because the estimated F-ratio is 8003.41, we can reject the null hypothesis of no significant linear relationship between X and Y. This conclusion is verified by the entry in the "P" column, which represents the probability of obtaining the regression results if the null hypothesis is correct. The value 0.00 suggests that there is a 0% chance that the null hypothesis of the F-test is correct.

---

[9] In fact, in simple regression, the F-statistic is the square of the t-statistic on the slope parameter. This follows from the formal definitions of the t- and F-distributions, and can be seen by referring to the relevant entries in the t- and F-tables. Notice that this is only true for simple regression; in multiple regression analysis, the F- and t-tests are quite different.

OUTLIERS AND THE IMPORTANCE OF *LOOKING* AT THE DATA

THE SUMMARY statistics produced by regression analysis are the usual criteria used in the analysis of the regression model. However, exclusive reliance on these statistics can occasionally be misleading— enough so that it is always a good idea to plot the data and look for anything peculiar. One important thing to look for is *outliers*—data points that are far from the norm—because regression analysis places excessive weight on extreme points. As an example of the problems posed by outliers, consider the two data sets below from Edward Tufte, *The Visual Display of Quantitative Information*[10]:

X1	Y1	X2	Y2
10.0	8.04	8.0	6.58
8.0	6.95	8.0	5.76
13.0	7.58	8.0	7.71
9.0	8.81	8.0	8.84
11.0	8.33	8.0	8.47
14.0	9.96	8.0	7.04
6.0	7.24	8.0	5.25
4.0	4.26	19.0	12.5
12.0	10.84	8.0	5.56
7.0	4.82	8.0	7.91
5.0	5.68	8.0	6.89

---

[10]Graphics Press, Cheshire, Connecticut, 1983, p. 13–14. Data used with permission.

continued on page 82

These are obviously very different sets of data; however, performing regression analysis on them yields almost exactly the same summary statistics and parameter estimates! A quick glance at the scatter plots tells the story: The extreme outlier in the second data set, $X_8 = 19$, is enough to affect the results considerably. Outliers that extreme are rare in real-world data and would have less of an impact with a reasonably sized data set; but you are advised to examine a plot of the data as well as the summary statistics very carefully before drawing to any conclusions. Outliers can be dealt with in several ways. The easiest way is simply to omit them, but without a well-defined decision rule, throwing away data can lead to even more serious problems.

```
Dep var:Y1  N: 11  R-squared: .667  SER: 1.24

Variable  Coefficient  Std Error    T    P(2 tail)
CONSTANT    3.00         1.12      2.67    0.03
    X1      0.50         0.12      4.24    0.00

              Analysis of Variance

  Source   Sum-of-Squares  DF  Mean-Square  F-Ratio   P
Regression     27.51        1    27.51       17.99  0.00
Residual       13.76        9    1.53
```

```
Dep var: Y2  N: 11  R-squared: .667  SER: 1.24

Variable  Coefficient  Std Error    T    P(2 tail)
CONSTANT     3.00        1.12     2.67     0.03
    X2       0.50        0.12     4.25     0.00

              Analysis of Variance

  Source   Sum-of-Squares  DF  Mean-Square  F-Ratio   P
Regression     27.49        1    27.49      18.00   0.00
Residual       13.74        9    1.53
```

continued on page 83

S I D E
■ B A R

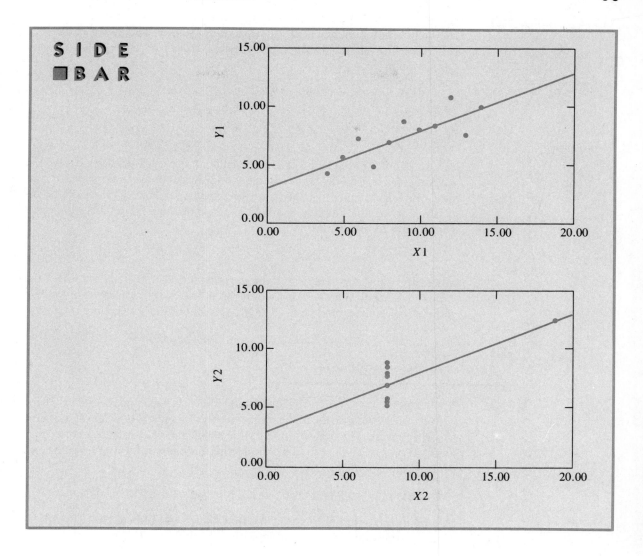

3.4

PREDICTION

Thus far, the regression model has been used simply to explain the relationship between DPI and CONS. The other main purpose of regression analysis is prediction or forecasting.

Once the regression model has been estimated, it is a simple matter to extrapolate the trend—merely estimate a future value of the independent variable and plug it into the regression equation. For example, if you have reason to believe that real DPI will rise to $2,800 billion next year, substituting this value into the regression equation yields a *point estimate* of next year's consumption[11]:

$$\widehat{CONS}_{T+1} = -33.38 + 0.93(2800) = \$2570.62 \text{ billion.}$$

Such a forecast is called a *conditional forecast* because its accuracy depends (among other things) on the accuracy of the estimated value of X_{T+1}.

If X_{T+1} is known, the resulting prediction is said to be *unconditional*. How can we know a *future* value of an independent variable? We can't. However, we can construct models that make unconditional forecasts possible. In fact, most models designed primarily for forecasting use lagged values of the independent variables as regressors. In the case of the CONS/DPI model, we would have to test the form:

$$CONS_t = \alpha_0 + \alpha_1 DPI_{t-1} + \varepsilon_t, \qquad [3.32]$$

where the subscript t indicates the current period and $t-1$ indicates the previous period. Whether this would be a reasonable forecasting model[12] depends, of course, on whether $CONS_t$ is a function of DPI_{t-1}.

3.4.1   The Prediction Interval

Point estimates—even for unconditional forecasts—can prove embarrassing to forecasters because the audience inevitably remembers how far off, not how close, you were. The best solution to this problem is to construct a confidence interval around the prediction. The prediction interval for a 5% significance level is calculated as:

$$\Pr(\hat{Y}_{T+1} - t_{0.05}s_p \le Y_{T+1} \le \hat{Y}_{T+1} + t_{0.05}s_p) = 0.95. \qquad [3.33]$$

Assuming our assumptions hold and that X_{T+1} is as predicted, Eq. [3.33] says that the true value of Y_{T+1} will lie within this interval 95% of the time. Note

---

[11] Notice that we are using the subscript "t" to indicate individual observations on X and Y. (The last observation in the series denotes T, so "$T+1$" in a one period prediction.) This is only to emphasize that we are dealing with time series data. The subscript "i" would work just as well and will be used throughout the text except when the point being discussed applies explicitly to time series data.

[12] In this particular case, the lagged version of the model fits almost as well as the current version: $R^2 = 0.99$ and $\hat{\beta}_1 = 0.93$. However, $\hat{\beta}_0$ rises to 6.13—an indication that the lagged model differs substantially from the model using current data. A different—and superior—version of the consumption function is tested in Chapter 5.

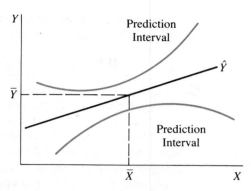

FIGURE 3.3   The prediction interval.

The prediction interval increases as the forecast moves farther from $\bar{X}$. The standard error of the prediction also increases with s^2; it decreases as the variance of X increases.

that we have used s_p, the *standard error of the prediction*, instead of the SER in the calculation of the prediction interval. The standard error of the prediction is defined as the square root of the forecast variance given in;

$$s_p^2 = s^2 \left[1 + \frac{1}{T} + \frac{(X_{T+1} - \bar{X})^2}{\sum (X_t - \bar{X})^2} \right] \qquad\qquad [3.34]$$

where T is the total number of observations in the data set.

The derivation of the formula for the forecast variance is quite tedious and, therefore, has been left for Appendix 3.A, but we should note three things about the prediction variance before proceeding. First, the prediction variance varies directly with s^2, the regression variance. Second, the denominator of the third term is $t - 1$ times the sample variance of X, so as the variance of X increases, s_p^2 decreases. This is an indication that, other things being equal, better predictions come from models with X variables that show a wide dispersion. Third, and perhaps most important, the presence of $\bar{X}$ in the numerator of the third term indicates that the prediction variance, and hence the standard error of the prediction and prediction interval, increases the farther the prediction is from $\bar{X}$. This is illustrated in Fig. 3.3

To calculate the actual prediction interval around Y_{T+1}, we need to find the information to plug into Eqs. [3.33] and [3.34]. We can get s^2 from two places. The "mean square" of the residual in Table 3.2 is the sum that is minimized in the process of calculating $\hat{\beta}_0$ and $\hat{\beta}_1$—otherwise known as s^2. Alternatively, we could simply square the SER. The mean of X, $\bar{X}$, was not provided by either printout, but can be found quite easily; it is 1860.68. To find $\sum (X_i - \bar{X})^2$, recall the definition of se($\hat{\beta}_1$): the SER divided by the square root of $\sum (X_i - \bar{X})^2$.

Because $se(\hat{\beta}_1) = 0.01$ and the SER = 25.78, a little manipulation shows that $\sum(X_i - \bar{X})^2 = 6646084$, which gives s_p^2 the following value:

$$s_p^2 = 25.78^2\left[1 + \frac{1}{28} + \frac{(2800 - 1860.68)^2}{6646084.0}\right] = 776.58.$$

The square root of 688.40 is 26.24, so a 95% confidence interval is 2570.62 $\pm 2.056(27.87)$.

Accurate prediction is an alternative test of the reliability of the regression model, but a quite different test than R^2, F-, or t-tests. In fact, a model may forecast well even if it has a bad R^2. It is also possible for a model to forecast very poorly even if it has good summary statistics—especially if the forecast is attempted during a period of structural change that was not captured in the model. For these reasons, many econometricians use the methods discussed in Chapter 9—time series forecasting—when their primary goal is forecasting.

PREDICTION AND THE SER   While construction of a confidence interval around the forecast may save some embarrassment, that interval should be very small if possible. How small? As a rule of thumb, many forecasters like the SER to be 15% or less of the mean value of the dependent variable. Like most "rules of thumb," there is no real statistical reason for the 15% rule; it is simply a convenient benchmark. Most forecasters, in fact, would prefer that the SER be much less than 15% of $\bar{Y}$.

3.5

ELASTICITIES

We often need to calculate *elasticity coefficients* for regression models. Elasticity measures the relative responsiveness of the dependent variable to a small change in the independent variable. For example, a concept used in microeconomics is the price elasticity of demand, η_p. When demand is inelastic, a change in price will result in a relatively small change in the quantity demanded. When demand is elastic, the opposite occurs: A change in price will result in a relatively large change in the quantity demanded. Among other things, elasticity of demand depends on the availability of substitutes—when more substitutes are available, demand will tend to be more elastic. Formally, price elasticity is defined as:

$$\eta_p = \frac{\%\Delta \text{ in quantity}}{\%\Delta \text{ in price}} = \frac{\Delta Q/Q}{\Delta P/P}. \qquad [3.35]$$

Elasticity is not limited to demand curves. In fact, elasticity coefficients can be derived for any system that has both independent and dependent variables—including regression analysis.

For the simple regression equation, $Y_i = \beta_0 + \beta_1 X_i + \varepsilon_i$, the relevant elasticity coefficient measures the percentage change in Y associated with a percentage change in X. We write the equation as:

$$\eta_x = \frac{\Delta Y/Y}{\Delta X/X}, \tag{3.36}$$

or, with a little manipulation,

$$\eta_x = \frac{\Delta Y}{\Delta X}\left(\frac{X}{Y}\right). \tag{3.37}$$

We can relate this directly to the regression printout by noting that β_1 is the slope of the regression equation, $\Delta Y/\Delta X$. Substitution into Eq. [3.37] gives:

$$\eta_x = \beta_1\left(\frac{X}{Y}\right). \tag{3.38}$$

We need to make one additional adjustment: Elasticity is closely related to slope, but it is definitely not the same thing. For example, a linear demand curve has a constant slope but is inelastic ($\eta < 1$) at high prices, elastic ($\eta > 1$) at low prices, and has a unitary elasticity coefficient ($\eta = 1$) at the midpoint. Because of this, we need to measure elasticity at a particular point on the regression line. Generally, this is done at the midpoint.[13] Thus, we substitute $\bar{X}$ and $\bar{Y}$ in Eq. [3.38]:

$$\eta_x = \beta_1\left(\frac{\bar{X}}{\bar{Y}}\right). \tag{3.39}$$

Now we return to the consumption model. Because the mean of $\mathrm{DPI}(\bar{X}) = 1860.7$, the mean of $\mathrm{CONS}(\bar{Y}) = 1688.0$ and $\hat{\beta}_1 = 0.93$, the income elasticity of consumption is: $0.93(1860.7/1688) = 1.025$, which means that a one percentage point change in income will result in a 1.025 percentage point change in consumption. The importance of elasticities is one reason why regression analysis is often performed using logs of the data. As shown in the appendix to Chapter 5, the regression coefficients from a model using logs of the data are elasticities, not slopes.

Do the assumptions hold?

Whenever conducting econometric studies, we need to be certain the assumptions have been satisifed before trusting the results. In this case, we have good reason to be skeptical: The sign and value of $\hat{\beta}_1$ make sense, but

---

[13] But not always. Elasticity is typically calculated at the end point when the model is intended for forecasting.

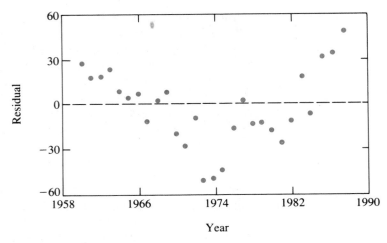

FIGURE 3.4   Residuals.

The pattern in the residuals—several positive residuals, followed by several negative residuals, etc.—is an indication of autocorrelation, a violation of A4.

we did not expect a negative value for $\hat{\beta}_0$, and an R^2 that exceeds 0.99 is almost certainly too good to be true. At least two of the assumptions must be called into question.

A1: Does the specified model accurately reflect the true model? Perhaps, but we have no way of knowing for sure. Suffice it to say that several theories of the consumption function—for example, the life cycle hypothesis—hold that the consumption function is nonlinear. Further, most theories of consumption include additional independent variables— an interest rate, wealth, expected inflation, etc. Thus, we must hold open the possibility that the model was misspecified. Specification errors can bias parameter estimates and could explain why we got a negative value for $\hat{\beta}_0$.

A4: Are the error terms independent? We will examine this problem in detail in later chapters, but for the time being, a simple inspection of a plot of the regression residuals in Fig. 3.4 is enough to spot the problem. Notice that the first several residuals are positive while the next several are negative, followed by several positive residuals. Thus, if you know the sign of e_1, you probably know the sign of e_2, etc. This is an indication that the errors are correlated with each other—clear evidence of autocorrelation, a violation of A4. As we will find out in Chapter 6, autocorrelation biases both the t-ratios and R^2 upward, making the model look better than it really is.

Data. We should also be wary of the data set used in this test. Most macroeconomists would prefer to use quarterly data instead of annual data for a test of this sort. Not only would quarterly data provide four times as many data points, but it better captures business fluctuations.[14] The small sample size—only 28 data points—leaves open the possibility that the particular sample we chose does not capture the true relationship between consumption and disposable income. This is always a possibility when working with sample data, but it is particularly acute with such a small sample.   ◆ ◆ ◆

CONCEPTS FOR REVIEW

This is an exceedingly important chapter so it is crucial that you understand the ideas well before proceeding. Be sure you:

- can state and understand the five assumptions;
- know how to interpret simple regression and ANOVA printouts;
- can differentiate between regression and correlation analysis;
- can calculate degrees of freedom for t- and F-tests;
- can read t- and F-tables and use them to test hypotheses;
- understand these important derivations: $\hat{\beta}_1$ is unbiased and R^2 is derived from $\sum(Y_i - \bar{Y})^2$;
- can calculate elasticities from regression results;
- can define and use the following terms in context.

KEY TERMS

ANOVA	prediction interval
autocorrelation	R^2
BLUE	SER
conditional, unconditional forecast	standard error of the prediction
elasticity	stochastic, nonstochastic
F-test	TSS, RSS, ESS
Gauss-Markov Theorem	t-test
heteroscedasticity	

---

[14]Since World War II, the typical recession has lasted just under a year. Thus, annual data may smooth over important consumption and income downturns.

EXERCISES

3.1 Suppose that $var(X) = var(Y)$. How would this affect the relationship between $\hat{\beta}_1$ and $corr(X, Y)$?

3.2 Calculate the t-ratios using the data from Table 1.1 in Chapter 1. Would you accept or reject the null hypothesis on the intercept? On the slope?

3.3 Suppose that $Y_i = \beta_0 + \beta_1 X_i + \varepsilon_i$. Given a sample of 18 observations and the following information: $\sum x_i^2 = 222527.6$, ESS $= 127.87$

$$\sum X_i = 4478; \qquad \sum Y_i = 706; \qquad \sum X_i Y_i = 209952;$$
$$\sum X_i^2 = 1336749; \qquad \sum Y_i^2 = 33106.$$

a. Find $\hat{\beta}_0$ and $\hat{\beta}_1$.   **b.** Find s^2.

c. Find $se(\hat{\beta}_1)$.   **d.** Calculate R^2.

3.4 Suppose that the mean of ε_i is nonzero. How will this affect parameter estimates?

3.5 Prove Eq. [3.2].

3.6 The hypothesis for the consumption function was $H_0: \beta_1 = 0$ versus $H_a: \beta_1 \neq 0$. This is a two-tailed test. Economic theory might suggest a one-tailed test. State the null and alternative hypotheses for such a test. How would this affect your interpretation of the regression results?

3.7 Would you be more confident of a model if $var(X)$ were large or small? Why?

3.8 Suppose you have reason to believe that Y is affected by X. To test this hypothesis, you collect ten data points and perform regression analysis. The computer gives the following information. What does it mean?

```
Estimated model parameters:

Variable    Estimate    t-value   P(Chance)   Sig.
--------    --------    -------   ---------   ----

Intercept   138.15205   16.39034   0.00000     *
X             0.61636    3.79317    0.00264     *

R squared is    0.64267
Estimated sigma squared is      66.12426
```

3.9 When you ask the computer to print the ANOVA table, you accidentally drag your foot across the carpet, and because you are wearing the latest 100% polyester leisure suit, you zap the computer with static electricity and blur some of the results. The only thing that prints is the following:

```
Analysis of Variance for Significance of Regression

Source          Sum Squares   Deg. Freedom   Mean Square
------          -----------   ------------   -----------

Regression        951.4059         ?           951.4059
Error             528.9941         ?            66.1243

Total            1480.4000

F-Value is ?
R squared is ?
```

Replace the question marks with the correct data.

3.10 Prove that:

$$\text{cov}(\hat{\beta}_0, \hat{\beta}_1) = \frac{-\bar{X}\sigma^2}{\sum x_i^2}.$$

3.11 Suppose that $\bar{Q}_d = 50$, $\bar{P} = \$8$, and $\hat{\beta}_1 = 1.5$. Is demand elastic or inelastic?

3.12 Suppose you wanted to determine if television advertising affects the sales at your department store. Explain how you could use regression analysis to answer this question.

3.13 Suppose you wanted to test if the level of personal savings (SAV) has an influence on the AAA bond rate. After performing simple regression on annual data over the 1977–87 period, you find the following:

```
Dep var: AAA  N: 11  R-squared: .799  SER: 1.01

Variable  Coefficient  Std Error    T     P(2 tail)

CONSTANT     -0.38       1.93    -0.20      0.85
     SAV      0.09       0.01     5.97      0.00

F-Ratio 35.70
```

a. Interpret these results. Are they consistent with economic theory?

b. After running that regression you realize that you had misspecified your model by assigning AAA as the dependent variable and SAV as the independent variable. A second regression yields the following. Interpret these results. Explain why some of the estimates are the same and some are different.

```
Dep var:SAV   N: 11   R-sq:  .799   SER:  10.38

Variable   Coefficient   Std Error    T     P(2 tail)

CONSTANT        29.89        17.22    1.74     0.12
   AAA           9.21         1.54    5.97     0.00

F-Ratio 35.70
```

c. Is there any way to tell from the two printouts which of the variables is actually independent and which is dependent?

3.14 The data used in Exercise 3.21 were input such that 5.5 represented a 5.5% unemployment rate and 11.8 stood for eleven and eight-tenths weeks duration. Suppose that the unemployment data were rescaled and input as 0.054, 0.065, etc.? How would this change $\hat{\beta}_0$ and $\hat{\beta}_1$?

3.15 Suppose the five assumptions are satisfied.

a. If $e_1, e_2, e_3 > 0$, which is the probability that $e_4 < 0$?

b. How would you change your answer if A4 were violated?

c. How would you change your answer if A5 were violated?

3.16 Simple Keynesian theory holds that the intercept of the consumption function should be positive. Use the information in Table 3.1 to conduct a one-tailed test on β_0. Can you reject the null hypothesis at the 5% significance level? At 10%?

3.17 One of the key ideas in finance is the *beta coefficient*, a measure of the risk associated with a particular stock or stock portfolio. The beta coefficient of a particular stock, Y, is the slope coefficient (β_1) from a simple regression using the rate of return for the stock as the dependent variable and the rate of return of the market as the independent variable. Suppose you ran regressions for stocks A and B and got the following results:

$$\hat{Y}_A = \beta_0 + 1.5X,$$

$$Y_B = \beta_0 + 0.5X,$$

with identical R^2's and significant t-ratios. Which stock would you rather have in your portfolio? Why?

3.18 Prove

$$R^2 = \hat{\beta}_i^2 \frac{\sum x_i^2}{\sum y_i^2}.$$

3.19 Prove RSS $= \hat{\beta}_1 \text{cov}(X, Y)$.

3.20 Show $R^2 = [\rho(\hat{Y}_i, Y_i)]^2$.

3.21 The average duration of unemployment (D) appears to increase when the unemployment rate (U) increases. Use the data below, from the *Economic Report of the President*, to test this hypothesis with regression analysis.

Year	U	D	Year	U	D
1960	5.4	12.8	1966	3.7	10.4
1961	6.5	15.6	1967	3.7	8.7
1962	5.4	14.7	1968	3.5	8.4
1963	5.5	14.0	1969	3.4	7.8
1964	5.0	13.3	1970	4.8.	8.6
1965	4.4	11.8			

Before you perform regression analysis:

a. What sign do you expect on $\hat{\beta}_1$? On $\hat{\beta}_0$?

b. Do you expect to get a high R^2?

After you perform the analysis:

c. Are your results consistent with your *a priori* hypothesis?

d. How would you improve the model?

3.22 The Conference Board compiles the *consumer confidence index* (CCI) to use as a leading indicator of economic activity. Generally, an upturn in the CCI suggests good economic times ahead while a downturn indicates the opposite. Data Set 2 from Appendix I gives monthly data for the CCI as well as real consumer durable (CD) and nondurable (CN) goods production for the period 1981–85. Construct two regression models to test the relationship between the CCI and CD and CCI and CN.

Before running the regression:

a. State your hypothesis regarding the expected signs on $\hat{\beta}_1$ and $\hat{\beta}_0$ for both models.

b. Do you expect to find a higher R^2 for the CD or CN model? Why?

After running the regression:

c. Interpret your results.

d. How would you improve the models?

APPENDIX 3.A

PROOFS

We left four demonstrations to the appendix. The first is quite simple, the others are a bit more tedious.

$E(\Sigma x_i \varepsilon_i) = 0$

One step in the proof that $\hat{\beta}_1$ was unbiased required the result $E(\sum x_i \varepsilon_i) = 0$. This step is critical not only in this proof, but we will use it later when we discuss specification errors and simultaneous equations estimation. Fortunately, the demonstration is quite easy.

First, the expected value operator can be moved inside the summation sign:

$$E\left(\sum x_i \varepsilon_i\right) = \sum E(x_i \varepsilon_i). \qquad [A.1]$$

However, while X can be a random variable, individual observations on X are fixed. Thus, we can write:

$$\sum E(x_i \varepsilon_i) = \sum x_i E(\varepsilon_i); \qquad [A.2]$$

but $E(\varepsilon_i) = 0$, so we are left with what we needed to demonstrate:

$$\sum x_i E(\varepsilon_i) = \sum x_i(0) = 0. \qquad [A.3]$$

The Variance of β_1

We can derive the $\text{var}(\hat{\beta}_1)$ by making a few substitutions, using assumptions A4 and A5, and recalling a definition from Chapter 2. First, note that $\hat{\beta}_1$ is a weighted sum of x_i and y_i:

$$\hat{\beta} = \frac{\sum x_i y_i}{\sum x_i^2}. \qquad [A.4]$$

We can simplify the derivation quite a bit if we denote the weight as:

$$w_i = \frac{x_i}{\sum x_i^2}. \qquad [A.5]$$

We need to use two results related to w_i. First, if we square and sum w_i we get:

$$\sum w_i^2 = \sum \left[\frac{x_i^2}{(\sum x_i^2)^2}\right]. \qquad [A.6]$$

We can take the denominator outside the sum because $\sum x_i^2$ is a constant. This leaves us with:

$$\sum w_i^2 = \frac{1}{(\sum x_i^2)^2} \sum x_i^2 = \frac{1}{\sum x_i^2}. \qquad [A.7]$$

Also, notice what happens if we sum and square $w_i x_i$:

$$\sum w_i x_i = \sum \frac{x_i^2}{\sum x_i^2} = \frac{\sum x_i^2}{\sum x_i^2} = 1. \qquad [A.8]$$

The definition of w_i allows us to rewrite $\hat{\beta}_1$ as:

$$\hat{\beta}_1 = \sum w_i y_i. \qquad [A.9]$$

Because $y_i = \hat{\beta}_1 x_i + \varepsilon_i$, substitution for y_i in Eq. [A.9] gives:

$$\hat{\beta}_1 = \sum w_i y_i = \sum w_i (\beta_1 x_i + \varepsilon_i). \qquad [A.10]$$

These results will be useful momentarily.

Now, because $E(\hat{\beta}_1) = \beta_1$, the definition of $\text{var}(\hat{\beta}_1)$ is:

$$\text{var}(\hat{\beta}_1) = E(\hat{\beta}_1 - \beta_1)^2. \qquad [A.11]$$

Equation [A.10] allows us to write $(\hat{\beta}_1 - \beta_1)$ as:

$$(\hat{\beta}_1 - \beta_1) = \sum w_i (\beta_1 x_i + \varepsilon_i) - \beta_1. \qquad [A.12]$$

Expanding the right side gives:

$$\sum w_i (\beta_1 x_i + \varepsilon_i) - \beta_1 = \beta_1 \sum w_i x_i + \sum w_i \varepsilon_i - \beta_1. \qquad [A.13]$$

Equation [A.8] allows us to simplify Eq. [A.13] considerably:

$$\beta_1 \sum w_i x_i + \sum w_i \varepsilon_i - \beta_1 = \beta_1(1) + \sum w_i \varepsilon_i - \beta_1 = \sum w_i \varepsilon_i. \qquad [A.14]$$

Hence,

$$(\hat{\beta}_1 - \beta_1)^2 = (\sum w_i \varepsilon_i)^2. \qquad [A.15]$$

Now we are ready to determine the variance of $\hat{\beta}_1$. Using the expected value of Eq. [A.15],

$$\text{var}(\hat{\beta}_1) = E(\hat{\beta}_1 - \beta_1)^2 = E(\sum w_i \varepsilon_i)^2, \qquad [A.16]$$

expanding the sum gives:

$$E(\sum w_i \varepsilon_i)^2 = E[(w_1 \varepsilon_1)^2 + (w_2 \varepsilon_2)^2 + 2(w_1 w_2 \varepsilon_1 \varepsilon_2) + \cdots + (w_n \varepsilon_n)^2]. \qquad [A.17]$$

However, A4 allows us to assume that the ε_i are uncorrelated, meaning that the expected values of all terms involving $E(\varepsilon_i \varepsilon_j)$, $i \neq j$, go to zero. Eq. [A.17] thus becomes:

$$\text{var}(\hat{\beta}_1) = E(\sum w_i \varepsilon_i)^2 = E[(w_1 \varepsilon_1)^2 + (w_2 \varepsilon_2)^2 + \cdots + (w_n \varepsilon_n)^2].$$

[A.18]

Because the weights are nonstochastic, they can come outside the expected value operator:

$$E(\sum w_i \varepsilon_i)^2 = w_1^2 E(\varepsilon_1^2) + w_2^2 E(\varepsilon_2^2) + \cdots + w_n^2 E(\varepsilon_n^2);$$

[A.19]

and because we assume the errors are homoscedastic, we have:

$$\text{var}(\hat{\beta}_1) = \sigma^2 \sum w_i^2.$$

[A.20]

Substituting Eq. [A.6] for $\sum w_i^2$ gives:

$$\text{var}(\hat{\beta}_1) = \frac{\sigma^2}{\sum x_i^2},$$

[A.21]

which completes the proof.

Finally, the standard error of $\hat{\beta}_1$, $\text{se}(\hat{\beta}_1)$, is just the positive square root of $\text{var}(\hat{\beta}_1)$.

$\Sigma(\hat{Y}_i - \bar{Y})(Y_i - \hat{Y}_i) = 0$

When we showed that R^2 was equal to the ratio of RSS to TSS, we had to assume that $\sum(\hat{Y}_1 - \bar{Y})(Y_i - \hat{Y}_1) = 0$. The demonstration is straightforward. First substitute, e_i for $Y_i - \hat{Y}_i$. This gives:

$$\sum(\hat{Y}_i - \bar{Y})(Y_i - \hat{Y}_i) = \sum(\hat{Y}_i - \bar{Y})e_i.$$

[A.22]

When we expand the right side and take the constant $\bar{Y}$ outside the sum, we have:

$$\sum(\hat{Y}_i - \bar{Y})e_i = \sum \hat{Y}_i e_i - \bar{Y} \sum e_i.$$

[A.23]

Now, the sum of the regression residuals is zero, so the second term on the right side goes to zero. Substituting for $\hat{Y}_i$ in the first term on the right side gives:

$$\sum \hat{Y}_i e_i = \sum(\hat{\beta}_0 + \hat{\beta}_1 X_i)e_i,$$

[A.24]

which, after expanding and taking the constants outside is

$$\sum(\hat{\beta}_0 + \hat{\beta}_1 X_i)e_i = \hat{\beta}_0 \sum e_i + \hat{\beta}_1 \sum X_i e_i.$$

[A.25]

Because the first term on the right side equals zero, Eq. [A.24] will equal zero only if the second term is also zero. To show this, substitute $x_i + \bar{X}$ for X_i and write:

$$\sum X_i e_i = \sum (x_i + \bar{X}) e_i = \sum x_i e_i + \bar{X} \sum e_i = \sum x_i e_i. \qquad \text{[A.26]}$$

Letting $y_i - \hat{\beta}_1 x_i = e_i$, we can write:

$$\sum x_i e_i = \sum x_i (y_i - \hat{\beta}_1 x_i) = \sum x_i y_i - \hat{\beta}_1 \sum x_i^2. \qquad \text{[A.27]}$$

Substituting the estimator for $\hat{\beta}_1$ completes the proof:

$$\sum x_i e_i = \sum x_i y_i - \frac{\sum x_i y_i}{\sum x_i^2} \left(\sum x_i^2 \right) = 0. \qquad \text{[A.28]}$$

Derivation of s_p

In Sec. 3.4.1, we noted that the standard error of the prediction (s_p) differs from the SER. The proof, [15] although somewhat tedious, is necessary to show why the prediction interval increases as the prediction gets farther from $\bar{X}$. The best prediction of the OLS model is:

$$\hat{Y}_{T+1} = \hat{\beta}_0 + \hat{\beta}_1 X_{T+1}, \qquad \text{[A.29]}$$

and the error of the prediction is:

$$e_{T+1} = \hat{Y}_{T+1} - Y_{T+1} = (\hat{\beta}_0 - \beta_0) + (\hat{\beta}_1 - \beta_1)X_{T+1} - \varepsilon_{T+1}. \qquad \text{[A.30]}$$

Equation [A.30] makes it apparent that there are two possible sources of error in any prediction: the true error (ε_{T+1}), and the errors in the estimation of the regression parameters. The error of the prediction has a zero mean as long as $\hat{\beta}_0$ and $\hat{\beta}_1$ are unbiased. It is also normally distributed because it is a linear combination of $\hat{\beta}_0$, $\hat{\beta}_1$, and ε_{T+1}.

Now to find the standard error of the prediction, we need to first derive the variance of e_{T+1}:

$$\sigma_p^2 = E(e_{T+1}^2) = E[(\hat{\beta}_0 - \beta_0)^2] + E[(\hat{\beta}_1 - \beta_1)^2]X_{T+1}^2 + E[(\varepsilon_{T+1})^2]$$
$$+ 2E[(\hat{\beta}_0 - \beta_0)(\hat{\beta}_1 - \beta_1)]X_{T+1}. \qquad \text{[A.31]}$$

What happened to the terms involving the estimated coefficients and e_{T+1}? They go to zero because $\hat{\beta}_0$ and $\hat{\beta}_1$ were estimated using only the first T observations and are thus independent of e_{T+1}.

Equation [A.31] can be written more simply by noting that the first three terms on the right side are variances and the fourth is a covariance:

$$\sigma_p^2 = \text{var}(\hat{\beta}_0) + \text{var}(\hat{\beta}_1)X_{T+1}^2 + \sigma^2 + 2\text{cov}(\hat{\beta}_0, \hat{\beta}_1)X_{T+1}. \qquad \text{[A.32]}$$

---

[15] This derivation follows Pindyck and Rubenfeld, *Econometric Models and Econometrics Forecasts* (New York: McGraw-Hill, 1981), p. 208–210.

Substituting Eqs. [3.16] and [3.14] for $\text{var}(\hat{\beta}_0)$ and $\text{var}(\hat{\beta}_1)$, respectively, and noting from Exercise 3.10 that the covariance between $\hat{\beta}_0$ and $\hat{\beta}_1$ is defined as:

$$\text{cov}(\hat{\beta}_0, \hat{\beta}_1) = \frac{-\bar{X}\sigma^2}{\sum(X_t - \bar{X})^2},$$ [A.33]

a little manipulation gives:

$$\sigma_p^2 = \sigma^2\left[\frac{\sum X_t^2}{T\sum(X_t - \bar{X})^2} - \frac{2\bar{X}X_{T+1}}{\sum(X_t - \bar{X})^2} + \frac{X_{T+1}^2}{\sum(X_t - \bar{X})^2} + 1\right].$$ [A.34]

Notice that the first term in the brackets on the right side of Eq. [A.34] can be written as:

$$\frac{\sum X_t^2}{T\sum(X_t - \bar{X})^2} = \frac{\sum(X_t - \bar{X})^2 + T\bar{X}^2}{T\sum(X_t - \bar{X})^2} = \frac{1}{T} + \frac{\bar{X}^2}{\sum(X_t - \bar{X})^2}.$$ [A.35]

This allows us to write Eq. [A.34] as:

$$\sigma_p^2 = \sigma^2\left[1 + \frac{1}{T} + \frac{\bar{X}^2 - 2\bar{X}X_{T+1} + X_{T+1}^2}{\sum(X_t - \bar{X})^2}\right].$$ [A.36]

Rewriting the numerator of the fraction on the right side gives:

$$\sigma_p^2 = \sigma^2\left[1 + \frac{1}{T} + \frac{(X_{T+1} - \bar{X})^2}{\sum(X_t - \bar{X})^2}\right].$$ [A.37]

Finally, recall that the estimated variance is:

$$s^2 = \frac{1}{T - 2}\sum(Y_t - \hat{Y}_t)^2.$$ [A.38]

Substitution into Eq. [A.38] gives the estimated prediction error variance:

$$s_p^2 = s^2\left[1 + \frac{1}{T} + \frac{(X_{T+1} - \bar{X})^2}{\sum(X_t - \bar{X})^2}\right].$$ [A.39]

The positive square root of Eq. [A.39] is the prediction error we have been trying to find.

Finally, Eq. [A.39] gives the variance for a point prediction, $\hat{Y}_{T+1}$. It is sometimes appropriate to predict the expected value of $\hat{Y}_{T+1}$. In this case, the variance $(\bar{s}_p^2)$ is slightly smaller:

$$\bar{s}_p^2 = s^2\left[\frac{1}{T} + \frac{(X_{T+1} - \bar{X})^2}{\sum(X_t - \bar{X})^2}\right].$$ [A.40]

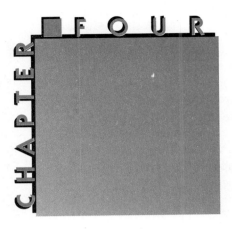

CHAPTER FOUR

MULTIPLE REGRESSION AND MULTICOLLINEARITY

One of the aphorisms of economics is that "Everything depends on everything else," so to expect a simple regression model to capture real economic behavior adequately is asking quite a lot. For example, in the *Caution* section that concluded Chapter 3, we noted a possible specification error: It is hard to imagine that disposable income is the only independent variable that affects aggregate consumption. Wouldn't high interest rates cause consumers to increase their saving and cut consumption? Isn't it possible that expected inflation causes people to increase current consumption to beat the price increases? Certainly. Without too much thought, you could list several more variables that might affect consumption. In fact, the models used by practicing econometricians often employ hundreds of variables and hundreds of equations. Fortunately, even though these models may look complex, they are really nothing more than a natural extension of the ideas we studied in Chapters 2 and 3. This chapter, then, takes a big step toward realistic econometrics by developing the key ideas behind *multiple regression analysis*, regression models with several independent variables.

Independent variables cannot be added haphazardly, however. The inclusion of additional independent variables should be based on *a priori* reasoning, and another assumption must be met before we can trust the resulting parameter estimates and summary statistics. The inclusion of multiple independent variables also affects interpretation of *t*- and *F*-statistics because the degrees of freedom change. We will develop these ideas first with reference to the three-variable model—one *Y* and two *X*'s—before we get into the general *k*-variable multiple regression model. We will also discuss multicollinearity, a common problem that crops up with multiple regression models.

4.1

THE THREE-VARIABLE MODEL

The extension of the simple regression model to the three-variable model is straightforward, though we need to be particularly careful about the notation. The three-variable multiple regression model is denoted as:

$$Y_i = \beta_0 + \beta_1 X_{1i} + \beta_2 X_{2i} + \varepsilon_i \qquad i = 1, 2, \ldots, n; \qquad j = 0, 1, 2.$$

[4.1]

The only difference between this equation and the simple regression equation (Eq. [3.1]) is that we have included a second independent variable. To distinguish clearly between observations, independent variables, and coefficients, double subscripts on the *X*'s are necessary. Thus "X_{1i}" is the *i*'th observation on the first independent variable, X_1; "X_{2i}" is the *i*'th observation on the second independent variable, X_2. Notice that the first subscript (*j*) indicates variables and coefficients, while the second subscript (*i*) indicates the data point. For the three-variable model the *j* subscripts begin at 0 and end at 2; thus, there are 2 slope estimates (β_1 and β_2) plus the intercept (β_0). The *i* subscripts begin at 1 and end at *n* to indicate there are *n* data points.[1]

---

[1]This is very common notation, but it does have its quirks. Among other things, the *j* subscript is listed first because there will be times when we need to indicate the *n*'th − 1 observation; i.e., $X_{2,n-1}$, which is preferred to $X_{n-1,2}$. Another common notation uses α instead of β_0. When the discussion relies on matrix algebra, for convenience the model is sometimes written as $Y_i = \beta_0 X_0 + \beta_1 X_1 + \beta_2 X_2 + \varepsilon_i$ and all observations on the "variable" X_0 equal 1.

Estimation is possible as long as there are more observations than parameters to be estimated; i.e., $n > k + 1$. However, interpretation of the t-ratios is unreliable unless there are approximately 30 more observations than there are parameter estimates.

Interpretation of the regression coefficients—now called *partial regression coefficients*—is slightly different than in the case of simple regression. The coefficient on X_1, β_1, is interpreted as the change in Y induced by a one unit change in X_1, *assuming that X_2 is held constant*. Likewise, β_2 is interpreted as the change in Y induced by a one unit change in X_2, *assuming that X_1 is held constant*. The error term obeys assumptions A3, A4, and A5 as outlined in Chapter 3.

When do we need to add additional independent variables? Recall that OLS parameter estimates are BLUE only if the model is correctly specified. Correct specification requires not only that the relationship between Y and X be linear, but that all of the "causal factors" that influence Y are included in the model. For example, trying to estimate a demand function with only one independent variable, price, would almost certainly lead to problems: As income increases, people often buy more goods even at higher prices. The result would be a positive regression coefficient on price—a suggestion that price and the quantity demanded vary directly. Thus, we have to include the additional independent variables to be sure that the parameter estimates will be BLUE. However, we cannot add just any new variable and expect to get BLUE parameter estimates. In fact, under certain circumstances, the incorrect inclusion of the independent variables may make it impossible for the computer program to generate any parameter estimates at all.

4.1.1   Assumption 6 (A6)

The sixth assumption of the classical OLS model relates to the relationship among the independent variables:

ASSUMPTION 6 (A6)

No exact linear relationship can exist between any combination of the independent variables.

Assumption 6 requires a new bit of terminology. When variables are exact linear combinations of each other, i.e., if $X_1 = 2X_2$, the variables are said to be *perfectly collinear*. The term *multicollinearity* refers to the general problem that exists when independent variables are linearly related to each other.

The purpose of A6 is twofold. First, for the mathematical reasons illustrated in Sec. 4.3.1, it is impossible to generate any parameter estimates at all if there is perfect collinearity.[2] Second, if two variables are almost but not perfectly collinear, it may be impossible to hold one constant while varying the other—a requirement in the computation of partial regression coefficients—making interpretation of the regression results difficult. That is, when X_1 and X_2 are collinear, it is hard to determine which variable is responsible for the change in Y. We discuss the problem of multicollinearity in more detail in Sec. 4.3.

4.1.2 A Three-Variable Model of the Consumption Function

To illustrate the three-variable model, the consumption function test of Chapter 3 has been modified to include an interest rate, specifically the interest rate on AAA corporate bonds (AAA). Our *a priori* hypothesis is that the relationship between AAA and consumption (CONS) will be negative: Because high interest rates increase the incentive to save, they should decrease consumption. As before, the data were in constant 1982 dollars and covered the period 1960–87. The results of the test are given in Table 4.1.

Interpretation of multiple regression results is similar to simple regression, with only a few changes. Because all of the *t*-ratios are significant at the 95% level, the fitted regression equation is:

$$\widehat{CONS}_t = -45.201 + 0.959DPI_t - 6.301AAA_t.$$

TABLE 4.1 **Multiple regression results**

```
Dep var: CONS  N: 28  R-sq: .997  Adj R-sq: .997  SER: 24.275

Variable  Coefficient  Std Error    T     P(2 tail)

CONSTANT    -45.201     19.532   -2.314    0.029
    DPI       0.959      0.019   50.662    0.000
    AAA      -6.301      3.028   -2.081    0.048

                Analysis of Variance

  Source    Sum-of-Squares  DF  Mean-Square   F-Ratio     P

Regression    5323328.600    2  2661664.300  4516.696  0.000
  Residual      14732.365   25    589.295
```

---

[2]This is not always true because computer programs typically use special algorithms—not the methods used in the Appendix 1.A—to solve least-squares problems. However, such results cannot be trusted.

This equation can be used in the same way a simple regression equation is used—for prediction, calculating elasticities, etc. However, interpretation of multiple regression results is slightly more complicated and requires that we look at the mathematics of multiple regression analysis.

4.1.3   Revised Parameter Estimates

We will not waste our time deriving the formulae for the parameter estimates of the three-variable model—much less a k-variable model—because a computer can carry out quite tedious calculations in an instant. However, it is instructive to take a careful look at the formulae for the three parameter estimates.[3]

$$\hat{\beta}_1 = \frac{(\sum x_{1i} y_i)(\sum x_{2i}^2) - (\sum x_{2i} y_i)(\sum x_{1i} x_{2i})}{(\sum x_{1i}^2)(\sum x_{2i}^2) - (\sum x_{1i} x_{2i})^2}, \qquad [4.2]$$

$$\hat{\beta}_2 = \frac{(\sum x_{2i} y_i)(\sum x_{1i}^2) - (\sum x_{1i} y_i)(\sum x_{1i} x_{2i})}{(\sum x_{2i}^2)(\sum x_{1i}^2) - (\sum x_{1i} x_{2i})^2}, \qquad [4.3]$$

$$\hat{\beta}_0 = \bar{Y} - \hat{\beta}_1 \bar{X}_1 - \hat{\beta}_2 \bar{X}_2. \qquad [4.4]$$

A quick inspection of these equations reveals something very important: Except under quite special conditions, using simple regression instead of multiple regression will result in biased parameter estimates. For example, notice in Eqs. [4.2] and [4.3] that the second term in the denominator and the last sum in the numerator are closely related[4] to the covariance between X_1 and X_2. Thus, unless X_1 and X_2 are linearly independent [i.e., if $cov(X_1, X_2) = 0$], the simple regression estimates of $\hat{\beta}_1 = \sum x_{1i} y_i / x_{1i}^2$ and $\hat{\beta}_2 = \sum x_{2i} y_i / x_{2i}^2$ will be incorrect. A glance at Eq. [4.4] shows that using simple regression instead of multiple regression will also bias the intercept unless one of the slope parameters happens to be zero—an indication that the "true" model can be estimated with simple regression.

The possibility of getting biased parameter estimates may seem to imply that the best technique is to include any variable that might have any chance of affecting Y. However, there are several reasons to avoid this strategy. Among

---

[3] Equations [4.2], through [4.4] are complex, but masochists could derive them in the same way $\hat{\beta}_0$ and $\hat{\beta}_1$ were derived in Appendix 1.B: Minimize the sum of squared errors by partially differentiating with respect to $\hat{\beta}_0$, $\hat{\beta}_1$, and $\hat{\beta}_2$, setting the three equations to zero, and solving simultaneously.

[4] Why are these terms related to the covariance? Recall that the sample covariance between X and Y is $1/(n-1) \sum (X_i - \bar{X})(Y_i - \bar{Y})$. Because X_1 and X_2 are written in deviation form, the terms in question are $(n-1)$ times the sample covariance between X_1 and X_2.

other things,[5] adding additional variables means that more parameters need to be estimated, which results in a loss in the degrees of freedom, an issue we discuss below.

4.1.4   *t*-tests on the Parameter Estimates

The same type of *t*-tests are used in multiple regression as in simple regression. Typical null and alternative hypotheses for a one-tailed test are:

$$H_0: \beta_j = 0 \quad \text{versus} \quad H_a: \beta_j > 0,$$

while the decision whether to reject the null hypothesis is based on evaluation of the *t*-ratio:

$$t_{n-3} = \frac{\hat{\beta}_j}{\text{se}(\hat{\beta}_j)}. \qquad\qquad [4.5]$$

We need to make two comments about the *t*-ratios used in multiple regression analysis. First, the denominator, $\text{se}(\hat{\beta}_j)$, is the standard error of the estimated value $\hat{\beta}_j$. The formula for $\text{se}(\hat{\beta}_j)$ needn't detain us here, but it is estimated from the regression residuals, as was the standard error of $\hat{\beta}_1$ in the simple regression model.[6] Second, because $\text{se}(\hat{\beta}_j)$ was estimated using the regression residuals, the *t*-ratio now has $n - 3$ degrees of freedom. Why? We began with n observations but lost three degrees of freedom because we had to estimate three parameters—two slopes ($\hat{\beta}_1$ and $\hat{\beta}_2$) and the intercept ($\hat{\beta}_0$). As before, the null hypothesis will be rejected if the *t*-ratio exceeds the critical value in the *t*-table. Referring back to Table 4.1, because there were 28 observations, there are 25 degrees of freedom for each of the *t*-tests. Thus, we could reject the null hypotheses for each parameter.[7]

4.1.5 R^2 and Corrected R^2 ($\bar{R}^2$)

Another complication arises when we begin adding additional independent variables to the model: Additional independent variables cannot lower R^2; if there is any effect at all, it will be to raise R^2. This means that it is possible to increase R^2 by picking data series at random and adding them to the model.

---

[5] As we note in the next chapter, the inclusion of extraneous independent variables will reduce the efficiency of all parameter estimates in the model.

[6] The precise formula for $\text{se}(\hat{\beta}_j)$ is used in Exercise 4.1.

[7] Because there are 25 degrees of freedom, the critical *t*-value for a 95% confidence interval, one-tailed test is 1.71; for a two-tailed test, it is 2.06.

Of course, serious econometricians resist such "data mining," but even well-intentioned investigators might inadvertently add variables that contain very little explanatory power. To determine whether additional variables increase the explanatory power of the model significantly, R^2 can be adjusted for degrees of freedom.[8] This new measure is called *corrected* or *adjusted* R^2 and will be denoted as "$\bar{R}^2$" in the text and "Adj R-sq" on most of the sample printouts. (Other common notations include "Corr-R^2" and "Adj-R^2.") For the three-variable model, $\bar{R}^2$ is found with the following formula:

$$\bar{R}^2 = 1 - \frac{\text{ESS}/df}{\text{TSS}/df} = 1 - \frac{\sum e_i^2/n - 3}{\sum y_i^2/n - 1}.$$

[4.6]

Why might $\bar{R}^2$ decrease as additional independent variables are added? Each time a new variable is added, the degrees of freedom associated with ESS will decline by one. However, if the new variable contains significant explanatory

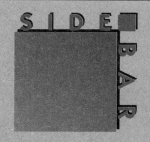

STANDARDIZED REGRESSION COEFFICIENTS

Many regression packages, including the Systat™ family, SAS™, and Minitab™, calculate what are known as standardized regression (beta) coefficients. Standardized regression coefficients are estimated from the regression model using all data in deviation form and divided by their own standard deviations. Standardized regression coefficients can be used to give some idea as to which variable is most important in explaining the dependent variable. The variable with the highest standardized regression coefficient (in absolute value) probably has the most explanatory power. However, this is not always a valid inference if the independent variables are collinear.

---

[8]F-tests can also be used to help determine whether additional independent variables offer significant explanatory power. One such test is discussed in Chapter 11.

power, ESS will decrease as well. These two effects will change the numerator of the second term on the left side of Eq. [4.6]. The result is that $\bar{R}^2$ is usually lower than R^2; it can never be higher. The hope of the investigator, of course, is that the difference between $\bar{R}^2$ and R^2 will be very small—an indication that the new variable(s) have increased explanatory power and thus improve the model.

What is the main use of $\bar{R}^2$? A "large" divergence between R^2 and $\bar{R}^2$ indicates that some of the variables are extraneous; that is, they do not contain significant explanatory power. Unfortunately, no standard rule says how close R^2 and $\bar{R}^2$ should be. In the case of the consumption function test in Table 4.1, the two are equal—an indication that both of the independent variables help explain variation in the dependent variable. On the other hand, because R^2 changed very little with the addition of the AAA variable, it is possible that the AAA variable contributed very little to the model.[9] Under these circumstances, it may be appropriate to conduct an additional test of the explanatory power of the suspect variable(s). The restricted F-test presented in Appendix 4.A is one such test.

4.1.6   The *F*-Test

The F-test was really superfluous when applied to the simple regression model of Chapter 3 because we could extract the same information[10] from the t-ratio on $\hat{\beta}_1$. In multiple regression models, the F-test is used to test the overall significance of the regression. In other words, it tests the *joint significance* of all of the independent variables.

The null and alternate hypotheses of the F-test in the three-variable regression model are:

$$H_0: \beta_1 = \beta_2 = 0 \quad \text{versus} \quad H_a: \text{at least one } \beta_j \neq 0.$$

Notice that the F-test does not test the significance of the intercept, β_0. As before, this test is conducted by forming a ratio of the explained variance to the unexplained variance. In the case of the three-variable model, the ratio is:

$$F_{2, n-3} = \frac{\text{RSS}/df}{\text{ESS}/df} = \frac{\sum \hat{y}_i^2 / 2}{\sum e_i^2 / n - 3}. \qquad [4.7]$$

Most regression programs print the F-statistic, but some merely calculate RSS and ESS—which means that we'd need to determine the degrees of freedom in order to calculate the F-ratio. The simple model had one degree of

---

[9] We should note here that the R^2's from both models are biased upward as a result of autocorrelation, an issue we discuss in Chapter 6.

[10] See note 8 in Chapter 3.

freedom in the numerator and $n - 2$ degrees of freedom in the denominator; the three-variable model has 2 degrees of freedom in the numerator and $n - 3$ in the denominator. You might be able to memorize this, but for the *k*-variable model determining degrees of freedom can be difficult, and memorization would be of no help when we have to determine the degrees of freedom in different situations. To determine the degrees of freedom for a standard *F*-test, recall from Chapter 3 that TSS = RSS + ESS. Remember also that TSS has $n - 1$ degrees of freedom because the only constraint on the data is $\sum Y_i / n = \bar{Y}$. The three parameter estimates ($\hat{\beta}_0$, $\hat{\beta}_1$, and $\hat{\beta}_2$) used in the calculation of ESS represent three constraints, so there are $n - 3$ degrees of freedom in the denominator of the *F*-statistic. Now, because TSS = RSS + ESS, only 2 degrees of freedom are left in RSS, the numerator of the *F*-statistic.

As before, the null hypothesis is rejected if the calculated *F*-statistic exceeds the value in the table. At the 5% significance level, the critical value for $F_{2,25}$ is 3.39. Because $4516.696 > 3.39$, we would reject the null hypothesis and conclude that at least one of the X_j's has a significant effect on Y.

OTHER *F*-TESTS   Actually, several varieties of *F*-tests are used in multiple regression analysis. As shown in Appendix 4.A, an *F*-test can be used to detect the joint significance of a subset of the independent variables. The test involves running OLS on the model with and without the suspect variable(s) and comparing ESS from the two regressions. Another *F*-test, the Chow test, is used to check for the existence of a structural shift in the model. The Chow test is presented in Chapter 5. Finally, in Chapter 11, we show how to use an *F*-test to check whether causality flows from X to Y or from Y to X in time series models.

4.2

THE *k*-VARIABLE MODEL

The step from the three-variable multiple regression model to the *k*-variable model is easier than the step from simple to multiple regression analysis. We need to be careful only about degrees of freedom and some related issues.

The general form of the *k*-variable model is:

$$Y_i = \beta_0 + \beta_1 X_{1i} + \beta_2 X_{2i} + \cdots + \beta_k X_{ki} + \varepsilon_i. \qquad [4.8]$$

As before, the index for observations is i; it runs from 1 to n. The index used for variables and coefficients is j; it runs from 0 to k. All of the concepts we discussed in the three-variable model apply to the *k*-variable model, and interpretation of regression results is identical—as long as we are careful to adjust for degrees of freedom.

As with simple regression, most of the important statistical tests make use of the estimated error variance, s^2, or its square root, the standard error of the regression (SER). As usual, s^2, is estimated by squaring and summing the regression residuals, and dividing by the degrees of freedom. Because one degree of freedom is lost for each of the parameter estimates, s^2 is given by:

$$s^2 = \frac{\sum e_i^2}{n - k - 1},$$ [4.9]

where k is the number of regressors.

The denominator of Eq. [4.9] makes it clear that there are $n - k - 1$ degrees of freedom in the t-ratios used to test the significance of the $\hat{\beta}_j$. Similar reasoning reveals that the F-statistic for multiple regression has $n - k - 1$ degrees of freedom in the denominator and k degrees of freedom in the numerator.

4.3

MULTICOLLINEARITY

The likelihood of ever encountering perfect multicollinearity is extremely small, but we can illustrate some of the problems of multicollinearity with a rather ridiculous example before we get to the more serious and very common problem of less than perfect multicollinearity. The basic problem caused by multicollinearity is the difficulty that arises when you try to separate the influences of the collinear variables. This makes regression coefficients untrustworthy.

4.3.1   Perfect Multicollinearity

Suppose you were trying to determine the effect of education on productivity growth. To do so you formulated a multiple regression model with productivity growth as the dependent variable and several independent variables— R&D expenditures, work effort, education, etc. Assume also that you included two measures of education: the number of years of education per worker, and the last grade completed per worker. (You should have noted that the number of years of education and last grade completed measure exactly the same thing! Unfortunately, you miss this key point and input the data into the computer anyway.) When you type the commands to ask for multiple regression analysis, the almost immediate answer is something like "RUN ABORTED, COULD NOT INVERT X MATRIX." Such a message may seem cryptic, but is really quite clear to people versed in matrix algebra: It means that there was an exact linear relationship between two or more of the independent variables—perfect multicollinearity.[11] However, even without matrix algebra, we can get some idea of what's happening by looking at Eq. [4.2] and recalling the definitions of variance and covariance from Chapter 2.

We have already noted that the sample covariance between X_1 and X_2 appears in the denominator of the expression for $\hat{\beta}_1$ (Eq. [4.2]). Likewise, the first two terms in the denominator are $(n-1)$ times the sample variance of X_1 and X_2, respectively. Further, if X_1 and X_2 are exact linear combinations of each other, that is, if $X_2 = cX_1$, then $\mathrm{var}(X_2) = c^2\mathrm{var}(X_1)$. Now, if we write cov (X_1, X_2) as cov (X_1, cX_1), drop the subscripts, and define covariance in terms of expected values we have:

$$
\begin{aligned}
\mathrm{cov}(X, cX) &= E\{[X - E(X)][cX - E(cX)]\} \\
&= E\{[cX^2 - XcE(X) - E(X)cX - cE(X)E(X)]\} \\
&= c\{E(X^2) - E(X)^2\} \\
&= c\,\mathrm{var}(X).
\end{aligned}
$$

Writing Eq. [4.2] with the denominator in terms of variance and covariance gives:

$$
\hat{\beta}_1 = \frac{(\sum x_{1i}y_i)(\sum x_{2i}^2) - (\sum x_{2i}y_i)(\sum x_{1i}x_{2i})}{\mathrm{var}(X_1)\mathrm{var}(X_2) - [\mathrm{cov}(X_1)(X_2)]^2}. \qquad [4.10]
$$

If we substitute cX_1 for X_2, we have:

$$
\hat{\beta}_1 = \frac{(\sum x_{1i}y_i)(\sum x_{2i}^2) - (\sum x_{2i}y_i)(\sum x_{1i}x_{2i})}{\mathrm{var}(X_1)c^2\mathrm{var}(X_1) - [c\,\mathrm{var}(X_1)]^2}, \qquad [4.11]
$$

which makes it apparent what happens in the case of perfect multicollinearity: The coefficients are undefined because the denominator goes to zero. (Exercise 4.2 demonstrates this point using a numerical example.)

4.3.2   Less than Perfect Multicollinearity

Perfect multicollinearity is rare and can often be detected before the regression analysis is performed. Unfortunately, less than perfect, but still severe multicollinearity is quite common and frequently makes it difficult to interpret

---

[11]Students familiar with matrix algebra know that matrix inversion is impossible when linear dependence exists between columns. Using matrix notation, the regression model is $\mathbf{Y} = \mathbf{X}\boldsymbol{\beta} + \boldsymbol{\varepsilon}$ and $\hat{\boldsymbol{\beta}}$ is found with the transformation $\hat{\boldsymbol{\beta}} = (\mathbf{X}'\mathbf{X})^{-1}\mathbf{X}'\mathbf{Y}$. The data matrix $\mathbf{X}$ cannot be inverted, and thus $\hat{\boldsymbol{\beta}}$ cannot be found, if A6 is violated.

T A B L E 4 . 2   **Multiple regression results**

```
Dep var: CONS  N: 28  R-sq: .997  Adj  R-sq: .997  SER: 23.681

Variable  Coefficient  Std Error      T      P(2 tail)

CONSTANT     -40.852     19.271   -2.120    0.045
     DPI       0.948      0.020   47.492    0.000
     AAA       0.484      5.384    0.090    0.929
   TBILL      -6.035      4.004   -1.507    0.145


                 Analysis of Variance

 Source     Sum-of-Squares  DF   Mean-Square   F-Ratio   P

Regression   5324602.256    3   1774867.419   3165.000  0.000
Residual       13458.709   24      560.780
```

regression results. To pick a rather contrived example, let us run the consumption model again, this time adding a third independent variable, the interest rate on three-month treasury bills (TBILL), which we know to be highly collinear with the interest rate on Aaa bonds. The results of this run are presented in Table 4.2. A quick glance at the results of Table 4.2 shows that the F-statistic and $\bar{R}^2$ are both good, but two of the t-ratios are too low. A high R^2 combined with low t-ratios is the classic symptom of severe multicollinearity. Notice what has happened to the coefficient on the AAA variable: It now has the wrong sign—positive instead of negative—and its t-ratio has fallen out of the significance range. The coefficient on TBILL has the correct sign, but it too has a low t-ratio. Multicollinearity often reverses the signs of regression coefficients. Strictly speaking, however, multicollinearity does not bias parameter estimates, though it does result in inefficient parameter estimates with large standard errors.[12] The only way multicollinearity can bias parameter estimates is indirectly through specification error—the low t-ratios could cause the investigator to drop a variable incorrectly from the model in subsequent regression runs. The result: We cannot "trust" parameter estimates when multicollinearity exists.

Conceptually, what is happening is that the two interest rate variables are so highly correlated—at least over the sample period used in this example—that we cannot tell which one is causing changes in the dependent variable. An obvious solution, of course, would be to drop one of the interest rate variables.

---

[12] If multicollinearity often reverses the signs of parameter estimates, doesn't this mean that it biases parameter estimates? No. There is an equal chance that the parameter estimates will be too high or too low when the model suffers from severe multicollinearity, so parameter estimates are unbiased but they cannot be trusted.

In fact, this is one recommended solution to the problem of multicollinearity; but dropping variables should not be done haphazardly. The fact that $\bar{R}^2$ fell so little when TBILL was added suggests that it might have some explanatory power, so dropping it would reduce the explanatory power of the model and could result in biased parameter estimates. For this reason, moderate multicollinearity is often ignored—especially when the model is intended primarily for prediction.

Another important reason to be careful about dropping suspect variables is that the usual symptoms of multicollinearity—high R^2 and low t-ratios—can be caused by factors other than multicollinearity, in which case dropping variables may cause more problems than it solves.

4.3.3 Detection of Multicollinearity

Before trying to deal with multicollinearity, you must be sure that the problem is really multicollinearity. Two simple ways to detect multicollinearity are by means of the simple correlation matrix and the tolerance coefficient. A third method involving auxiliary regressions is presented as Exercise 4.7.

CORRELATION MATRIX   The simplest way to check for multicollinearity is to calculate a correlation matrix for the dependent and all of the independent variables. If any of the independent variables are more highly correlated with each other than with the dependent variable, multicollinearity is severe enough to be a problem. That is, multicollinearity is serious if:

$$\rho(X_1, X_2) > \rho(Y, X_1) \quad \text{or} \quad \rho(Y, X_2). \qquad [4.12]$$

Most computer programs can calculate a correlation matrix between several different variables. The correlation matrix for the consumption function data is presented in Table 4.3. Reading a correlation table is straightforward. The

TABLE 4.3   Correlation check for multicollinearity

```
        PEARSON CORRELATION MATRIX

              CONS      DPI      AAA      3TB

     CONS     1.000
      DPI     0.998    1.000
      AAA     0.845    0.858    1.000
    TBILL     0.671    0.692    0.904    1.000

    NUMBER OF OBSERVATIONS:   28
```

1.00's along the diagonal indicate that the variables are perfectly correlated with themselves. The entries in the first column represent the correlation between consumption (CONS), itself, and the three independent variables. The entries in the second column represent the correlations between DPI, itself, AAA, and TBILL. There are only three entries in this column because the correlation between DPI and CONS was already calculated in the first column.

To check for the presence of multicollinearity, we need to compare the entries in the first column with the other columns. Notice that the correlation between AAA and TBILL is 0.904, but the correlation between AAA and CONS is only 0.845 and the correlation between TBILL and CONS is only 0.671. Because $\rho(\text{AAA, TBILL}) > \rho(\text{CONS, AAA})$ and $\rho(\text{AAA, TBILL}) > \rho(\text{CONS, TBILL})$, multicollinearity is severe enough to be a problem. The correlation between AAA and DPI is more of a judgment call. Because $\rho(\text{AAA, DPI}) = 0.858$ is slightly greater than $\rho(\text{CONS, AAA}) = 0.845$, multicollinearity *may* be a problem for this sample. However, both coefficients have the correct sign and good t-ratios, so it is probably safe to leave them in the three-variable model. On the other hand, the fact that R^2 did not change significantly with the addition of the AAA variable suggests that AAA could be extraneous.

THE TOLERANCE COEFFICIENT　　Some programs compute a statistical measure, called the *tolerance coefficient*, that can be helpful in the detection of multicollinearity. The tolerance coefficient is defined as one minus the squared multiple correlation between each X variable and every other X in the model. If the X variables are highly collinear, the tolerance coefficient will approach zero. On the other hand, if the tolerance coefficient approaches one, the X variables are not linearly related and there is little chance of multicollinearity. A potential advantage of the tolerance coefficient over simple correlations is that the tolerance coefficient can detect multicollinearity that is caused by the interaction of three or more variables. For example, multicollinearity of the $X_1 = c_1 X_2 + c_2 X_3$ variety might not be detected with simple correlations; it normally would be detected with the tolerance coefficient.

The tolerance coefficients for the model presented in Table 4.2 were DPI = 0.227, AAA = 0.080, and TBILL = 0.157. These values are all quite low—an indication of potentially serious multicollinearity—which is what we suspected from an examination of the correlation matrix in Table 4.3.

4.3.4　Correcting for Multicollinearity

We have already mentioned one solution to the problem of multicollinearity: Drop the suspect variable. This is often the most practical solution, but it is far from the best solution because dropping variables can lead to specification errors that can bias parameter estimates.[13] Other solutions worth trying include the following.

OBTAIN MORE DATA   Multicollinearity is a sample problem, not a population problem. This suggests that the solution may be to enlarge the sample by obtaining more data. Why would this work? The larger the data set, the more of the variation in the series that can be captured. For example, in the case of the interest rate series, the correlation between Aaa bonds and three-month treasury bills was only 0.85 in the 1940s and 1950s—significantly less than it was over the sample period used in the test. The problem with collecting more data as a solution to multicollinearity is that the data might not be available, because all available data are usually used in the original study.

DIFFERENCE THE DATA   Multicollinearity can show up in both cross-sectional and time series data, but it seems to be more common in time series data. When this is the case, the influence of multicollinearity can often be reduced by running the model using first differences of the data. First differences represent the change in the data from period to period and are calculated by subtracting consecutive observations from each other—a task that the computer will do for you. Letting the asterisks represent differenced data, we have:

$$Y_t^* = Y_t - Y_{t-1}; \qquad X_{jt}^* = X_{jt} - X_{jt-1}. \tag{4.13}$$

Why does differencing eliminate multicollinearity? In time series data, data often correlate because of an underlying trend—DPI, CONS, AAA, and TBILL all followed an upward though somewhat erratic trend over the sample period. By differencing the data, the trend is removed and thus much of the correlation between the regressors.[14] Later we will discuss several other reasons for wanting to difference the data.

In addition to differencing the data, it is sometimes possible to reduce the influence of multicollinearity by using percent changes. In some cases, converting the data from levels into per capita or real terms also works. One caution should be kept in mind when using any of the transformations: Transforming the data also transforms the model. Interpretation of a model using per capita GNP is quite different from one using aggregate GNP.

---

[13] We should mention, however, that temporarily dropping a variable is a very crude but often effective way to check for multicollinearity. For example, suppose the model in Table 4.2 was the initial regression run. The high R^2 and low t's suggest possible multicollinearity. If either of the interest rate variables is dropped, the coefficient on the other interest rate variable will change drastically. This extreme sensitivity of parameter estimates to model specification is another indication of possible multicollinearity.

[14] Exercise 4.4 presents the consumption test with differenced data.

ADVANCED TECHNIQUES If none of these techniques works, you can always take refuge in advanced techniques. One of the most common methods for dealing with multicollinearity is called *factor analysis*. This technique involves the construction of artificial variables (factors) as a weighted average of the original collinear variables. By construction, the factors are perfectly independent of each other so multicollinearity is eliminated completely. Factor analysis and a related method, *principle components*, are also used for data reduction when degrees of freedom are a problem.[15]

How to deal with multicollinearity

Multicollinearity is almost always present in multiple regression models, so the question is not whether it is there, but how serious it is. Unfortunately, the methods designed to detect multicollinearity cannot always determine how serious it is, so dealing with multicollinearity, like so many issues in applied econometrics, is something of a judgment call. For forecasting purposes, many econometricians simply dismiss the problem. If the model is designed for explanatory purposes, the decision must be made as to whether multicollinearity creates more problems than do the practical solutions designed to eliminate multicollinearity.   ◆ ◆ ◆

THE PROBLEM OF MULTICOLLINEARITY

1. Multicollinearity is almost always present in multiple regression models, especially those using time series data.

2. Multicollinearity can be detected by calculating a correlation matrix between all of the variables in the model. If some of the X's are more highly correlated with each other than they are with Y, multicollinearity is serious. A low tolerance coefficient also indicates multicollinearity.

3. The classic symptoms of multicollinearity are low t-ratios and high R^2.

4. Multicollinearity does not bias parameter estimates, but it makes them untrustworthy and can reverse signs. Parameter estimates have a large variance.

5. Because multicollinearity is a sample problem, the best way to correct for it is to collect more data. If this is not possible, dropping suspect variables or differencing the data may work.

---

[15] Exercise 4.5 presents a very simple version of factor analysis as a solution to the multicollinearity in the consumption function test.

CONCEPTS FOR REVIEW

Chapters 3 and 4 form the basis for the rest of the book, so be sure you get the details down before proceeding. Make sure you:

- can write out the general form of the k-variable multiple regression model, including the subscripts and index notation;
- know the six assumptions of the classical OLS model;
- know symptoms of multicollinearity;
- know how multicollinearity affects parameter estimates;
- know how to eliminate multicollinearity;
- can define and use the following key terms in context.

KEY TERMS

Assumption 6

corrected R^2

correlation matrix

covariance

first differences

F-test

multicollinearity

multiple regression model

partial regression
coefficients

perfect multicollinearity

tolerance coefficient

EXERCISES

4.1   One of the problems with multicollinearity is that it results in inefficient parameter estimates. Noting that the estimated variance of $\hat{\beta}_2$ in the three-variable model is:

$$\widehat{\text{var}}(\hat{\beta}_2) = \frac{s^2}{\sum x_{2i}^2(1 - r^2)},$$

where r is the sample correlation coefficient between X_1 and X_2, show that $\text{se}(\hat{\beta}_2) \to \infty$ when there is perfect multicollinearity.

4.2   Suppose that the X_1 data series is: 1, 2, 3, 1, 2, 5, 3, 2, 7, 5, 9. Define X_2 as $X_2 = 2X_1$ and show that the denominator of Eq. [4.2] goes to zero. (*Hint:* It is much easier to do this on a computer but few computers calculate covariance. Can you think of a way around this?)

4.3   Suppose you conclude that the only practical solution to the multicollinearity problem in the AAA/TBILL consumption test is to drop one of the variables. Which one would you recommend dropping? Why?

4.4   In an attempt to rid the model of multicollinearity, the
      CONS/DPI/AAA/TBILL data were differenced and another
      regression was run on the differenced data. The results were:

```
Dep var: DCONS  N: 27  R-sq: .805  Adj  R-sq: .779  SER: 14.613

Variable  Coefficient  Std Error  Tolerance     T     P(2 tail)

CONSTANT      19.938     7.218                 2.762    0.011
   DDPI        0.634     0.107   0.6208978     5.938    0.000
   DAAA      -11.254     4.832   0.3371241    -2.329    0.029
  DTBILL      -0.057     2.891   0.3813942    -0.020    0.985

                    Analysis of Variance

  Source    Sum-of-Squares  DF  Mean-Square  F-Ratio    P

Regression     20228.332    3    6742.777    31.574   0.000
 Residual       4911.742   23     213.554
```

a. Interpret these results. Remember that the model that was run
   was specified as DCONS = f(DDPI, DAAA, DTBILL) where
   DCONS = $CONS_t - CONS_{t-1}$, etc.

b. Do you think multicollinearity has been eliminated?

c. If you were to run another regression, how would you change the
   model specification?

d. How do you interpret the constant term? (*Hint:* Take first
   differences of a simple regression equation and see what
   happens to the intercept.)

4.5   Rather than dropping one of the collinear variables, AAA and TBILL
      were added together to make a new variable, FACTOR. A new
      regression on CONS was run using DPI and FACTOR. The results
      were:

$$CONS = -44.14 + 0.96DPI - 3.30FACTOR; \bar{R}^2 = 0.997,$$
$$ (18.55) \quad (0.02) \qquad (1.30)$$

where the standard errors are in parentheses.

a. Interpret these results. Do you think that multicollinearity has
   been eliminated?

b. What is the economic meaning of the new variable FACTOR?

4.6   In an effort to improve the results of the accelerator test of Chapter 1,
      a second independent variable was added to the model, business fixed

investment lagged one year (LBFI). The results of this regression run are:

```
Dep var: BFI  N: 16  R-sq: .975  Adj R-sq: .972  SER: 12.89

Variable   Coefficient  Std Error    T     P(2 tail)
CONSTANT      31.66        22.61    1.40     0.18
   DRGNP       0.49         0.04   11.79     0.00
    LBFI       0.89         0.04   20.57     0.00

                        Analysis of Variance
   Source    Sum-of-Squares  DF  Mean-Square  F-Ratio   P

Regression       85995.93    2    42997.97    258.65   0.00
Residual          2161.13   13      166.24
```

a. Interpret these results. Would you be confident using this model to forecast BFI?

b. Are the classic signs of multicollinearity present in this printout? Is there any other reason to suspect multicollinearity?

c. Still concerned about the possible multicollinearity, you check the correlation matrix and find the following. Does it provide any evidence of multicollinearity?

```
                  Correlation Matrix

                  BFI        DRGNP      LBFI
          BFI    1.00
        DRGNP    0.41        1.00
         LBFI    0.84       -0.10      1.00
```

4.7 An alternative way to check for multicollinearity is to run *auxiliary regressions* of the independent variables on all of the other independent variables. If the R^2 from any of these regressions approaches 1.0, multicollinearity is serious enough to be a problem.

a. The R^2's from the independent variable regressions from the consumption model are shown below. What variable seems to be the source of the multicollinearity? Is this consistent with the results from Table 4.3?

$$DPI = f(AAA, TBILL), \quad R^2 = 0.773,$$

$$AAA = f(DPI, TBILL), \quad R^2 = 0.920,$$

$$TBILL = f(DPI, AAA), \quad R^2 = 0.843.$$

b. Some econometricians feel that this is a better way to check for multicollinearity than using the simple correlation matrix. Do you agree or disagree? Why?

c. How does this method compare to the tolerance coefficient?

4.8 One of the problems with multicollinearity is that it increases the standard errors of the parameter estimates. A recommended solution for dealing with multicollinearity is to increase the sample size. With reference to the formula for $se(\hat{\beta}_1)$, explain the conditions under which increasing the sample size will reduce $se(\hat{\beta}_1)$.

4.9 Automobile thefts have risen at an alarming rate in the past decade; however, the rise in thefts varies significantly among the states. To try to determine the causes of automobile thefts, a regression model was developed. Automobile thefts for the 48 contiguous states were used as the dependent variable (AUTOTHEF) and population density (POPDEN) and personal income by state (INCOME) were used as the independent variables. The initial results of this regression are shown in the printout below. Data for this example are in Data Set 3 in Appendix I.

```
Dep var: AUTOTHEF  N: 48  R-sq: .622  Adj R-sq: .605  SER: 125.410

Variable  Coefficient  Std Error     T     P(2 tail)

CONSTANT    -339.894     124.233   -2.736    0.009
 POPDEN        0.308       0.100    3.082    0.004
 INCOME        0.191       0.038    5.026    0.000

               Analysis of Variance

 Source     Sum-of-Squares  DF  Mean-Square  F-Ratio   P

Regression   1162368.436    2   581184.218   36.953  0.000
 Residual     707745.043   45    15727.668
```

a. Do you think the model specification is reasonable? What signs would you expect on the independent variables?

b. Interpret the results of the printout.

c. What additional information would you like to have to supplement the printout?

4.10 Carefully explain why there are k degrees of freedom in the numerator and $n - k - 1$ degrees of freedom in the denominator of the F-test used in the k-variable multiple regression model.

4.11 Refer to Exercise 3.22 and Data Set 2 of Appendix I. The University of Michigan computes the *index of consumer sentiment* (ICS), an index similar to but not identical to the consumer confidence index compiled by the Conference Board. In this exercise, use multiple regression analysis to test whether inclusion of the ICS and the interest rate on six-month certificates of deposit (CD6) improve the explanatory power of the simple regression consumer durables model. (This exercise is continued in Appendix 4.A and Exercise 6.12.)

Before analysis:

a. What signs do you expect on CD6 and ICS?

b. Do you expect to find multicollinearity in this model? If so, between which regressors?

After performing multiple regression analysis:

c. Is there any sign of multicollinearity? If so, correct for it and explain why it is there.

4.12 Predicting movements on the stock market is notoriously difficult—if it weren't, we'd all be rich! However, a connection does seem to exist between movements in the money supply, interest rates, and stock market. Monthly data on the Dow Jones Industrial index (DJ), Federal Funds Rate (FFR), and the percentage change in the real M2 money supply (M2) are provided in Data Set 4 of Appendix I.

Before your analysis:

a. Write out the model. What signs do you expect to find on the regressors? Do you expect to get a good R^2?

b. Are you comfortable using monthly data? Would you prefer to have daily? Annual? Do you think five years of monthly data is enough information?

c. Both DJ and the change in DJ (DDJ) are provided in Data Set 4. Which one do you think would serve as a more interesting dependent variable?

After performing regression analysis:

d. Run the model using both DJ and DDJ as dependent variables and interpret the printouts. Are the results as expected?

e. Now run simple regression using one regressor at a time. What do these results tell you?

f. Suggest how you might improve the model.

APPENDIX 4.A

RESTRICTED F-TESTS

As mentioned in Sec. 4.2.1, a common use of the F-test is to check for the joint significance of a subset of the independent variables. That is, suppose a model is specified as:

$$Y_i = \beta_0 + \beta_1 X_{1i} + \beta_2 X_{2i} + \cdots + \beta_{k-r} X_{k-ri} + \cdots + \beta_k X_{ki} + \varepsilon_i$$

and that there is reason to question whether significant explanatory power is provided by the r variables, $X_{k-r} + \cdots + X_k$. The joint significance of $X_{k-r} + \cdots + X_k$ can be tested by comparing the error sum of squares from the model, which includes the suspect variables (the *unrestricted* model), to the error sum of squares from the model with the suspect variables omitted (the *restricted* model). If the suspect variables contain significant explanatory power, the error sum of squares from the restricted model (ESS_r) will be large relative to the error sum of squares from the unrestricted model (ESS_u).

The null and alternative hypotheses to test for joint significance are:

H_0: all parameters from omitted independent variables $= 0$,

H_a: at least one β_j from the omitted variables is nonzero.

The steps to this test are as follows:

1. Perform OLS on the unrestricted model and collect ESS_u.

2. Omit the suspect variables and perform OLS on the restricted model to collect ESS_r.

3. Form the F-ratio:

$$F_{r,n-k-1} = \frac{(ESS_r - ESS_u)/r}{ESS_u/n - k - 1},$$

where r is the number of restrictions (omitted variables) in the test and $n - k - 1$ is the degrees of freedom from ESS_u.

4. If the calculated F-statistic is greater than the table value at the chosen level of significance, the null hypothesis is rejected.

This test is most useful in large models when it can be used to test for the joint significance of several variables, but it can be illustrated with a simple test for the significance of one variable, the AAA variable in the model reported in Table 4.1. This is a reasonable test because, even though the sign on AAA is correct and the t-ratio indicates significance, inclusion of AAA had almost no effect on R^2.

The null and alternative hypothesis for this test is:

$$H_0: \beta_2 = 0,$$

$$H_a: \beta_2 \neq 0.$$

No additional regressions are necessary because both ESS's were reported earlier: $ESS_r = 17285.16$ was reported in Table 3.2 and $ESS_u = 14732.37$ is in Table 4.1. Because $r = 1$ and $n - k - 1 = 25$, the test statistic is:

$$F_{1,25} = \frac{(17285.16 - 14732.37)/1}{14732.37/25} = 4.33.$$

The null hypothesis is rejected because 4.33 is greater than 4.24, the critical *F*-value at the 5% significance level.

Exercises

A4.1 Using the information in Tables 3.2 and 4.2, test the joint hypothesis that $\beta_2 = \beta_3 = 0$ in the model reported in Table 4.2. How can you reconcile this result with the example above?

A4.2 Use an *F*-test to see whether the POPDEN variable in Exercise 4.9 offered significant explanatory power. The results from the restricted regression were:

```
Dep var: AUTOTHFT  N: 48  R-sq: .542  Adj R-sq: .532  SER: 136.500

Variable  Coefficient  Std Error    T      P(2 tail)

CONSTANT    -515.020    120.242   -4.283    0.000
  INCOME       0.255      0.035    7.374    0.000

                   Analysis of Variance

  Source    Sum-of-Squares  DF  Mean-Square  F-Ratio  P

Regression    1013023.928   1  1013023.928  54.369  0.000
  Residual     857089.551  46    18632.382
```

A4.3 Conduct a restricted *F*-test on the consumer durables model from Exercise 4.11 to determine whether CD6 and ILS significant explanatory power.

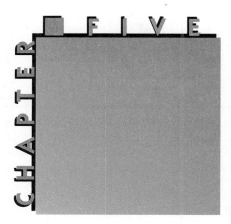

CHAPTER FIVE

MODEL
SPECIFICATION

The consumption function we tested in Chapters 3 and 4 was chosen for two reasons. First, it is a basic topic in the first economics course so most students are familiar with it. Second, it is quite reasonable to estimate the consumption function with the simple linear form as in Eqs. [3.1] and [4.1]. Unfortunately, we can only go so far with simple linear functions. Many economic relationships, in fact, are non-linear. Does this mean that linear regression is inappropriate in most real-world analyses? No. Several kinds of nonlinearities can be handled with linear regression models. In this chapter we will show how models can be specified to handle a wide variety of nonlinearities and other functional forms. We will also show how to deal with some types of qualitative data and note some of the problems associated with specification errors.

5.1

FUNCTIONAL FORMS

The fact that linear regression models can be applied to certain types of non-linear relationships does not mean that the methodology has been mis-named. Several different kinds of nonlinearities exist, and linear regression analysis can be applied only to certain types. As illustrations, consider the four models below:

$$Linear\ model: \qquad Y_i = \beta_0 + \beta_1 X_i + \varepsilon_i, \qquad\qquad [5.1]$$

$$Polynomial\ model: \quad Y_i = \beta_0 + \beta_1 X_i^2 + \varepsilon_i, \qquad\qquad [5.2]$$

$$Reciprocal\ model: \quad Y_i = \beta_0 + \beta_1 \left(\frac{1}{X_i}\right) + \varepsilon_i, \qquad\qquad [5.3]$$

$$Exponential\ model: \quad Y_i = \beta_0 X_{1i}^{\beta_1} X_{2i}^{\beta_2} \varepsilon_i. \qquad\qquad [5.4]$$

Equation [5.1] is the same model we have been using since Chapter 1 and is obviously linear. Note that there are no exponents higher than 1 and that no variables are multiplied by each other. The squared term in Eq. [5.2] indicates a nonlinear relationship between X_1 and Y; however, this type of nonlinear-ity can be handled quite easily with linear methods: Simply define a new variable — $Z_i = X_i^2$ — and perform regression analysis as usual. We will use a polynomial to estimate a total cost function in Sec. 5.1.3. Equation [5.3] is also inherently linear, even though a graph in (X, Y)-space would not be a straight line. If β_1 is positive, the graph will be downward sloping and approach both axes asymptotically, as required by the Phillips curve, which we will estimate in Sec. 5.1.2. Equation [5.4] is nonlinear because the independent variables are entered as a product and the coefficients to be estimated are exponents. It must be transformed before it can be estimated with linear regression. The appropriate transformation is a log transformation, the topic of Sec. 5.1.1.

5.1.1 Log Transformations

One of the most useful forms of the production function is the *Cobb-Douglas production function*. Developed in the 1920s, the Cobb-Douglas production function gained popularity quite rapidly for several reasons. First, it seemed to fit a variety of real-world situations. Just as importantly, it is mathematically elegant and consistent with neoclassical distribution theory.[1] One of the main attributes of neoclassical theory captured by the Cobb-Douglas production

---

[1] Some of the mathematical properties of the Cobb-Douglas production function are discussed in Appendix 5.A.

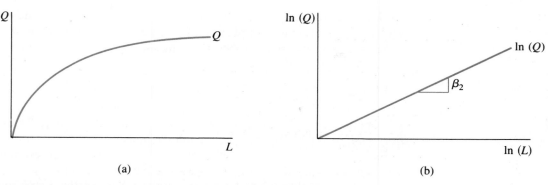

FIGURE 5.1   Diminishing marginal product-log transformation

Neoclassical distribution theory indicates that the marginal product of labor will be diminishing—that additional labor will increase output but at a diminishing rate, as shown in (a). To estimate this relationship with linear regression analysis, a log transformation is used. The result (b) is a linear relationship between ln(Q) and ln(L). Note that both of these curves are drawn for a fixed capital stock. An increase in the capital stock would cause an upward shift of the curves.

function is that the factors of production exhibit diminishing marginal product; that is, if the capital stock is fixed, additions of labor will increase output at a diminishing rate.

A simple two-factor version of the Cobb-Douglas production function is:

$$Q_t = \beta_0 L_t^{\beta_1} K_t^{\beta_2} \varepsilon_t,$$ [5.5]

where:

Q_t = output
L_t = labor input
K_t = capital input
ε_t = random error term
β_j = parameters to be estimated.

Figure 5.1(a) is a plot the Cobb-Douglas function in (L, Q)-space. The non-linear shape is an indication of the diminishing marginal product of labor: As more labor is added to a fixed capital stock, the output per unit of labor added diminishes. This result holds only if $0 < \beta_1, \beta_2 < 1$, a result demonstrated in Appendix 5.A.

The Cobb-Douglas function cannot be estimated with linear regression analysis as it is written. However, a log transformation of the equation will convert it into an expression that is "log linear" and permit estimation with linear regression. Taking natural logs of each side of Eq. [5.5] yields:

$$\ln(Q_t) = \ln(\beta_0) + \beta_1 \ln(L_t) + \beta_2 \ln(K_t) + \ln(\varepsilon_t).$$ [5.6]

Figure 5.1(b) plots the linear relationship between ln(Q) and ln(L).

Note that log transformations are appropriate only when the entire right side of the equation is multiplicative. For example, Eq. [5.7] cannot be converted into a linear equation because it has an "additive error" not a "multiplicative error" as does Eq. [5.5]:

$$Q_t = \beta_0 L_t^{\beta_1} K_t^{\beta_2} + \varepsilon_t. \qquad\qquad [5.7]$$

If economic theory suggests a model specification such as Eq. [5.7], estimation is impossible using linear regression methods.[2]

Estimation of Eq. [5.6] will result in BLUE parameter estimates— assuming of course that all of the classical assumptions hold—with only one potential new problem: The log transformation changes the distribution of the errors. However, this is not necessarily a problem, so most investigators rely on standard t- and F-tests as usual.[3]

Two additional advantages of estimating the log form of a regression model are: First, if the original model was multiplicative, the $\hat{\beta}_j$ are elasticities, not slopes. This is a simple point to demonstrate, but is best done with calculus so it has been relegated to Appendix 5.A. Direct estimation of elasticities eliminates the need to go through the manipulation discussed in Chapter 3 to calculate the elasticities. Second, as we point out in Chapter 7, a log transformation can sometimes be an effective and simple way to eliminate heteroscedasticity.

■ EXAMPLE 5.1

A TEST OF THE COBB–DOUGLAS PRODUCTION FUNCTION

The Cobb-Douglas production function has been fitted to many production functions, including those of macroeconomics. An immediate problem with testing aggregate production functions is that very substantial differences are likely to exist between the measured capital stock and capital utilization, and between the number of people working and the hours and education levels of those working. Adjustments for these factors were made by Christensen and Jorgenson in their study, "U.S. Real Product and Real Factor Input, 1929–67."[4]

---

[2] It must be pointed out, however, that economic theory rarely indicates the shape of the error term. Other than intuition, the only recourse is often to plot the residuals after performing the initial regressions.

[3] A rather technical discussion of the log-normal distribution can be found in George G. Judge, et al., *The Theory and Practice of Econometrics*, 2nd ed. (New York: Wiley, 1980) p. 438–444.

[4] L. R. Christensen and D. W. Jorgenson, "U.S. Real Product and Real Factor Input, 1929–67," *Review of Income and Wealth*, March 1970. Data used with permission.

Data from the Christensen-Jorgenson study were used to test the Cobb-Douglas production function. The initial results are shown in the printout below. A quick glance shows that this model seems to fit well. The summary statistics—R^2, $\bar{R}^2$, and the F-test—are all very good. Because the t-tests on the individual regressors are also very high, there appears to be little chance of multicollinearity. The coefficient on LNL (the log of labor, adjusted for hours and education) is 1.45. This is the elasticity of real output with respect to labor; thus a 1% change in the labor force results in a 1.45% change in real output. The coefficient on LNK (the log of capital, adjusted for capacity utilization) is 0.38, meaning that a 1% change in the capital stock results in only a 0.38% change in real output. Finally, the intercept is negative and significant.

```
DEP var: LNQ   N: 39   R-sq: .995   Adj  R-sq: .994   SER: 0.03

Variable   Coefficient   Std Error      T      P(2 tail)

CONSTANT      -3.94         0.24       -16.67      0.00
     LNL       1.45         0.08        17.49      0.00
     LNK       0.38         0.05         8.01      0.00

                        Analysis of Variance

   Source    Sum-of-Squares  DF  Mean-Square  F-Ratio    P

Regression         8.03       2      4.02     3344.11   0.00
  Residual         0.04      36      0.00
```

Do these results make sense? Why is labor input so much more effective than capital input? What is the economic content of the negative intercept? All studies of aggregate production functions are the subject of ongoing debate, but any number of reasonable "as if" stories are possible. It is reasonable to suspect that capital adds less to output growth than labor because much capital is used for capital *deepening*—more capital per worker. Because worker productivity depends in part on the amount of capital they have to work with, capital deepening will raise labor productivity—and could explain the 1.38 elasticity coefficient with respect to labor. On the other hand, the addition of capital to a growing capital stock will, because of the law of diminishing returns, result in a decline in the marginal product of capital. Unfortunately, the fact that $\hat{\beta}_1 + \hat{\beta}_2$ sums to greater than one suggests rather strong increasing returns to scale, an implication contrary to most assumptions regarding aggregate production. This may be caused by specification errors, specifically omitted variables.

One of the debates surrounding such studies is in the size and significance of the intercept. Recall that economic significance is rarely attached to the intercept and that it is usually interpreted as the combined effect of omitted variables. Growth models have been an ongoing study of Edward Denison, who has used the term *residual* to refer to this combined effect of omitted variables.[5] Denison believes that the residual has been a main source of economic growth throughout the post-war period and that perhaps 80% of the productivity slowdown of the 1970s was caused by the residual. The question, of course, is just what is the economic content of the residual. Denison is still studying that, but a recent working definition was, "advances in knowledge and other miscellaneous determinants. . . ." Other investigators have suggested that the omitted variables represent social variables—work effort, the effectiveness of management control, worker alienation, etc.—and have tried to construct proxy variables to measure them.[6]

SEMI-LOG TRANSFORMATION   A variant of the log transformation is the semi-log transformation. Only some of the variables are transformed into logs with a semi-log transformation. For example, in the model:

$$Y_t = \beta_0 + \beta_1 X_{1t} + \beta_2 \ln X_{2t} + \varepsilon_t, \qquad\qquad [5.8]$$

the slope coefficients would have a different interpretation. As usual, $\hat{\beta}_1$ would represent the slope in (Y, X_1)-space—the change in Y in response to a one unit change in X_1, holding X_2 constant. However, $\hat{\beta}_2$ represents the slope in $(Y, \ln X_2)$-space, not (Y, X_2)-space. This means that, for a constant $\hat{\beta}_2$, a graph in (Y, X_2)-space will be nonlinear.

The semi-log transformation is used whenever there is reason to believe that the responsiveness of the dependent variable to the independent variable changes over time. It is often used in models involving growth rates. For example, a constant percentage rate of increase in the labor force will result in ever larger increases in the size of the labor force over time. This could be captured with a simple regression equation using the log of the labor force on the left side and time on the right side. Another example is consumption: As an individual's income increases, there will be smaller and smaller increments in consumption. To model this relationship, consumption would be regressed against the log of income.

---

[5] Edward Denison, *Trends in American Economic Growth, 1929–1982* (Washington, D.C.: Brookings, 1985).
[6] Samuel Bowles, David Gordon, and Thomas E. Weisskopf, "Hearts and Minds: A Social Model of U.S. Productivity Growth," *Brookings Papers*, Vol. 2, 1983.

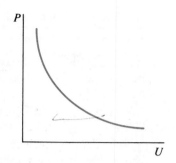

FIGURE 5.2   The Phillips curve, a reciprocal model

5.1.2   Reciprocal Models

One of the most important relationships in Keynesian macroeconomics is the Phillips curve.[7] The Phillips curve is a plot of the inverse and nonlinear relationship between inflation and unemployment. While the theory behind the Phillips curve is still a much debated issue, its downward slope is usually associated with labor market conditions: When unemployment is high, wage demands and hence inflation will be low; when unemployment is low, the reverse will occur. Explanations for its nonlinear shape are a bit more complicated, but are usually based on market rigidities or contracts that put a floor on wage demands and inflation despite excessive unemployment. A typical Phillips curve is shown in Fig. 5.2. While this figure is clearly nonlinear, it is linear in the coefficients and can be estimated with linear regression analysis by using the reciprocal of the unemployment rate as the independent variable.[8]

---

[7]A. W. Phillips, "The Relation Between Unemployment and the Rate of Change of Money Wages in the United Kingdom, 1861–1957," *Economica*, November 1958, p. 283–299; or see W. S. Brown, *Macroeconomics* (Englewood Cliffs, N.J.: Prentice-Hall, 1988), Chapter 5. A useful survey monograph on the development of the Phillips curve literature is Thomas M. Humphrey, *A History of the Phillips Curve*, Federal Reserve Bank of Richmond, October 1986.

[8]Students often have a difficult time understanding why the reciprocal model generates a nonlinear relationship. A numerical example might help: Let $\beta_0 = -0.06$ and $\beta_1 = 20.0$, and let $U_t = \{.04, .05, .06, .07, .08, .09\}$. The resulting values for P_t are $\{4.94, 3.94, 3.27, 2.80, 2.44, 2.16\}$. A plot of these points in (P_t, U_t)-space is nonlinear and downward sloping as required.

■ **EXAMPLE 5.2**

ESTIMATING A SIMPLE PHILLIPS CURVE

After A. W. Phillips discovered what appeared to be a stable relationship between wage growth and unemployment in the United Kingdom, a number of economists extended Phillips's initial insights. One of the first extensions was the development of what we know today as the Phillips curve—the relationship between inflation and unemployment. Unfortunately, almost as soon as this modified Phillips curve was developed, its stability came into question. In particular, between 1957 and 1958 and again in the 1970s, rising unemployment was accompanied by rising, not falling, inflation as the Phillips curve hypothesis suggested. Most economists felt this was caused by an outward shift of the Phillips curve. The question then became *why*.

This issue is far from settled, but most economists feel there are two main reasons for the outward shift of the Phillips curve: inflationary expectations and a rise in the natural rate of unemployment. Why these variables should shift the Phillips curve is straightforward: An increase in expected inflation will cause workers to demand higher wages at every unemployment rate. This would raise production costs and inflation. A precise definition of the natural rate of unemployment is beyond the scope of this book (the interested reader is invited to look at any intermediate-level macroeconomics text), but it is usually defined as a rate of unemployment, which, by definition, is consistent with a nonaccelerating rate of inflation. When unemployment falls below the natural rate, there is pressure on wages and inflation; an unemployment rate above the natural rate will eventually bring about a reduction in the rate of inflation. It follows that, for a given rate of unemployment, a rise in the natural rate of unemployment will arise inflationary pressures. Unfortunately, the natural rate of unemployment cannot be observed, so it must be estimated. During the 1970s and 1980s, however, most investigators reached roughly the same conclusions regarding the natural rate of unemployment: It rose from about 5% to about 6% due to changes in labor force participation rates and other factors.

To test the Phillips curve hypothesis, a multiple regression model was specified as:

$$P = \beta_0 + \beta_1 RECIPU + \beta_2 LAGP + \beta_3 NATU + \varepsilon,$$

where

  P = current rate of inflation; calculated as the percentage change in
     GNP deflator
  RECIPU = reciprocal of the unemployment rate
  LAGP = one year lag in P
  NATU = estimated natural rate of unemployment.[9]

Before explaining the results in the printout below, two comments are in order. First, it is impossible to measure expected inflation accurately, so it must be estimated. Several estimation techniques have been suggested, but the simplest method is to use a one period lag of the current rate. This explains the inclusion of the LAGP variable. Second, theory requires the inclusion of the NATU variable; however, because this series is little more than a smooth trend from 5.0 to 6.0 over the sample period, the coefficient on this variable must be regarded with caution. Data Set 5 of Appendix 1 provides the data used in this example.

```
Dep var: P  N: 25  R-sq: .770  Adj  R-sq: .737  SER: 1.381

Variable  Coefficient  Std Error     T     P(2 tail)

CONSTANT     -13.391     10.749   -1.246    0.227
  RECIPU      14.688      6.593    2.228    0.037
    LAGP       0.842      0.166    5.060    0.000
    NATU       2.029      1.903    1.066    0.299

                    Analysis of Variance

  Source    Sum-of-Squares  DF  Mean-Square  F-Ratio    P

Regression      134.209     3     44.736     23.472  0.000
Residual         40.025    21      1.906
```

The results of the test were as anticipated. A reasonable amount of the variation in P has been captured ($\bar{R}^2 = 0.737$ and F is significant at the 1% level) and the signs of all of the coefficients are correct. Both LAGP and RECIPU are significant at the 5% level for one-tailed tests; however, the t-score on NATU is quite low. Economic theory says to include this variable, and its low t-score may be partially accounted for by the fact that this series shows very little variation over the sample period. Still, inclusion of an "extra" variable costs us degrees of freedom. Should it be dropped? There is no definitive answer, but as we will find out in Sec. 5.2, the omission of a significant variable can potentially bias *all* of the remaining parameter estimates. Unless the evidence is clear that the inclusion of NATU has adverse effects on the model, it is probably best to retain it. Exercise 5.17 conducts another test of the Phillips curve model.

[9]NATU estimates are from Robert J. Gordon, *Macroeconomics*, 4th ed. (Boston: Little-Brown, Inc., 1987), Appendix A. Inflation and unemployment data are from the 1989 *Economic Report of the President*, Tables B-3 and B-34, respectively.

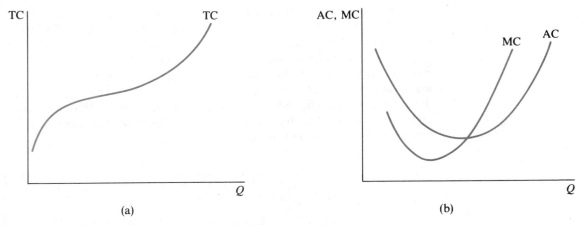

(a)   (b)

FIGURE 5.3   The total cost function, a cubic polynomial

The shape of the total cost function (TC) is derived from neoclassical
theory and can be fitted to a third-order (cubic) polynomial equation.
Marginal cost (MC) is found by differentiating the total cost function
with respect to quantity, or as $\Delta TC / \Delta Q$. Average cost is found by
dividing total cost by quantity, TC/Q.

5.1.3   Polynomial Models

The total cost function in much standard microeconomic analysis is the cubic cost function, shown in Fig. 5.3(a). The shape of the total cost function
is derived from the neoclassical production function. The cubic cost function exhibits the three stages of production—increasing marginal product,
diminishing marginal product, and decreasing marginal product. Micro-
economists (and microeconometricians) are also concerned with the average
cost function (defined as TC/Q) and marginal cost function (defined as $\Delta TC/$
ΔQ). According to theory, these curves should be "U" shaped as shown in
Fig. 5.3(b).

Equation [5.9], a third-order or *cubic polynomial* equation, can be used to
estimate the cubic cost function.

$$TC \equiv C = \beta_0 + \beta_1 Q + \beta_2 Q^2 + \beta_3 Q^3. \qquad [5.9]$$

The distinguishing characteristic of a polynomial equation is the inclusion of
several terms involving the independent variable—Q, Q^2, and Q^3 in the case
of a third-order polynomial. The signs and significance of the coefficients on
these terms will determine whether the shape of the curve is consistent with
theory. The coefficients of a well-behaved cubic cost function will fit these
requirements[10]: $\beta_0, \beta_1, \beta_3 > 0$; $\beta_2 < 0$, and $\beta_2^2 < 3\beta_1\beta_3$.

---

[10] Alpha C. Chiang, *Fundamental Methods of Mathematical Economics*, 3rd ed. (New
York: McGraw-Hill, 1984) p. 250–251.

■ EXAMPLE 5.3

STATISTICAL COST STUDIES

One of the classic works in econometrics is Jack Johnston's *Statistical Cost Analysis* (New York: McGraw-Hill, 1960). One of Johnston's main goals in writing *Statistical Cost Analysis* was to survey the then-recent empirical work on cost functions. The final chapter, "A Summary of the Empirical Evidence," presents a survey of more than 30 statistical cost studies. As would be expected, the results from diverse studies—leather belts, hosiery, retail department stores, steel production, etc.—differ quite substantially, but Johnston did reach one important generalization: The conventional U-shaped cost curve could not be verified by the evidence. In *none* of the studies listed in the final chapter was the cubic term (Q^3) significant! Many of the total cost functions were linear with respect to quantity; others were found to be log-linear or nonlinear with respect to time.

Listed below are the cost functions for several of the studies cited by Johnston:

Leather belts: $TC = -60,178 + 0.77Q + 70,181.3W,$

Hosiery: $TC = -13,634.83 + 2.068Q + 1,308.04T - 22.28T^2,$

Retail coats: $TC = -35.44 + 1.05NT - 0.00NT^2 + 0.79AVT,$

Light plant: $TC = 16.68 + 0.13Q + 0.004Q^2,$

Steel: $TC = 182,100,000 + 55.73Q,$

Electricity: $LTC = -0.12LC - 0.41LL,$

where

TC = total cost
Q = output
W = weight of belting
T = time
T^2 = time-squared
NT = number of transactions
AVT = average value per transaction
LTC = log of total costs
LC = log of generator capacity
LL = log of load factor.

What should we make of these results? At least two things. First, they explain why so many applied econometricians rejected the textbook U-shaped cost curves long ago. Instead, costs are assumed to be linear or perhaps log-linear. Second, we should *not* conclude that there is no reason to check the fit of a third-order polynomial. It may be unlikely to find a significant β on a cubic term in a cost function, but there are many other places where cubic terms are quite significant. This is especially true in time series analysis, a subject we look at in Chapter 9.

5.1.4   Interaction Effects

A literally *infinite* number of model specifications could be discussed, but we want to illustrate one final specification and ask the student to work through the exercises to see other examples.

Sometimes, the effect of one variable on the model depends on the level of another variable. For example, consider Eq. [5.10]:

$$Y_i = \beta_0 + \beta_1 X_{1i} + \beta_2 X_{2i} + \beta_3 X_{1i} X_{2i} + \varepsilon_i. \qquad [5.10]$$

The partial regression coefficients β_1 and β_2 are interpreted as usual: β_1 is the effect of a unit change in X_1 on Y, assuming that X_2 is constant, and so on for β_2. However, β_3 has a different interpretation. Notice that the effect of X_1 on Y_1, via β_3, depends on the *level* of X_2.[11] That is, a unit change in X_1 will cause Y to change by:

$$\frac{\Delta Y}{\Delta X_1} = \beta_1 + \beta_3 X_2, \qquad [5.11]$$

while the effect of X_2 on Y is given by:

$$\frac{\Delta Y}{\Delta X_2} = \beta_2 + \beta_3 X_1. \qquad [5.12]$$

As an example, it is plausible that the level of wealth affects the propensity to consume disposable income. That is, in Eq. [5.10], we could call X_1 disposable income and X_2 the level of assets. *A priori*, we would expect all coefficients to be positive. The interaction effect would be interpreted as follows: When wealth (X_2) is "low," a small change in disposable income (X_1) will affect consumption by only β_1 plus only a small amount, $\beta_3 X_{2i}$; when wealth is "high," a small change in disposable income will affect consumption by a larger amount, $\beta_1 + \beta_3 X_{2i}$. Another example of an interaction term is given in Exercise 5.12.

---

[11] This can be shown quite easily with some simple calculus. Taking partial derivatives with respect to X_1 and X_2 gives: $\partial Y / \partial X_1 = \beta_1 + \beta_3 X_2$, and $\partial Y / \partial X_2 = \beta_2 + \beta_3 X_1$.

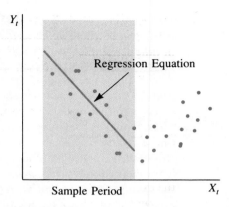

FIGURE 5.4   Incorrect functional form

Incorrect functional form can create problems when trying to make forecasts out of sample. In this case, the linear model has been incorrectly fitted to a quadratic polynomial. Notice that within the sample, the model fits pretty well; however, any forecast is likely to be quite wide of the mark.

5.1.5   Problems with Incorrect Functional Forms

The functional form of the model must be based on economic theory for at least two reasons. First, if the wrong form is selected, even a model that appears to fit the sample data well may result in incorrect inferences outside of the sample. For example, Fig. 5.4 shows what could happen if a linear form was selected but the model is actually quadratic polynomial. Forecasts based on values of $X_{T+\tau}$ outside the sample would be wildly incorrect.

A second problem is that, without the guidance of economic theory, the tendency is to try alternative functional forms and select the one with the highest R^2. Not only does this fall into the realm of unethical data mining, but it can also result in incorrect inferences about functional form: The R^2's of alternative models cannot be compared if the dependent variable has been transformed — Y, $\ln(Y)$, etc. The R^2 term is rarely a good criteria for model selection.

5.2
DUMMY VARIABLES

All of the variables and data used thus far in the text have been *quantitative*; that is, they could be counted. Interest rates (6%, 6.4%, 7%, etc.) and consumption expenditures (640 billion, 660 billion, etc.) are two of the quantitative variables we have used in the regression models we have estimated. Economic theory often suggests the inclusion of variables that are nonquantitative. For example, a study of voting patterns might necessitate some indication of the political party—Democrat or Republican—of the voters. Likewise, it could be important to distinguish between races in a study of labor force participation rates. In both cases, the recommended technique is to distinguish between the two outcomes (Democratic/Republican, black/white) by assigning values of zero and one. These are just two examples where *qualitative* variables—variables that cannot be counted—are used in econometric analysis. The most important qualitative variables used in econometric analysis are *dummy variables*. This section demonstrates how to use dummy independent variables to test for structural shifts in the model; Chapter 10 discusses the use of dummies as dependent variables.

5.2.1 Intercept Dummies

Suppose you believe that saving behavior is affected by the state of East/West tensions. For example, if people fear that nuclear war is imminent, they may be inclined to adopt a "live for today" attitude and reduce their saving. On the other hand, if they believe in a long and peaceful future, their saving may increase. To test this hypothesis, we would have to measure fear of impending war, which is not an easy task.[12] The obvious solution, a survey, would be costly, time-consuming, and perhaps inaccurate. A second best solution is to use a dummy variable, which captures the negotiation tactics of the government in power.

The hypothesized relationship is shown in Figure 5.5. Notice that the effect of the structural shift is to shift the intercept of the savings function downward. The hypothesis of this figure can be tested by setting up an equation using an intercept dummy variable. To simplify the example, suppose that income (Q_t) is the only independent variable besides the dummy that affects aggregate saving. The regression equation is:

$$S_t = \beta_0 + \beta_1 Q_t + \beta_2 D_t + \varepsilon_t. \qquad [5.13]$$

Dummy variables are always given a value of zero or one. In this case, let $D_t = 0$ when a "dove" government is in power, and let $D_t = 1$ when a "hawk" government is in power.

---

[12] In NBER Working paper 887, "Post-War Capital Accumulation and the Threat of Nuclear War," May 1982, Joel Slemrod suggests using the "minutes before midnight" measure calculated by the Union of Concerned Scientists. Slemrod's results were interesting, but tentative.

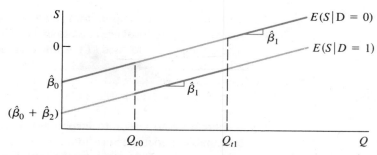

FIGURE 5.5   Intercept dummy

An intercept dummy can be used to capture a structural shift, which affects the intercept of the regression equation. In this example, fear of nuclear war during time period $Q_{t0} \rightarrow Q_{t1}$ is hypothesized to cause a downward shift in the entire savings function, from $\hat{\beta}_0$ to $(\hat{\beta}_0 + \hat{\beta}_2)$.

Taking the expected values of Equation [5.13] gives:

$$E(S_t) = \beta_0 + \beta_1 Q_t, \text{ during a "dove" government because } D_t = 0$$

$$E(S_t) = (\beta_0 + \beta_2) + \beta_1 Q_t, \text{ during a "hawk" government because } D_t = 1.$$

The two regression lines in Fig. 5.5 represent these two outcomes. Notice that the slopes of both lines are the same, $\hat{\beta}_1$, while the intercepts have changed. The sign and significance of the dummy variable will determine whether the "hawkishness" of the government affects saving behavior. The hypothesis will be verified if $\hat{\beta}_2$ is negative and has a significant t-ratio.

An especially important application of intercept dummy variables is in the correction for seasonal fluctuations, a subject discussed in Example 5.4.

■ EXAMPLE 5.4

USING DUMMY VARIABLES TO TEST FOR SEASONAL EFFECTS

One of the most common uses of dummy variables is to check for seasonal fluctuations. Seasonal fluctuations occur because of weather and custom. For example, unemployment typically rises in June when school ends and teenagers begin looking for summer jobs; and retail sales often boom in the fourth quarter due to the Christmas shopping season. Analysts need to distinguish between such seasonal fluctuations and other changes in the data.

As an example, suppose that retail sales (S) of a particular department store depend on local area employment (E) and traffic through the mall where the store is located (T). A linear specification of this relationship might be:

$$S = \beta_0 + \beta_1 E + \beta_2 T + \varepsilon. \tag{1'}$$

If there were no reason to suspect seasonal effects, this would be a reasonable model specification. However, most retail sales do have seasonal effects, so a model containing seasonal dummies is probably preferred.

To check for seasonality, one time period must be selected as the control period and separate dummies must be used for every remaining time period within the year. For example, with monthly data, there should be 11 dummies plus a control, and for quarterly data there should be 3 dummies plus the control period. As mentioned in Sec. 5.2.4, the dummy variable trap precludes the use of 12 and 4 dummies.

If the retail sales data are quarterly, the correct model specification would be:

$$S = \beta_0 + \beta_1 E + \beta_2 T + \beta_3 D_1 + \beta_4 D_2 + \beta_5 D_3 + \varepsilon, \tag{2'}$$

where

$D_1 = 1$, in the first quarter; 0 otherwise
$D_2 = 1$ in the second quarter; 0 otherwise
$D_3 = 1$ in the third quarter; 0 otherwise.

In this case, the fourth quarter was selected as the control quarter, but it is possible to use any quarter.

Now, if we take expected values of Eq. [2'], we find:

First quarter: $E(S) = (\beta_0 + \beta_3) + \beta_1 E + \beta_2 T,$

Second quarter: $E(S) = (\beta_0 + \beta_4) + \beta_1 E + \beta_2 T,$

Third quarter: $E(S) = (\beta_0 + \beta_5) + \beta_1 E + \beta_2 T,$

Fourth quarter: $E(S) = \beta_0 + \beta_1 E + \beta_2 T.$

What signs should we expect on β_3, β_4, and β_5? If it is true that retail sales boom in the fourth quarter, they should be significant and negative. If they are positive or statistically insignificant, then we would conclude that retail sales do not boom in the fourth quarter.

An alternative method for dealing with seasonal effects is presented in Chapter 9.

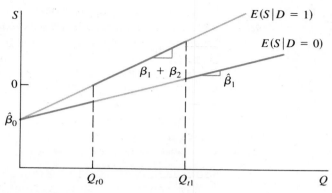

FIGURE 5.6   Slope dummy

A slope dummy will cause the slope of the regression function to change over the period of the structural change, $Q_{t0} \to Q_{t1}$. Notice that there has been no change in the intercept. In this case, the marginal propensity to save rises from β_1 to $(\beta_1 + \beta_2)$ from time Q_{t0} to Q_{t1} because people fear a collapse of the Social Security system. At time Q_{t1} people realize that their fears were unfounded, so their saving behavior returns to normal, β_1.

5.2.2   Slope Dummies

Dummy variables can also be used to test for the presence of a structural change that affects the slope of the regression equation. As an example, suppose that in year t_0 a rumor is circulated that the Social Security system is on the verge of bankruptcy. This might result in an increase in the marginal propensity to save (MPS) as people try to save for retirement. If this rumor is proved false in year t_1, the MPS will return to its previous level. Such a scenario is shown graphically in Fig. 5.6.

Specification of a slope dummy is only a bit more complex than an intercept dummy. The equation to be estimated is:

$$S_t = \beta_0 + \beta_1 Q_t + \beta_2 Q_t D_t + \varepsilon_t, \qquad [5.14]$$

with the dummy defined as $D_t = 0$, when there is no fear of Social Security bankruptcy, and $D_t = 1$, when savers fear Social Security will go bankrupt.

Taking expected values of Eq. [5.14] gives:

$$E(S_t) = \beta_0 + \beta_1 Q_t, \quad \text{when} \quad D_t = 0,$$

$$E(S_t) = \beta_0 + (\beta_1 + \beta_2)Q_t, \quad \text{when} \quad D_t = 1.$$

As before, the sign and statistical significance of the dummy will allow us to accept or reject the hypothesis of a structural shift in the slope of the saving function. Notice that because of the way the model was specified, we would expect $\hat{\beta}_2$ to be positive; had the dummy variables been assigned differently (i.e., $D_t = 1$ when people feared bankruptcy), we would have expected $\hat{\beta}_2$ to be negative.

5.2.3   Piecewise Linear Models

A structural change could affect both the slope and the intercept. For example, in most universities, tenure decisions are based partially on the number of articles published in refereed journals. The ability to publish is partially an acquired skill, so the rate of publication is likely to increase over time with experience. Once tenure is granted, many professors begin to devote their time to writing textbooks—an activity that can be lucrative, but one that is too risky before being granted tenure because texts do not "count" as much as journal articles.

Such a scenario is pictured in Fig. 5.7 where the structural change (tenure) is assumed to occur at time t_0. The dependent variable, Y_t, represents published articles; the independent variable, X_t, represents time or experience. Notice that publications increase over time until point t_0 when tenure is assumed to be granted. The experience the professor has acquired up to point t_0 permits a continuing increase in journal publication, but the fact that tenure has been

FIGURE 5.7   Piecewise linear model

Both the slope and intercept change in a piecewise linear model. Before the structural change occurs at point X_{t0}, the intercept is $\hat{\beta}_0$ while the slope is $\hat{\beta}_1$. After the structural shift, the intercept is $(\hat{\beta}_0 - \hat{\beta}_2 X_{t0})$ and the slope is $(\hat{\beta}_1 + \hat{\beta}_2)$.

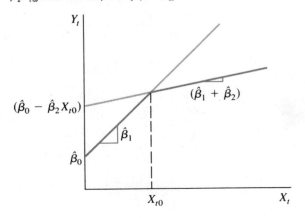

granted allows a reordering of scholarly activity priorities. This model is called a *piecewise linear model* because it is linear in sections.[13]

Despite the fact that both the slope and the intercept have changed, the possibility of such a structural change can be tested with a model using only one dummy variable. The general form of a piecewise linear model is:

$$Y_t = \beta_0 + \beta_1 X_t + \beta_2 (X_t - X_{t0}) D_t + \varepsilon_t, \qquad [5.15]$$

where

Y_t = dependent variable (publications)
X_t = independent variable (time or experience)
X_{t0} = when the structural shift takes place (tenure)
$D_t = 0$ if $t < t_0$
$D_t = 1$ if $t > t_0$
ε_t = error term.

Taking expected values of Eq. [5.15] gives:

$$E(Y_t) = \beta_0 + \beta_1 X_t \text{ before the structural shift at } X_{t0},$$

$$E(Y_t) = (\beta_0 - \beta_2 X_{t0}) + (\beta_1 + \beta_2) X_t \text{ after the structural shift.}$$

Notice that because X_{t0} is a constant, the term $\beta_2 X_{t0}$ becomes part of the intercept. As before, the sign and significance of $\hat{\beta}_2$ will determine whether the hypothesized structural shift has taken place. In the case of Fig. 5.7, we would expect $\hat{\beta}_2$ to be negative.

5.2.4   Restrictions on the Use of Dummy Variables

Dummy variables are a powerful tool if used correctly, but a number of restrictions must be kept in mind when using them. First, we have discussed the use of dummies only as independent variables; dummy dependent variables are a separate subject we delay until Chapter 10. Second, dummy variables must take on values of zero and one; there are several statistical problems if they are assigned values of, for instance, 0, 1, 2, 3.

Another potentially serious problem with dummy variables is known as the *dummy variable trap*. The dummy variable trap can occur when multiple dummies are used incorrectly to capture multiple structural shifts. If multiple dummies add up to exactly one, there will be perfect multicollinearity between them and the intercept, making it impossible to compute any regression estimates. As an example, suppose that two intercept dummies, D_{1t} and D_{2t}, were used to test the same thing—the effect of the fear of war on savings. If the

---

[13] Piecewise linear models are also called *spline functions* or *jack-knife models*.

assigned values were $D_{1t} = 0$ when the hawks run the govenment and $D_{1t} = 1$ during the time the doves are in power, and $D_{2t} = 1$ when the hawks run the government and $D_{2t} = 0$ when the doves are in power, it would follow that $D_{1t} + D_{2t} = 1$, which is perfectly collinear with the intercept.

The dummy variable trap can be avoided as long as the number of dummies is less than the number of outcomes. In the savings example, there are two outcomes—"normal" and "reduced" saving in response to fear of war. In fact, only one dummy is needed because the determination that saving decreased when the hawks are in power implies the opposite—that saving rises when the doves are in office.[14]

5.2.5   The Chow Test

An alternative way to check for the existence of structural change is the *Chow test*.[15] The Chow test is most often used to check for the presence of a structural change in a model using time series data. For example, suppose you run a model using annual data for the period 1950–90 and you suspect that there was a structural change in 1975. To conduct a Chow test, the model is run three times: once for the entire 1950–90 period, and once over each of the subperiods. The model run over the entire period is called a *restricted model* because it is constrained such that the β_j from both subperiods must be equal.

The premise of the Chow test is that if a structural change has occurred, the error sum of squares for a *restricted model* (ESS_r) will be larger than the error sum of squares for the unrestricted models (ESS_u) covering the two subperiods. Determining whether ESS_r is large relative to ESS_u is done with an F-test.

The Chow test is conducted as follows:

1.   Run the model over both periods to calculate ESS_r. There will be n_1 observations before the structural shift and n_2 observations after the shift for a total of $n = n_1 + n_2$ observations. The number of parameters to be estimated will be $k + 1$, so ESS_r will have $n - k - 1$ degrees of freedom.

---

[14] The dummy variable trap can also be avoided by suppressing the intercept in the regression model, a technique that was alluded to in Example 5.4. However, suppression of the intercept can lead to the violation of A3. Among other things, this can bias the remaining parameter estimates because the effects of omitted variables will be captured in included variable coefficients. For a discussion of this issue, see A. H. Studenmund and Henry J. Cassidy, *Using Econometrics* (Boston: Little-Brown, 1987), p. 163–65.

[15] Gregory C. Chow, "Tests for Equality Between Sets of Coefficients in Two Linear Regressions," *Econometrica*, Vol. 28, No. 3, 1960.

2. Run the model over the two subperiods to find ESS_1 and ESS_2, with $n_1 - k - 1$ and $n_2 - k - 1$ degrees of freedom, respectively. Sum ESS_1 and ESS_2 to get ESS_u, which will have $n - 2k - 2$ degrees of freedom.

3. Form the F-ratio:

$$F_{(k+1),\ (n-2k-2)} = \frac{ESS_r - ESS_u/(k+1)}{ESS_u/(n-2k-2)}.$$ [5.16]

If this ratio is greater than the table value, the null hypothesis of no structural change can be rejected.

The Chow test has become a standard tool for econometricians, but two cautions regarding its use must be mentioned. First, if the errors are heteroscedastic, the Chow test is inappropriate, so it is important to first check the model for hetersocedasticity, a topic we cover in Chapter 7. Second, the need to split the data into two groups means that there can be a degree-of-freedom problem with small data sets.   ◆ ◆ ◆

5.3

DISTRIBUTED LAG MODELS

Most of the models we have looked at thus far have been contemporaneous in the sense that the indpendent and dependent variables are from the same point in time; that is, Y_t was assumed to be a function of X_{jt}. This is often a reasonable specification, but not always. For example, a farmer's decision to plant may depend more on last year's price than the current price. Likewise, monetary theorists have long argued that changes in the money supply affect economic activity after a lag of six months or more, and that the effects continue for several months. No special econometric problems occur when there is only one lagged variable on the right side of the regression equation, but when there are several lags—as economic theory often suggests there should be—several difficulties arise that necessitate proper model specification.

5.3.1   The Nature of Distributed Lags

Many phenomena in economics take place over time. For example, the OPEC supply shocks of the 1970s affected the world over a period of years. There was an initial effect—inflation accelerated and GNP growth slowed almost immediately—but there were also lag effects for several years as the higher oil costs were passed on to different sectors of the economy. Such a relationship might be captured with a distributed lag model:

$$Y_t = \beta_0 + \beta_1 X_t + \beta_2 X_{t-1} + \beta_3 X_{t-2} + \beta_4 X_{t-3} + \cdots + \varepsilon_t, \qquad [5.17]$$

where

Y_t = current inflation rate
X_{t-s} = OPEC price of oil lagged s years
ε_t = random error.

A priori, it is reasonable to suspect that the influence of the oil price shock declines over time so that $\beta_1 > \beta_2 > \beta_3$. This is true of most distributed lag models.

Unfortunately, trying to estimate Eq. [5.17] is fraught with difficulties. First, the X_{t-s} regressors are likely to suffer from severe multicollinearity, making it difficult to trust the $\hat{\beta}_j$. Second, the potentially large number of lags will reduce the degrees of freedom. These are the main reasons why the Koyck and other distributed lag models were developed.

5.3.2 The Koyck Model

The simplest and one of the most useful distributed lag models is the Koyck model.[16] This model eliminates both of the problems mentioned above: multicollinearity and loss of degrees of freedom.

The Koyck model assumes that the influence of the X_{t-s} regressors declines smoothly over time. This can be captured with the equation:

$$\beta_j = \beta_1 \lambda^s, 0 < \lambda < 1, \qquad j = 1, \ldots, k, \qquad s = 0, \ldots, k, \qquad [5.18]$$

where s is the length of the lag. To see how this works, suppose that $\lambda = 0.5$; then substitute Eq. [5.18] into Eq. [5.17]:

$$Y_t = \beta_0 + \beta_1(X_t + 0.5X_{t-1} + 0.25X_{t-2} + 0.125X_{t-3} + \cdots) + \varepsilon_t.$$
$$[5.19]$$

We should make two comments about Eq. [5.19]. First, notice that the intercept, β_0, remains outside of the parentheses. Second, because $0 < \lambda < 1$, the influence of X_{t-s} becomes insignificant at some time lag. This will be important momentarily when we derive an alternative expression for the Koyck lag. Figure 5.8 illustrates how the relative influence of the lagged variables declines over time.

---

[16] L. M. Koyck, *Distributed Lags and Investment Analysis* (Amsterdam: North-Holland, 1954).

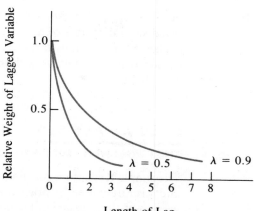

FIGURE 5.8   The Koyck Lag

The influence of X_{t-s} regressors declines over time. Smaller values of λ cause the influence of X_{t-s} to decline more quickly.

Thus far, we have done little more than rewrite Eq. [5.17], the equation we just finished saying was difficult to estimate. How does the Koyck lag help? A few manipulations will show. We rewrite Eq. [5.19] in its general form:

$$Y_t = \beta_0 + \beta_1(\lambda^0 X_t + \lambda^1 X_{t-1} + \lambda^2 X_{t-2} + \lambda^3 X_{t-3} + \cdots) + \varepsilon_t.$$

[5.20]

Now, lag and multiply by λ:

$$\lambda Y_{t-1} = \lambda\beta_0 + \beta_1(\lambda^1 X_{t-1} + \lambda^2 X_{t-2} + \lambda^3 X_{t-3} + \lambda^4 X_{t-4} + \cdots) + \lambda\varepsilon_{t-1}.$$

[5.21]

Subtract Eq. [5.21] from [5.20]:

$$Y_t - \lambda Y_{t-1} = (\beta_0 - \lambda\beta_0) + \beta_1 X_t + \beta_1(\lambda^1 X_{t-1} + \lambda^2 X_{t-2} + \lambda^3 X_{t-3} + \cdots)$$
$$- \beta_1(\lambda^1 X_{t-1} + \lambda^2 X_{t-2} + \lambda^3 X_{t-3} + \lambda^4 X_{t-4} + \cdots) + (\varepsilon_t - \lambda\varepsilon_t).$$

[5.22]

The common terms cancel and the last lag on X_{t-s} approaches zero. Some rearranging gives:

$$Y_t = \beta_0^* + \beta_1 X_t + \lambda Y_{t-1} + \varepsilon_t^*,$$

[5.23]

where $\beta_0^* = \beta_0 - \lambda\beta_0$ and $\varepsilon_t^* = \varepsilon_t - \lambda\varepsilon_t$.

Equation [5.23] is the equation to be estimated in a Koyck distributed lag model. Once $\hat{\beta}_0^*$, $\hat{\beta}_1$, and $\hat{\lambda}$ have been found, the coefficients on the X_{t-s} terms can be found by substitution. By removing the X_{t-s} terms from the right side, the Koyck transformation has eliminated much of the multicollinearity and saved several degrees of freedom. Other problems may have been created by the lagged endogenous variable on the right side—especially if ε_t^* suffers from autocorrelation—but we will find out how to deal with that problem in the next chapter.

■ EXAMPLE 5.5

THE PERMANENT INCOME HYPOTHESIS

The simple Keynesian consumption function we estimated in Chapters 3 and 4 is rarely used by practicing economists today. Most economists use a version of the permanent income hypothesis developed by Milton Friedman.[17] Friedman argued that the consumption decision depends on the perception of *permanent* income—a guess made about the flow of income over time—not current income. Among other things, this means that consumers may not respond to temporary or *transitory* changes in their income. Friedman developed a precise utility maximizing framework to describe how individuals would estimate their permanent income, but the basic idea was that people use the pattern of their past income to form expectations of current permanent income. This can be expressed as a distributed lag model:

$$\text{CONS}_t = \beta_0 + \beta_1 \text{DPI}_t + \beta_2 \text{DPI}_{t-1} + \beta_3 \text{DPI}_{t-2} + \beta_4 \text{DPI}_{t-3} + \cdots + \varepsilon_t, \tag{1'}$$

where

CONS_t = real consumption expenditures at time period t
DPI_{t-s} = real disposable personal income at time period $t - s$
ε_t = random error term.

As we know, estimation of Eq. [1′] will be difficult because of multicollinearity, but we will estimate it to compare it to a Koyck version of the same equation:

$$\text{CONS}_t = \beta_0^* + \beta_1 \text{DPI}_t + \lambda \text{CONS}_{t-1} + \varepsilon_t^*. \tag{2'}$$

The same data in Data Set 1—real annual data, 1960–87—were used in this example. The regression results from Eq. [1′] are shown. As expected, there are clear signs of multicollinearity: R^2 is extremely high, but the t-ratios on DPIL1, DPIL2, and DPIL3 (1, 2, and 3 period lags on

---

[17]Milton Friedman, *The Theory of the Consumption Function* (Cambridge, Mass.: NBER, 1957).

```
Dep var: CONS  N: 25  R-sq: .997  Adj  R-sq: .996  SER: 26.01

Variable  Coefficient  Std Error    T     P(2 tail)

CONSTANT       -72.90      27.25   -2.68     0.01
    DPI          1.03       0.15    6.76     0.00
  DPIL1          0.08       0.22    0.36     0.73
  DPIL2         -0.17       0.23   -0.74     0.47
  DPIL3         -0.01       0.16   -0.04     0.97
```

DPI) are insignificant. Notice too what has happened to the coefficient on DPI: It is now greater than one—something that did not happen in any of the regressions run in Chapters 3 or 4. Parameter estimates than cannot be trusted are another symptom of multicollinearity. Finally, the coefficients do not decline smoothly as we would expect in a distributed lag model.

When the same data are used in a Koyck version of the model, Eq. [2'], the results are much more reasonable:

```
Dep var: CONS  N: 27  R-sq: .997  Adj  R-sq: .997  SER: 23.29

Variable  Coefficient  Std Error    T     P(2 tail)

CONSTANT       -20.11      21.13   -0.95     0.35
    DPI          0.60       0.13    4.43     0.00
  CONSL1         0.36       0.15    2.47     0.02
```

Assuming that these results can be trusted, we can work backward to find the distributed lag coefficients. Recall that the coefficient on Y_{t-1} ($=$ CONSL 1) is an estimate of λ. Substituting $\lambda = 0.36$ and $\beta_1 = 0.6$ into Eq. [5.20] gives:

$$\widehat{\text{CONS}}_t = \beta_0^* + 0.60\text{DPI}_t + 0.6(0.36)\text{DPI}_{t-1} + 0.6(0.36)^2\text{DPI}_{t-2} + 0.6(0.36)^3\text{DPI}_{t-3},$$

$$\widehat{\text{CONS}}_t = 0 + 0.6\text{DPI}_t + 0.22\text{DPI}_{t-1} + 0.08\text{DPI}_{t-2} + 0.03\text{DPI}_{t-3}.$$

These results are quite reasonable, and *much* more reliable than those obtained from the initial regression.

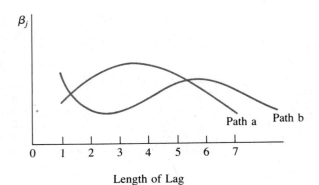

Length of Lag

FIGURE 5.9   Almon lag possibilities

The Almon lag is quite general and can be used to specify many different coefficient paths, including the two above. Path a indicates that the independent variable has less effect on Y in period 1 than in period 2 or 3, but that after period 4 the effect diminishes. Path b indicates that there is a large initial effect which tapers off until period 3 when it increases again.

5.3.3   Other Distributed Lag Models

Many other distributed lag models exist, but most are beyond the scope of an introductory treatment. One useful lag model is the *Almon* or *polynomial lag*.[18] Unlike the Koyck model, this model does not assume that $\beta_1 > \beta_2 > \beta_3$. For example, models can be formulated with either of the patterns shown in Fig. 5.9 below. Other lag structures include the Pascal lag and the rational lag.[19]

5.4

SPECIFICATION ERRORS

In addition to specifying the correct functional form, it is important that all relevant variables but no extraneous variables be included in the model to be

---

[18] Shirley Almon, "The Distributed Lag Between Capital Appropriations and Expenditures," *Econometrica*, Vol. 33, January 1965, p. 178–196.
[19] The interested reader can find a good discussion of the Almon lag in Chapter 5 of Harry H. Kelejian and Wallace E. Oates, *Introduction to Econometrics* (New York: Harper and Row, 1989). Other lag structures are covered in Chapter 11 of Jan Kmenta, *Elements of Econometrics* (New York: Macmillan, 1986).

estimated. If important relevant variables are omitted, parameter estimates are likely to be biased.[20] If extraneous variables are included, parameter estimates will be unbiased but inefficient.

Unfortunately, it is not always clear whether a particular variable should be included or excluded from a model. Both economic theory and statistical criteria must be relied on, but ultimately modeling is an art as much as a science. This section will point out some of the problems associated with misspecification; Chapter 11 explores the subject of econometric modeling in more detail.

5.4.1 Omitted Variables

Suppose that a model is constructed to study the influence of fertilizer on crop yield. The expectation, of course, is that fertilizer increases yield. However, if a simple regression model were used, $\text{YIELD} = \beta_0 + \beta_1 \text{FERTILIZER}$, $\hat{\beta}_1$ could be biased. For example, if the sample were taken over a period of declining rainfall, $\hat{\beta}_1$ might turn out negative. The correct specification—inclusion of a rainfall variable and all other significant explanatory variables—is necessary to eliminate this source of bias.

In general, parameter estimates will be biased if significant variables are omitted from the estimated model. Suppose that the "true" model involves two independent variables:

$$y_i = \beta_1 x_{1i} + \beta_2 x_{2i} + \varepsilon_i. \tag{5.24}$$

However, only one independent variable is used in the estimated model:

$$y_i = \beta_1^* x_{1i} + \varepsilon_i^*. \tag{5.25}$$

Application of OLS to Eq. [5.25] would yield:

$$\hat{\beta}_1^* = \frac{\sum x_{1i} y_i}{\sum x_{1i}^2}, \tag{5.26}$$

which is biased.

The bias in $\hat{\beta}_1^*$ can be shown by substituting Eq. [5.24] for y_i into the numerator of Eq. [5.26],

$$\hat{\beta}_1^* = \frac{\sum x_{1i}(\beta_1 x_{1i} + \beta_2 x_{2i} + \varepsilon_i)}{\sum x_{1i}^2} = \beta_1 \frac{\sum x_{1i}^2}{\sum x_{1i}^2} + \beta_2 \frac{\sum x_{1i} x_{2i}}{\sum x_{1i}^2} + \frac{\sum x_{1i}\varepsilon_i}{\sum x_{1i}^2}, \tag{5.27}$$

---

[20] As shown in Chapter 6, omission of significant variables can also lead to autocorrelation.

and taking the expected value. If the OLS assumptions hold, the third term on the left side goes to zero and we are left with:

$$E(\hat{\beta}_1^*) = \beta_1 + \beta_2 E\left(\frac{\sum x_{1i}x_{2i}}{\sum x_{1i}^2}\right) + 0. \tag{5.28}$$

Thus, $\hat{\beta}_1^*$ will be unbiased only if the expected value of $\sum x_{1i}x_{2i}$ is zero, which it probably is not. This term is the covariance between X_1 and X_2. Because we began the exercise assuming that a relevant independent variable, X_2, was omitted from the estimated equation, we must assume that it is correlated with the dependent variable. Because X_1 is correlated with the dependent variable, it is almost a certainty that X_1 and X_2 are also correlated. This fact allows us to reach an important conclusion regarding the extent of the bias: If the omitted variable is highly correlated with included variable(s), the bias is likely to be large; if the correlation between the omitted variable and the included variable(s) is low, the bias will tend to be small.

5.4.2 Extraneous Variables

The inadvertent inclusion of extraneous variables in the fitted model will not bias parameter estimates, but it can result in inefficient parameter estimates and low t-scores, which can cause the investigator to drop a relevant variable incorrectly and thus bias the remaining parameter estimates. This too can be shown quite easily.

Suppose now that the "true" model is a simple regression model:

$$y_i = \beta_1 x_{1i} + \varepsilon_i, \tag{5.29}$$

but the estimated model is

$$y_i = \beta_1^* x_{1i} + \beta_2^* x_{2i} + \varepsilon_i^*. \tag{5.30}$$

Using OLS to estimate $\hat{\beta}_1^*$ from Eq. [5.30] would yield:

$$\hat{\beta}_1^* = \frac{(\sum x_{1i}y_i)(\sum x_{2i}^2) - (\sum x_{2i}y_i)(\sum x_{1i}x_{2i})}{(\sum x_{1i}^2)(\sum x_{2i}^2) - (\sum x_{1i}x_{2i})^2}, \tag{5.31}$$

with an estimated variance of:

$$\widehat{\text{var}}(\hat{\beta}_1^*) = \frac{s^{*2}}{\sum x_{1i}^2(1 - r_{12}^2)}. \tag{5.32}$$

As always, s^{*2}, the estimated variance, is the sum of the squared residuals divided by the degrees of freedom, and r_{12}^2 is the correlation between X_1 and X_2.

To demonstrate that $\hat{\beta}_1^*$ is inefficient, we need to compare $\widehat{\text{var}}(\hat{\beta}_1^*)$ to $\widehat{\text{var}}(\hat{\beta}_1)$. Recall that $\widehat{\text{var}}(\hat{\beta}_1)$ is defined as:

$$\widehat{\text{var}}(\hat{\beta}_1) = \frac{s^2}{\sum x_{1i}^2}. \qquad [5.33]$$

The variance in Eq. [5.32] is, in general, greater than the variance in Eq. [5.33] for two reasons. First, even if X_2 is truly extraneous, it is likely that there will be some spurious correlation between X_1 and X_2 and thus r_{12}^2 will be a nonzero value. This will decrease the denominator of Eq. [5.31] and thus raise the variance of $\hat{\beta}_1^*$. Second, the numerator of $\widehat{\text{var}}(\hat{\beta}_1^*)$ is probably larger than the numerator of $\widehat{\text{var}}(\hat{\beta}_1)$ as well. Note that the error term for the misspecified model is actually:

$$\varepsilon_i^* = \varepsilon_i - \beta_2 x_2. \qquad [5.34]$$

To calculate s^{*2}, this is squared, summed, and divided by degrees of freedom:

$$s^{*2} = \frac{\sum(\varepsilon_i^2 - 2\beta_2 x_{2i} + \beta_2^2 x_{2i}^2)}{n-3} = \frac{\sum \varepsilon_i^2 - 2\beta_2 \sum x_{2i} + \beta_2^2 \sum x_{2i}^2}{n-3}. \qquad [5.35]$$

The middle term on the right side, however, goes to zero because $\sum x_{2i} = 0$. The result is that s^{*2} is greater than s^2 except for *very* small samples[21]:

$$s^{*2} = \frac{\sum(\varepsilon_i^2 + \beta_2^2 x_{2i}^2)}{n-3} > s^2 = \frac{\sum \varepsilon_i^2}{n-2}. \qquad [5.36]$$

Of course, extraneous variables *should* have such low *t*-scores that they are left out of the model after the initial regression run. However, for any particular sample, there can be a spurious correlation between X_j and Y that will translate into a high *t*-ratio. In this case—and anytime you wonder whether a variable should be included in the model—the *F*-test developed in Appendix 4.A can be used to determine whether the suspect variable(s) adds significant explanatory power to the model.

5.5

SUMMARY: SPECIFICATION SEARCHES

In practice, model specification may be more of an art than a science. Economic theory rarely suggests a precise functional form or the complete list of independent variables to include in the model. Further, almost all

---

[21] The reason we must qualify this statement with the phrase "except for *very* small samples" is that the residual sum of squares from the two- and three-variable models will not be identical for any particular sample.

regression models have omitted variables, because "everything depends on everything else" in economics. The result is that *all* parameter estimates are potentially biased. Does this mean that we should throw out regression analysis entirely? Not at all. The key is the extent of the bias. Models that contain most of the important variables can be trusted, within limits, and we often do know the most important variables to be included in the model. Still, most econometricians check several model specifications and try several different independent variable combinations before settling on a model.

The model that is finally selected depends on several factors, and is ultimately a very personal decision. Some econometricians tend to place as much or more value on economic theory as statistical criteria. These people are inclined to leave in variables suggested by theory even if their individual *t*-ratios are low. They are also less inclined to keep trying alternative model specifications until they hit on one that "works." Other econometricians rely on statistical criteria to verify or refute their *a priori* beliefs. These econometricians are somewhat less inclined to keep variables with low *t*-scores. Obviously, the trade-off between bias (omitted variables) and inefficiency (extraneous variables) can serve only as a partial guide. These and other methodological issues are discussed in Chapter 11.

We must add one final item before going on: Unlike multicollinearity (or heteroscedasticity or autocorrelation), specification errors can lead to biased parameters, potentially a very serious problem. Another likely source of bias is *simultaneous equation bias*. As we will point out in Chapter 8, estimation of a single equation that is really part of a simultaneous equation system can also lead to biased parameter estimates. Because most economic relationships are drawn from simultaneous systems, this is another very common source of bias.

CONCEPTS FOR REVIEW

This has been a long chapter, but it has barely covered the variety of functional forms and model specifications used in econometric models. You'll certainly want to refer back to this chapter when you begin to formulate the model for your class project. Don't expect to find the precise model specification you need; invariably it will be a variation of the models we have just outlined.

This has been the last chapter in the foundation of econometric modeling techniques. Beginning with Chapter 6, most of our attention will be on real-world problems that inevitably crop up—biased parameter estimates, poorly behaved errors, etc. Before you are ready to go on, make sure you know:

- why linear regression analysis is called "linear" even though it can be applied only to models that, when plotted, are nonlinear
- how and why dummy variables are used in regression models
- what problems are likely to crop up when estimating distributed lag models and how the Koyck transformation solves these problems

- how specification errors affect parameter estimates
- how to define and use the following key terms in context.

KEY TERMS

Almon lag	log transformation
Chow test	omitted variable
Cobb-Douglas production function	Phillips curve
	piecewise linear model
cubic cost function	polynomial model
distributed lag	qualitative variable
dummy variable trap	quantitative variable
extraneous variable	reciprocal model
interaction effects	slope dummy
intercept dummy	specification error
Koyck lag	

EXERCISES

5.1 The Phillips curve was specified with both parameters positve. What would the curve look like if β_1 were negative? To what kind of economic relationship might this apply?

5.2 Would you expect there to be a problem with multicollinearity when estimating polynomial equations? Why or why not?

5.3 In Sec. 5.2.1, we noted that the bias associated with an omitted variable depends on the correlation between the omitted and included variables. How does this fact complicate the problems associated with multicollinearity?

5.4 Refer back to Example 5.4. Can you think of an alternative way to check for seasonal effects that would save degrees of freedom?

5.5 Suppose you believe that the relationship between Y and X_1 is:

$$Y_t = \frac{1}{\beta_0 + \beta_1 X_{1t} + \varepsilon_t}.$$

a. Sketch how the graph would look.

b. Transform this model to allow estimation with linear regression.

5.6 Suppose you have reason to believe that the relationship between Y and X_1 is $Y_t = \exp(\beta_0 + \beta_1 X_{1t} + \varepsilon_t)$

   a. Sketch a graph of this function.

   b. Transform this model to allow estimation with linear regression and sketch a graph of the transformed equation.

5.7 Suppose you have reason to believe that the relationship between X_t and Y_t underwent a structural shift at time period X_{t0} such that the graph looks like the figure below:

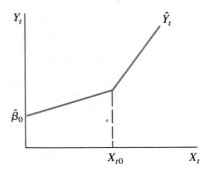

   a. Set up a piecewise linear model to test this hypothesis.

   b. Set up a model using two dummies to test this relationship. Will you fall into the dummy variable trap?

5.8 Is there any evidence of multicollinearity in the Phillips curve test? What additional information would you like to have to be sure?

5.9 How is it possible to talk about a *residual* in the Cobb-Douglas production test of Example 5.1 given that $\bar{R}^2$ exceeds 0.99?

5.10 Interest rates are notoriously difficult to forecast. One reason for this is because of the dynamics involved in interest rate determination. A plausible specification for an interest rate model is:

$$R_t = \beta_0 + \beta_1 \text{DPI} + \beta_2 \sum M_t + \beta_3 \sum P_t + \varepsilon_t,$$

where:

   R_t = interest rate on AAA bonds
   DPI_t = disposable personal income
   $\sum M_t$ = moving sum of changes in the money supply:
   $\quad \sum M_t = \Delta M_t + \Delta M_{t-1} + \Delta M_{t-2}$
   $\sum P_t$ = moving sum of the inflation rate:
   $\quad \sum P_t = P_t + P_{t-1} + P_{t-2}.$

a. Why do you think the money supply and inflation variables were specified as they were?

b. What signs would you expect to find on the regression coefficients?

5.11 In the 1972 publication, *The Inflation Process in the United States, A Study Prepared for the Use of the Joint Economic Committee,* Otto Eckstein and Roger Brinner argued that inflation affected wage demands only after it reached a level of 2.5%. Use this information to respecify the Phillips curve model of Example 5.2.

5.12 Winter usage of natural gas (G) depends on temperature (T) as well as price (P). However, it is possible that the effect of T depends on P, that is, people may turn down the thermostat when the price of natural gas rises. Specify a regression model that could be used to test this hypothesis.

5.13 In Sec. 5.3.2, we stated, "By removing the X_{t-s} terms from the right side, the Koyck transformation has eliminated *much* of the multicollinearity . . . ." Why didn't it say removed *all* of the multicollinearity?

5.14 Assume that the model tested in Exercise 4.6, Chapter 4, is a Koyck lag. Write out the distributed lag equation. Where would you cut off the lag?

5.15 Suppose population growth is given by:

$$P_t = \beta_0(1 + g)^t e^{\varepsilon_t},$$

where

P_t = population growth
g = compound rate of growth of P_t
β_0 = parameter
e = the base of natural logs,
ε_t = error.

a. Take a log transformation of the population growth function.

b. Show that P_t and t are nonlinearly related but that $\ln(P_t)$ and t are linearly related.

5.16 We noted in the text that the regression coefficients of a log-linear model are actually elasticities and that the elasticity of a linear model is given by $\hat{\beta}_1(\bar{X}/\bar{Y})$. Find the elasticity expressions for the reciprocal model and the semi-log model.

5.17 Many investigators believe that supply shocks were significant causes of inflation in the 1970s, especially the OPEC oil price hikes of 1974–75 and 1978–79. Test this proposition by adding an intercept dummy to the Phillips curve model estimated in Example 5.2. The data used in Example 5.2 are provided in Data Set 5 of Appendix I. You will need to have the computer calculate LAGP and RECIPU and will have to input the (1, 0) values for the dummy variable.

Before beginning the analysis:

a. What sign do you expect to find on your dummy variable?

b. Do you think inclusion of a dummy will improve the R^2?

After completing the initial regression runs:

c. Interpret the results. Are they what you expected? Did the dummy improve the explanatory value of the model?

d. The NATU variable had a low *t*-score in Example 5.2. Is there any reason to suspect that the low *t*-score was caused by multicollinearity?

e. Run the model using U instead of RECIPU as one of the regressors. Is this model superior or inferior to the RECIPU model? Why or why not?

APPENDIX 5.A

SOME MATHEMATICAL PROPERTIES

We skimmed over some important mathematics to allow us to concentrate on the econometrics in this chapter. The material in this appendix should help you in other economics courses, especially intermediate theory and managerial economics.

The Cobb-Douglas Production Function

The Cobb-Douglas production function is a popular starting place for neoclassical growth models. It is consistent with most neoclassical distribution theory and is easy to manipulate mathematically. Most importantly, perhaps, is that it also seems to fit quite a bit of the real-world growth experience since World War II. The attractive properties of the Cobb-Douglas function can be illustrated fairly easily to students who remember their calculus.

Recall that the Cobb-Douglas production function is written as[22]:

$$Q = \beta_0 L^{\beta_1} K^{\beta_2}. \tag{A.1}$$

First we find the marginal product of capital and labor by taking the partial derivatives with respect to K and L, or:

$$MP_K = \frac{\partial Q}{\partial K} = \beta_2 \beta_0 L^{\beta_1} K^{\beta_2 - 1}, \tag{A.2}$$

$$MP_L = \frac{\partial Q}{\partial L} = \beta_1 \beta_0 L^{\beta_1 - 1} K^{\beta_2}. \tag{A.3}$$

Neoclassical production theory requires that the marginal product be positive but diminishing. This is apparent from Eqs. [A.2] and [A.3]. Substitute any fractions, $0 < \beta_1, \beta_2 < 1$, and both expressions are positive. For example, if $\beta_1 = \beta_2 = 1$, Eq. [A.2] becomes:

$$MP_K = \frac{\partial Q}{\partial K} = \beta_1 \beta_0 L^{\beta_1} K^{-\beta_1} > 0. \tag{A.4}$$

Thus, the marginal product will be positive because all components of Eq. [A.4] are greater than zero.

---

[22] To reduce the clutter, observation subscripts and error terms are omitted in this appendix.

To show that the marginal product diminishes as more of a factor is added, differentiate Eqs. [A.2] and [A.3] a second time to get:

$$\frac{\partial^2 Q}{\partial K^2} = (\beta_2 - 1)\beta_2 \beta_0 L^{\beta_1} K^{\beta_2 - 2}, \qquad\qquad \text{[A.5]}$$

$$\frac{\partial^2 Q}{\partial L^2} = (\beta_1 - 1)\beta_1 \beta_0 L^{\beta_1 - 2} K^{\beta_2}. \qquad\qquad \text{[A.6]}$$

Both of these expressions are less than zero because the terms in parentheses are less than zero.

The Cobb-Douglas production function also exhibits constant returns to scale if $\beta_1 + \beta_2 = 1$. This can be shown by doubling inputs and checking to see if output doubles. We will substitute $2K$ and $2L$ for L and K in Eq. [A.1]. If this doubles output, we have demonstrated constant returns to scale. We must determine whether:

$$\beta_0 (2L)^{\beta_1} (2K)^{\beta_2} = 2Q. \qquad\qquad \text{[A.7]}$$

Because $\beta_1 + \beta_2 = 1$, it follows that $2^{\beta_1} 2^{\beta_2} = 2^1 = 2$, so Eq. [A.7] can be written as:

$$2(\beta_0 K^{\beta_1} L^{\beta_2}) = 2Q \qquad\qquad \text{[A.8]}$$

and we have proven constant returns to scale.

Another interesting property of the Cobb-Douglas production function is that the factors are paid incomes equal to their marginal product. To simplify things, let us assume that technology is fixed for the moment. This means that only two factors of production exist, L and K. If the factors are paid their marginal products and this exhausts all income payments, then it follows that:

$$Q = MP_K K + MP_L L \qquad\qquad \text{[A.9]}$$

To see if this is correct, we substitute for MP_K and MP_L from Eqs. [A.2] and [A.3]:

$$Q = K\beta_2 \beta_0 L^{\beta_1} K^{\beta_2 - 1} + L\beta_1 \beta_0 L^{\beta_1 - 1} K^{\beta_2}. \qquad\qquad \text{[A.10]}$$

We divide this by $Q = \beta_0 L^{\beta_1} K^{\beta_2}$ to get:

$$\frac{Q}{Q} = \frac{K\beta_2 \beta_0 L^{\beta_1} K^{\beta_2 - 1}}{\beta_0 L^{\beta_1} K^{\beta_2}} + \frac{L\beta_1 \beta_0 L^{\beta_1 - 1} K^{\beta_2}}{\beta_0 L^{\beta_1} K^{\beta_2}}. \qquad\qquad \text{[A.11]}$$

After cancelling we are left with:

$$1 = \beta_2 + \beta_1, \qquad\qquad \text{[A.12]}$$

which is what we have been assuming all along.

Proof that Coefficients are Elasticities

One of the advantages to the log transformation is that the estimated coefficients are elasticities instead of slopes. In Chapter 3, we showed how to calculate elasticities for models using data in levels rather than logs. The log transformation allows us to skip that step. The explanation requires a bit of calculus.

Suppose the model to be estimated is a demand function with only one independent variable:

$$Q = \beta_0 P^{\beta_1}. \tag{A.13}$$

A log transformation is necessary to estimate this model with linear regression:

$$\ln Q = \ln \beta_0 + \beta_1 \ln P. \tag{A.14}$$

We need to show that β_1 (and all of the β_j in a multiple regression model) are elasticities.

Differentiating Eq. [A.13] with respect to P gives:

$$\frac{dQ}{dP} = \beta_1 \beta_0 P^{\beta_1 - 1}. \tag{A.15}$$

Recall that the definition of price elasticity is

$$\eta_p = \frac{dQ/Q}{dP/P} = \frac{dQ}{dP}\left(\frac{P}{Q}\right). \tag{A.16}$$

Substituting Eq. [A.15] for dQ/dP and Eq. [A.13] for Q gives:

$$\eta_p = \beta_1 \beta_0 P^{\beta_1 - 1}\left(\frac{P}{\beta_0 P^{\beta_1}}\right) = \beta_1, \tag{A.17}$$

which is what we wanted to show.

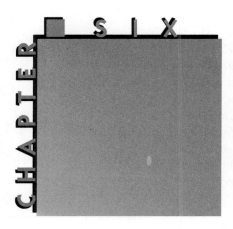

CHAPTER SIX

AUTOCORRELATION

Ask people on the street what they think of economists and you will probably hear something to the effect that economists are the ones with crystal balls, *cloudy* crystal balls. The reason for this is because the main times the public hears from economists is when they make econometric forecasts. A lot of effort goes into the construction of the models used for making those forecasts, maybe too much given the accuracy of forecasts over the past two decades. An *a priori* theory must be developed, data collected and input into the computer, etc. Invariably, that process also involves dealing with autocorrelation. Autocorrelation is the most common problem that crops up in studies of time series data. Unless corrected, autocorrelation will generate parameter estimates that are not BLUE. More important to the forecaster, however, is that autocorrelation often causes models to miss turning points. When the expansion you predicted turns into a recession, your crystal ball looks pretty cloudy. Welcome to the world of econometric forecasting!

Autocorrelation, or serial correlation as it is often called, is a violation of assumption A4, the requirement that error terms be independent. It has two main effects on the regression model: (1) Though unbiased, parameter estimates are inefficient, and (2) R^2 and t-ratios are biased upward, making the model look better than it actually is. There are numerous ways to correct for autocorrelation, and some computer programs even do it with a simple command. However, the methods for dealing with autocorrelation are as much an art as a science—especially with small data sets—so it is vitally important to understand the "whys" behind autocorrelation before beginning to analyze time series data.

6.1

DEFINITIONS AND CAUSES

Autocorrelation exists when error terms are correlated with each other. The simplest and most common kind of autocorrelation, *first-order autocorrelation*, occurs when consecutive errors are correlated.[1] First-order autocorrelation can be expressed by a simple equation:

$$\varepsilon_t = \rho\varepsilon_{t-1} + v_t, \qquad\qquad [6.1]$$

where

ε_t = error at time period t
ε_{t-1} = error one period in the past
ρ = simple correlation coefficient between ε_t and ε_{t-1}, $|\rho| < 1$
v_t = normally distributed random error obeying the classical assumptions; i.e., $v_t \sim \mathcal{N}(0, \sigma_v^2)$.

The shorthand notation for an error that exhibits first-order autocorrelation is $\varepsilon_t \sim AR(1)$, where "AR" stands for "autoregressive process." Because autocorrelation represents a violation of one of the six assumptions of the OLS model, Gauss-Markov no longer applies and parameter estimates are not BLUE.

Two types of autocorrelation are possible, positive and negative. Positive first-order autocorrelation occurs when consecutive errors usually have the

---

[1] Higher order autocorrelated errors occasionally arise. For example, quarterly data often exhibit fourth-order autocorrelated errors—$\varepsilon_t = \rho\varepsilon_{t-4} + v_t$—especially if the data have not been seasonally adjusted. This chapter discusses only first-order autocorrelation.

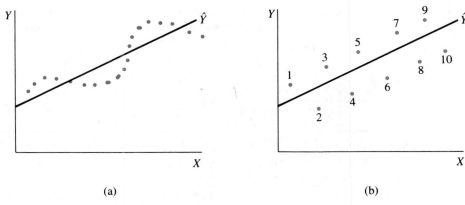

(a)   (b)

FIGURE 6.1   First-order autocorrelated errors

(a) Illustration of positive first-order autocorrelation ($\rho > 0$). Positive autocorrelation is very common in time series models. Notice that positive residuals are almost always followed by positive residuals. While negative residuals are almost always followed by negative residuals. Such a pattern implies that errors are not random, a violation of the classical assumptions. (b) Illustration of negative first-order autocorrelation ($\rho < 0$). Notice that positive errors are almost always followed by negative residuals and vice versa.

same sign. For example, if $\varepsilon_t > 0$, so is ε_{t-1}, etc. Negative first-order autocorrelation exists when most positive errors are followed by negative errors, and *vice versa*. These cases are illustrated in Fig. 6.1.

Autocorrelation can be caused by several factors, but the two most common causes are probably inertia and omitted variables. In macroeconomic models, inertia is a main source of business cycles. For example, when an economic recovery begins, most macroeconomic series turn upward, begin to build momentum, and continue upward until the cycle peak is reached. The result: Successive observations—and their errors—are dependent on each other; i.e., they are autocorrelated.

The other main cause of autocorrelation is omitted variables. To understand why, suppose that the "true" model is:

$$y_t = \beta_1 x_{1t} + \beta_2 x_{2t} + \varepsilon_t. \tag{6.2}$$

If x_{2t} is erroneously omitted, the fitted model will be:

$$y_t = \beta_1 x_{1t} + \varepsilon_t^*. \tag{6.3}$$

Subtracting Eq. [6.2] from [6.3] shows that the error term for the misspecified model is:

$$\varepsilon_t^* = \beta_2 x_{2t} + \varepsilon_t. \tag{6.4}$$

In most cases, ε_t^* will exhibit a systematic pattern (autocorrelation)[2] because the effect of x_{2t} on y_t will continue over time and be captured in ε_t^*.

6.2

CONSEQUENCES OF AUTOCORRELATED ERRORS

Autocorrelation has two main effects on regression estimates. Parameter estimates are inefficient though unbiased, and both R^2 and the t-ratios are biased upward. To understand why autocorrelation has these effects, we need to derive the variance and covariances of the autocorrelated errors.

6.2.1   Large Error Variance

Because we are still assuming that $E(\varepsilon_t) = 0$, the variance[3] of the error, σ_ε^2, can be found by taking the expected value of ε_t^2:

$$\sigma_\varepsilon^2 = E(\varepsilon_t^2) = E[(\rho\varepsilon_{t-1} + v_t)^2] = E(\rho^2\varepsilon_{t-1}^2 + v_t^2 + 2\rho\varepsilon_{t-1}v_t). \quad \text{[6.5]}$$

Applying the expected value operator term by term and noting that ε_{t-1} and v_t are independent gives:

$$\sigma_\varepsilon^2 = \rho^2\sigma_\varepsilon^2 + \sigma_v^2. \quad \text{[6.6]}$$

Rewriting Eq. [6.6] gives us a convenient way to express σ_ε^2:

$$\sigma_\varepsilon^2 = \frac{\sigma_v^2}{1 - \rho^2}. \quad \text{[6.7]}$$

Equation [6.7] makes it apparent that if there is no correlation between errors (i.e., if $\rho = 0$), then $\sigma_\varepsilon^2 = \sigma_v^2$. Because we assume that v_t is well behaved, we are assured that parameter estimates are BLUE. Likewise, if perfect correlation exists between errors (i.e., if $|\rho| = 1$), σ_ε^2 is undefined. The most common case is when $|\rho| < 1$, which implies that $\sigma_v^2 < \sigma_\varepsilon^2$. This is significant. As we will see shortly, the basic technique for eliminating autocorrelation is to modify the

---

[2]David Hendry has argued that what is often called autocorrelation in macroeconomic series is usually the result of omitted variables and other specification errors. In fact, he contends that true autocorrelation is extremely rare in real macroeconomic processes. We discuss Hendry's views in more detail in Chapter 11.

[3]Notice that we are using σ_ε^2 to indicate the model variance to distinguish it from σ_v^2, which is the variance of the error of the $AR(1)$ error.

model so that its error is v_t, which is well behaved, instead of ε_t, which is autocorrelated. Because $\sigma_v^2 < \sigma_\varepsilon^2$, the residual variance for the modified model will be less than the residual variance for the autocorrelated model, which leads to a better fitting model.

6.2.2   Biased se $(\hat{\beta}_j)$

Because errors are correlated, the error in one period feeds back on the errors in every other period. The result is that the standard errors are biased. To show this, we need to calculate the covariance between errors in different periods.

Because $E(\varepsilon_t) = 0$, the covariance between consecutive errors is defined as:

$$\text{cov}(\varepsilon_t, \varepsilon_{t-1}) = E[(\rho\varepsilon_{t-1} + v_t)\varepsilon_{t-1}] = E(\rho\varepsilon_{t-1}^2 + \varepsilon_{t-1}v_t). \qquad [6.8]$$

Because ε_t and v_t are uncorrelated, application of the expected value operator gives:

$$\text{cov}(\varepsilon_t, \varepsilon_{t-1}) = \rho\sigma_\varepsilon^2. \qquad [6.9]$$

Similar manipulations can be used[4] to derive the covariance between errors in periods t and $t - s$:

$$\text{cov}(\varepsilon_t, \varepsilon_{t-s}) = \rho^s\sigma_\varepsilon^2 \qquad [6.10]$$

Notice that because $|\rho| < 1$, $\rho^s < |\rho|$ so the correlation between errors diminishes as they become farther apart in time.

We can now see why OLS methods will bias R^2 and t-ratios upward. Recall from Eq. [3.12] that $\text{var}(\hat{\beta}_1)$ for a simple regression model is defined as:

$$\text{var}(\hat{\beta}_1) = \frac{\sigma_\varepsilon^2}{\sum x_t^2}. \qquad [6.11]$$

As we show in Appendix 6.A, this result is correct only if the covariance between errors is zero; i.e., if there is no autocorrelation. If errors are correlated, $\text{var}(\hat{\beta}_1)$ increases, perhaps quite substantially.[5] The correct formula for the variance of $\hat{\beta}_1$ if errors are autocorrelated is:

$$\text{var}(\hat{\beta}_1)^* = \frac{\sigma_\varepsilon^2}{\sum x_t^2}\left(1 + 2\rho\frac{\sum x_t x_{t-1}}{\sum x_t^2} + 2\rho^2\frac{\sum x_t x_{t-2}}{\sum x_t^2} + \cdots\right). \qquad [6.12]$$

---

[4]Simply substitute ε_{t-2} for ε_{t-1} to get $\text{cov}(\varepsilon_t, \varepsilon_{t-2}) = \rho^2\sigma^2$ and so on. This is demonstrated in Appendix 6.A.

[5]In *Introduction to Econometrics* (New York: Macmillan, 1988), p. 197–198, G. S. Maddala presents an example with $T = 20$ and $\rho = 0.8$, which shows that $\text{var}(\hat{\beta}_1)$ is underestimated by more than 80%.

However, if the autocorrelation has gone undetected and OLS is incorrectly used for estimation, $\text{var}(\hat{\beta}_1)$ will be underestimated by the amount of the term in parentheses. Because the t-ratio is defined as the ratio of $\hat{\beta}_1$ to $\text{se}(\hat{\beta}_1)$, underestimation of $\text{var}(\hat{\beta}_1)$ will bias the t-ratio upward and make the model appear better than it really is.

A comparison of Eq. [6.11] and [6.12] also explains why autocorrelation tends to inflate $\bar{R}^2$. Recall that $\bar{R}^2$ is defined as:

$$\bar{R}^2 = 1 - \frac{\text{unexplained variation}/d.f.}{\text{total variation}/d.f.} = 1 - \frac{\sum e_i^2/T - k - 1}{\sum (Y_i - \bar{Y})^2/T - 1},$$

[6.13]

where, as always, e_t^2 is the square of the regression residuals. The variance of the regression residuals is underestimated in the presence of autocorrelation, so $\bar{R}^2$ will be overestimated.

6.2.3   Parameter Estimates Cannot be Trusted

We can easily show that parameter estimates remain unbiased in the presence of autocorrelated errors.[6] However, simply proving that an estimate is unbiased does not mean that it should be trusted; remember how we could not trust parameter estimates in the presence of multicollinearity. Recall the definition of statistical bias. A parameter is said to be biased if there is a tendency for it to be, on average, too high or, on average, too low. Autocorrelated errors result in parameter estimates that have an equal chance of being too high or too low. These chances "cancel" each other out, meaning that parameter estimates are statistically unbiased. However, any particular parameter estimate may miss the mark by a substantial amount and the confidence intervals around such estimates are distorted. The conclusion: Parameter estimates from models with autorocelated errors cannot be trusted.

6.3

DETECTION: THE DURBIN-WATSON STATISTIC

We can check for autocorrelation in several ways, but none is quite foolproof. Severe autocorrelation is often obvious from an inspection of a plot of the residuals to see if it resembles Fig. 6.1. However, to correct for autocorrelation, it is necessary to find $\hat{\rho}$, an estimate of ρ, and this cannot be done merely by

---

[6]Simply take the expected value of Eq. [A.10] in Appendix 6.A.

SECTION 6.3   DETECTION: THE DURBIN-WATSON STATISTIC   **169**

inspecting the residuals. The most popular method[7] for detecting autocorrelation, the *Durbin-Watson statistic*, is more accurate than merely looking at the residuals and also can be used to generate a preliminary estimate of $\hat{\rho}$.

6.3.1   The Durbin–Watson Statistic (*d*)

Most computer programs automatically calculate the Durbin-Watson statistic, but because it is notoriously imprecise, it is important to understand how it is calculated before trying to use it.

The Durbin-Watson statistic tests the null hypothesis of zero first-order autocorrelation against the alternative, the presence of first-order autocorrelation, with the following formula:

$$d = \frac{\sum\limits_{t=2}^{T} (e_t - e_{t-1})^2}{\sum\limits_{t=1}^{T} e_t^2}.$$

[6.14]

Several statistical complications were involved in the development of this formula, but the basic premise was quite simple: If consecutive residuals are usually "close" to each other, positive first-order autocorrelation is probably present; if they are usually "far apart," negative autocorrelation is indicated. The question, of course, is how close is *close*, and how far is *far*; this is a statistical proposition and requires use of the Durbin-Watson table.

Two comments are necessary before we can interpret the Durbin-Watson statistic. First, notice that the numerator of Eq. [6.14] is indexed from $t = 2$ to T, while the denominator is indexed from $t = 1$ to T. This is necessary because of the presence of e_{t-1} in the numerator. Second, there must be enough data points to make it reasonable to assume that:

$$\sum\limits_{t=1}^{T} e_t^2 \cong \sum\limits_{t=2}^{T} e_t^2 \cong \sum\limits_{t=2}^{T} e_{t-1}^2.$$

[6.15]

These assumptions partially account for the existence of an indeterminant region in the Durbin-Watson table.

6.3.2   Interpreting the Durbin–Watson Statistic

The Durbin-Watson statistic (*d*) is calculated to test the null hypothesis of no first-order autocorrelation versus the alternative hypothesis of first-order

---

[7]J. Durbin and G. S. Watson, "Testing for Serial Correlation in Least Squares Regression," *Biometrika*, 1950, p. 409–428; 1951, p. 159–178.

autocorrelation:

$H_0: \rho = 0$ (No first-order autocorrelation is present.)

$H_a: \rho \neq 0$ (First-order autocorrelation is present.)

The calculated value for d is helpful, but not always definitive, in the detection of autocorrelation.

• $d = 0$ if $\rho = 1$.   Suppose there is perfect positive first-order autocorrelation; i.e., $\rho = 1$. This would allow us to write Eq. [6.1] as:

$$\varepsilon_t = \varepsilon_{t-1} + v_t.$$

Because we assume that $E(v_t) = 0$, this implies that $\varepsilon_t = \varepsilon_{t-1}$, on average. Now, if we substitute e_t for e_{t-1} in Eq. [6.14], the numerator will vanish so that $d = 0$. Therefore, $d \to 0$ if $\rho \to 1$.

• $d = 4$ if $\rho = -1$.   Suppose there is perfect negative first-order autocorrelation; i.e., $\rho = -1$. If $E(v_t) = 0$, it follows that $\varepsilon_{t-1} = -\varepsilon_t$. If we expand Eq. [6.14] and accept the assumptions in Eq. [6.15], perfect negative autocorrelation implies that:

$$d = \frac{\sum_{t=2}^{T} e_t^2 + \sum_{t=2}^{T} e_t^2 - 2\sum_{t=2}^{T} e_t(-e_t)}{\sum_{t=1}^{T} e_t^2} \cong \frac{\sum_{t=2}^{T} e_t^2}{\sum_{t=1}^{T} e_t^2} + \frac{\sum_{t=2}^{T} e_t^2}{\sum_{t=1}^{T} e_t^2} + 2\left(\frac{\sum_{t=2}^{T} e_t^2}{\sum_{t=1}^{T} e_t^2}\right) \cong 4$$

• $d = 2$ if $\rho = 0$.   Finally, if there is no autocorrelation, $\rho = 0$, so $\varepsilon_t = v_t$, which is well behaved. One characteristic of well-behaved error terms is zero covariance between consecutive errors. Thus, $\sum e_t e_{t-1}$, the sample covariance[8] between e_t and e_{t-1}, approaches zero if $\rho = 0$. Expanding Eq. [6.14], substituting for $\sum e_t e_{t-1} = 0$, and again applying the assumptions in Eq. [6.15] gives:

$$d = \frac{\sum_{t=2}^{T} e_t^2 + \sum_{t=2}^{T} e_{t-1}^2 - 2\sum_{t=2}^{T} e_t e_{t-1}}{\sum_{t=1}^{T} e_t^2} \cong \frac{\sum_{t=2}^{T} e_t^2}{\sum_{t=1}^{T} e_t^2} + \frac{\sum_{t=2}^{T} e_t^2}{\sum_{t=1}^{T} e_t^2} + 0 \cong 2.$$

Unfortunately, the Durbin-Watson statistic has two possibly rather large indeterminant regions, partially as a result of making so many assumptions in the calculation of d. These regions are between d_L (lower bound) and d_U (upper

---

[8]Recall that the sample covariance is defined as $[1/(n-1)]\sum(x - \mu_x)(y - \mu_y)$. Because we are assuming that $E(\varepsilon_t) = E(\varepsilon_{t-1}) = 0$, $\sum e_t e_{t-1}$ is actually $(n-1)$ times the sample covariance.

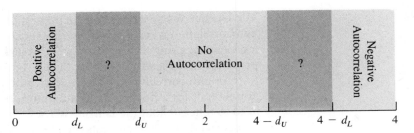

FIGURE 6.2   The Durbin–Watson statistic

A d value sufficiently close to 2 indicates the absence of first-order
autocorrelation; a d value close to zero indicates positive
autocorrelation, and a value close to 4 indicates negative
autocorrelation. The determinant regions are larger for small data sets.

bound) and between $4 - d_L$ and $4 - d_U$. Figure 6.2 illustrates the determinant
and indeterminant regions of the Durbin-Watson statistic.

6.3.3   Using the Durbin–Watson Table

Two parameters are necessary to use the Durbin-Watson table: the number of
observations (T) and the number of explanatory variables in the model (k).
Knowing those two parameters, the procedure of matching the number of
observations in the first column of the Durbin-Watson table and the number
of explanatory variables across the top row is simple. The corresponding
entries in the table are d_L and d_U. Durbin-Watson tables are commonly
tabulated for 1 and 5% significance levels.

• **Positive autocorrelation is probably present when d is "close" to 0.**   If d
is between 0 and d_L, there is a statistically significant chance that positive
first-order autocorrelation is present; if d is greater than d_U but less than
2.0, the chance of positive first-order autocorrelation is statistically
insignificant. If the calculated d is between d_L and d_U, the test is
inconclusive.[9]

• **Negative autocorrelation is probably present when d is "close" to 4.**
When the calculated d is greater than 2.0, the Durbin-Watson statistic tests
for negative first-order autocorrelation. A d value greater than $4 - d_L$
indicates the presence of negative first-order autocorrelation; a value
between 2 and $4 - d_U$ suggests the absence of negative autocorrelation. The
region between $4 - d_L$ and $4 - d_U$ is indeterminant.

---

[9]Many investigators avoid the indeterminant region and use d_U as the decision
point: If $d < d_U$, positive autocorrelation is assumed to exist; if $d > 4 - d_U$, negative
autocorrelation is assumed to be present.

The Durbin-Watson statistic is an inappropriate test for first-order autocorrelation when a lagged endogenous variable is used as an independent variable. The recommended test is the *Durbin h-test*, which is presented in Appendix 6.B. Also, the Durbin-Watson test—and most other tests for autocorrelation—are accurate only with large samples. Small sample tests for autocorrelation are notoriously unreliable. Finally, we need to reiterate that the Durbin-Watson test can detect only first-order autocorrelation. Different tests are necessary for higher order autocorrelation.   ◆ ◆ ◆

6.4

CORRECTING FOR AUTOCORRELATION: QUASI- DIFFERENCING

The general approach to correct for autocorrelation (and many other violations of the classical assumptions) is called *generalized least squares* (GLS). GLS methods modify the model so that the original error is replaced by an error that obeys the classical assumptions. In the case of autocorrelation, the autocorrelated error, ε_t, is replaced by the well-behaved error term, v_t. The specific GLS technique used to correct for autocorrelation is called *quasi-differencing*.

6.4.1   Quasi-Differencing

If $\hat{\rho}$ is known, autocorrelation can usually be eliminated with a four-step procedure:

1. Lag the data to get Y_{t-1} and X_{jt-1}.

2. Multiply the lagged values by $\hat{\rho}$. That is, calculate $\hat{\rho}Y_{t-1}$ and $\hat{\rho}X_{jt-1}$.

3. Define new variables by subtracting $\hat{\rho}Y_{t-1}$ and $\hat{\rho}X_{jt-1}$ from the original data:

$$Y_t^* = Y_t - \hat{\rho}Y_{t-1} \qquad X_{jt}^* - \hat{\rho}X_{jt-1}. \qquad [6.16]$$

4. Perform OLS on the transformed data.

If $\hat{\rho}$ is estimated correctly, quasi-differencing will result in well-behaved errors and thus BLUE parameter estimates. To show this, suppose that the model is:

$$Y_t = \beta_0 + \beta_1 X_t + \varepsilon_t; \qquad \varepsilon_t \sim AR(1). \qquad [6.17]$$

Lagging and multiplying by ρ gives:

$$\rho Y_{t-1} = \rho\beta_0 + \beta_1\rho X_{t-1} + \rho\varepsilon_{t-1}.$$ [6.18]

If we subtract Eq. [6.18] from [6.17] we have:

$$Y_t - \rho Y_{t-1} = \beta_0 - \rho\beta_0 + \beta_1 X_t - \beta_1\rho X_{t-1} + \varepsilon_t - \rho\varepsilon_{t-1}.$$ [6.19]

The reason this technique works can be seen by noting that the last two terms in Eq. [6.19] equal v_t. Rearranging and using the definitions in Eq. [6.16], Eq. [6.19] becomes:

$$Y_t^* = \beta_0(1 - \rho) + \beta_1 X_t^* + v_t.$$ [6.20]

Because v_t is well behaved, $\hat{\beta}_0$ and $\hat{\beta}_1$ will be BLUE. When OLS is performed on the transformed model, the Durbin-Watson statistic will be close to 2.

■ EXAMPLE 6.1

CORRECTING THE CONSUMPTION FUNCTION REGRESSION FOR AUTOCORRELATION

We can illustrate quasi-differencing by correcting the multiple regression consumption function from Chapter 4. The regression results and a plot of the residuals are shown below. The residuals plot gives us strong reason to suspect that autocorrelation exists, and a check of the Durbin-Watson statistic confirms our suspicions. The calculated value, $d = 0.521$, is less than 1.26, which is d_L for a 5% significance level with $k = 2$ and $n = 28$. This indicates positive first-order autocorrelation.

INITIAL MULTIPLE REGRESSION RUN

```
Dep var: CONS  N: 28  R2: .997  Adj-R2: .997  SER: 24.28

Variable  Coefficient  Std Error     T       P(2 tail)

CONSTANT   -45.20         19.53     -2.31        0.03
    DPI      0.96          0.02     50.66        0.00
    AAA     -6.30          3.03     -2.08        0.05

                 Analysis of Variance

  Source     Sum-of-Squares  DF  Mean-Square  F-Ratio   P

Regression     5323328.60     2   2661664.30  4516.70  0.00
  Residual       14732.36    25       589.29


Durbin-Watson D Statistic     .521
First Order Autocorrelation   .668
```

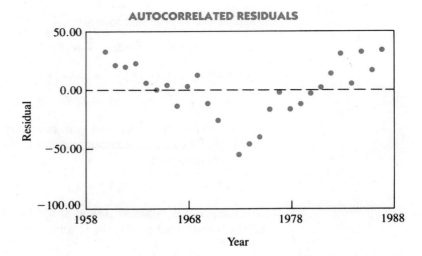

Fortunately, the regression program used in this study, Fastat,™ is able to calculate $\hat{\rho}$, so we can correct for autocorrelation with the GLS procedure outlined above. Lag all observations one period, multiply by $\hat{\rho} = 0.668$ (estimated on the initial regression run), and subtract from the original data; i.e.,

$$\text{CONS}_t^* = \text{CONS}_t - 0.668\ \text{CONS}_{t-1},\ \text{DPI}_t^* = \text{DPI}_t - 0.668\ \text{DPI}_{t-1},$$
$$\text{and AAA}_t^* = \text{AAA}_t - 0.668\ \text{AAA}_{t-1}.$$

A new regression was run after these transformations. A quick inspection of the Durbin-Watson statistic and residual plot indicates that autocorrelation has been eliminated.

SECOND REGRESSION RUN, AC CORRECTED

```
Dep var: CONS*  N: 27  R2: .989  Adj-R2: .988  SER: 16.49

Variable  Coefficient  Std Error       T   P(2 tail)

CONSTANT      -24.68      13.95     -1.77     0.09
   DPI*         0.97       0.02     40.58     0.00
   AAA*        -6.72       3.06     -2.20     0.04

                Analysis of Variance

  Source    Sum-of-Squares  DF  Mean-Square  F-Ratio    P

Regression      587792.97    2    293896.49  1081.29  0.00
  Residual        6523.25   24       271.80


Durbin-Watson D Statistic    2.265
First Order Autocorrelation  -.161
```

Correction for autocorrelation often changes the parameter estimates and summary statistics substantially. In this case, there was only a small change in $\hat{\beta}_1$ or $\hat{\beta}_2$, their t-scores, or R^2. Such small changes are somewhat unusual. As expected, the SER decreased after correction for autocorrelation, an indication that the transformed model fits the data better than the original model.

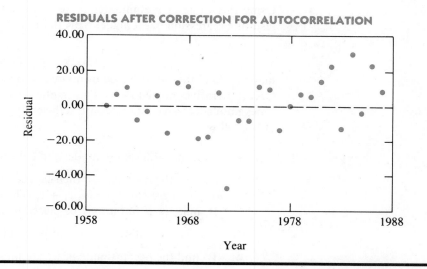

RESIDUALS AFTER CORRECTION FOR AUTOCORRELATION

6.4.2 Methods for Estimating $\hat{\rho}$

The GLS procedure just outlined is simple enough, but only after $\hat{\rho}$ has been estimated. The real problem is how to estimate $\hat{\rho}$. Some computer programs do it automatically, and if there is a large data set, this is the preferred method. However, not all programs calculate $\hat{\rho}$, and with small data sets, it may be possible to find a better estimate of $\hat{\rho}$ than the one generated by a computer. Below are four common methods for estimating $\hat{\rho}$.

ESTIMATE ρ FROM d   A first approximation of $\hat{\rho}$ can be found with a simple manipulation of the Durbin-Watson statistic[10]:

$$d \approx 2(1 - \hat{\rho}).$$

[6.21]

The advantage to this method is that it is very quick; however, it does not always generate a good estimate of $\hat{\rho}$.

[10]The proof of this statement is left as Exercise 6.4.

For the consumption example, the calculations would be:

$$0.521 \approx 2(1 - \hat{\rho}).$$

$$\hat{\rho} \approx 0.740,$$

which is fairly close to the value estimated by the computer program (0.668). Using this value of $\hat{\rho}$ eliminates some of the autocorrelation; however, the resulting regression has a higher SER than the previous attempt.

THE COCHRAN–ORCUTT PROCEDURE   The most common method for estimating $\hat{\rho}$ (and the method used by many computer programs) is the Cochran-Orcutt iterative procedure.[11] This method requires estimating $\hat{\rho}$ several times until successive estimates are sufficiently close to each other. The steps are as follows:

1. Perform OLS on the model and collect the residuals, e_t.

2. Regress the residuals on their lagged values; i.e., perform OLS on the regression $e_t = \hat{\rho} e_{t-1} + v_t$. The estimate $\hat{\rho}$ is a consistent estimate of ρ, but it may be biased in small samples.

3. Use $\hat{\rho}$ as an estimate of ρ and perform GLS to calculate the $\hat{\beta}_j$.

4. To find the best estimate of ρ, you must reestimate the residuals and again calculate $\hat{\rho}$. Substitute the parameter estimates from step 3 into the *original* regression equation (use Y_t and X_{jt} instead of the transformed values) to collect a new set of residuals, e_t^*:

$$e_t^* = Y_t - \hat{\beta}_0^* - \hat{\beta}_1^* X_{1t} - \hat{\beta}_2^* X_{2t} - \cdots.$$

5. Finally, regress e_t^* on e_{t-1}^* to calculate $\hat{\hat{\rho}}$. Continue until successive iterations generate estimates of ρ that are very close to each other, say, no more than 0.01 apart. Generally no more than three or four iterations are necessary.

When Cochran-Orcutt was performed on the consumption model, the first regression of e_t on e_{t-1} gave an estimate of $\hat{\rho}$ of 0.434—quite far off the mark—but $\hat{\rho}$ approached 0.7 after just three iterations. While it can be shown that this method results in consistent and efficient estimates of ρ, it is a bit tedious unless the statistical package contains a Cochran-Orcutt routine. The same might be said about the next method for estimating ρ.

---

[11] D. Cochran and G. H. Orcutt, "Application of Least Squares Regressions to Relationships Contain Autocorrelated Error Terms," *Journal of the American Statistical Association*, Vol. 44, 1949, p. 32–61.

HILDRETH–LU PROCEDURE   This procedure[12] involves setting up a grid of possible values for $\hat{\rho}$, and running several GLS regressions to find the transformation that minimizes ESS. The steps are as follows:

1. Establish a grid of possible $\hat{\rho}$ values and perform GLS with each possible value. For positive autocorrelation, the recommended initial grid is to let $\hat{\rho}$ take the values $\{0.1, 0.2, 0.3, \ldots, 0.9\}$. Nine GLS regressions are then run, one with each value in the grid.

2. The regression with the lowest ESS is selected. Suppose this is $\hat{\rho} = 0.4$. A grid is then constructed around this value, $\hat{\hat{\rho}} = \{0.36, 0.37, \ldots, 0.45\}$. Nine more regressions are run and again the regression with the lowest ESS is selected.

3. The process is repeated until ESS does not vary considerably between iterations. This generally occurs after three or four iterations.

The Cochran-Orcutt and Hildreth-Lu methods are popular but they share a common and potentially serious weakness: It is possible to find a value of $\hat{\rho}$ that minimizes ESS locally, but not globally.

THE DURBIN TWO-STEP METHOD   Durbin has suggested a very simple method[13] for estimating $\hat{\rho}$ that can be quite successful for large data sets. Notice that if we add ρY_{t-1} to both sides of Eq. [6.19] we have:

$$Y_t = \beta_0 - \rho\beta_0 + \beta_1 X_t - \beta_1\rho X_{t-1} + \rho Y_{t-1} + \varepsilon_t - \rho\varepsilon_{t-1}, \qquad \text{[6.22]}$$

which can be written as:

$$Y_t = \theta_0 + \theta_1 X_t + \theta_2 X_{t-1} + \theta_3 Y_{t-1} + u_t. \qquad \text{[6.23]}$$

OLS is then run on Eq. [6.23] and the coefficient on Y_{t-1}, $\hat{\theta}_3$, is used as an estimate of $\hat{\rho}$. With a very large data set, $\hat{\theta}_1$ is a consistent estimate of $\hat{\beta}_1$ so GLS is not necessary; however, Durbin recommends using $\hat{\theta}_3$ as an estimate for $\hat{\rho}$ and performed GLS as usual.[14]

---

[12]G. Hildreth and J. Y. Lu, "Demand Relations with Autocorrelated Disturbances," *Technical Bulletin 276*, Michigan State University (November 1960).

[13]J. Durbin, "Estimation of Parameters in Time Series Regression Models," *Journal of the Royal Statistical Society*, Series B, Vol. 22 1960, p. 139–153.

[14]In "Econometric Modelling: The 'Consumption Function' in Retrospect," *Scottish Journal of Political Economy*, November 1983, p. 193–219, David Hendry suggests an interesting check on model specification by looking at the relationship between θ_1, θ_2, and θ_3. By comparing Eqs. [6.22] and [6.23], it is apparent that θ_2 should be equal to the negative product of θ_1 and θ_3. If this relationship does not hold, Hendry suggests that the model has been misspecified and that what appears to be autocorrelation is in fact caused by omitted variables.

The Durbin method is recommended only for large data sets, but it was applied to the consumption regression as an illustration. The results from the initial regression were $\hat{\theta}_3 \equiv \hat{\rho} = 0.388$ and $\hat{\theta}_1 \equiv \hat{\beta}_1 = 0.615$—quite different from the values calculated by Fastat.

TWO QUICK-AND-DIRTY METHODS   To reduce the number of iterations often involved in the estimation of $\hat{\rho}$, two recommendations are offered.

First Differences   If $\rho = 1$, GLS can be performed by first differencing; that is, use $\Delta Y_t \equiv Y_t^* = Y_t - Y_{t-1}$, $\Delta X_{jt} \equiv X_t^* = X_{jt} - X_{jt-1}$, etc. Because almost all computer programs have a differencing function, this can be a very quick way to deal with extreme autocorrelation; however, there are two potential problems. First, it is never clear that $\rho = 1$. The only time it *may* be reasonable to use the method for dealing with autocorrelation is when d has a very low value. Second, as shown in Exercise 6.7, taking first differences will eliminate the intercept term of the transformed regression model, an issue that may be important in some studies.

Simple Grids   The Hildreth-Lu method can be tiring with less sophisticated statistical packages. An alternative is to estimate $\hat{\rho}$ with the Durbin method or from the Durbin-Watson statistic, and then form a small grid around this estimate and evaluate ESS after each run. For example, suppose that $d = 1$. Substitution into Eq. [6.21] would give an initial estimate of $\hat{\rho}$ as 0.5. Run GLS with this value and calculate ESS. Then run GLS using $\hat{\rho} = 0.4$ and $\hat{\rho} = 0.6$ and compare ESS. If $\text{ESS}(\hat{\rho} = 0.6) < \text{ESS}(\hat{\rho} = 0.4)$, run GLS using $\hat{\rho} = 0.7$, etc. This method will reduce the number of GLS runs by 50%, but it is also more likely to result in a local rather than a global minimum ESS.

GLS is not always appropriate

Autocorrelation shows up so often in regression models using time series data that you might be tempted to estimate $\hat{\rho}$ automatically and apply GLS. This is often the correct procedure, but not always. At least two cautions must be kept in mind before proceeding with GLS estimation:

1. When autocorrelation is caused by omitted variables, a better solution is to respecify the model. GLS may make the errors look well behaved, but it will do nothing about the likely bias resulting from the specification error.

2. With a small sample, it may be best to ignore autocorrelation. Why? Finding a good estimate of ρ is difficult with small samples, and if $\hat{\rho}$ is estimated incorrectly, GLS may be inferior to OLS. Remember, OLS parameter estimates are inefficient, but they are not biased. GLS performed with the wrong $\hat{\rho}$ may do more harm than good.   ◆ ◆ ◆

■ **E X A M P L E 6 . 2**

AUTOCORRELATION AND TURNING POINTS

As mentioned in the introduction to this chapter, autocorrelation makes it difficult to predict turning points—often the most important piece of information for forecasters. This can be shown quite well with a very simple—and quite likely misspecified—model of the interest rate.

Suppose you have reason to believe that movements in the three-month treasury bill rate (TB3) are caused primarily by two factors, inflation (INF) and M1 money supply growth (M1):

$$TB3_t = \beta_0 + \beta_1 M1_t + \beta_2 INF_t + \varepsilon_t.$$

```
Dep var: TB3  N: 29  R-sq: .688  Adj  R-sq: .664  SER: 1.6644

Variable  Coefficient  Std Error    T      P(2 tail)

CONSTANT      0.6489     0.8011   0.8100    0.4253
      M1      0.0074     0.0018   4.1217    0.0003
     INF      0.6568     0.1188   5.5261    0.0000

                  Analysis of Variance

  Source    Sum-of-Squares  DF  Mean-Square  F-Ratio    P

Regression      158.9569    2     79.4784   28.6918  0.00
  Residual       72.0218   26      2.7701


Durbin-Watson D Statistic    .587
First Order Autocorrelation  .662
```

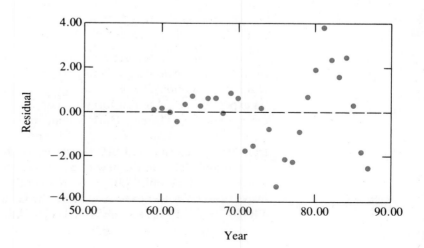

To check this relationship, OLS is run on annual data for the period 1959–87. The results are shown in the table below. The *t*'s and summary statistics are good, but the Durbin-Watson statistic suggests autocorrelation, and a glance at a plot of the residuals confirms this suspicion.

If this model had been used for forecasting without correcting for autocorrelation, the turning points in the series would be missed. The graph below, a plot of the dependent variable (TB3) and the fitted values against time illustrates this problem. The fitted line shows interest rates falling in 1970 when they were actually rising, and shows them rising in 1976 when they were actually falling. But the biggest error, as is often the case with autocorrelation, occurs at the end of the series: A forecast made in 1987 would suggest higher interest rates in 1988 even though the actual data series was declining considerably.

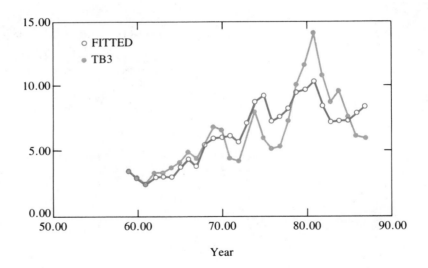

Correction for autocorrelation makes it much easier to predict turning points. After transforming the model with GLS ($\hat{\rho} = 0.662$), another regression was run. The results are given in the table on the next page. As expected, the GLS transformation appears to have eliminated autocorrelation: The new Durbin-Watson statistic is between 2.0 and the critical value (= 1.56 at the 5% significance level) and a plot of the transformed residuals (RESID*) appears random.

An initial glance at the new plot seems to suggest that the new fitted values (FITSTAR) miss TB3 by more than the OLS fitted values. Closer inspection shows this to be incorrect: The GLS transformation (TB3$_t$* = TB3$_t$ − 0.662TB3$_{t-1}$, etc.) gives the FITSTAR series a different magnitude

```
Dep. var: TB3*  N: 28  R-sq: .471  Adj R-sq: .429  SER: 1.20

Variable   Coefficient   Std Error      T     P(2 tail)

CONSTANT      0.4031       0.5413    0.7448    0.4634
     M1*      0.0045       0.0032    1.4264    0.1661
    INF*      0.7173       0.1565    4.5832    0.0001

                  Analysis of Variance

  Source     Sum-of-Squares  DF  Mean-Square  F-Ratio    P

Regression       32.1468      2     16.0734   11.1355  0.0003
Residual         36.0857     25      1.4434

Durbin-Watson D Statistic        1.507
First Order Autocorrelation       .246
```

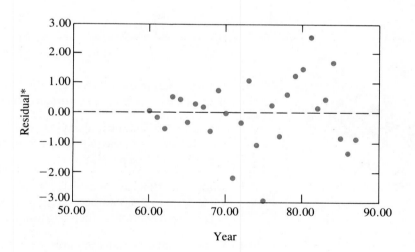

than TB3. This does not create any problems because actual forecasts would be made with the GLS parameter estimates using untransformed data. In fact, GLS does improve the model some; FITSTAR catches most of the turning points in the TB3 series. It incorrectly predicts a decline between 1980 and 1981, but is close everywhere else, except after 1983. Still, this fit is far from ideal, which is an indication that $\hat{\rho}$ was estimated incorrectly or that there are other problems with the model. We will look at this model again in the next chapter when we take up the problem of heteroscedasticity.

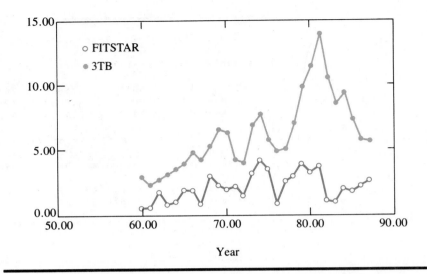

Year

THE PROBLEM OF AUTOCORRELATION

1. Autocorrelation exists when error terms are correlated. It is most often caused by inertia or omitted variables.

2. Autocorrelation almost always crops up in models using time series data, at least when the data are entered in levels form instead of as first differences or percentage changes.

3. Autocorrelation can be detected with the Durbin-Watson statistic. If d is close to 2, no autocorrelation is likely to be present. If it is close to zero or four, autocorrelation may be present.

4. Autocorrelation results in unbiased but inefficient parameter estimates, inflated t-scores and R^2. Forecasts made with models containing autocorrelated errors often miss turning points.

5. GLS is used to eliminate autocorrelation.

CONCEPTS FOR REVIEW

Autocorrelation is one of the most common problems encountered with models using time series data. Because it can make parameter estimates unreliable and the model appear better than it really is, it is vital that you know how to detect and eliminate autocorrelation. Be sure you know:

- what factors can cause autocorrelation;
- how autocorrelation affects parameter estimates, t-ratios, and R^2;
- what information is necessary to use the Durbin-Watson table and when the Durbin-Watson statistic is inappropriate;
- how to use quasi-differencing to eliminate autocorrelation;
- several methods for estimating $\hat{\rho}$;
- how to define and use the following terms in context.

KEY TERMS

autocorrelation	Hildreth-Lu
Cochran-Orcutt	indeterminant region
Durbin method	inertia
Durbin-Watson statistic	quasi-differencing
first differences	serial correlation
GLS	specification error

EXERCISES

6.1 Autocorrelation can be illustrated by plotting e_t versus e_{t-1}. Sketch a graph of positive and negative first-order autocorrelation with e_{t-1} on the horizontal axis and e_t on the vertical axis. Does this plot tell you more or less than the plot in Fig. 6.1?

6.2 Autocorrelation does not bias parameter estimates. However, few econometricians would trust parameter estimates derived from models with autocorrelated residuals. Why?

6.3 Suppose that the true model is:

$$Y_t = \beta_0 + \beta_1 X_{1t} + \beta_2 X_{2t} + \varepsilon_t,$$

where ε_t is well behaved and all parameter coefficients are positive. If the fitted model is:

$$Y_t = \beta_0^* + \beta_1^* X_{1t} + \varepsilon_t^*,$$

would you expect to find positive or negative first-order autocorrelation? Why?

6.4 Prove Eq. [6.21]. (*Hint:* Recall the relationship between covariance and correlation.)

6.5 The residuals from the Cobb-Douglas production function tested in Chapter 5 are plotted below.

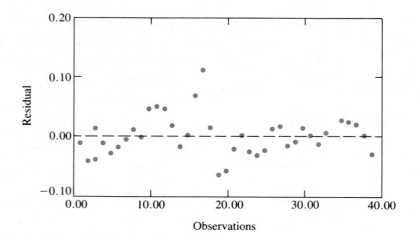

a. Is there evidence of autocorrelation?

b. The Durbin-Watson statistic for the log version of the Cobb-Douglas test was 0.858. There were 39 observations and 2 independent variables. Does this confirm your analysis from part (a)?

c. When the Cobb-Douglas production function was tested using levels of K and L, the Durbin-Watson statistic was 0.635. Why do you think there was more apparent autocorrelation in this run than the log version?

6.6 Suppose that a model is correctly specified as

$$Y_t = \beta_0 + \beta_1 X_t + \varepsilon_t$$

and that a preliminary regression reveals that there is severe autocorrelation.

a. Show that first differencing will eliminate the intercept of the transformed model.

b. Suppose that a model was run in first differenced form and the results showed that there was a statistically significant intercept. How could you explain this result?

c. Suppose that there is a time trend in the model; i.e.,

$$Y_t = \beta_0 + \beta_1 X_t + \beta_2 t + \varepsilon_t.$$

Difference this equation and show what happens to β_2.

6.7 Refer to Example 6.1.

  a. What are the critical t-values for the corrected regression?

  b. What is the estimated value of β_0 in the corrected run?

6.8 In an attempt to solve the autocorrelation problem, the consumption function test was run with first differences. The results are presented in the table below.

```
Dep var: DCONS  N: 27  R-sq: .809  Adj R-sq: .793  SER: 14.13

Variable  Coefficient  Std Error   T    P(2 tail)

CONSTANT      20.35       6.00    3.39    0.00
    DDPI       0.63       0.09    7.21    0.00
    DAAA     -11.64       2.93   -3.97    0.00

                     Analysis of Variance

   Source     Sum-of-Squares  DF  Mean-Square  F-Ratio   P

Regression       20346.72      2    10173.36    50.94   0.00
  Residual        4793.35     24      199.72

Durbin-Watson D Statistic     2.177
First Order Autocorrelation   -.096
```

  a. Interpret these results.

  b. Has autocorrelation been eliminated?

  c. Is this method better or worse than the method used in Example 6.1?

6.9 Do you think autocorrelation is more likely to be found in annual or monthly data? Why?

6.10 The "cobweb" model often describes agricultural markets well. In this model, the farmer's decision to plant (supply) this year depends on the price that prevailed last year. A simple regression model of this phenomenon might be:

$$S_t = \beta_0 + \beta_1 P_{t-1} + \varepsilon_t.$$

  a. Sketch a graph of this model to illustrate why it is called a "cobweb."

  b. Explain why a cobweb model is likely to exhibit autocorrelation.

6.11 Economic theory holds that, other things equal, appreciation of a nation's currency (**XR**) will lead to an increase in the size of the trade deficit (BT). Test this hypothesis using the data in Data Set 7 of Appendix I.

Before running the model:

a. What sign do you expect to find on $\hat{\beta}_1$? Other than the fact that the main topic of this chapter is autocorrelation, why might you expect to find autocorrelation?

After running the model:

b. Interpret the results.

c. If necessary, correct for autocorrelation and interpret the revised results. Did correction for autocorrelation affect the regression results in the usual manner?

6.12 Check the consumer durables model run in Exercise 4.11 for autocorrelation. If present, correct for it and interpret your results.

APPENDIX 6.A

SOME MATHEMATICS

We left two important implications of autocorrelation for the appendix because they involve rather tedious manipulations.

All Past Errors Are Correlated

If ε_t is correlated with ε_{t-1}, it is also correlated with all past errors. Intuitively, this is one reason why autocorrelation biases R^2 upward—the correlation between errors imparts a strong trend to the data. The correlation between past errors can be demonstrated by manipulating and generalizing Eq. [6.9] from the chapter.

We found in Eq. [6.9] that the covariance between consecutive errors is:

$$\text{cov}(\varepsilon_t, \varepsilon_{t-1}) = \rho\sigma_\varepsilon^2. \tag{A.1}$$

Replacing ε_{t-1} with ε_{t-2} will give the covariance between ε_t and ε_{t-2}:

$$\text{cov}(\varepsilon_t, \varepsilon_{t-2}) = E[(\rho\varepsilon_{t-1} + v_t)\varepsilon_{t-2}] = E(\rho\varepsilon_{t-1}\varepsilon_{t-2} + \varepsilon_{t-2}v_t). \tag{A.2}$$

The definition of first-order autocorrelation, however, allows us to write ε_{t-1} as:

$$\varepsilon_{t-1} = \rho\varepsilon_{t-2} + v_t. \tag{A.3}$$

Substituting this into Eq. [A.2] and applying the expected value operator gives:

$$E[\rho(\rho\varepsilon_{t-2} + v_t)\varepsilon_{t-2} + \varepsilon_{t-2}v_t] = \rho^2\sigma_\varepsilon^2. \tag{A.4}$$

With only a little imagination, we can generalize from Eq. [A.1] to [A.2]. Note that

$$\text{cov}(\varepsilon_t, \varepsilon_{t-1}) = \rho^1\sigma_\varepsilon^2, \tag{A.5}$$

and that

$$\text{cov}(\varepsilon_t, \varepsilon_{t-2}) = \rho^2\sigma_\varepsilon^2. \tag{A.6}$$

Similar substitutions will give:

$$\text{cov}(\varepsilon_t, \varepsilon_{t-s}) = \rho^s\sigma_\varepsilon^2, \tag{A.7}$$

which is the general result we needed.

β_i Are Unbiased but Inefficient

We stated that the $\text{var}(\hat{\beta}_1)$ is larger for a model with autocorrelated errors than for one with well-behaved errors. This is an especially devious problem because unless autocorrelation is detected and corrected for, the model will appear to be much better than it actually is. To show this, recall that $\hat{\beta}_1$ is defined as:

$$\hat{\beta}_1 = \frac{\sum x_t y_t}{\sum x_t^2}.$$

[A.8]

In Chapter 3, we proved that $\hat{\beta}_1$ was unbiased by first substituting for y_t:

$$\hat{\beta}_1 = \frac{\sum x_i(\beta x_t + \varepsilon_t)}{\sum x_t^2} = \beta \frac{\sum x_t^2}{\sum x_t^2} + \frac{\sum x_t \varepsilon_t}{\sum x_t^2},$$

[A.9]

and taking the expected value:

$$E(\hat{\beta}_1) = \beta_1 + E\left(\frac{\sum x_t \varepsilon_t}{\sum x_t^2}\right).$$

[A.10]

We concluded that $\hat{\beta}_1$ was unbiased if the second term on the right side went to zero. Autocorrelation does not negate this result.

We can also use Eq. [A.10] to derive $\text{var}(\hat{\beta}_1)^*$, the variance of $\hat{\beta}_1$ for a model with autocorrelated errors. Because $\hat{\beta}_1$ is unbiased, $E(\hat{\beta}_1) = \beta_1$ and thus $E(\hat{\beta}_1 - \beta_1) = E(\hat{\beta}_1) - E(\hat{\beta}_1) = 0$. The definition of variance allows us to write:

$$\text{var}(\hat{\beta}_1)^* = E(\hat{\beta}_1 - \beta_1)^2.$$

[A.11]

If we subtract β_1 from each side of Eq. [A.10] and square the result, we have:

$$\text{var}(\hat{\beta}_1)^* = E(\hat{\beta}_1 - \beta_1)^2 = E\left(\frac{\sum x_t \varepsilon_t}{\sum x_t^2}\right)^2.$$

[A.12]

This equation is the key to the demonstration, but it must be manipulated quite a bit. First, because x_t is a constant, $\sum x_i^2$ can be taken outside the expected value operator, resulting in:

$$E\left(\frac{\sum x_t \varepsilon_t}{\sum x_t^2}\right)^2 = \frac{1}{(\sum x_t^2)^2} E(\sum x_t \varepsilon_t)^2.$$

[A.13]

Now consider the first three terms in the sum $(\sum x_t \varepsilon_t)^2$:

$$(\sum x_t \varepsilon_t)^2 = x_1^2 \varepsilon_1^2 + x_2^2 \varepsilon_2^2 + x_3^2 \varepsilon_3^2 + 2x_1 x_2 \varepsilon_1 \varepsilon_2$$
$$+ 2x_1 x_3 \varepsilon_1 \varepsilon_3 + 2x_2 x_3 \varepsilon_2 \varepsilon_3.$$

[A.14]

Because $E(\varepsilon_t^2) = \sigma_\varepsilon^2$, and $E(\varepsilon_t \varepsilon_{t-s}) = \rho^s \sigma_\varepsilon^2$, this can be written as:

$$\sigma_\varepsilon^2(\sum x_t^2 + 2\rho \sum x_t x_{t-1} + 2\rho^2 \sum x_t x_{t-2}).$$

[A.15]

Substituting this into Eq. [A.6] and generalizing for T periods gives:

$$\text{var}(\hat{\beta}_1)^* = \frac{\sigma_\varepsilon^2}{(\sum x_t^2)^2}\left(\sum x_t^2 + 2\rho \sum x_t x_{t-1} + 2\rho^2 \sum x_t x_{t-2} + \cdots\right).$$

[A.16]

We are getting close. To compare $\text{var}(\hat{\beta}_1)^*$ with $\text{var}(\hat{\beta}_1)$, we only need to factor $1/\sum x_t^2$ out of the denominator:

$$\text{var}(\hat{\beta}_1)^* = \frac{\sigma_\varepsilon^2}{\sum x_t^2}\left(\frac{\sum x_t^2}{\sum x_t^2} + 2\rho \frac{\sum x_t x_{t-1}}{\sum x_t^2} + 2\rho^2 \frac{\sum x_t x_{t-2}}{\sum x_t^2} + \cdots\right).$$

[A.17]

Finally, because $\sum x_t^2 / \sum x_t^2 = 1$ and $\text{var}(\hat{\beta}_1) = \sigma_\varepsilon^2 / \sum x_t^2$, Eq. [A.17] can be written as

$$\text{var}(\hat{\beta}_1)^* = \text{var}(\hat{\beta}_1)\left(1 + 2\rho \frac{\sum x_t x_{t-1}}{\sum x_t^2} + 2\rho^2 \frac{\sum x_t x_{t-2}}{\sum x_t^2} + \cdots\right),$$

[A.18]

which is clearly greater than $\text{var}(\hat{\beta}_1)$.

APPENDIX 6.B

DURBIN'S *h*-TEST

One of the *Cautions* mentioned in Chapter 6 noted that it was inappropriate to use the Durbin-Watson test in models containing lagged dependent variables. This is because the Durbin-Watson statistic is biased toward 2.0 when there is a lagged dependent variable. Because many econometric models incorporate lagged dependent variables, it is important to be able to detect autocorrelation in these cases.

A three-variable model containing a lagged dependent variable is shown in Eq. [B.1]:

$$Y_t = \beta_0 + \beta_1 Y_{t-1} + \beta_2 X_t + \varepsilon_t. \tag{B.1}$$

The correct test statistic for autocorrelation in models containing a lagged dependent variable is *Durbin's h-test*.[15] The *h*-test is also appropriate when there are longer lags, such as Y_{t-2}, Y_{t-3}, etc.

The *h*-test is calculated as:

$$h = \hat{\rho} \left\{ \frac{T}{1 - T[\text{var}(\hat{\beta}_j)]} \right\}^{1/2}, \tag{B.2}$$

where

T = number of observations
$\text{var}(\hat{\beta}_j)$ = variance of the coefficient on the lagged dependent variable.
$\hat{\rho}$ = estimated value of ρ, assuming $e_t = \rho e_{t-1} + v_t$.

How do we estimate $\hat{\rho}$? The easiest way is from Eq. [6.19], i.e.,

$$h = \left(1 - \frac{d}{2}\right) \left\{ \frac{T}{1 - T[\text{var}(\hat{\beta}_j)]} \right\}^{1/2}. \tag{B.3}$$

The *h*-test checks the null hypothesis of no first-order autocorrelation versus the alternative of first-order autocorrelation. For large samples, it can be shown that the *h*-statistic is approximately normally distributed with a variance of one. Thus, once the calculations in Eq. [B.3] are carried out, the test is performed by comparing *h* to the critical value in the normal table. If the calculated *h* is higher than the normal table, the null hypothesis of no autocorrelation is rejected.

As an example, consider the model discussed in Exercise 4.6 of Chapter 4. The printout for that model is repeated below, along with the Durbin-Watson

---

[15] J. Durbin, "Testing for Serial Correlation in Least-Squares Regression when Some of the Regressors are Lagged Dependent Variables," *Econometrica*, Vol. 38, 1970, p. 410–421.

statistic and an estimate of $\hat{\rho}$ that was calculated with the Cochran-Orcutt procedure by the computer program.

```
Dep var: BFI  N: 16  Squared  Multiple  R: .975
Adj-Squared  Multiple  R: .972  SER: 12.89

Variable  Coefficient  Std Error    T    P(2 tail)
CONSTANT       31.66      22.61    1.40     0.18
   DRGNP        0.49       0.04   11.79     0.00
    LBFI        0.89       0.04   20.57     0.00

                Analysis of Variance

  Source    Sum-of-Squares  DF  Mean-Square  F-Ratio    P

Regression      85995.93    2    42997.97   258.65    0.00
 Residual        2161.13   13      166.24

Durbin-Watson D Statistic    2.265
First Order Autocorrelation  -.161
```

At first glance, there does not appear to be any autocorrelation: $d = 2.265$ is less than 2.46, the critical value for $n = 16, k = 2$. However, the presence of the lagged dependent variable (LBFI) means that the *h*-test is necessary. Using the computer-generated estimate of $\hat{\rho}$ of -0.161, the calculations are:

$$h = (-0.161)\left[\frac{16}{1 - 16(0.0016)}\right]^{1/2} = -0.65.$$

Because $|-0.65|$ is less than the critical value of $|1.64|$, we cannot reject the null hypothesis of no autocorrelation. Had the calculated *h* exceeded $|1.64|$, we would have concluded that there was first-order autocorrelation.

Strictly speaking, Durbin's *h*-test is correct only for large samples, so we must regard the results from this example as tentative. Unfortunately, no simple test exists that is clearly superior to the *h*-test for small samples. We should also note that the test cannot be performed when $T[\text{var}(\hat{\beta}_j)]$ is greater than one.[16] Finally, some computer programs calculate *h* automatically. To do so, of course, it is necessary to know which of the independent variables is the lagged dependent variable. Most often, the correct procedure is to make the lagged dependent variable the first independent variable.

---

[16] R. Pindyck and D. Rubenfeld, *Econometric Models and Economic Forecasts* (New York: McGraw-Hill, 1981), p. 194–195 for a technique for dealing with situations when $T[\text{var}(\hat{\beta}_j)] > 1$.

CHAPTER SEVEN

HETEROSCEDASTICITY

The consumption function example that we developed in previous chapters used time series data. This was the correct specification given that we were interested in studying the relationship between consumption and disposable income over time. But what if we were interested in studying the relationship between consumption and disposable income at a particular point in time? In other words, suppose we were interested in the relationship:

$$C_i = \beta_0 + \beta_1 DPI_i + \epsilon_i,$$

where the i subscripts refer to individual families instead of years. We would still expect β_1 to be between zero and one, but interpretation of the regression results would be entirely different. The estimated slope parameter would depend on the distribution of income because higher income families tend to spend a lower fraction of their income on consumption than do low-income families. Just as important, the problem we dealt with in Chapter 6, autocorrelation, is usually irrelevant in this kind of cross-sectional study.[1] Unfortunately, another violation of the OLS assumptions is likely to crop up in this and other cross-sectional studies: heteroscedasticity, or nonconstant error variances. Why would we expect it in this model? People with very low incomes have little choice as to how to spend their income. They have few options other than spending it on food, shelter, and the necessities of life, so low-income people almost always spend a very high fraction of their income on consumption. People in upper income brackets, on the other hand, have many options. They could spend 50% and save 50%, spend 99% and save 1% or even go into debt and spend 120% while saving −20%. The result is that the variance of the consumption/income relationship and, hence, the spread of the errors about the fitted regression line will widen as income rises. Why does heteroscedasticity create problems for regression analysis? Think back to the Outliers sidebar in Chapter 3. The least-squares technique tends to place too much weight on outliers, so the points with the widely scattered errors (high income and consumption levels) will have more weight than points with tight errors (low income and consumption). The result is parameters that are inefficient, though unbiased.

7.1

DEFINITIONS AND CAUSES

Heteroscedasticity is a violation of Assumption 5, the requirement that error variances be *homoscedastic* or constant. That is, heteroscedasticity exists when:

$$\sigma_i^2 \neq \sigma_j^2 \ \forall \ i, j. \tag{7.1}$$

Notice that we are using subscripts on σ^2 to indicate that var(ε_i) is not constant. When subscripts are omitted from σ^2, the errors are assumed to be homoscedastic.

While it is possible to find heteroscedasticity in time series studies, it is most common in cross-sectional analysis. Typically, heteroscedasticity is associated with one or more of the independent variables. For example, in the

---

[1] Some authors would qualify this statement: Spatial autocorrelation is possible and can be detected in the same way as time series autocorrelation. However, the correction procedures recommended for time series autocorrelation (lag, multiply by $\hat{\rho}$, etc.) are illogical with spatial autocorrelation.

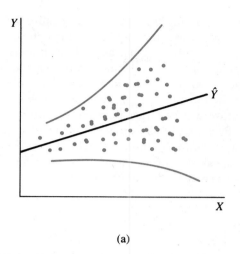

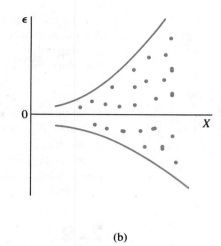

(a)   (b)

FIGURE 7.1   Heteroscedastic errors

(a) Plot of heteroscedastic errors in (X, Y)-space. A plot of the individual X_{ji} against Y_i can often detect the presence of heteroscedasticity.
(b) Heteroscedasticity from a different

perspective, in (X, ϵ)-space. Notice that in both cases var(ϵ_i) increases as X increases. Heteroscedasticity also exists when var(ϵ_i) decreases as X increases.

cross-sectional consumption/disposable income example discussed above, the source of the heteroscedasticity is disposable income. A hypothetical plot of such errors is shown in Fig. 7.1(a). Heteroscedasticity may also be detected by examination of a plot in (X, ε)-space. Heteroscedasticity is indicated if the errors increase or decrease as X increases, as shown in Fig. 7.1(b).

Heteroscedasticity can be caused by several things. In general, it is more likely to exist when the data set has a large range of observations. For example, the range of incomes in any one year in the United States will stretch from nothing to billions of dollars. The "discretionary income" earned by people in upper income brackets allows a wide range of options in their consumption and saving behavior. Such options are not available to low-income people, so a cross-sectional study will probably exhibit heteroscedasticity. Similar reasoning would suggest the possibility of heteroscedasticity in a cross-sectional study of industry sales when there is a large variation in firm size.

Two examples of time series heteroscedasticity might be mentioned. As factory workers acquire skills over time, the likelihood of production defects decreases. Thus, a time series study of factory defects as a function of sales could show a declining variance over time. Time series heteroscedasticity also may be associated with the technology of data collection. As data collection techniques improve, measurement errors decline, as does the residual variance.

Finally, omitted variables can sometimes result in errors that appear heteroscedastic. For example, suppose that a simple regression model was constructed to test the hypothesis that high interest rates cause the number of unemployed workers to rise. Clearly, the number of unemployed workers also depends on population and other factors as well as the interest rate. Therefore, omission of population as an explanatory variable will probably bias parameter estimates, but it may also result in what appears to be heteroscedasticity: The variation in the number of unemployed workers associated with a larger population will be larger than the variation associated with a smaller population. Because population is not included in the tested model, this effect will be captured in the residual, giving the appearance of heteroscedasticity. Strictly speaking, however, this is a problem of model specification, not heteroscedasticity. Some economists call this *impure heteroscedasticity*.

7.2
CONSEQUENCES OF HETEROSCEDASTIC ERRORS

As stated, the main problem caused by heteroscedasticity is that the $\hat{\beta}_j$ are inefficient, though they do remain unbiased. Additionally, the standard errors of the parameter estimates will be biased and inconsistent, meaning that the hypothesis tests on the $\hat{\beta}_j$ may not be valid.

7.2.1   Unbiased Parameter Estimates

The reason parameter estimates remain unbiased may not be obvious at first. Recall that $\hat{\beta}_1$ is unbiased only if X_i and ε_i are uncorrelated. How is this possible if σ_i^2 is a function of X_i, a common cause of heteroscedasticity? The key is that a relationship between σ_i^2 and X_i does not mean that ε_i and X_i are correlated. As long as the *distribution* of the ε_i around X_i is symmetrical, the expected value of ε_i is still zero for any value of X_i. This means that X_i and ε_i are uncorrelated and that $\hat{\beta}_1$ remains unbiased. This can be seen by looking back at Fig. 7.1(a). Because OLS minimizes the sum of squared errors, which are distributed symmetrically around $\hat{Y}_i$, $\hat{\beta}_1$ remains unbiased because there is no reason to suspect that it will be too high or too low.

7.2.2   Biased Standard Errors

Heteroscedasticity does, however, bias the standard errors of the parameter estimates, $se(\hat{\beta}_j)$, and it is usually difficult to determine whether they are biased upward or downward. To understand why the standard errors are biased, recall that the variance of $\hat{\beta}_1$ is defined for the two-variable model as:

$$\text{var}(\hat{\beta}_1) = \frac{\sigma^2}{\sum x_i^2}.$$ [7.2]

However, as shown in Appendix 7.A, the correct parameter variance in the presence of heteroscedasticity is:

$$\mathrm{var}(\hat{\beta}_1) = \frac{\sum x_i^2 \sigma_i^2}{\left(\sum x_i^2\right)^2},$$ [7.3]

which clearly differs from Eq. [7.2].

Two implications result. First, if heteroscedasticity is ignored and the variance formula in Eq. [7.2] is used in the calculation of t-ratios and confidence intervals around the $\hat{\beta}_j$, the resulting hypothesis tests will be invalid. Any inferences based on these estimates will be suspect. Second, if heteroscedasticity is recognized and the formula in Eq. [7.3] is used, the parameter estimates will not be best because an alternative estimation technique—weighted least squares—can generate more efficient parameter estimates.

7.3
DETECTION OF HETEROSCEDASTICITY: A STUDY OF A REGIONAL HOUSING MARKET

The literature on housing markets and home ownership is replete with examples of heteroscedasticity. For example, in a simple model of home ownership as a function of family income, we would expect heteroscedastic errors because people with higher incomes can choose to buy or rent large or small houses, while lower income families are often priced out of the home ownership market entirely. In the extended example that follows, we illustrate how to detect heteroscedasticity with a simple model of the housing market. Then, in Sec. 7.4, we show how to correct for heteroscedasticity using the same model.

7.3.1   The OLS Model

It is reasonable to think that the proportion of a community that owns their home is a positive function of median family income.[2] To test this hypothesis, 1980 census data from Pierce County, Washington, were collected. The independent variable was median family income by census tract (INCOME), and the dependent variable was the ratio of the number of families who own

---

[2] Recall that the median is the middle data point—the point where half of the observations lie above it and half lie below it. The median is often used in income distribution studies because of the wide dispersion of the data, something that is not captured with the mean.

DATA SET 7.1   Housing data

Tract	Income	Ownratio	Tract	Income	Ownratio
601	24909	7.220	630	15784	1.751
602	11875	1.094	631	18917	5.074
603	19308	3.587	632	17431	4.272
604	20375	5.279	633	17044	3.868
605	20132	3.508	634	14870	2.009
606	15351	0.789	635	19384	2.256
607	14821	1.837	701	18250	2.471
608	18816	5.15	705	14212	3.019
609	19179	2.201	706	15817	2.154
609	21434	1.932	710	21911	5.190
610	15075	0.919	711	19282	4.579
611	15634	1.898	712	21795	3.717
612	12307	1.584	713	22904	3.720
613	10063	0.901	713	22507	6.127
614	5090	0.128	714	19592	4.468
615	8110	0.059	714	16900	2.110
616	4399	0.022	718	12818	0.782
616	5411	0.172	718	9849	0.259
617	9541	0.916	719	16931	1.233
618	13095	1.265	719	23545	3.288
619	11638	1.019	720	9198	0.235
620	12711	1.698	721	22190	1.406
621	12839	2.188	721	19646	2.206
623	15202	2.850	724	24750	5.650
624	15932	3.049	726	18140	5.078
625	14178	2.307	728	21250	1.433
626	12244	0.873	731	22231	7.452
627	10391	0.410	731	19788	5.738
628	13934	1.151	735	13269	1.364
629	14201	1.274			

SOURCE: 1980 Census, Pierce County, Washington.

their homes to the number who rent (OWNRATIO). The data for this test are presented in Data Set 7.1.

The first step in this test was to perform OLS on a simple regression model. The results are presented in Table 7.1. A first glance shows that the model seems to fit well: Both R^2 and F are adequate, and our *a priori* hypothesis regarding the sign of β_1 is verified. However, because this is a cross-sectional study and we have good reason to suspect heteroscedasticity, it is important to

TABLE 7.1   OLS results

```
Dep var:OWNRATIO  N: 59  R-sq: .597  SER: 1.21

Variable  Coefficient  Std Error   T      P(2 tail)

CONSTANT    -2.22        0.54     -4.09    0.00
  INCOME    2.97E-4      3.23E-5   9.18    0.00

              Analysis of Variance

  Source    Sum-of-Squares  DF  Mean-Square  F-Ratio   P

Regression       123.65     1      123.65    84.31   0.00
Residual          83.59    57        1.47
```

check for its presence before accepting these results. As with autocorrelation, a first check for heteroscedasticity is to examine a plot of the residuals. If the residuals show any indication of possible heteroscedasticity, or if there are strong *a priori* reasons to suspect heteroscedasticity, more rigorous methods for detection must be used.

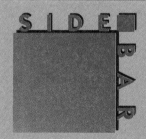

SCIENTIFIC NOTATION

The slopes and standard errors on the regression printout in Table 7.1 are expressed in what is called scientific or exponential notation to save space. The number "2.97E−4" is shorthand for 0.000297. The E−4 indicates that 2.97 is multiplied times 1/10,000, or 10 to the minus 4 power. The easiest way to do this is to just move the decimal 4 places to the left. The standard error, 3.23E−5 could be written 0.0000323 or $3.23 * 10^{-5}$. Scientific notation is also used for large numbers. For example, 2.56E6 means move the decimal six places to the right: 2,560,000.

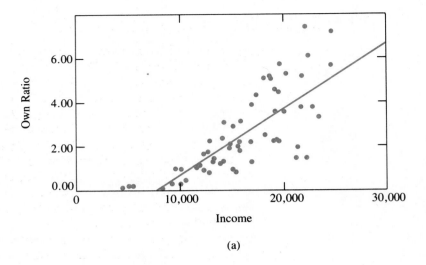

(a)

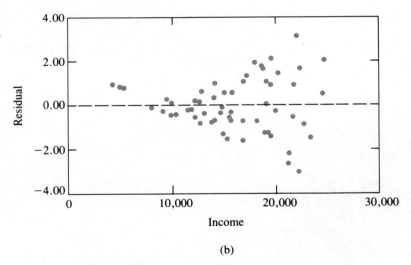

(b)

FIGURE 7.2   Plots from housing OLS regression

(a) Scattergram of the data used in the OLS regression on the housing market. The wider spread of points at higher INCOME values is an indication of heteroscedasticity. (b) Plot of the regression residuals against INCOME, the independent variable.

7.3.2 Plot and Inspect the Residuals

A preliminary check for heteroscedasticity that can be done is to plot the data and residuals, as was done in Figs. 7.2(a) and (b). Figure 7.2(a) shows the scatter of data points around the fitted line in (X, Y)-space. Notice that the spread of the data increases as INCOME increases, a strong indication of heteroscedasticity. The second graph, Fig. 7.2(b), plots the residuals against INCOME, the only independent variable in this model. This graph provides essentially the same information as Fig. 7.1(a), but from a different perspective. It too indicates heteroscedasticity. Why do we need both graphs? In simple regression we may not, but in multiple regression any—or none—of the independent variables is a potential source of the heteroscedasticity, so it can be useful to plot each independent variable against the residuals to isolate the source of the heteroscedasticity.

Graphical analysis is useful, but it is not very precise, so more rigorous methods are necessary to test for heteroscedasticity in all but the most obvious examples. Unfortunately, no method is generally regarded as the best method for detecting heteroscedasticity, partially because the effectiveness of detection techniques depends on the source of the heteroscedasticity. In the next three sections, we will look at three of the most popular methods and encourage the interested reader to pursue the matter further in the references cited in the bibliography.

7.3.3 The Park Test

Perhaps the simplest method for detecting heteroscedasticity is the Park test.[3] The Park test begins with the assumption that a relationship exists between the error variance and one of the independent variables in the model such that:

$$\text{var}(\varepsilon_i) = \sigma_i^2 = \sigma^2 X_1^\delta e^{v_i}, \qquad\qquad [7.4]$$

where

σ^2 = homoscedastic portion of the heteroscedastic error;
X_i = independent variable thought to be the source of heteroscedasticity
δ = parameter to be estimated
e = base of natural logarithms
v_i = error term that obeys the OLS assumptions.

---

[3] R. E. Park, "Estimation with Heteroscedastic Error Terms," *Econometrica*, Vol. 34, No. 4, October 1966, p. 888.

To perform the Park test, take the log of Eq. [7.4] to obtain:

$$\ln(\sigma_i^2) = \ln(\sigma^2) + \delta \ln(X_i) + v_i. \qquad [7.5]$$

If it were possible to perform OLS on Eq. [7.5], a significant t-ratio on the parameter estimate $\hat{\delta}$ would suggest that the error variance was a function of X_i. Unfortunately, we cannot observe the true error or its variance. The solution, of course, is to use the regression residuals as proxies. Thus, the Park test is performed in the following steps:

1. Disregard heteroscedasticity and perform OLS on the original model. Collect the regression residuals.

2. Square the regression residuals and take logs of both the suspect X_j and the squared residuals.

3. Perform OLS on Eq. [7.6]:

$$\ln(e_i^2) = \delta_0 + \delta_1 \ln(X_i) + v_i. \qquad [7.6]$$

4. If the t-ratio on $\hat{\delta}_1$ is statistically significant, the null hypothesis of homoscedasticity can be rejected.

The Park test is simple to perform and, as we will see shortly, may even provide information helpful for eliminating heteroscedasticity. However, it is not without its problems. First, like most tests for heteroscedasticity, it requires that the investigator determine which variable is the source of the heteroscedasticity. Second, it requires an assumption regarding the particular functional form of the heteroscedastic errors. Equation [7.4] is only one possibility; several others have been suggested and should be tried in a complete test. For example, Glejser has developed[4] a similar test that uses the absolute value of the regression residuals as the dependent variable and recommends running regressions on several functional forms, for example, $|e_i| = a + bX_i + v_i$, $|e_i| = a + bX_i^{-1} + v_i$, etc. Finally, Goldfeld and Quandt point out that it is possible for the v_i errors to be heteroscedastic, so the t-ratio on $\hat{\delta}_1$ may be invalid.[5]

A Park test was performed on the regression residuals from the housing study. The transformed data necessary for the Park test are presented in Data Set 7.2, and the resulting regression results are shown in Table 7.2. As expected, the t-ratio on LNINCOME is significant. This verifies the hypothesis of heteroscedasticity that we formed from looking at the plots in Fig. 7.2. We do not need any other information from Table 7.2 for the moment, but we will find out in Sec. 7.4 that the coefficient on LNINCOME will be of use when we correct for heteroscedasticity.

---

[4]H. Glejser, "A New Test for Heteroscedasticity," *Journal of the American Statistical Association*, Vol. 64, 1969, p. 316–323.

[5]S. M. Goldfeld and R. E. Quandt, *Nonlinear Methods in Econometrics* (Amsterdam: North-Holland, 1972), Chapter 3.

DATA SET 7.2   Park test data

Tract	LNINCOME (X)	RESID	RESID^2	LNRESID^2 (Y)
601	10.123	2.055	4.223	1.440
602	9.382	−0.206	0.043	−3.157
603	9.868	0.083	0.007	−4.982
604	9.922	1.458	2.126	0.754
605	9.910	−0.241	0.058	−2.849
606	9.639	−1.542	2.378	0.866
607	9.604	−0.337	0.113	−2.176
608	9.842	1.791	3.208	1.166
609.1	9.862	−1.266	1.602	0.471
609.2	9.973	−2.202	4.851	1.579
610	9.621	−1.330	1.770	0.571
611	9.657	−0.517	0.267	−1.321
612	9.418	0.155	0.024	−3.722
613	9.217	0.138	0.019	−3.954
614	8.535	0.840	0.705	−0.349
615	9.001	−0.125	0.016	−4.163
616.1	8.389	0.939	0.882	−0.126
616.2	8.596	0.788	0.621	−0.476
617	9.163	0.308	0.095	−2.357
618	9.480	−0.397	0.158	−1.847
619	9.362	−0.211	0.045	−3.107
620	9.450	0.150	0.023	−3.792
621	9.460	0.602	0.362	−1.016
623	9.629	0.563	0.317	−1.150
624	9.676	0.546	0.298	−1.211
625	9.559	0.324	0.105	−2.253
626	9.413	−0.537	0.288	−1.243
627	9.249	−0.450	0.203	−1.596
628	9.542	−0.760	0.577	−0.549
629	9.561	−0.716	0.513	−0.668
630	9.667	−0.708	0.502	−0.690
631	9.848	1.685	2.84	1.044
632	9.766	1.324	1.752	0.561
633	9.744	1.035	1.071	0.068
634	9.607	−0.179	0.032	−3.439
635	9.872	−1.271	1.616	0.480
701	9.812	−0.72	0.518	−0.658
705	9.562	1.025	1.052	0.050
706	9.669	−0.315	0.099	−2.308
710	9.995	0.914	0.835	−0.180
711	9.867	1.082	1.170	0.157

(continued)

DATA SET 7.2 *Continued*

Tract	LNINCOME (X)	RESID	RESID²	LNRESID² (Y)
712.2	9.989	−0.524	0.275	−1.291
713.1	10.039	−0.851	0.724	−0.323
713.2	10.022	1.674	2.802	1.030
714.1	9.883	0.879	0.773	−0.257
714.2	9.735	−0.680	0.462	−0.771
718.1	9.459	−0.798	0.636	−0.452
718.2	9.195	−0.441	0.194	−1.639
719.1	9.737	−1.566	2.453	0.897
719.2	10.067	−1.473	2.169	0.774
720	9.127	−0.272	0.074	−2.606
721.2	10.007	−2.953	8.720	2.166
721.3	9.886	−1.399	1.957	0.671
724.2	10.117	0.532	0.283	−1.262
726	9.806	1.920	3.686	1.305
728	9.964	−2.647	7.008	1.947
731.1	10.009	3.081	9.494	2.251
731.2	9.893	2.091	4.373	1.475
735	9.493	−0.349	0.122	−2.104

To conduct the Park test, run OLS on the original model and collect the residuals (RESID). Square (RESID²) and take the logs of these residuals (LNRESID²). Using the log of the variable thought to be the source of the heteroscedasticity (LNINCOME), perform an OLS regression using LNINCOME as the independent variable and LNRESID² as the dependent variable. If the coefficient on LNINCOME is statistically significant, heteroscedasticity is probably present.

7.3.4 The Goldfeld–Quandt Test

This may be the most popular method for detecting heteroscedasticity. It is computationally simple and requires fewer assumptions about the nature of heteroscedasticity than does the Park test. However, unlike the Park test, it provides little information as to how to eliminate heteroscedasticity once it has been detected.

The idea behind the Goldfeld-Quandt test is that the variances associated with high values of X should be significantly different from the variances associated with low values of X. This is checked by forming an F-ratio, which is used to test the null hypothesis of homoscedasticity. There are four steps in the Goldfeld-Quandt test:

T A B L E 7 . 2   **Park test regression**

```
Dep var:LNRESIDS  N: 59  R-sq: .177  SER: 1.59

Variable  Coefficient  Std Error     T     P(2 tail)

CONSTANT      -19.59      5.39     -3.64      0.00
LNINCOME        1.96      0.56      3.50      0.00

                  Analysis of Variance

  Source    Sum-of-Squares  DF  Mean-Square  F-Ratio    P

Regression        31.14     1      31.14     12.25   0.00
  Residual       144.90    57       2.54
```

KEY: LNRESIDS = log of the square of the regression residuals;
LNINCOME = log of INCOME, the independent variable in the preliminary
regression.

1. Sort the data by magnitude of the X variable thought to be the source of heteroscedasticity. Most computer programs can do this with a simple SORT command.

2. Omit the middle d observations, perhaps one-fifth of the sample size.[6]

3. Run two separate regressions, one for the low values of X and one for the high values of X. Each regression will have $(n - d)/2$ data points and $[(n - d)/2] - 2$ degrees of freedom. Calculate ESS_1 and ESS_2 from the two regressions.

4. Form the ratio ESS_2/ESS_1 with residuals from the higher valued X_i in the numerator. This ratio will be distributed as an F-ratio with $(n - d - 4)/2$ degrees of freedom in both the numerator and the denominator. If this ratio exceeds the critical value from the F-table, the null hypothesis of homoscedasticity is rejected.

A Goldfeld-Quandt test was performed on the housing data as well. The data were first sorted by income in ascending order and the middle 13 ($\cong 0.2n$)

---

[6]There is no way to determine how many observations to omit. With a very small data set, it may not be possible to omit any data points; but the more that are omitted, the more powerful the test. Most investigators recommend omission of between one-fifth and one-third. For a discussion of this issue, see George G. Judge et al., *The Theory and Practice of Econometrics*, 2nd ed. (New York: Wiley, 1980), p. 449.

observations were deleted. This left 23 observations for each regression and the calculation of ESS_1 and ESS_2. The sorted data are shown in Data Set 7.3. Table 7.3 presents the ANOVA portion of the regression printouts from the separate runs.

To test the null hypothesis of homoscedasticity against the alternative of heteroscedasticity, an F-statistic was formed:

$$F_{21,21} = \frac{61.49/21}{5.19/21} = 11.85.$$

Because this is greater than the critical value for the 95% significance level, $F_{20,20} = 2.12$, we reject the null hypothesis of homoscedasticity.

7.3.5 The Breusch–Pagan Test

A final test for heteroscedasticity is the Breusch-Pagan test.[7] This test is somewhat more powerful than the previous tests because it can be used to test whether heteroscedasticity is caused by more than one independent variable. Like the Park test, it involves regression of the residuals on the independent variables, but it uses a χ^2 statistic to test for heteroscedasticity.[8] This test requires that the regression residuals be approximately normally distributed so it is best applied to large sample sets.

Suppose the regression model has two or more X variables and that the suspect variables are X_1 and X_2. Testing the null hypothesis of homoscedasticity versus the alternative hypothesis of heteroscedasticity involves five steps:

1. Run OLS on the model and collect the regression residuals.

2. Estimate the variance of the regression residuals as $\hat{\sigma}^2 = \sum e_i^2/n$.

3. Compute the square of the standardized residuals, $s_i^2 = e_i^2/\hat{\sigma}^2$.

4. Run OLS on the equation $s_i^2 = \alpha_0 + \alpha_1 X_{1i} + \alpha_2 X_{2i}$.

5. The ratio RSS/2 is distributed as a χ^2 distribution with k degrees of freedom, where k is the number of independent variables in the regression run in step 4. If the calculated value is greater than the critical value from the χ^2-table, the null hypothesis of homoscedasticity is rejected.

---

[7]T. S. Breusch and A. R. Pagan, "A Simple Test for Heteroskedasticity and Random Coefficient Variation," *Econometrica*, Vol. 47, 1979, p. 1287–1294.
[8]This is the first time we have used a χ^2-test. The χ^2-table is read like a t-table: Line up the degrees of freedom and level of significance. In this case, interpretation is just like a standard F-test: If the value calculated from the Breusch-Pagan test is greater than the table entry, reject the null hypothesis of homoscedasticity. Other χ^2-tests are used in Chapters 9 and 10.

DATA SET 7.3   **Sorted data for Goldfeld-Quandt test**

Tract	Income	Ownratio	
616.1	4399	0.022	
614	5090	0.128	
616.2	5411	0.172	
615	8110	0.059	
720	9198	0.235	
617	9541	0.916	
718.2	9849	0.259	
613	10063	0.901	
627	10391	0.410	
619	11638	1.019	
602	11875	1.094	Low X values
626	12244	0.873	
612	12307	1.584	
620	12711	1.698	
718.1	12818	0.782	
621	12839	2.188	
618	13095	1.265	
735	13269	1.364	
628	13934	1.151	
625	14178	2.307	
629	14201	1.274	
705	14212	3.019	
607	14821	1.837	
634	14870	2.009	
610	15075	0.919	
623	15202	2.850	
606	15351	0.789	
611	15634	1.898	
630	15784	1.751	
706	15817	2.154	OMIT $d = 13 (\approx 0.2\,n)$ observations
624	15932	3.049	
714.2	16900	2.110	
719.1	16931	1.233	
633	17044	3.868	
632	17431	4.272	
726	18140	5.078	
701	18250	2.471	
608	18816	5.150	
631	18917	5.074	
609.1	19179	2.201	
711	19282	4.579	*(continued)*

D A T A S E T 7 . 3   *Continued*

Tract	Income	Ownratio	
603	19308	3.587	High X values
635	19384	2.256	
714.1	19592	4.468	
721.3	19646	2.206	
731.2	19788	5.738	
605	20132	3.508	
604	20375	5.279	
728	21250	1.433	
609.2	21434	1.932	
712.2	21795	3.717	
710	21911	5.190	
721.2	22190	1.406	
731.1	22231	7.452	
713.2	22507	6.127	
713.1	22904	3.720	
719.2	23545	3.288	
724.2	24750	5.650	
601	24909	7.220	

To perform the Goldfeld-Quandt test, sort the data in ascending order according to the variable thought to be the source of the heteroscedasticity, INCOME in this case. Then omit the middle $d \approx 0.2n$ observations and perform separate OLS regressions on the two data sets. Form an F-ratio of the ESS from the two regressions to test for heteroscedasticity.

T A B L E 7 . 3   Goldfeld-Quandt ANOVA statistics

	Low Income Analysis of Variance				
Source	Sum-of-Squares	DF	Mean-Square	F-Ratio	P
Regression	8.59	1	8.59	34.77	0.00
Residual	5.19	21	0.25		
	High Income Analysis of Variance				
Source	Sum-of-Squares	DF	Mean-Square	F-Ratio	P
Regression	7.53	1	7.53	2.57	0.12
Residual	61.49	21	2.93		

TABLE 7.4   Breusch-Pagan ANOVA

```
                      Analysis of Variance

      Source      Sum-of-Squares  DF  Mean-Square  F-Ratio    P

   Regression        15.493       1     15.493     19.961   0.000
   Residual          44.242      57      0.776
```

The Breusch-Pagan test was performed on the housing model. The first step, OLS, was reported in Table 7.1. That table provides the information needed for step 2, calculation of the variance of the regression residuals. Divide ESS by n: $83.59/59 = 1.42$. Step 3 is accomplished by dividing the regression residuals by 1.42 and squaring the result to get s_i^2. In step 4, this column of data is used as the dependent variable in an OLS regression on all of the independent variables in the model, INCOME in this case. The ANOVA table from that regression is shown in Table 7.4. The χ^2-statistic is formed by dividing RSS by 2, to give $15.493/2 = 7.75$. This is greater than the critical value at the 1% significance level for one degree of freedom $[\chi^2_{df=1}(0.01) = 6.63]$, so the null hypothesis of homoscedasticity is rejected.

7.4
CORRECTING FOR HETEROSCEDASTICITY: WEIGHTED LEAST SQUARES

The process we just went through to detect heteroscedasticity may have seemed very detailed but, in practice, it often is a good idea to use a couple of different methods to detect heteroscedasticity because none of the methods is very powerful. The question then becomes: How do we correct for heteroscedasticity?

Correction for heteroscedasticity is much like correction for autocorrelation: Modify the model to make the error terms well behaved. This can be done with the method of *weighted least squares* (WLS), one type of GLS regression. As the name suggests, WLS involves weighting each observation to eliminate the tendency of counting large variance terms more heavily than small variance terms. When WLS is performed correctly, the resulting parameter estimates are BLUE—as long as all of the other OLS assumptions are satisfied. We will look at two kinds of WLS: correction when the individual variances are known, and the more likely situation when the individual variances are unknown.

7.4.1 Correction When Variances are Known

In the unlikely case that the individual heteroscedastic variances are known, WLS is performed by dividing each observation by its standard deviation. As we will show shortly, this transformation will convert the heteroscedastic errors into homoscedastic errors. The transformation is straightforward, but it does affect the interpretation of the intercept and slope parameters. The mechanics will be simplified somewhat if we multiply the intercept by the "variable" $X_{0i} = 1$ and write the equation as:

$$Y_i = \beta_0 X_{0i} + \beta_1 X_{1i} + \varepsilon_i, \qquad\qquad [7.7]$$

where

Y_i = dependent variable
$X_{0i} = 1 \ \forall \ i$
X_{1i} = independent variable
$\beta_0 = \beta_0 X_{0i}$ = intercept
β_1 = slope
ε_i = heteroscedastic error term.

Weighted least squares is performed by dividing Eq. [7.7] by the known σ_i to give:

$$\frac{Y_i}{\sigma_i} = \beta_0 \frac{X_{0i}}{\sigma_i} + \beta_1 \frac{X_i}{\sigma_i} + \frac{\varepsilon_i}{\sigma_i}. \qquad\qquad [7.8]$$

Letting β_0^* and β_1^* be the regression parameters from the transformed model, Eq. [7.8] can be rewritten as:

$$Y_i^* = \beta_0^* X_{0i}^* + \beta_1^* X_i^* + \varepsilon_i^*,$$

where

$$Y_i^* = \frac{Y_i}{\sigma_i} \qquad X_{0i}^* = \frac{X_{0i}}{\sigma_i} = \frac{1}{\sigma_i} \qquad X_{1i}^* = \frac{X_{1i}}{\sigma_i} \qquad \varepsilon_i^* = \frac{\varepsilon_i}{\sigma_i}.$$

We can easily show that the errors of the transformed model are homoscedastic. Because $E(\varepsilon_i^*) = 0$, we can write the variance as:

$$\operatorname{var}(\varepsilon_i^*) = E(\varepsilon_i^{*2}) = E\left(\frac{\varepsilon_i}{\sigma_i}\right)^2. \qquad\qquad [7.9]$$

We are still assuming that σ_i^2 is known, so we can take it outside the expected value operator to get:

$$\frac{1}{\sigma_i^2} E(\varepsilon_i^2) = \frac{\sigma_i^2}{\sigma_i^2} = 1. \qquad\qquad [7.10]$$

Because one is a constant, the variance of the transformed error is homoscedastic and the $\hat{\beta}_j^*$ will be BLUE.

As mentioned, a potential problem with WLS is that it complicates interpretation of the regression coefficients. However, when WLS is performed by dividing by σ_i, only the intercept has a different interpretation; the slope parameter(s) are interpreted in the same way as with OLS. Note that the WLS regression coefficients are found by minimizing the expression:

$$\sum \left(\frac{y_i - \hat{\beta}_1 x_i}{\sigma_i} \right)^2. \qquad [7.11]$$

The WLS estimates of the slope parameters are consistent estimates of the OLS slope parameters.[9] However, when the WLS regression is run, it is necessary to suppress the intercept because the coefficient on $(1/\sigma_i)$, $\hat{\beta}_0^*$, is the estimated intercept from the original model. This complicates the interpretation slightly, but as we have pointed out repeatedly, there is rarely any economic content to the intercept. Interpretation is slightly different when performing WLS on models with unknown variances.

GROUPED DATA   Because it is extremely unlikely that we would ever know the actual variances, performing WLS by σ_i division has limited applicability. However, a simple extension of this method is sometimes applicable to grouped data. For example, in the case of the housing study, it might be feasible to group INCOME into brackets of, for example, 8,000–9,999, 10,000–11,999, etc., and estimate the sample standard deviation of the OWNRATIO for each income bracket. INCOME and OWNRATIO would then be divided by these estimated standard deviations. If we have enough data points, this method will yield BLUE parameter estimates.[10]

7.4.2   Correction When Variances Are Unknown

The most common situation is one in which you do not know the error variances. This requires another version of WLS—dividing the model by some function of the independent variable that is thought to be the source of the heteroscedasticity.

To understand why this method works, again suppose that the correct specification of the model is as in Eq. [7.7] and that the X_{1i} variable is the

---

[9]Exercise 7.14 asks you to prove that $E(\hat{\beta}_1^*) = \beta_1$.

[10]There are not enough data points within each bracket to make this kind of WLS transformation feasible. However, the standard deviation of OWNRATIO does increase from 0.077 for the 4,000–5,999 income bracket and to 2.396 for the 22,000–23,999 bracket. It declines to 1.11 for the 24,000–25,999 bracket, but there are only two data points in this bracket.

source of the heteroscedasticity. Suppose further that the relationship between X_{1i} and ε_i is:

$$\text{var}(\varepsilon_i) = CX_{1i}^2, \qquad\qquad [7.12]$$

where C is some unknown constant. If we weight the model by dividing by X_i, we would have:

$$Y_i^* = \frac{Y_i}{X_{1i}}; \qquad X_{0i}^* = \frac{X_{0i}}{X_{1i}}; \qquad X_{1i}^* = \frac{X_{1i}}{X_{1i}} = 1; \qquad \varepsilon_i^* = \frac{\varepsilon_i}{X_{1i}}, \qquad [7.13]$$

and the model to be tested will be:

$$\frac{Y_i}{X_{1i}} = \beta_0^* \frac{1}{X_{1i}} + \beta_1^* \frac{X_{1i}}{X_{1i}} + \varepsilon_i^*. \qquad\qquad [7.14]$$

Thus, if Eq. [7.12] is correct, WLS is performed by regressing the weighted dependent variable (Y_i/X_{1i}) on the *reciprocal* of the independent variable. Notice how this affects interpretation of the parameter estimates. Because $X_{1i}/X_{1i} = 1$, the intercept of the transformed regression is actually the slope of the untransformed model, and the slope of the transformed model is actually the intercept. We will analyze this more carefully when we perform WLS on the housing study.

To show that division by X_{1i} will generate homoscedastic errors in the transformed model, we need to solve for the variance of ε_i^*. Write:

$$\text{var}(\varepsilon_i^*) = \text{var}\left(\frac{\varepsilon_i}{X_{1i}}\right). \qquad\qquad [7.15]$$

Because X_{1i} is a constant, it is squared when it comes outside the variance operator, giving us:

$$\frac{1}{X_{1i}^2} \text{var}(\varepsilon_i) = C, \qquad\qquad [7.16]$$

which is a constant.

The problem with this method is that we do not know the particular function of X_{1i} to use in the weighting process. For example, if the relationship between $\text{var}(\varepsilon_i)$ and X_{1i} does not involve a square term; i.e., if $\text{var}(\varepsilon_i) = CX_{1i}$, it would be necessary to weight by the square root of X_{1i} because:

$$\text{var}\left(\frac{\varepsilon_i}{\sqrt{X_{1i}}}\right) = \frac{1}{X_{1i}} \text{var}(\varepsilon_i) = \frac{1}{X_{1i}} CX_{1i} = C. \qquad [7.17]$$

The Park test can be used to determine the correct weights to use. Recall that the Park test begins with the assumption that the heteroscedastic error variance is equal to a homoscedastic error times X_{1i} raised to some power $[\text{var}(\varepsilon_i) = \sigma_i^2 = \sigma^2 X_1^\delta e^{v_i}]$ and that it is performed by regressing a double log function. This means that the estimated slope parameter ($\hat{\delta}$) is the exponent to which X_{1i} is raised. Finally, as we just demonstrated in Eq. [7.12] through [7.16], if X_{1i} is raised to the second power, the correct weighting scheme is division by X_{1i}^1. The conclusion[11]: If $\hat{\delta}$ is significant, the correct weighting factor is $X_i^{\delta/2}$.

7.4.3   WLS Estimation of the Housing Model

To correct for heteroscedasticity in the housing model (Table 7.1), WLS was performed using a weighting factor estimated from the Park test (Table 7.2). Because $\hat{\delta}$ was estimated as 1.96, the proper WLS transformation is division by $0.98X_{1i} \cong 1X_{1i}$. OLS was then performed on the model:

$$\text{ORINC}_i = \beta_0^* + \beta_1^*\text{RECINC}_i + \varepsilon_i^*,$$

where

$\text{ORINC}_i = \text{OWNRATIO/INCOME}$
$\text{RECINC}_i = 1/\text{INCOME}$
$\beta_0^* = $ intercept of the transformed model, but the slope of the original model
$\beta_1^* = $ slope of the transformed model but the intercept of the original model
$\varepsilon_i^* = $ transformed error, now homoscedastic.

The results of this regression are shown in Table 7.5. A comparison of Tables 7.1 and 7.5 shows some important differences:

1. Because of WLS, the constant term in Table 7.5 (2.40E − 4) is actually the slope, which is comparable to the slope estimate from the OLS run in Table 7.1. (2.97E − 4) This is to be expected because heteroscedasticity does not bias parameter estimates.

2. The corresponding t-ratio rose from 9.18 to 12.0. This may be an indication that the transformed model has generated a more efficient estimate of the slope parameter.

3. R^2 fell from 0.597 in Table 7.1 to 0.352 in Table 7.5. However, this does not necessarily mean that the heteroscedasticity correction was incorrect because the dependent variable changed between the two models.

---

[11] We need to reiterate that the Park test is not without its detractors and that this method of estimating the weighting factor is especially suspect. Unfortunately, without taking refuge in advanced techniques, the only other simple way to estimate the weights is by trial and error.

TABLE 7.5   **WLS regression**

```
Dep var: ORINC  N: 59  R-sq: .352  SER: 0.0674

Variable  Coefficient  Std Error      T      P(2 tail)

CONSTANT     2.40E-4     0.020     .12E+02     0.00
  RECINC    -1.370       0.246    -5.56920     0.00

             Analysis of Variance

  Source    Sum-of-Squares  DF  Mean-Square  F-Ratio  P

Regression     0.141         1     0.141     31.0160  0.000
Residual       0.259        57     0.005
```

To compare the two models, we must calculate a new R^2 as the square of the correlation coefficient between the original dependent variable, $\widehat{\text{OWNRATIO}}_i$, and the fitted values, $\widehat{\text{OWNRATIO}}_i$, derived from the transformed model using the efficient parameter estimates. The fitted values are calculated as:

$$\widehat{\text{OWNRATIO}}_i = -1.37 + 0.00024 \text{INCOME}.$$

The correlation between $\widehat{\text{OWNRATIO}}$ and OWNRATIO is 0.772, which when squared gives an R^2 of 0.596. Thus, the WLS transformation did not cause the model to lose any explanatory power, and did result in more efficient parameter estimates.

The standard technique for dealing with heteroscedasticity is WLS. The two varieties of WLS that we have just illustrated — dividing by known variances and dividing by a function of the independent variable thought to be the source of the heteroscedasticity — are often successful, but not always. We invariably run into difficulties when trying to determine the best weighting factor, though, in practice, division by X_i or $\sqrt{X_i}$ is usually adequate. Also, the examples we discussed involved simple regression. In the real world, multiple regression is the norm, and it is possible for heteroscedasticity to be associated with two or more of the independent variables so the Breusch-Pagan or a similar method must be used for detection. However, even when this is the case, it is usually best to try to adjust for heteroscedasticity by dividing by just one of the independent variables because interpretation of the parameter estimates from the

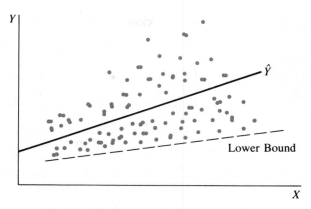

FIGURE 7.3   Heteroscedastic errors

transformed model gets complicated when the weighting factor is a product of two independent variables. It is sometimes appropriate to weight by $\hat{Y}_i$ or $\sqrt{\hat{Y}_i}$ if the heteroscedasticity is associated with multiple regressors. Alternatively, the scale of the data may often be compressed by taking logs of the data, thus eliminating most of the heteroscedasticity.

Finally, while the focus of this chapter has been on the detection and elimination of heteroscedasticity, we should point out that the discovery of heteroscedasticity can sometimes lead to important insights about the model and data being investigated. For example, *a priori* reasoning is enough to raise suspicions regarding heteroscedasticity in the housing model or a cross-sectional consumption function, but in many cases the detection of heteroscedasticity comes as something of a surprise. It is still appropriate to use WLS to eliminate the problem, but before doing so it is always important to try to figure out *why* the relationship between X and Y is heteroscedastic. Does the model fail to capture an important relationship? Has a variable been omitted? Is there a wide range of observations on the independent variable? For example, consider a plot such as the one in Fig. 7.3 where the lower bound of the 95% confidence interval is well defined but the upper bound is not.[12] This might indicate that X is a sufficient condition for increasing Y, but not necessary because other factors, including the error, interact with X.   ◆ ◆ ◆

---

[12] This example comes from George W. Downs and David M. Rocke, "Interpreting Heteroscedasticity," *American Journal of Political Science*, Vol. 23, No. 4, November 1979, p. 823–824.

HETEROSCEDASTICITY AND WLS

1. Heteroscedasticity occurs when error variances are not constant.

2. It is most common in cross-sectional data.

3. Heteroscedasticity does not bias parameter estimates, but it does make them inefficient relative to alternative estimates.

4. Popular methods for detecting heteroscedasticity include the Park, Goldfeld-Quandt, and Breusch-Pagan tests.

5. The most common method for eliminating heteroscedasticity is weighted least squares. WLS is usually performed by dividing (weighting) the data by a function of the independent variable thought to be the source of the heteroscedasticity.

CONCEPTS FOR REVIEW

Heteroscedasticity is a common problem in cross-sectional studies so it is important that you recognize it and take corrective measures. Be sure you can:

- define heteroscedasticity and know how it affects parameter estimates;
- know how to detect heteroscedasticity graphically and with the Park, Goldfeld-Quandt, and Breusch-Pagan tests;
- know how to correct for heteroscedasticity with weighted least squares;
- define and use the following terms in context.

KEY TERMS

Breusch-Pagan test	homoscedasticity
χ^2 test	inefficiency
F-test	Park test
Goldfeld-Quandt test	weighted least squares
heteroscedasticity	(WLS)

EXERCISES

7.1 Define multicollinearity, autocorrelation, heteroscedasticity, and specification error and explain how they affect parameter estimates, t-ratios, and R^2.

7.2 Explain how multicollinearity, autocorrelation, heteroscedasticity, and specification error are detected. Under what conditions is an incorrect diagnosis likely?

7.3 Suppose you wanted to study crime rates by city in the United States. Specify the model, etc. Would you expect to find heteroscedasticity in your study?

7.4 Would you expect to find heteroscedasticity in these models?

    a. Cross-sectional study of industry profits.

    b. Production function.

    c. Firm's sales and advertising expenditures.

    d. Rent $= f$(sex, population density, school children per household).

7.5 Why are cross-sectional studies so infrequently subject to autocorrelation? Can you think of an example that might have cross-sectional autocorrelation?

7.6 **a.** Redraw Fig. 7.1(b) using ε_i^2 instead of ε_i.

    b. Draw the relationship between $\hat{Y}_i$ and ε_i and ε_i^2.

7.7 Figure 7.1 provided two plots of the same hypothetical heteroscedastic errors. Would the two plots ever provide different information in a simple regression model? In a multiple regression model?

7.8 The R^2 for the Park test was low, only 0.177. Does this mean that the null hypothesis of homoscedasticity should not have been rejected? Why or why not?

7.9 In Sec. 7.4.3, R^2 for the transformed model was calculated by computing the simple correlation coefficient between Y_i and $\hat{Y}_i$. Can you think of an alternative way to calculate R^2?

7.10 **a.** When is it necessary to suppress the intercept when correcting for heteroscedasticity?

    b. Under what conditions is what appears to be a slope parameter actually the intercept?

7.11 Refer to Example 6.2. Does it look like the residuals are heteroscedastic? What do you think causes it? How would you correct for it?

7.12 The discussion in Sec. 7.4 illustrated how the correct choice of the weights to be used in WLS can eliminate heteroscedasticity. We also mentioned that the Park test can be used to help estimate the weights. However, some computer programs have WLS routines that automatically use X_i^2 or $\sqrt{X_i}$ weights.

   a. Why is this a reasonable method for dealing with heteroscedasticity?

   b. Another common technique is to weight by $\hat{Y}_i$ or $\sqrt{\hat{Y}_i}$. Does this seem reasonable?

7.13 One recommendation for dealing with heteroscedasticity is to take logs of the data.

   a. Explain why this might eliminate heteroscedasticity.

   b. Based on the material in Chapter 5, do you think this is a good method? Why or why not?

7.14 Prove that WLS parameter estimates are unbiased; i.e., prove that $E(\hat{\beta}_1^*) = \beta_1$.

7.15 Use the data in Data Set 8 of Appendix 1 to test the hypothesis that life expectancy in less developed countries (LIFE) depends on per capita GNP (PCGNP) and an index of food production (FOOD).

   Before beginning analysis:

   a. What signs do you expect on the regressors?

   b. This is cross-sectional data, so the possibility of heteroscedasticity exists. What variable do you think is a potential source?

   c. Are there any other problems you foresee with the model?

   After performing the regression:

   d. Interpret the results. Is the overall model significant? Are the signs as you expected?

   e. Use the Park test to check for heteroscedasticity.

   f. Use the Breusch-Pagan test to check for heteroscedasticity.

   g. If necessary, correct for heteroscedasticity and any other problems.

7.16 Using the housing example data in Data Set 7.1 in this chapter, correct for heteroscedasticity with weights of $\sqrt{X_i}$ instead of X_i as was done in Table 7.5. Compare your results to those obtained in Table 7.5.

APPENDIX 7.A

DERIVATION OF VAR ($\hat{\beta}_1$) FOR A MODEL WITH HETEROSCEDASTIC ERRORS

This derivation begins with Eq. [A.16] from Appendix 3.A. One step in the process of deriving var($\hat{\beta}_1$) showed that:

$$\text{var}(\hat{\beta}_1) = E(\hat{\beta}_1 - \beta_1)^2 = E(\sum w_i \varepsilon_i)^2, \qquad [A.1]$$

where

$$w_i = \frac{x_i}{\sum x_i^2}. \qquad [A.2]$$

After expanding the sum in Eq. [A.1], we have:

$$E(\sum w_i \varepsilon_i)^2 = E[(w_1 \varepsilon_1)^2 + (w_2 \varepsilon_2)^2 + 2(w_1 w_2 \varepsilon_1 \varepsilon_2) + \cdots + (w_n \varepsilon_n)^2].$$

$$[A.3]$$

The ε_i are assumed to be uncorrelated, so the expected value of all terms involving $E(\varepsilon_i \varepsilon_j)$, $i \neq j$, goes to zero. Eq. [A.3] thus becomes:

$$\text{var}(\hat{\beta}_1) = E(\sum w_i \varepsilon_i)^2 = E[(w_1 \varepsilon_1)^2 + (w_2 \varepsilon_2)^2 + \cdots + (w_n \varepsilon_n)^2]. \quad [A.4]$$

The weights can come outside the expected value operator because they are nonstochastic. This gives:

$$E(\sum w_i \varepsilon_i)^2 = w_1^2 E(\varepsilon_1^2) + w_2^2 E(\varepsilon_2^2) + \cdots + w_n^2 E(\varepsilon_n^2). \qquad [A.5]$$

Now, if the errors were homoscedastic, we could let $E(\varepsilon_n^2) = \sigma^2$ and write:

$$\text{var}(\hat{\beta}_1) = \sigma^2 \sum w_i^2 = \frac{\sigma^2}{\sum x_i^2}, \qquad [A.6]$$

which is var($\hat{\beta}_1$) for the two-variable model with homoscedastic errors. However, the presence of the heteroscedastic error means that we cannot factor out σ^2. This means Eq. [A.4] becomes:

$$E(\sum w_i \varepsilon_i)^2 = w_1^2 \sigma_1^2 + w_1^2 \sigma_n^2 + \cdots + w_n^2 \sigma_n^2 = \sum w_i^2 \sigma_i^2. \qquad [A.7]$$

Substituting for w_i gives:

$$\text{var}(\hat{\beta}_1) = \sum w_i^2 \sigma_i^2 = \sum \left(\frac{x_i}{\sum x_i^2} \right)^2 \sigma_i^2. \qquad [A.8]$$

Once x_i^2 has been summed, it is a constant, so it can come outside the first summation sign to give:

$$\text{var}(\hat{\beta}_1) = \left(\frac{1}{\sum x_i^2}\right)^2 \sum x_i^2 \sigma_i^2 = \frac{\sum x_i^2 \sigma_i^2}{(\sum x_i^2)^2}, \qquad \text{[A.9]}$$

which completes the derivation. Notice that it is not permissible to "cancel" the $\sum x_i^2$ terms in the numerator and denominator because x_i^2 is multiplied by σ_i^2 before the summation takes place.

CHAPTER EIGHT

SIMULTANEOUS EQUATIONS AND TWO-STAGE LEAST SQUARES

The step from simple to multiple regression was an important one that enabled us to develop some useful techniques and models. This chapter takes us one step closer to real-world econometrics as we learn how to estimate systems of simultaneous equations. Most economic theory is couched in a general equilibrium framework—the idea that the economy can best be described as an inter-action between several interrelated markets. For example, market prices are determined not by a single equation, but by the intersection of the demand and supply equations. Thus, trying to forecast price from a single equation would probably be unsuccessful. In fact, we show in this chapter that using OLS to estimate the parameters of a single equation that is actually part of a multiequation system will result in biased parameter estimates. The recommended solution to this problem is *two-stage least squares*, an extension of regression analysis.

8.1

THE IDENTIFICATION PROBLEM

The terms "demand curve" and "supply curve" are very common even though such curves are actually observed very rarely. Most often we see only the selling price and quantities—the single point of intersection between the two equations. To trace or *identify* the demand curve, we must assume that it is fixed and then shift the supply curve along it. The resulting points of intersection would be the demand curve of Fig. 8.1. The same technique is used to identify the supply curve: Assume the supply curve is fixed and shift the demand curve. This is the essence of what is called the *identification problem* in simultaneous equation estimation. Before we can begin to solve the identification problem, however, we need to establish a few definitions.

8.1.1 Definitions

The reason we could identify the demand curve in Fig. 8.1 is because a variable in the supply equation that was absent from the demand equation acted as the shift parameter to trace the demand curve. This is the key to solving the identification problem: Find variables in one equation that are not in the other equation(s) and use them as "shift parameters" to identify the individual equations. As you might expect, not all variables can serve the role of shift parameters in the identification process.

FIGURE 8.1   The Identification Problem

Because we observe only the intersection between the supply and demand curves, it is necessary to fix one curve and shift the other along it to trace out the entire curve. In this case, the supply curve is shifting along a fixed demand curve, which allows us to identify the demand curve.

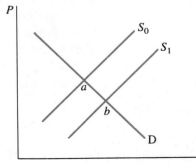

Three kinds of variables are important in simultaneous equation estimation: exogenous, endogenous, and predetermined variables. The supply and demand system presented below illustrates each of these kinds of variables. All variables are expressed in deviation form

$$Supply: \quad q_t^s = \beta_1 p_t + \beta_2 r_t + \beta_3 p_{t-1} + \varepsilon_{1t}, \tag{8.1}$$

$$Demand: \quad q_t^d = \alpha_1 p_t + \alpha_2 y_t + \varepsilon_{2t}, \tag{8.2}$$

$$Equilibrium: \quad q_t^s = q_t^d = q_t, \tag{8.3}$$

where

q_t^d = quantity of wheat demanded
q_t^s = quantity of wheat supplied
p_t = current price of wheat
p_{t-1} = last year's price of wheat
r_t = annual rainfall
y_t = aggregate personal income
ε_{1t} and ε_{2t} = random errors.

An *exogenous variable* is a variable whose value is determined by factors outside of the equation system. For example, the supply of wheat is influenced by rainfall. Because rainfall affects the supply of wheat, but nothing in the wheat market influences the amount of rainfall, rainfall can be considered to be an exogenous variable in the supply equation. Likewise, aggregate personal income affects the demand for wheat, but the wheat market has little noticeable impact on aggregate income, so it is considered exogenous to the demand equation.

Endogenous variables are determined by the equation system. For a supply and demand system, both price and quantity are determined by the system and are thus considered endogenous. As in any equation system, the number of endogenous variables cannot exceed the number of equations if a solution is to exist. Notice that Eq. [8.3], an identity, allows us to treat q_t^d and q_t^s identically, so we really have only two equations and two unknowns in this model.

Predetermined variables are a special class of exogenous variables—they are endogenous variables whose values have been determined in a previous period. The only predetermined variable in the supply and demand model is p_{t-1}, a one period lag of the price. Because last period's price is fixed, it cannot be influenced by current values in the system; thus, it is treated exactly like an exogenous variable. In fact, the terms "predetermined variable" and "exogenous variable" are often used interchangeably, a practice that we will follow in this chapter.

In summary, the supply equation has two exogenous variables and two endogenous variables; the demand equation has two endogenous variables and one exogenous variable. This is important information that will be used to determine if equation identification is possible.

8.1.2   The Order Condition

An equation is identified if it satisfies two criteria, the rank and order conditions.[1] The order condition is a necessary, but not sufficient, condition for identification. To determine if the order condition is satisfied, we must count the number of endogenous and exogenous variables in the equation system to see which ones, and how many, are included or excluded from each equation.

In the equation system of [8.1] through [8.3], the supply equation is *just identified*, because there is exactly one exogenous variable (y_t) in the demand equation that is not in the supply equation. Conceptually at least, y_t allows us to trace the supply curve by shifting the demand curve. Just-identified systems can be estimated with several econometric techniques.[2] Unfortunately, just-identified systems are exceedingly rare in practice.

An equation is *under identified* if there are no exogenous variables in any equation that are excluded from it; i.e., an under-identified equation contains all of the exogenous variables from the entire equation system. Under-identified equations cannot be estimated with any econometric technique.

Equations are most often *over identified* in large econometric models.[3] Equation [8.2], the demand curve, is over identified because there is more than one exogenous variable (r_t and p_{t-1}) in the supply equation that is absent from the demand equation. The thought experiment we used to identify just-identified equations—to allow income shifts to trace the supply curve—does not work with over-identified equations because we cannot tell which of the exogenous variables is causing the supply curve to shift along the fixed demand curve. When equations are over identified, they can be estimated with *two-stage least squares* (2SLS), the main topic of this chapter.

The order conditions can be determined simply enough for a two-equation model, but when the model gets larger, it becomes imperative to use a more general approach. One approach is summarized in the Order Condition box; an equivalent method is presented in Exercise 8.5. These methods are generalizations of the process we just went through to identify the supply and demand equations. Using the notation from the Order Condition box, the

---

[1] The terms "rank" and "order" owe their existence to matrix algebra. Very briefly, order refers to the order or number of rows and columns in the matrix. Rank refers to the largest number of linearly independent rows or columns in the matrix.
[2] Instrumental variables and indirect least squares as well as 2SLS can be used to estimate just-identified equations. These methods are discussed in Appendix 8.A.
[3] In fact, this statement may not be true. Christopher Sims, Robert Lucas, and others contend that in large econometric models it is difficult to find enough truly exogenous variables to identify the equations. Their approach has been to develop a new branch of econometrics—vector autoregression—and a new school of macroeconomics—the new classical school. Vector autoregression is discussed briefly in Chapter 9.

system in Eqs. [8.1] through [8.3] have two endogeneous variables ($G = 2$), and three exogeneous variables ($H = 3$). There is one exogenous variable in the demand equation ($h = 1$), and two endogenous variables ($g = 2$). Because $H - h > g - 1$, the demand equation is over identified, just as we had previously determined. For the supply equation, $h = 2$ and $g = 2$, so $H - h = g - 1$, an indication that it is just identified.

THE ORDER CONDITION

Let: G = number of endogenous variables in the system;
g = number of endogenous variables in the equation;
H = number of exogenous variables in the system; and
h = number of exogenous variables in the equation.

Then:
If $H - h > g - 1$, the equation is over identified.
If $H - h = g - 1$, the equation is just identified.
If $H - h < g - 1$, the equation is under identified.

8.1.3 The Rank Condition[4]

Because the order condition is a necessary but not sufficient condition for identification, it is possible (though rare in practice) for an equation to satisfy the order condition but still not be identified. The rank condition is sufficient for identification. The reasoning behind the rank condition may seem arbitrary because it is based on matrix algebra, but the basic idea is that the exogenous variables counted for identification purposes must be independent of each other. Otherwise, you may not be able to obtain unique parameter estimates.

Determining whether the rank condition is satisfied involves the construction of an array of the equation system and the performance of a series of steps that involve counting equations and variables. This is best illustrated with a system containing three or more equations. Consider the three-equation system:

$$y_1 = \alpha_1 y_2 + \alpha_2 x_1 + \alpha_3 x_2 + \varepsilon_1,$$ [8.4]

$$y_2 = \beta_1 x_1 + \beta_3 x_2 + \varepsilon_2,$$ [8.5]

$$y_3 = \psi_1 x_1 + \psi_2 x_3 + \varepsilon_3,$$ [8.6]

---

[4]This section is optional and can be omitted without loss of continuity.

where the y's are endogenous and the x's are exogenous. By the order condition, $H = 3$ and $G = 3$, so:

Eq. [8.4] is just identified: $h = 2, g = 2, H - h = g - 1$;

Eq. [8.5] is over identified: $h = 1, g = 2, H - h > g - 1$; and

Eq. [8.6] is over identified: $h = 1, g = 2, H - h > g - 1$.

The rank condition shows this not to be the case.

To determine whether or not the rank condition is satisfied, first construct an array to indicate if each variable is included in each equation. Second, for each equation, strike out the corresponding row and form an array of the columns having zeros in that equation's row. Then, if the number of rows and columns containing nonzero elements equals or exceeds $G - 1$, the rank condition is satisfied and estimation is possible.

The array for the three-equation system of [8.4] through [8.6] is shown below. An "x" indicates that a particular variable is in the equation; "0" indicates that it is not.

Equation	y_1	y_2	y_3	x_1	x_2	x_3
8.4	x	x	0	x	x	0
8.5	0	x	0	x	x	0
8.6	0	0	x	x	0	x

The steps required for checking the rank of Eq. [8.4] are illustrated on the array. (1) A line has been drawn through the first row, and the columns with zeros have been boxed. (2) The elements in the columns containing zeros have been circled, and an array has been formed of the circled elements:

0	0
x	x

(3) The information we need to determine rank is in this array. If there are less than $G - 1$ rows and columns containing some nonzero entries, the rank condition fails and estimation of the equation is impossible. For Equation [8.4], there are two columns but only one row that contain nonzero entries. Because $G - 1 = 2$, this equation fails the rank test and estimation is impossible—a result contrary to our inference from examination of the order condition.

The second row has three zeros, so the array for Eq. [8.5] consists of three columns of two rows:

$$
\begin{array}{ccc}
x & 0 & 0 \\
0 & x & x
\end{array}
$$

The rank condition is satisfied because there are three columns and two rows containing some nonzero elements. This is the same conclusion we reached from the order condition.

Equation [8.6] also passes the rank test. After deleting the third row and isolating the columns with zeros, the resulting array is:

$$
\begin{array}{ccc}
x & x & x \\
0 & x & x
\end{array}
$$

Both the number of columns and the number of rows containing nonzero entries equals or exceeds $G - 1$, so estimation of this equation is possible. This is the same conclusion we reached from looking at the order condition. The reader can verify that both of the equations in the supply and demand system pass the rank test.

THE RANK CONDITION

1. Construct a table listing each equation in the first column and each variable in the equation system across the top row. Place an "x" if a variable is in each equation; place a zero if that variable is not.
2. Delete the row for the equation being checked.
3. Form an array of the columns that have zeros in the deleted row.
4. The rank condition is satisfied if there are $G - 1$ or more rows and columns that are not all zeros. If there are less than $G - 1$ rows and columns that are not all zeros, the rank condition is not satisfied and estimation is impossible.

8.2

STRUCTURAL AND REDUCED FORMS

Equations [8.1] through [8.3] are called the *structural equations* of the supply and demand model because they were developed to describe the hypothesized structure of the wheat market. Simple economic theory suggests that the supply of wheat would be a positive function of all of the variables on the right side of Eq. [8.1]: Farmers should be willing to offer more wheat at higher prices, good rainfall increases crop yield, and a high price last year will result in additional acreage being planted this year. Similar arguments can be made about the demand equation.

In the first stage of 2SLS, we have to construct the *reduced form equations* from the structural equations. The reduced form equations will also make it easy to show that OLS parameter estimates from equations systems are biased—the main reason why 2SLS is used instead of OLS.

8.2.1 Reduced Form Equations

Reduced form equations are derived from the structural model by putting one endogenous variable on the left side and all of the exogenous and predetermined variables on the right side. One reduced form equation must exist for each endogenous variable in the system. In this case, there are two endogenous variables in the system, so there must be two reduced form equations.

Before we derive the reduced form equations for the supply and demand model, we simplify[5] our task somewhat by dropping the variables y_t and p_{t-1}. The simplified equation system is:

$$\text{Supply:} \qquad q_t^s = \beta_1 p_t + \beta_2 r_t + \varepsilon_{1t}, \tag{8.7}$$

$$\text{Demand:} \qquad q_t^d = \alpha_1 p_t + \varepsilon_{2t}, \tag{8.8}$$

$$\text{Equilibrium:} \ q_t^s = q_t^d = q_t. \tag{8.9}$$

To solve for the first reduced form equation, use Eq. [8.9] to set supply equal to demand:

$$\alpha_1 p_t + \varepsilon_{2t} = \beta_1 p_t + \beta_2 r_t + \varepsilon_{1t}. \tag{8.10}$$

---

[5] However, notice that by dropping the y_t variable we have made it impossible to estimate the supply equation because it is no longer identified. This simplification also makes it easier to show the source of bias in the next section.

Next, subtract $\beta_1 p_t$ and ε_{2t} from each side of the equation and factor:

$$p_t(\alpha_1 - \beta_1) = \beta_2 r_t + \varepsilon_{1t} - \varepsilon_{2t}. \qquad [8.11]$$

After dividing by $(\alpha_1 - \beta_1)$ we have:

$$p_t = \frac{\beta_2}{(\alpha_1 - \beta_1)} r_t + \frac{\varepsilon_{1t} - \varepsilon_{2t}}{(\alpha_1 - \beta_1)}. \qquad [8.12]$$

The second reduced form equation can be found by substituting the right side of Eq. [8.12] into Eq. [8.8]:

$$q_t = \alpha_1 \left[\frac{\beta_2}{(\alpha_1 - \beta_1)} r_t + \frac{\varepsilon_{1t} - \varepsilon_{2t}}{(\alpha_1 - \beta_1)} \right] + \varepsilon_{2t}. \qquad [8.13]$$

After distributing the α_1, we have:

$$q_t = \frac{\alpha_1 \beta_2}{(\alpha_1 - \beta_1)} r_t + \frac{\alpha_1 \varepsilon_{1t} - \alpha_1 \varepsilon_{2t}}{(\alpha_1 - \beta_{21})} + \varepsilon_{2t}. \qquad [8.14]$$

In practice, it is rarely necessary to carry out the derivations in Equations [8.10] through [8.14] because we usually do not need to separate estimates of the α_j or β_j in the reduced form equations. As shown below, only the fitted values from the reduced form equations are used in the second stage of 2SLS.

The most important aspect of this is the composition of the reduced form equation system. There must be one equation for each endogenous variable in the simultaneous system, and each equation must have exactly one endogenous variable on the left side and all of the exogenous and predetermined variables on the right side. Thus, the reduced form equations are written most often as simply general linear functions that obey these criteria. The common notation for reduced form equations is to label parameter estimates π_{ij} where the first subscript represents the equation and the second represents the coefficient on the exogenous variable. Because there are two equations in this system, i runs from 1 to 2. There is only one exogenous variable in this system, so j runs from 0 (for the intercept) to 1. For our system, the notation is:

$$p_t = \pi_{11} r_t + u_{1t}, \qquad [8.15]$$

$$q_t = \pi_{21} r_t + u_{2t}, \qquad [8.16]$$

where

$$\pi_{11} = \frac{\beta_2}{\alpha_1 - \beta_1}, \qquad \pi_{21} = \frac{\alpha_1 \beta_2}{\alpha_1 - \beta_1},$$

$$u_{1t} = \frac{\varepsilon_{1t} - \varepsilon_{2t}}{\alpha_1 - \beta_1}, \qquad u_{2t} = \frac{\alpha_1 \varepsilon_{1t} - \alpha_1 \varepsilon_{2t}}{\alpha_1 - \beta_1} + \varepsilon_{2t}.$$

8.2.2   Biased OLS Parameter Estimates

The main problem with using OLS to estimate simultaneous equations is that the potential exists for biased and inconsistent[6] parameter estimates. For example, if OLS is applied to the structural demand equation (Eq. [8.8]), the resulting parameter estimate is:

$$\hat{\alpha}_1 = \frac{\sum q_t p_t}{\sum p_t^2}.$$

[8.17]

For this to be unbiased, it must be true that $E(\hat{\alpha}_1) = \alpha_1$. To check this, substitute for q_t from Eq. [8.8]:

$$\hat{\alpha}_1 = \frac{\sum p_t(\alpha_1 p_t + \varepsilon_{2t})}{\sum p_t^2} = \alpha_1 \frac{\sum p_t^2}{\sum p_t^2} + \frac{\sum p_t \varepsilon_{2t}}{\sum p_t^2}.$$

[8.18]

Obviously, $\hat{\alpha}_1$ is unbiased if and only if $E(\sum p_t \varepsilon_{2t})$ goes to zero. Does it? Almost certainly not. The term $E(\sum p_t \varepsilon_{2t})$ represents the covariance between p_t and ε_{2t}, and because p_t appears in both of the structural equations, the errors could feed back between equations and be correlated with the endogenous variables. The result: $E(\sum p_t \varepsilon_{2t})$ may be nonzero, making OLS estimates potentially biased and inconsistent. To show this, substitute Eq. [8.15], the reduced form price equation for p_t:

$$E\left(\frac{\sum p_t \varepsilon_{2t}}{\sum p_t^2}\right) = E\left(\frac{\sum(\pi_{11} r_t + u_{1t})\varepsilon_{2t}}{\sum p_t^2}\right)$$

[8.19]

which can be written as:

$$E\left(\frac{\sum(\pi_{11} r_t \varepsilon_{2t} + u_{1t}\varepsilon_{2t})}{\sum p_t^2}\right) = E\left(\frac{\sum \pi_{11} r_t \varepsilon_{2t}}{\sum p_t^2}\right) + E\left(\frac{\sum u_{1t}\varepsilon_{2t}}{\sum p_t^2}\right).$$

[8.20]

The first term on the right side may go to zero, but the second term does not. Substitution for u_{1t} gives:

$$E\left(\frac{\sum u_{1t}\varepsilon_{2t}}{\sum p_t^2}\right) = E\left(\frac{\sum \frac{(\varepsilon_{1t} - \varepsilon_{2t})}{(\beta_1 - \alpha_1)}\varepsilon_{2t}}{\sum p_t^2}\right) = \frac{T}{\alpha_1 - \beta_1}\,\text{var}(\varepsilon_{2t}) \neq 0,$$

[8.21]

where T is the number of observations and ε_{1t} is assumed to be independent of ε_{2t}.

To find a consistent—though perhaps still biased in small samples—estimate of α_1, we need to use a method that assures a zero correlation be-

---

[6] Recall that consistency is a large sample property. Thus, an inconsistent parameter estimate is biased even for a large sample.

tween the errors and the endogenous variables as the sample gets large. This can be accomplished by constructing an *instrument* for p_t that has a zero correlation with ε_{2t} but a positive correlation with p_t. One method for doing this is 2SLS.

8.3

TWO-STAGE LEAST SQUARES

The most popular method for finding consistent parameter estimates in simultaneous equations models is two-stage least squares (2SLS). As the name suggests, 2SLS involves estimating the equation system in two stages. In the first stage, OLS is performed on the reduced form equations in order to find the fitted values of the endogenous variables. The fitted values are usually called *instruments*. In the second stage, OLS is performed on the structural equations that have been modified by replacing the endogenous variables that appear on the right side with the fitted values from the first-stage regressions. The resulting parameter estimates are consistent, though they may still be biased in small samples.

We will estimate a very simple Keynesian national income model as an illustration of 2SLS, but must mention three caveats before beginning. First, the main purpose of 2SLS is to eliminate simultaneous equation bias. However, it is unlikely that the five-equation system we are going to estimate will eliminate parameter bias. As shown in Example 8.2, most macroeconometric models have hundreds of equations. Second, we will be ignoring autocorrelation in this example. A technique for dealing with autocorrelation in simultaneous equation models is presented in Sec. 8.3.2. Finally, only a very small data set is used in this example, far too small to generate the consistent parameter estimates possible with a larger sample.

8.3.1 A Keynesian Macroeconomic Model

The system we will estimate is a standard Keynesian national income model consisting of consumption, interest rate and investment equations, and two identities. The equations in the system are:

$$C_t = \alpha_0 + \alpha_1 DY_t + \varepsilon_{1t}, \tag{8.22}$$

$$R_t = \beta_0 + \beta_1 Y_t + \beta_2 M_t + \varepsilon_{2t}, \tag{8.23}$$

$$I_t = \gamma_0 + \gamma_1 Y_t + \gamma_2 R_t + \varepsilon_{3t}, \tag{8.24}$$

$$DY_t \equiv Y_t - T_t, \tag{8.25}$$

$$Y_t \equiv C_t + I_t + G_t + X_t, \tag{8.26}$$

where

C_t = real (1982 dollars) personal consumption expenditures
DY_t = "disposable income"; i.e., real GNP − real tax revenues
R_t = the Aaa bonds rate
M_t = real $M2$ money supply
I_t = real GPDI
Y_t = real GNP
T_t = real government tax revenue
G_t = real government spending
X_t = real net exports
ε_{jt} = random errors.

The five endogenous variables are C_t, DY_t, R_t, Y_t, and I_t. The four exogenous variables are M_t, T_t, G_t, and X_t. All of the equations in the system are over identified, a point that you are asked to verify in Exercise 8.8.

For later comparison, OLS was performed on Eqs. [8.22], [8.23], and [8.24] using annual data for the period 1960–87. The data are found in Data Set 9 of Appendix I. The essential results were:

$$\hat{C}_t = -377.07 + 0.919DY_t, \qquad \bar{R}^2 = 0.99,$$

$$\hat{R}_t = 8.02 + 0.009Y_t - 0.049M_t, \qquad \bar{R}^2 = 0.89,$$

$$\hat{I}_t = -71.60 + 0.23Y_t - 11.381R_t, \qquad \bar{R}^2 = 0.94.$$

All t-ratios were significant at the 95% level. These results are consistent with our *a priori* expectations: Consumption should be positively related to disposable income; interest rates should be positively related to income and negatively related to the money supply; and investment should be positively related to income and negatively related to interest rates. However, these results may suffer from simultaneous equation bias so it is necessary to estimate the equations with 2SLS

STAGE 1: PERFORM OLS ON THE REDUCED FORM EQUATIONS After verifying that the rank and order conditions are met, the first step in 2SLS estimation is derivation of the reduced form equations. Recall that exactly one reduced form equation exists for each endogenous variable in the system, and each reduced form equation must have all of the exogenous variables on the right side. There are, therefore, five reduced form equations for the system, but we need to estimate only the Y_t, DY_t, and R_t equations because these are the only endogenous variables that appear on the right side of the structural equations we want to estimate. The reduced form equations we need are:

$$Y_t = \pi_{10} + \pi_{11}M_t + \pi_{12}T_t + \pi_{13}G_t + \pi_{14}X_t + u_{1t}, \qquad [8.27]$$

$$DY_t = \pi_{20} + \pi_{21}M_t + \pi_{22}T_t + \pi_{23}G_t + \pi_{24}X_t + u_{2t}, \qquad [8.28]$$

$$R_t = \pi_{30} + \pi_{31}M_t + \pi_{32}T_t + \pi_{33}G_t + \pi_{34}X_t + u_{3t}. \qquad [8.29]$$

OLS was performed on the reduced form equations to find the instruments (fitted values) to use in the second-stage regressions. Other than the fitted values themselves, the only important information from the first-stage regressions is the coefficient of determination, R^2. Significant multicollinearity will probably exist among the regressors and there is no theoretical justification to include all of the variables on the right side, so individual t-ratios are inconsequential. However, two problems result if the R^2's from the first-stage regressions are low. First, a low R^2 indicates that the instruments are not highly correlated with the endogenous variables they are replacing. Second, it can be shown that when OLS is used in the second stage, the standard errors of the regression coefficients are biased and inconsistent.[7] If a low R^2 is found in the first stage, it is necessary to adjust the standard errors with a correction factor; a high R^2 on the first-stage regressions eliminates the need to use a correction factor. Sophisticated computer programs do this automatically; with more low-level programs, it must be done by hand.[8] In this case, a correction factor is probably not needed because the first-stage regressions all had R^2's exceeding 0.90.

STAGE 2: PERFORM OLS ON THE MODIFIED STRUCTURAL EQUATIONS

The second stage involves running OLS on the structural equations while replacing endogenous variables that appear on the right side with the instruments constructed in the first-stage regressions. The results from the second-stage regressions are shown below:

$$\hat{C}_t = -389.90 + 0.925\widehat{DY}_t; \qquad R^2 = 099,$$

$$\hat{R}_t = 8.66 + 0.009\hat{Y}_t - 0.053M_t; \qquad \bar{R}^2 = 0.90,$$

$$\hat{I}_t = -64.77 + 0.225\hat{Y}_t - 10.896\hat{R}_t; \qquad \bar{R}^2 = 0.89.$$

All t-ratios were significant at the 90% level.

A comparison of the OLS and 2SLS results shows little change from the original OLS estimates. However, we should be careful before making too much of these results because of the small sample, the extremely simple model specification, and the fact that we have ignored autocorrelation. Among other things, the negative intercept on the consumption function is cause for worry—economic theory suggests it should be zero or positive.[9]

---

[7] These problems are illustrated in the cost-push inflation example that follows.
[8] The bias and correction factor can be found in D. Gujarati, *Basic Econometrics*, 2nd ed. (New York: McGraw-Hill, 1988), p. 620–621.
[9] Additionally, the multipliers associated with this model turn out to be negative—a rather clear sign that something is wrong.

8.3.2   2SLS in the Presence of Autocorrelation

As we stressed in Chapter 6, autocorrelation is likely to be present in models using time series data, especially when the data are expressed in levels form. The Keynesian macromodel we have just estimated is no exception: The Durbin-Watson statistics from the preliminary OLS regressions indicated autocorrelation in both the consumption and interest rate equations. A modified version of 2SLS must be used when autocorrelation is present. This procedure is not complicated, but it is tedious and requires a larger data set than was used in the Keynesian model example. The steps for estimating an equation system with autocorrelated errors are:

1. Run preliminary OLS regressions on the structural equations to check for possible autocorrelation.

2. If autocorrelation is present, the first-stage regressions must use current as well as lagged values of the exogenous variables. For example, instead of Eq. [8.27], the first-stage regression for the GNP equation should have been:

$$Y_t = \pi_{10} + \pi_{11}M_t + \pi_{12}T_t + \pi_{13}G_t + \pi_{14}X_t + \pi_{15}M_{t-1}$$
$$+ \pi_{16}T_{t-1} + \pi_{17}G_{t-1} + \pi_{18}X_{t-1} + u_{1t}. \qquad [8.30]$$

3. Using the fitted values from the first-stage regressions, estimate the second-stage regressions with quasi-differences; i.e., the second-stage consumption equation would be:

$$C_t^* = \beta_0(1 - \hat{\rho}) + \alpha_1 \hat{D}Y_t^*,$$

where $C_t^* = C_t - \hat{\rho}C_{t-1}$ and $\hat{D}Y_t^* = \widehat{DY_t} - \hat{\rho}\widehat{DY_{t-1}}$.

This technique will yield efficient and consistent parameter estimates for a large data set.

■ EXAMPLE 8.1

2SLS ESTIMATION OF A COST–PUSH INFLATION MODEL

Two main schools of thought on inflation have been pursued since the 1950s. Monetarists, and most orthodox economists, have argued that inflation is primarily a monetary phenomenon. They cite numerous econometric studies as evidence. Keynesians counter that inflation is primarily a cost-push phenomenon and that wage growth, not money growth, is the primary source of inflation. The Keynesian theory makes sense only if labor markets are imperfect and inflation affects wage demands. The feedback between wages and inflation means that 2SLS is required to test the Keynesian theory.

Annual data for the period 1948–87 were collected from the *Economic Report of the President* and used to test a simple two-equation version of the Keynesian cost-push model. The structural equations were:

$$IPD = \alpha_0 + \alpha_1 CPH + \alpha_2 OPH + \alpha_3 LIPD + \varepsilon_1,$$

$$CPH = \beta_0 + \beta_1 OPH + \beta_2 IPD + \beta_3 U + \varepsilon_2,$$

where

IPD = percent change in the implicit price deflator, business sector
CPH = compensation per hour, business sector
OPH = real output per hour, business sector
LIPD = one year lag on IPD
U = unemployment rate, all civilian workers
ε_1 and ε_2 = random errors.

The endogenous variables are IPD and CPH; all other variables are exogenous. Both equations are just identified and fulfill the rank condition. *A priori*, α_1, α_3, β_1, and β_2 are expected to be positive while α_2 and β_3 should be negative.

For later comparison, OLS was performed on the structural equations. The results are given below. The OLS results are reasonable—the *t*-ratios

```
Dep var: IPD  N: 39  R-sq: .839  Adj  R-sq: .825  SER: 1.198

Variable  Coefficient  Std Error   T       P(2 tail)

CONSTANT      -1.133      0.746   -1.519      0.138
     CPH       0.861      0.102    8.402      0.000
     OPH      -0.419      0.137   -3.063      0.004
    LIPD       0.158      0.095    1.656      0.107

F-ratio: 60.666   DW: 2.064
```

```
Dep var: CPH  N: 40  R-sq: .810  Adj  R-sq: .795  SER: 1.033

Variable  Coefficient  Std Error   T       P(2 tail)

CONSTANT       4.176      0.744    5.613      0.000
     OPH       0.237      0.107    2.215      0.033
     IPD       0.795      0.067   11.889      0.000
       U      -0.286      0.103   -2.782      0.009

F-ratio: 51.321   DW: 2.117
```

and summary statistics are adequate and all of the coefficients have the expected signs. However, the presence of IPD on the rightside of the CPH equation indicates possible simultaneous equation bias.

FIRST-STAGE REGRESSIONS   As always, one first-stage equation was constructed for each endogenous variable and all of the exogenous variables were used as regressors. The first-stage equations that were estimated were:

$$IPD = \pi_{10} + \pi_{11}OPH + \pi_{12}LIPD + \pi_{13}U + u_{1t},$$

$$CPH = \pi_{20} + \pi_{21}OPH + \pi_{22}LIPD + \pi_{23}U + u_{2t},$$

The results from the first-stage regressions are shown below. Unfortunately, the low R^2's from these runs indicate that the fitted values (IPDHAT and CPHHAT) will not be good instruments for the second-stage regressions. Additionally, inferences drawn from the t-ratios of the second-stage parameter estimates will be suspect because the standard errors are probably biased.

```
Dep var: IPD  N: 39  R-sq: .517  Adj R-sq: .476  SER: 2.072

Variable  Coefficient  Std Error    T       P(2 tail)

CONSTANT       3.041     1.407    2.162       0.038
     OPH      -0.353     0.239   -1.479       0.148
    LIPD       0.596     0.168    3.551       0.001
       U      -0.127     0.240   -0.528       0.601

F ratio: 12.501  DW: 1.69
```

```
Dep var: CPH  N: 39  R-sq: .417  Adj R-sq: .367  SER: 1.815

Variable  Coefficient  Std Error    T       P(2 tail)

CONSTANT       6.380     1.232    5.180       0.000
     OPH       0.131     0.209    0.629       0.534
    LIPD       0.650     0.147    4.426       0.000
       U      -0.537     0.210   -2.556       0.015

F ratio: 8.357  DW: 1.837
```

SECOND-STAGE REGRESSIONS   Despite the poor results from the first-stage regressions, the second-stage regressions were performed. The fitted values from the first-stage regressions, IPDHAT and CPHHAT, were used as instruments for the endogenous variables that appear on the right side of the structural equations. The results are shown below.

```
Dep var: IPD  N: 39  R-sq: .517  Adj  R-sq: .476  SER: 2.072

Variable  Coefficient  Std Error     T      P(2 tail)

CONSTANT      1.536      2.176    0.706       0.485
  CPHHAT      0.236      0.447    0.528       0.601
     OPH     -0.384      0.237   -1.616       0.115
    LIPD      0.442      0.240    1.776       0.084

F ratio: 12.510  DW: 1.69
```

```
Dep var: CPH  N: 39  R-sq: .417  Adj R-sq: .367  SER: 1.815

Variable  Coefficient  Std Error     T      P(2 tail)

CONSTANT      3.062      1.563    1.959       0.058
     OPH      0.516      0.268    1.923       0.063
  IPDHAT      1.091      0.247    4.426       0.000
       U     -0.398      0.196   -2.037       0.049

F ratio: 8.355  DW: 1.837
```

A comparison of the OLS and second-stage regressions is instructive. Some of the coefficient estimates have changed significantly—the sign on the constant term in the IPD equation changed. More important, perhaps, is the fact that both R^2's fell significantly and both SERs increased. Often, R^2 does decrease in the second-stage regression, but not this much. The magnitude of the decline is probably caused by the poor instruments, IPDHAT and CPHHAT. This is almost certainly the reason why the t-ratio on CPHHAT fell so much. Given that the t-ratios are suspect as well, the OLS results may be more reliable than the 2SLS specification.

This has been an exceedingly brief introduction to simultaneous equation estimation; so brief, in fact, that some rather detailed *cautions* are warranted. We have already mentioned several factors that must be taken into consideration before proceeding with 2SLS estimation, but they should be repeated.

Our initial interest in 2SLS estimation was prompted by the fact that OLS estimation of single equations of simultaneous systems can result in biased parameter estimates. Remember also that 2SLS estimates can be biased as well; hopefully, however, they will be consistent with a large sample.

As we illustrated in the cost-push inflation example, unless the first-stage regressions have reasonably high R^2's, the second-stage regressions will be unreliable. Additionally, the standard errors from the second stage will be incorrect and require adjustment. If the first-stage regressions have very high R^2's, there is often little difference between OLS and 2SLS parameter estimates.

Estimating single equations that should be part of simultaneous systems results in specification errors. However, the elimination of specification errors may require models with hundreds of equations, not two or three as we used in our examples; this point is illustrated in Example 8.2. Also, unless the simultaneous model is a very close approximation of the "true" model, 2SLS parameter estimates will remain biased and inconsistent.

Serious 2SLS estimations must be done on a high-level statistics program that is capable of computing unbiased standard errors. Microcomputer programs with 2SLS modules includes SAS™, SPSS™, RATS™, SHAZAM™, and the MS-DOS version of Systat™. Although 2SLS is the most popular method for estimating systems of equations, it is not the only one. Three-stage least squares is a more advanced technique that is used when we have reason to believe that there is significant correlation across equations. Under these conditions, 3SLS generates more efficient estimates[10] than 2SLS.

Finally, other perhaps more significant issues must be mentioned before proceeding. Much recent work in the methodology and philosophy of econometrics has focused on the identification problem, the starting point for this chapter. Many investigators now question whether it is legitimate to treat variables as being truly exogenous, and if it is not, whether identification is *ever* possible. For example, in the macromodel developed in Sec. 8.2, we classified government spending as an exogenous variable. Is it? Not completely, at least not if policymakers change government

---

[10] A discussion of 3SLS is beyond the scope of this book, but the interested reader can find a fairly elementary discussion and some examples in Robert S. Pindyck and Daniel L. Rubenfeld, *Econometric Models and Economic Forecasts*, 2nd ed. (New York: McGraw-Hill, 1981), p. 334–335.

spending in response to the state of economic activity; i.e., the rate of GNP growth. This and related issues have led to new econometric methods (some of which we introduce in the next chapter) and important research into causality and model specification. Those issues must be deferred until Chapter 11.   ◆ ◆ ◆

SIMULTANEOUS EQUATION ESTIMATION

1. Estimation of a single equation that is part of an equation system can lead to biased parameter estimates.

2. To estimate an equation system with 2SLS, we must first identify the equations. Only just- and over-identified equations can be estimated.

3. The first step in 2SLS is to form the reduced form equations.

    a. There should be one reduced form equation for each endogenous variable in the system.

    b. Each reduced form equation will have one endogenous variable on the left side and all of the exogenous variables on the right side.

4. The reduced form equations are estimated in order to collect the fitted values. The fitted values are then used as instruments for endogenous variables that appear on the right side of the structural equations.

5. Parameters estimated in the second stage will be consistent, but they may be biased in small samples.

■ EXAMPLE 8.2

THE FEDERAL RESERVE BOARD MULTICOUNTRY MODEL

The examples we used to illustrate 2SLS were extremely simplified; so much so that there is little question that simultaneous equation bias still exists in them. The simplifications were necessary, however, because, as this case study shows, actual 2SLS econometric models are so unwieldy that their pedagogical usefulness is limited, at best.

As an example of a real-world simultaneous equation model, consider one of the biggest, the Federal Reserve Board's multicountry model (MCM). This MCM is a quarterly macroeconomic model that links the G-5

TABLE 8.1
Prototype of an MCM country model

Demand		Variable definitions	
$C = C[R, A(L)Y_d]$	consumption	BU = unborrowed monetary base	(exogenous)
$I = I(K_{-1}, \Delta UC, \Delta Y)$	investment	C = real consumption expenditure	
$X_{gs} = X(Y^*, P/EP^*)$	real exports of goods and services	CAB = current account balance	
$M_{gs} = M(Y, P/EP^*)$	real imports of goods and services	$DNFAG$ = change in net foreign assets of private sector	(exogenous)
$Y = C + I + G + X_{gs} - M_{gs}$	goods market equilibrium	E = nominal exchange rate (local currency per unit of foreign currency)	
$Y_d = Y + (TR - T)/P$	real disposable income	$\dot{E}^e$ = expected change in nominal exchange rate	
		$\bar{E}$ = expected long-term nominal exchange rate	
Money market		G = real government expenditure	(exogenous)
$M/P = M_d(Y, i_s)$	money demand	I = real investment expenditure	
$RF = RF(M, i_s, i_d)$	bank demand for free reserves	i_d = nominal discount rate	(exogenous)
		i_s = nominal short-term interest rate	
$RR = \zeta M$	required reserves	i_l = nominal long-term interest rate	
$BU = RR + RF$	unborrowed money base (assuming no currency holdings)	i_s^* = foreign nominal short-term interest rate	(exogenous)
		K = stock of physical capital	
$i_l = C(L)i_s$	term structure equation	L = labor employed	
		$\bar{L}$ = labor force	(exogenous)
$R = i_l - \dot{P}^e$	real long-term interest rate	M = money supply	
		M_{gs} = real imports of goods and services	
Supply		M_i = imports of intermediate inputs	
		P = price of domestic absorption	
$Q = F(K, L, M_i)$	production function	P^* = price of foreign absorption	(exogenous)
$Y = Q - (P_{mi}/P_q)M_i$	definition real GNP	$\dot{P}$ = domestic inflation rate (absorption deflator)	
$P_q = P_q[P(UC), W, P_{mi}, Y]$	supply curve of domestic output	$\dot{P}^e$ = expected domestic inflation rate (absorption deflator)	
$P = P(P_q, P_{mf})$	price of domestic absorption	$\dot{P}^{e*}$ = foreign expected inflation rate (absorption deflator)	
$UC = UC(R, \delta, t)$	real user cost of capital	P_{mf} = price of final imports	(exogenous)
		P_{mf} = price of intermediate imports	(exogenous)
$\dot{P}^e = B(L)\dot{P}_{-1}$	expected inflation	P_q = price of domestic output	
$K = \delta K_{-1} + I$	capital stock	Q = gross output	
$W - W_{-1} = \dot{P}^e - \lambda(\bar{L} - L)$	Phillips curve	R = real long-term interest rate	
$M_i = F_{mi}^{-1}(P_{mi}/P)$	imported intermediates	RF = free reserves of banks	
		RR = required reserves of banks	
		t = corporate tax rate	(exogenous)

(continued)

TABLE 8.1 (*Continued*)

Exchange rate and balance of payments		Variable definitions	
$\dot{E}^e = i_s - i_s^*$	open interest parity condition	T = nominal government tax revenue	(exogenous)
$\dot{E}^e = \gamma(\ln \bar{E} - \ln E) + \dot{P}^e - \dot{P}^{e*}$	exchange rate expectations	TR = nominal government transfers	(exogenous)
		UC = real user cost of capital	
$\bar{E} = \bar{X}[(\dot{P}^e - P_{-1})/(\dot{P}^{e*} - P^*_{-1})]$	long-term equilibrium exchange rate	W = nominal wage rate	
		X_{gs} = real exports of goods and services	
$CAB = P(X_{gs}) - EP^*(M_{gs})$	current account balance	$\bar{X}$ = expected long-term real exchange rate	(exogenous)
$CAB - DNFAP - DNFAG = 0$	balance of payments identity	Y = real GNP	
		Y_d = real disposable income	
		Y^* = foreign real GNP	(exogenous)
		δ = real rate of depreciation	(exogenous)
		ζ = required reserve ratio	(exogenous)

KEYS : An asterisk (*) indicates a foreign variable; $A(L)$, $B(L)$, and $C(L)$ are polynomials in a distributed lag operator; γ and λ are scalar coefficients; $F_x(\cdot)$ is the partial derivative of $F(\cdot)$ with respect to x; and a dot over the variable indicates percentage rate of change.

nations, the United States, West Germany, Canada, Japan, and the United Kingdom. Each of the models for the individual countries consists of between 150 and 250 behavioral equations and identities. The MCM has been under development since the early 1970's and is still being modified as time, techniques, and the availability of data permit.

Despite the fact that there are almost 1,000 equations in the linked model, several simplifying assumptions still have to be made. The basic structure of the model is Keynesian and there are four principal markets—output, labor, money, and bonds. Nominal wages are assumed to be "sticky," which allows output to change in response to demand and supply shocks. Prices are assumed to be marked up over variable costs. Financial markets are assumed to be perfectly competitive, people are risk neutral, and short- and long-term financial assets are treated as perfect substitutes. Foreign and domestic bonds are also treated as substitutes so that interest rate parity exists between nations.

Table 8.1 (a replication of Table 1, p. 116, from Edison et al.[11]) presents a prototype of an MCM country model.

---

[11] H. J. Edison, J. R. Marquez, and R. W. Tryon, "The Structure and Properties of the Federal Reserve Board Multicountry Model," *Economic Modelling*, Vol. 4, No. 2, April 1987, p. 115–315.

The MCM has several uses, but one of the most important is policy simulation. For example, the MCM predicts that a sustained 1% increase in U.S. government purchases will increase real GNP 2% after one year, but taper off to 1.7% in the second year, 1.2% in the third year, etc. The increase in inflation would be insignificant in year one (0.2%) but rise steadily to 2.9% by year eight. The MCM can also be used to simulate coordinated fiscal policy changes. For example, if all five countries increase government purchases by 1% per year, U.S. real GNP will increase 2.5% in year one, 2.2% in year two, and 1.5% in year three—but inflation would accelerate to almost 3% within five years. The MCM is also useful for simulating the effects of monetary policies, supply shocks, and exchange rate multipliers.

CONCEPTS FOR REVIEW

OLS estimation of isolated equations that should be part of a simultaneous system can lead to biased parameter estimates, so most real-world econometrics involves systems of equations. Even if you don't feel ready to tackle a 100-equation system, it is vitally important that you understand the process of 2SLS estimation. You'll have a good start on that understanding if you can:

- explain why simultaneous equation bias exists
- identify structural equations and construct reduced form equations
- determine the rank and order of equations in simultaneous systems
- outline the steps to 2SLS estimation
- define and use the following terms in context.

KEY TERMS

consistent parameter estimates	over identified
endogenous variable	predetermined variable
exogenous variable	reduced form equation
identification problem	structural equation
instrument	2SLS
just identified	under identified

EXERCISES

8.1 Suppose you estimated a demand equation, $Q_t^d = \beta_0 + \beta_1 P_t + \varepsilon_t$, and found that $\hat{\beta}_1$ was statistically significant and positive. Does this mean that you actually estimated the supply equation instead?

8.2 Suppose that the consumption equation is given by $c_t = \beta_1 y_t + \varepsilon_t$ while GNP is defined as $y_t \equiv c_t + i_t + g_t$.

a. Show that OLS estimation of $\hat{\beta}_1$ will be biased.

b. Can you determine the direction of bias; that is, will $E(\hat{\beta}_1)$ be greater or less than β_1?

8.3 A linear version of the ISLM model could be written as:

$$\textit{Money market: } R_t = \beta_0 + \beta_1 Y_t + \beta_2 M_t^s + \varepsilon_{1t},$$

$$\textit{Goods market: } Y_t = \alpha_0 + \alpha_1 R_t + \alpha_2 I_t + \alpha_3 G_t + \varepsilon_{2t},$$

where Y_t is real GNP, R_t is the real interest rate, I_t is real investment, G_t is real government purchases, M_t^s is the real money supply, and ε_{1t} and ε_{2t} are errors; Y_t and R_t are endogenous.

a. Write the reduced form equations.

b. Determine whether this system can be estimated with 2SLS.

8.4 Consider a model composed of three structural equations:

$$Y_{1t} = \alpha_0 + \alpha_1 X_{1t} + \varepsilon_{1t},$$

$$Z_{1t} = \beta_0 + \beta_1 Y_{1t} + \beta_3 Z_{2t-1} + \varepsilon_{2t},$$

$$X_{1t} = Y_{1t} + Z_{1t} + Z_{2t}.$$

a. Are the Y and Z equations identified well enough to permit 2SLS estimation?

b. Construct the reduced form equations.

c. Suppose that the Y equation were estimated with OLS. Could you trust your estimate of $\hat{\alpha}_1$?

8.5 An alternative means of determining the order of an equation is the following: In a model with M simultaneous equations, an equation is identified if it excludes at least $M - 1$ of the variables in the model. This includes both exogenous and endogenous variables. If exactly $M - 1$ variables are excluded, the equation is just identified. If more than $M - 1$ variables are excluded, it is over identified. If less than

$M - 1$ variables are excluded, it is under identified and estimation is not possible.

a. Perhaps using a two-equation example, explain why this criteria is equivalent to the criteria used in the text.

b. Use this criteria to determine the order conditions of the system in Eqs. [8.1] through [8.3].

8.6 Determine the rank conditions for the cost-push inflation model in Example 8.1.

8.7 In Sec. 8.1.2, we stated, "Equations are often *over identified* in large econometric models." Would you consider fiscal and monetary policy variables exogenous in a system used to model aggregate macroeconomic variables? Why or why not?

8.8 Suppose that the macromodel estimated in the text is modified such that Eq. [8.22] is replaced with the consumption function we estimated in Chapter 4 and the investment function is the revised accelerator model of Exercise 4.6; i.e.,

$$C_t = \alpha_0 + \alpha_1 DY_t + \alpha_2 R_t + \varepsilon_{1t},$$

$$R_t = \beta_0 + \beta_1 Y_t + \beta_2 M_t + \varepsilon_{2t},$$

$$I_t = \gamma_0 + \gamma_1 \Delta Y_t + \gamma_2 I_{t-1} + \varepsilon_{3t},$$

$$DY_t \equiv Y_t - T_t,$$

$$Y_t \equiv C_t + I_t + G_t + X_t.$$

a. Determine the rank and order conditions of these equations.

b. Can any of these equations be estimated correctly as a single equation?

c. Calculate the spending multipliers for this system.

8.9 Suppose you tried to estimate the system in Eqs. [8.7] through [8.9]. Would you expect to get good results? Why or why not?

8.10 *Review Question:* Autocorrelation.

a. The OLS regressions on the structural equations of the Keynesian macromodel resulted in the following Durbin-Watson statistics: consumption: 0.822; interest rate: 0.647; and investment: 1.86. Calculate $\hat{\rho}$ for each equation and carefully explain how to eliminate autocorrelation with quasi-differencing.

b. The OLS regressions for the cost-push inflation model show no evidence of autocorrelation, yet the model uses time series data. Why?

8.11 *Review Question: F-ratio.* Interpret the *F*-ratios from the OLS, first, and second-stage regressions from the cost-push inflation model.

8.12 Use 2SLS on the data in Data Set 11 of Appendix I to estimate the structural coefficients of the model:

$$CONS = \alpha_0 + \alpha_1 GNP + \varepsilon_1,$$

$$GNP = \beta_0 + \beta_1 CONS + \beta_2 GPDI + \beta_1 DEF + \varepsilon_2,$$

where

   CONS = quarterly real personal consumption, 1982 dollars
   GNP = quarterly real GNP
   GPDI = quarterly real gross private domestic investment
   DEF = quarterly real government deficit.

Before 2SLS estimation:

a. Run OLS on the structural equations to check for possible autocorrelation and to compare with later 2SLS results.

b. Write out the reduced form equations.

After completing the first-stage regressions:

c. If you found autocorrelation in part (a), follow the steps in Sec. 8.3.2 when performing the first-stage regressions. What do the first-stage results indicate regarding possible bias of the standard errors?

d. Do the first-stage results suggest that the second-stage regressions will have a good fit?

After completing the second-stage regressions:

e. Compare the MPC estimated with OLS to the MPC estimated with 2SLS. Could you have expected this result?

ERRORS IN VARIABLES, INSTRUMENTAL VARIABLES, AND INDIRECT LEAST SQUARES

Two topics closely related to 2SLS are *instrumental variables* and *indirect least squares*. We used a version of instrumental variables when we substituted the fitted values from the first-stage regressions into the second stage. Another use of instrumental variables, correction for errors in variables, is the first topic we discuss in this appendix. The other topic, indirect least squares, is an alternative method that can sometimes be used for estimating systems of simultaneous equations. For practical purposes, 2SLS is usually the best approach, but a quick look at indirect least squares should improve your understanding of the identification problem and 2SLS. Most important, indirect least squares permits estimation of the structural coefficients from the reduced form equations for systems that are just identified.

Errors in Variables and Instrumental Variables

We have assumed to this point that the variables used in the regression equation are measured accurately. This is not always the case, and, unfortunately, *errors in variables* can result in serious problems. What can cause errors in the variables? Several things, but incorrect reporting—very likely in the case of aggregate macroeconomic data—and small, nonrandom samples are obvious causes. The problems caused by errors in variables depend on which variables are measured with error. If one of the independent variables is measured with error, the $\hat{\beta}_j$ will be biased. If the dependent variable is measured with error, the $\hat{\beta}_j$ remain unbiased, but the SER will increase.

***X* IS MEASURED WITH ERROR**　　Suppose the "true" regression model is:

$$y_i = \beta_1 x_i + \varepsilon_i, \tag{A.1}$$

but that x_i is measured with error such that x_i^* is observed instead; i.e.,

$$x_i^* = x_i + u_i, \tag{A.2}$$

where u_i obeys the OLS Assumptions 3, 4, and 5. The presence of measurement error means the model that is actually tested is:

$$y_i = \beta_1 x_i^* + \varepsilon_i. \tag{A.3}$$

To prove this measurement error results in bias, substitute Eq. [A.2] into [A.3]:

$$y_i = \beta_1(x_i + u_i) + \varepsilon_i = \beta_1 x_i + \beta_1 u_i + \varepsilon_i. \tag{A.4}$$

Because only x_i^* can be observed, however, regression analysis will be performed on

$$y_i = \beta_1 x_i^* + \varepsilon_i^* \qquad\qquad\qquad\qquad [A.5]$$

so that

$$\varepsilon_i^* = \varepsilon_i - \beta_1 u_i. \qquad\qquad\qquad\qquad [A.6]$$

Recall that in order for $\hat{\beta}_1$ to be unbiased, x_i must be noncorrelated with the error. This is not the case if X is measured with error. Notice that

$$\text{cov}(\varepsilon_i^*, x_i^*) = E[(\varepsilon_i - \beta_1 u_i)(x_i + u_i)] = -\beta_1 \sigma_u^2 \qquad\qquad [A.7]$$

so the $\hat{\beta}_j$ are biased.

Y IS MEASURED WITH ERROR   The situation is not as severe when Y is measured with error. If the true model is again Eq. [A.1], but Y is measured with error such that:

$$y_i^* = y_i + v_i, \qquad\qquad\qquad\qquad [A.8]$$

the fitted model would be:

$$y_i^* = \beta_1 x_i + (\varepsilon_i + v_i). \qquad\qquad\qquad\qquad [A.9]$$

There are two implications of regression on Eq. [A.9]. First, $\hat{\beta}_1$ will be unbiased as long as we can assume that x_i and v_i are uncorrelated. Second, the error variance of the model will increase because we will be squaring $(\varepsilon_i + v_i)$ instead of just ε_i. However, the larger error variance will be captured in the estimated variance and the SER, so F- and t-tests remain valid. Because the problems associated with measurement errors on the dependent variable are less serious than those associated with errors on the independent variables, many econometricians simply dismiss this problem.

INSTRUMENTAL VARIABLES   Instrumental variables can be used to eliminate the problems caused by measurement errors. Unfortunately, there is a significant difference between this use of instrumental variables and their use in the second stage of 2SLS. In 2SLS the choice of an instrument is obvious — the fitted values from the first-stage regression. In the case of measurement errors, there is rarely such a clear choice of what to use as an instrument. The obvious choice would be the actual variable purged of the measurement error, but if this were available, we would have no measurement error in the first place.

The best way to select instrumental variables is to use economic theory to find an instrument (Z) that has two characteristics:

1.   a high correlation between Z and X as the sample size gets large

2.   correlations between Z and ε, u, and v that approach zero as the sample size gets large.

Assuming such an instrument can be found, the instrumental variable estimate of β_1 for the two-variable model with X measured with error is:

$$\hat{\beta}_1^* = \frac{\sum y_i z_i}{\sum x_i^* z_i}.$$

[A.10]

This equation can easily be shown to be consistent, although, like 2SLS, it is biased for small samples. Interestingly, if the denominator of Eq. [A.10] is replaced by z_i^2, the resulting parameter is not consistent.

The formula in Eq. [A.10] is only as good as the instrument found for x_i^*, and estimates of $\hat{\beta}_j^*$ do depend on the selected instrument. In practice, the search for a suitable instrument can be quite difficult, and the fact that parameter estimates are only consistent, not unbiased, makes errors in variables a particularly difficult problem.

Indirect Least Squares

The method of indirect least squares can generate consistent parameter estimates when equations are just identified, but does not yield unique parameter estimates when applied to over-identified equations. As an example, consider the structural equations for a two-equation system:

$$y_{1t} = \beta_1 y_{2t} + \varepsilon_{1t},$$

[A.11]

$$y_{2t} = \alpha_1 y_{2t} + \alpha_2 x_{1t} + \varepsilon_{2t},$$

[A.12]

where y_{st} are endogenous variables; x_{1t} is exogenous; and ε_{st} are the error terms. It is easy to show that Eq. [A.11] is just identified and that Eq. [A.12] is under identified, so 2SLS estimation is possible only for Eq. [A.11]. The reduced form equations for this system are:

$$y_{1t} = \pi_{11} x_{1t} + u_{1t},$$

[A.13]

$$y_{2t} = \pi_{21} x_{1t} + u_{2t}.$$

[A.14]

We know that OLS estimation of Eq. [A.11] would result in biased parameter estimates because the correlation between y_2 and ε_1 is likely to be nonzero. However, suppose that x_1 is used as an instrument for y_2. Is this a reasonable instrument? Perhaps. Because it was assumed to be exogenous, it is not correlated with the error term, and because it is in the structural model, it should be correlated with y_2. The resulting parameter estimate would be:

$$\hat{\beta}_1^* = \frac{\sum y_{1t} x_{1t}}{\sum y_{2t} x_{1t}}, \qquad \text{[A.15]}$$

which will be consistent as long as x_1 fulfills the requirements of a good instrument: $\rho(y_2, x_1) \neq 0$ and $\rho(\varepsilon_1, x_1) \to 0$ as the sample size gets large.

Indirect least squares is an alternative method of estimation and will generate the same parameter estimates as the instrumental variable technique, but only if the equation being estimated is just identified. Notice what happens if we use OLS on the reduced form equations:

$$\hat{\pi}_{11} = \frac{\sum y_{1t} x_{1t}}{\sum x_{1t}^2}, \qquad \text{[A.16]}$$

$$\hat{\pi}_{21} = \frac{\sum y_{2t} x_{1t}}{\sum x_{1t}^2}, \qquad \text{[A.17]}$$

If we take the ratio $\hat{\pi}_{11}/\hat{\pi}_{21}$, we have:

$$\frac{\hat{\pi}_{11}}{\hat{\pi}_{21}} = \frac{\sum y_{1t} x_{1t}/\sum x_{1t}^2}{\sum y_{2t} x_{1t}/\sum x_{1t}^2} = \frac{\sum y_{1t} x_{1t}}{\sum y_{2t} x_{1t}}, \qquad \text{[A.18]}$$

which is identical to Eq. [A.15].

This is a simple method of estimation, but rarely useful given that most equations in large systems are over identified. To understand why indirect least squares is inappropriate for over-identified equations, suppose that the equation system contains another exogenous variable, i.e.,

$$y_{1t} = \beta_1 y_{2t} + \varepsilon_{1t}, \qquad \text{[A.19]}$$

$$y_{2t} = \alpha_1 y_{1t} + \alpha_2 x_{1t} + \alpha_3 x_{2t} + \varepsilon_{2t}. \qquad \text{[A.20]}$$

The corresponding reduced form equations would be:

$$y_{1t} = \pi_{11} x_{1t} + \pi_{12} x_{2t} + u_{1t}, \qquad \text{[A.21]}$$

$$y_{2t} = \pi_{21} x_{1t} + \pi_{22} x_{2t} + u_{2t}. \qquad \text{[A.22]}$$

We know from Eq. [4.2] that OLS estimates of π_{11} and π_{21} are:

$$\hat{\pi}_{11} = \frac{(\sum x_{1t} y_{1t})(\sum x_{2t}^2) - (\sum x_{2t} y_{1t})(\sum x_{1t} x_{2t})}{(\sum x_{1t}^2)(\sum x_{2t}^2) - (\sum x_{1t} x_{2t})^2}, \qquad \text{[A.23]}$$

$$\hat{\pi}_{21} = \frac{(\sum x_{1t} y_{2t})(\sum x_{2t}^2) - (\sum x_{2t} y_{2t})(\sum x_{1t} x_{2t})}{(\sum x_{1t}^2)(\sum x_{2t}^2) - (\sum x_{1t} x_{2t})^2}; \qquad \text{[A.24]}$$

and if we form the ratio $\hat{\pi}_{11}/\hat{\pi}_{21}$, we again have $\hat{\beta}_1^*$:

$$\hat{\beta}_1^* = \frac{\hat{\pi}_{11}}{\hat{\pi}_{21}} \cong \frac{\sum x_{1t}y_{1t}}{\sum x_{1t}y_{2t}}. \tag{A.25}$$

This would seem to be an alternative way to find parameter estimates from the structural equations. Unfortunately, this is not the case. We cannot be sure we will obtain unique parameter estimates because there is no reason to select x_1 over x_2 as the instrument.

If x_2 were chosen, the OLS estimates of π_{12} and π_{22} would be:

$$\hat{\pi}_{12} = \frac{(\sum x_{2t}y_{1t})(\sum x_{1t}^2) - (\sum x_{1t}y_{1t})(\sum x_{1t}x_{2t})}{(\sum x_{1t}^2)(\sum x_{2t}^2) - (\sum x_{1t}x_{2t})^2}, \tag{A.26}$$

$$\hat{\pi}_{22} = \frac{(\sum x_{2t}y_{2t})(\sum x_{1t}^2) - (\sum x_{1t}y_{2t})(\sum x_{1t}x_{2t})}{(\sum x_{1t}^2)(\sum x_{2t}^2) - (\sum x_{1t}x_{2t})^2}, \tag{A.27}$$

and their ratio would reduce to:

$$\hat{\beta}_1^{**} = \frac{\hat{\pi}_{12}}{\hat{\pi}_{22}} \cong \frac{\sum x_{2t}y_{1t}}{\sum x_{2t}y_{2t}}. \tag{A.28}$$

In general, both $\hat{\beta}_1^*$ and $\hat{\beta}_1^{**}$ will be consistent, but they will not be identical for any particular sample. Our conclusion: Indirect least squares is an inappropriate estimation technique unless equations are just identified.

KEY TERMS AND CONCEPTS

consistent estimate   instrumental variables

errors in variables   unbiased estimate

indirect least squares

Exercises

A.1 Show that Eq. [A.10] is an unbiased estimator of $\hat{\beta}_1$.

A.2 Replace the denominator of Eq. [A.10] by z_i^2, and show that the resulting parameter estimate is inconsistent.

A.3 Using the rank and order conditions, show that Eq. [A.11] is just identified and that Eq. [A.12] is under identified.

A.4 Use indirect least squares to estimate α_2 in Eq. [8.8].

A.5 Show that 2SLS, instrumental variables, and indirect least-squares estimates of parameters in just-identified equations are identical.

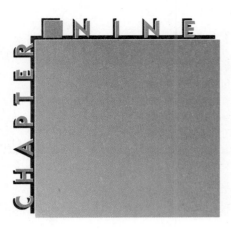

CHAPTER NINE

TIME SERIES MODELS AND FORECASTING

The econometric models we have discussed thus far in the text are known as *structural models* because they were based on economic theory and developed in order to capture the underlying structure of the economy. In contrast, *time series models* do not presuppose an underlying economic structure. In fact, they are often called "atheoretical" because they are only loosely based on economic theory. Obviously, this means that time series models are of little use in trying to explain the phenomena under question. This is not a problem, however, because these models are used almost exclusively for forecasting. In fact, in many circles—especially in business and areas of contemporary macroeconomics—time series models have replaced traditional structural models as the technique of choice for forecasting.

The basic approach of time series analysis is to forecast variables from their own past values. For example, a simple time series model is:

$$X_t = \alpha X_{t-1} + \epsilon_t;$$

that is, X_t is a linear function of itself lagged one period, X_{t-1}, plus a random error. This equation should look familiar: It is of the same form as the equation for first-order autocorrelation that we developed in Chapter 6. As we will find out in this chapter, we are often looking explicitly for autocorrelation in time series analysis, not trying to get rid of it as we did earlier.

9.1

TREND FORECASTING

Many time series analysts begin their studies by fitting a trend—either linear or nonlinear—to the data. In fact, until more modern methods were developed, time series analysis was little more than fancy trend fitting.

The first step in trend forecasting is to plot the data to note any special characteristics. If the plot is especially erratic, the second step is to smooth or *filter* the data to eliminate some of the random components. Filtering usually entails an arithmetic transformation of the data to reduce the influence of outliers, sharp peaks, etc. Finally, an attempt is made to fit the series to a mathematical model.[1] These steps will be illustrated by constructing a simple model to forecast consumer price inflation.

9.1.1 Forecasting Consumer Price Inflation

Suppose we suspect that most of the variation in consumer price inflation is the result of inflationary inertia; that is, that the current inflation rate is determined primarily by past inflation rates. If this is correct, a time series model should be reasonably successful for forecasting future inflation. The steps involved in constructing a forecast are:

---

[1] Early time series analysis tried to break the data into four components: trend, cycle, random elements, and, if the data were collected more often than yearly, seasonal. Few modern analysts believe that business cycles are regular enough to be detected consistently in economic data, so the component method is used infrequently today. For a discussion of the component approach to time series analysis, see Lloyd Valentine, *Business Cycles and Forecasting*, 7th ed. (Cincinnati: Southwestern, 1987), Chapter 3.

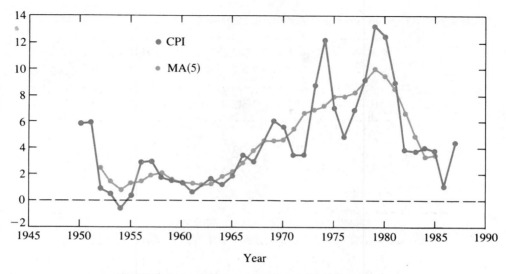

FIGURE 9.1   Consumer price inflation, 1950–87

1. PLOT THE DATA   Figure 9.1 plots annual inflation rates from 1950–87 in both raw and smoothed form. At first glance, the data seem to have very little pattern—a trend line would show an upward slope followed by a sharp decline—but the salient characteristic of the data is their erratic nature. Most investigators regard this as an indication that filtering is probably necessary.

2. FILTER THE SERIES IF NECESSARY   Several filters are possible, but the most common is probably the *moving average*.[2] Most computer programs have moving average functions, or they can be constructed by hand for small data sets with the formula in Eq. [9.1]:

$$y_t = \frac{1}{2m+1} \sum_{j=-m}^{+m} x_{t-j};$$ [9.1]

that is, add x_t to m observations on either side of x_t then divide by $2m + 1$. To construct a five-period ($= 2m + 1$) moving average, set $m = 2$. For the moving average centered around x_{10}, the calculations would be $(x_8 + x_9 + x_{10} + x_{11} + x_{12})/5$. The next element is found by dropping x_8, adding x_{13}, again dividing by 5, etc. The resulting series will have $n - 2m$ data points because the first two and the last two are lost. Part of the data from the

---

[2] Exercises 9.2 and 9.3 present other filtering techniques.

TABLE 9.1 Consumer price inflation, 1950–87

%ΔCPI	MA(5)	%ΔCPI	MA(5)
5.8	●	—	
5.9	●	13.3	10.1
0.9	2.5	12.4	9.5
0.6	1.5	8.9	8.5
−0.5	0.9	3.9	6.6
0.4	1.3	3.8	4.9
2.9	1.5	4.0	3.3
3.0	1.9	3.8	3.4
—		1.1	●
—		4.4	●

The moving average filter is used to smooth data series. The calculations for the first entry in the five-period series are: (5.8 + 5.9 + 0.9 + 0.6 − 0.5)/5 = 2.5; the second entry is (5.9 + 0.9 + 0.6 − 0.5 + 0.4)/5 = 1.5. Note that the five-period series loses two observations at either end of the data; a three-period series would lose only one observation at either end. The complete data set is in Data Set 12, of Appendix I.

original and the five-period moving average smoothed series are presented in Table 9.1; both were plotted on Fig. 9.1. Notice that the moving average series is smoother and has fewer spikes than the original series. Smoothing over a longer period would result in an even less erratic series, but would have also lost additional observations. The period used in the smoothing process is somewhat arbitrary, and many econometricians resist any smoothing at all because it hides some of the information in the data series.

3. REGRESSION ON TIME After smoothing the series, the next step is to use regression analysis to fit the data to a mathematical model. Because real data rarely fit hypothesized mathematical forms precisely, most investigators check several functional forms and choose the one with the best summary statistics. Three possible mathematical forms are linear, exponential, and parabolic.[3]

---

[3]There are, literally, an infinite number of possible mathematical forms. Exercise 9.8 uses an additional mathematical form.

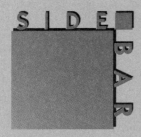

SEASONAL ADJUSTMENT

THE CPI data we are using are annual, but when series are compiled more often than annually, it is often necessary to adjust for the *seasonal component* before trends can be forecast. Fortunately, data from government sources are usually available both seasonally adjusted (SA) and not seasonally adjusted (NSA). Seasonal fluctuations are periodic components that take place over the course of the year and are due to weather, cultural, or other factors. For example, retail sales often peak in the fourth quarter due to holiday shopping; unemployment rises in the summer when school lets out; housing starts fall in the winter; etc. The monthly or quarterly forecaster needs to know whether high December retail sales are due to the seasonal component, or whether there has been an increase in sales beyond the normal seasonal fluctuation. Several methods can be used to isolate the seasonal component, the simplest of which is probably the *ratio to moving average* technique. This technique is illustrated below with hypothetical quarterly data representing the sales of an ice cream store. To simplify the calculations, only 12 data points were used in this example. For practical purposes, it is best to have at least ten years of data before calculating seasonals.

The first step is to take a moving average of the data that spans a year. For quarterly data, this is a four-period moving average; for monthly data a twelve-period moving average is necessary. Next, the ratio of the raw data to the moving average is formed. This is a preliminary seasonal index. Preliminary seasonal indices are computed for every data point then averaged to arrive at the unadjusted seasonal factors. These are calculated in column "MA(4)" below. Theoretically, the seasonal factors should sum to 4.000—giving each quarter an average weight of 1. Because they do not—and will not for any particular sample—we must calculate an adjustment factor by dividing 4.000 by the sum of the four unadjusted seasonal factors. This gives the adjusted seasonal factors shown in the bottom panel. Once the seasonal factors have been calculated, the raw data are divided by the seasonal factors to arrive at seasonally adjusted data in the last column of the

continued on page 256

top panel. For example, the NSA sales in first quarter 1985 were 100; on a seasonally adjusted basis, this is equivalent to $100/0.899 = 111.235$.

Seasonal Adjustment Calculations

Year: Q	Raw data	MA(4)	Raw data/MA(4)	Seasonally adjusted
1985:1	100	•	•	$100/.890 = 112.360$
1985:2	107	•	•	$107/.955 = 112.042$
1985:3	145	•	•	$145/1.240 = 116.936$
1985:4	98	112.5	0.871	$98/.917 = 106.870$
1986:1	110	115.0	0.957	$110/.890 = 123.596$
1986:2	124	119.25	1.040	$124/.955 = 129.843$
1986:3	158	122.50	1.290	$158/1.240 = 127.419$
1986:4	122	128.50	0.949	$122/.890 = 137.079$
1987:1	122	131.50	0.928	$131/.955 = 137.173$
1987:2	131	133.25	0.983	$188/1.240 = 151.613$
1987:3	188	140.75	1.336	$166/.917 = 181.025$
1987:4	166	151.75	1.094	

Unadjusted seasonal factors:

Q1: $(0.957 + 0.928)/2 =$ 0.943
Q2: $(1.040 + 0.983)/2 =$ 1.012
Q3: $(1.290 + 1.336)/2 =$ 1.313
Q4: $(0.871 + .949 + 1.094)/4 =$ 0.971
                                    ——
                                    4.239   Adjustment
                                               factor: $4.000/4.239 = 0.944$

Adjusted seasonals:

Q1: $(0.943)(0.944) = 0.890$
Q2: $1.012(0.944) = 0.955$
Q3: $1.313(0.944) = 1.240$
Q4: $0.971(0.944) = 0.917$
                     ——
                     4.002

Why do we bother to do all of this? We do it for two major reasons. First, without knowing the seasonal pattern of sales, you will not know whether the sales in any particular quarter are good or bad. For example, ice cream sales in the fourth quarter tend to drop below the third quarter, but how much? The seasonal factors tell us that they should fall to no less than $0.917/1.240 = 74\%$ of the third quarter; a greater decline is a cause for worry. A second reason to calculate the seasonal fluctuations is to eliminate them from the data series in order to concentrate on other components of the series. This is especially important when regression analysis is to be performed on the data. If the seasonal fluctuations are severe, trend forecasts may be incorrect because regression analysis tends to place too much weight on outliers.

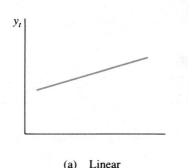

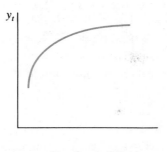

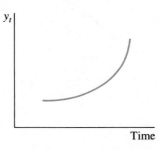

Time

(a) Linear   (b) Parabolic   (c) Exponential/Parabolic

FIGURE 9.2 Mathematical models

(a) The linear model is from the linear model $Y_t = a + bt$; $a, b, > 0$.
(b) A parabolic model, $Y_t = a + bt + ct^2$, b and c of different signs.
(c) Either an exponential function, $Y_t = \exp[a + b(t)]$, $b > 0$ or
a parabolic function, $Y_t = a + bt + ct^2$: $b, c > 0$.

The equations for these functional forms are:

Linear model: $y_t = a + bt + e_t.$

Exponential model: $y_t = \exp[a + b(t) + e_t] \Rightarrow \ln(y_t) = a + bt + e_t.$

Parabolic model: $y_t = a + bt + ct^2 + e_t.$

These three models are illustrated in Fig. 9.2. Unfortunately, none of the
functional forms shown in Fig. 9.2 captures the prominent inflation spikes that
appear in the late 1970s and early 1980s. While more complex mathematical
forms might be able to do this, most economists would argue that the dramatic
decline in inflation was due to a sudden shift in monetary policy. Policy shocks
are even more difficult to capture with time series models than with structural
models. Thus, the only simple way to fit the data is to divide them into two
segments: 1950–79 and 1980–87 is one reasonable division. The results are
presented below.

Estimation over 1950–79   The data from the five-period smoothed series
were used as the dependent variable and regressed against time in linear, parabolic, and exponential models. The summary statistics were:

Linear: $\hat{y}_t = -0.642 + 0.322t;$ $R^2 = 0.84,$ SER $= 1.18,$
                 $\bar{y}_t = 4.027.$

Exponential: $\widehat{\ln(y_t)} = -0.096 + 0.0841t;$ $R^2 = 0.82,$ SER $= 0.329,$
                 $\overline{\ln(y_t)} = 1.124.$

Parabolic: $\hat{y}_t = 1.887 - 0.184t + 0.017t^2;$ $R^2 = 0.97,$ $\bar{R}^2 = 0.96,$
    $\text{SER} = 0.548,$ $\bar{y}_t = 4.027.$

All coefficients were significant at the 95% level.

Estimation over 1980–1987   To save data, estimation was done with a three-period moving average. The summary statistics were:

Linear: $\hat{y}_t = 11.02 - 1.35t;$ $R^2 = 0.82,$ $\text{SER} = 1.48,$
    $\bar{y}_t = 5.61.$

Exponential: $\widehat{\ln(y_t)} = 2.51 + -0.23t;$ $R^2 = 0.91,$ $\text{SER} = 0.17,$
    $\overline{\ln(\bar{y}_t)} = 1.60.$

Parabolic: $\hat{y}_t = 15.21 - 4.15t + 0.35t^2;$ $R^2 = 0.99,$ $\bar{R}^2 = 0.98,$
    $\text{SER} = 0.43,$ $\bar{y}_t = 5.61.$

All coefficients were significant at the 95% level.

4. FORECASTING   The parabolic model appears to have the best fit over both time periods. Its standard error (SER) is the smallest fraction of the mean value of the dependent variable, and it also has the highest R^2 of the three models tested.[4] Figures 9.3(a) and (b) show the tight fit between the fitted parabolic equations and the smoothed data series.

Forecasting with simple time series models is accomplished just like any other regression model: Plug in the forecast value of the independent variable(s) and calculate the forecast estimate. When fitting the regression equations, time was input as consecutive numbers from 1 through 31 for the 1950–79 period, and 1 through 7 for the separate 1980–87 estimation. Thus, to construct a one-step forecast, we substitute 8 and 8^2 into the parabolic model to forecast CPI inflation. The calculations are:

$$\hat{y}_{t+1} = 15.21 - 4.147(8) + 0.35(64) = 4.43.$$

We have an immediate check on this forecast because we lost one observation in the smoothing process. Thus, the one-step forecast from the three-period

---

[4]We should be careful before attaching too much significance to the relative R^2's, however, because the dependent variable of the exponential model is different from the dependent variable of the two other models.

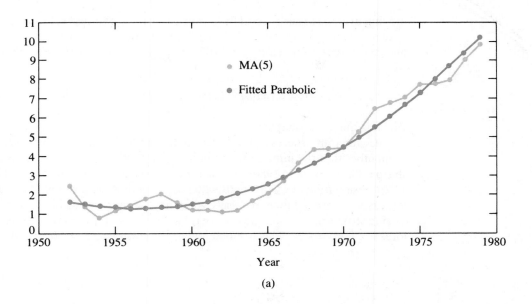

(a)

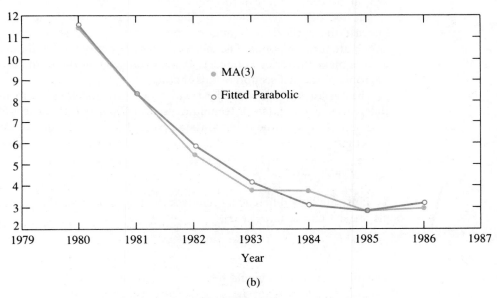

(b)

FIGURE 9.3   The fitted parabolic equation

(a) 1950–79 and (b) 1980–87.

moving average series is actually a forecast of the smoothed value of the last data point in the raw series. The last entry in the raw CPI series was 4.4, so the one-step forecast missed by just 0.03 percentage points. A two-step forecast would be:

$$\hat{y}_{t+2} = 15.21 - 4.147(9) + 0.35(81) = 6.24,$$

which is quite reasonable.

The apparent success of the parabolic model should not be oversold. Remember that the initial inspection of the data plot forced us to ignore the sharp inflation peak in 1980. Among other things, this meant that we had only seven observations to work with when constructing the forecast. Also, often forecasts are needed most precisely when time series analysis breaks down— during structural shifts. Note too what happens if we try to make a three-step forecast: $\hat{y}_{t+3} = 8.74$. This is much higher than what actually occurred.

9.1.2   Removing the Trend

We often need to remove the trend from the series ("detrend") in order to isolate the other components of the data. This allows the investigator to forecast the cyclical and random components of the series and perhaps anticipate turning points. The methods used for removing the trend are also used to make the series *stationary*, an important step in Box-Jenkins analysis, the topic of the last section of this chapter.

The easiest and often the best way to remove the trend is to take first differences of the data—a technique used in Chapter 6 to correct for auto-correlation. If x_t is the original data series, then y_t is the differenced series such that:

$$y_t = x_t - x_{t-1}. \tag{9.2}$$

To illustrate how differencing removes the trend, suppose that x_t has a simple linear trend of time, i.e.,

$$x_t = a + bt. \tag{9.3}$$

The differenced series would be:

$$y_t = x_t - x_{t-1} = (a + bt) - [a + b(t - 1)] = b. \tag{9.4}$$

Because b is a constant, y_t has no trend.

First differencing should be used as a first attempt to remove the trend, but other filters are sometimes appropriate. If the underlying model is parabolic, it may be necessary to employ second differences. To understand why second differencing is necessary with a parabolic series, consider the typical parabolic form, $x_t = a + bt + ct^2$, and take first differences:

$$
\begin{aligned}
y_t = x_t - x_{t-1} &= a + bt + ct^2 - [a + b(t-1) + c(t-1)^2] \\
&= a + bt + ct^2 - [a + bt - b + c(t^2 - 2t + 1)] \\
&= b - c + 2ct.
\end{aligned}
\tag{9.5}
$$

The presence of the t indicates a trend, but differencing once again will remove the trend:

$$
\begin{aligned}
z_t = y_t - y_{t-1} &= b - c + 2ct - [b - c + 2c(t-1)] \\
&= 2ct - 2ct - 2c = -2c,
\end{aligned}
\tag{9.6}
$$

which is a constant. If second differencing does not remove the trend, taking logs often works—especially if the underlying model is exponential. (Exercise 9.3 illustrates trend removal for an exponential series.) Figure 9.4 illustrates how first differencing removes the trend.

FIGURE 9.4   Trend removal

The trend can usually be removed from data by first differencing as this figure illustrates. Notice that the unemployment rate (U) shows an upward trend over the 1950–87 period. When the data are first differenced, $DU = U_t - U_{t-1}$, the trend is removed as indicated by the zero slope of the transformed series. The data are in Data Set 13 of Appendix I.

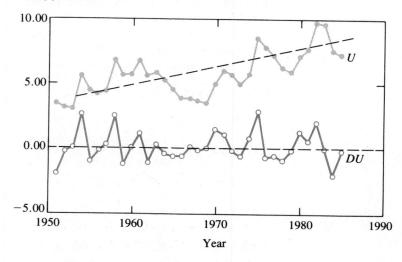

9.2

MA, AR, AND ARMA MODELS

Modern time series analysis has gone beyond the techniques mentioned in the previous section. The basic approach is still to plot the data, smooth it, and then try to fit it to a mathematical form. However, it has been shown analytically that almost all economic time series fit into one of three classes of models: moving average (MA), autoregressive (AR), or mixed autoregressive–moving average (ARMA). Thus, modern time series analysis is primarily a set of techniques for fitting series to one of these three forms. The most popular technique for doing this, *Box-Jenkins analysis*, is the topic of Sec. 9.3.

9.2.1 Moving Average Models

Suppose you wanted to forecast the interest rate, specifically, the rate on three-month treasury bills. We could do this with a structural model, but construction of such a model could be quite difficult. Because both real and financial factors affect interest rates, the model will probably be multiequation. It would also have to incorporate proxies for expected inflation, policy changes, etc. A simpler and perhaps just as successful model for forecasting the TBILL rate would be a time series model, perhaps a moving average model.[5]

Month-to-month changes in interest rates are often erratic, but next month's interest rate is constrained at least somewhat by the rate that prevails this month. In fact, the interest rate next month often simply appears to be this month's rate plus *white noise*, the term used in time series analysis to refer to a well-behaved random error term. (Remember, a well-behaved error term obeys Assumptions 3, 4, and 5 from Chapter 3.) If this is correct, a reasonable model to capture the behavior of interest rates might be:

$$x_{t+1} = x_t + \varepsilon_{t+1}, \qquad t = 1, 2, \ldots, T, \qquad [9.7]$$

where

x_t = interest rate that prevails this month
x_{t+1} = the interest rate next month
ε_{t+1} = white noise random error.

---

[5] We have a terminology problem here. An MA model is not quite the same thing as a moving average filter. MA models may better be called "weighted sums," but we will use the standard practice and call them moving average models.

If we subtract x_t from each side of Eq. [9.7], we have:

$$x_{t+1} - x_t = \varepsilon_{t+1}.$$ [9.8]

Now let us define y_{t+1} to be a one-period change in x_t, or:

$$y_{t+1} \equiv x_{t+1} - x_t = \varepsilon_{t+1}.$$ [9.9]

Because $E(\varepsilon_t) = 0$, it follows that $E(y_{t+1}) = 0$. That is, the best one-period forecast of the change in x_t, given no other information, is zero.

What if the effect of the random shock is not felt completely in one period? That is, suppose that the shock takes two periods to work itself out:

$$x_{t+2} = x_{t+1} + \varepsilon_{t+2} + \beta\varepsilon_{t+1},$$ [9.10]

where β reflects the effect of the random shock in the next period.

Letting y_{t+2} be the change in x_t between periods x_{t+2} and x_{t+1}, we have:

$$y_{t+2} = x_{t+2} - x_{t+1} = \varepsilon_{t+2} + \beta\varepsilon_{t+1},$$ [9.11]

which is called a *one-period moving average model*, MA(1), because the effect of the random shock lasts for one period into the future. By extension, if the effect of the shock lasts q periods, we would have an MA(q) model:

$$y_t = \varepsilon_t + \beta_1\varepsilon_{t-1} + \beta_2\varepsilon_{t-2} + \cdots + \beta_q\varepsilon_{t-q}.$$ [9.12]

The order of the model depends on how long the shock exerts influence on the y_t. An MA model is of order q if $\rho(y_t, y_{t-j}) = 0$, $j > q$. As shown in Appendix 9.A, the correlation between y_t and y_{t-j} is a function of β. For an MA(1) model it is:

$$\rho_{t,t-1} = \frac{\beta}{1 + \beta^2}.$$ [9.13]

The analogous expression for an MA(q) model is too complex to detain us and much too cumbersome to do by hand. For practical purposes, it would have to be estimated by the computer.[6]

After the β_j have been estimated ($\hat{\beta}_j = b_j$), we must then estimate the ε_t before the model can be used for forecasting. In structural models, errors are usually estimated directly from the regression residuals, but in MA models, more roundabout methods must be used. One method is to use an iterative technique. Letting $f_{T,1}$ represent a one-step forecast from the last observation in the data series (T), a one-step forecast for the MA(1) model is:

$$f_{T,1} = e_{T+1} + be_T.$$ [9.14]

---

[6]The interested student can find the expression in George E. P. Box and Gwilym M. Jenkins, *Time Series Analysis: Forecasting and Control*, revised ed. (San Francisco: Holden-Day, 1976), p. 68.

Because e_{T+1} cannot be observed, it is estimated as $E(e_{T+1}) = 0$. Equation [9.14] thus becomes:

$$f_{T,1} = be_T. \qquad [9.15]$$

Unfortunately, e_T cannot be observed either, so Eq. [9.15] is of little use by itself. However, consider the forecast errors associated with the model:

$$e_t = y_t - f_{t-1,1}. \qquad [9.16]$$

We know the y_t and could use Eq. [9.15] to find all of the one-step forecasts, $f_{t-1,1}$. However, a "startup problem" remains. What is the error on the forecast of the first observation on y_t? The recommended solution is to set it to zero, which is reasonable given that $E(e_t) = 0$. Some computer programs use a similar technique for estimating MA errors, but this method is not practical by hand.[7]

Another method of estimating the errors in an MA(1) model is to use the following equation:

$$e_t = y_t - by_{t-1} + b^2 y_{t-2} - b^3 y_{t-3} + \cdots + (-b)^k y_{t-k} + \cdots. \qquad [9.17]$$

As shown in Appendix 9.A, Eq. [9.17] is equivalent to Eq. [9.12]. To use this method, first use Eq. [9.13] to estimate β, then substitute known past values of y_t. This is the method we will use to estimate an interest rate series shortly.

9.2.2   Autoregressive Models

The moving average process developed above seems reasonable enough, but it is by no means the only way to represent the influence of past interest rates on their future. Consider Eq. [9.18]:

$$x_t = \alpha x_{t-1} + \varepsilon_t \qquad -1 < \alpha < +1. \qquad [9.18]$$

This is a *first-order difference equation* that tells us the current interest rate is a linear function of last month's interest rate plus a random error. The term αx_{t-1} suggests the influence of inertia while ε_t represents random shocks or "innovations" that impart fluctuations to the series. Notice that we have put stability constraints on α, $-1 < \alpha < +1$. If $|\alpha| > 1$, interest rates would increase or decrease without limit and cause the model to "explode." The

[7]An example of this method can be found in C. W. J. Granger, *Forecasting in Business and Economics*, revised ed., (New York: Academic Press, 1989), p. 50.

requirement that $|\alpha| < 1$ ensures us that the influence of past values diminishes over time. Models that have this structure are called *autoregressive models*.

The coefficient α represents the correlation between current and past values.[8] However, because x_t and x_{t-1} are correlated, so are x_{t-1} and x_{t-2}, x_{t-2} and x_{t-3}, x_{t-1} and x_{t-3}, etc. Thus, a more complete representation of Eq. [9.18] is:

$$x_t = \alpha_1 x_{t-1} + \alpha_2 x_{t-2} + \alpha_3 x_{t-3} + \cdots + \alpha_p x_{t-p} + \varepsilon_t. \qquad [9.19]$$

As shown in Appendix 9.A, the correlation between the individual terms in the series is given by:

$$\rho(x_t, x_{t-k}) = \alpha^k \ \forall \ k. \qquad [9.20]$$

The order of an autoregressive process is determined by analyzing the correlation coefficient between terms, which can be done by analysis of the partial autocorrelation function, a concept we introduce in the next section.

Once the α^k have been estimated ($\hat{\alpha}^k = a^k$), forecasts can be made iteratively. If the model is determined to be AR(1), a one-step forecast would be:

$$f_{T,1} = ax_T + \varepsilon_{T+1}. \qquad [9.21]$$

Because we assume that $E(\varepsilon_{T+1}) = 0$, this becomes:

$$f_{T,1} = ax_T. \qquad [9.22]$$

Likewise, a two-step forecast would be:

$$f_{T,2} = ax_{T+1} + \varepsilon_{T+2} = ax_{T+1}. \qquad [9.23]$$

We can substitute $f_{T,1}$ for x_{T+1} and let $E(\varepsilon_{T+2})$ be zero. Substituting Eq. [9.22] into [9.23] gives an equivalent two-step forecast:

$$f_{T,2} = a(ax_T) = a^2 x_T. \qquad [9.24]$$

9.2.3 Mixed Models: ARMA

How do we pick between moving average and autoregressive models? We often don't have to choose. Suppose that the TBILL series x_t can be represented as an AR(p) process with an MA(q) error:

$$x_t = \alpha_1 x_{t-1} + \alpha_2 x_{t-2} + \cdots + \alpha_p x_{t-p} + y_t, \qquad [9.25]$$

---

[8] We make this statement without proof. However, recall the equation of a first-order autoregressive error—$\varepsilon_t = \rho \varepsilon_{t-1} + v_t$—and note that ρ was a correlation coefficient.

where y_t is defined as:

$$y_t = \varepsilon_t + \beta_1 \varepsilon_{t-1} + \beta_2 \varepsilon_{t-2} + \cdots + \beta_q \varepsilon_{t-q}. \qquad [9.26]$$

This is an autoregressive–moving average process of order (p, q) and is denoted ARMA(p, q). ARMA processes may seem complex, and their statistical properties are quite complicated, but they are extremely important in real-world time series analysis. Further, almost all *stationary* economic time series can be represented with very low order ARMA processes. A series is stationary if the covariance between terms depends only on the time interval between the terms, not on time itself. That is, stationarity requires that the covariance between, say, x_{1960} and x_{1964} be equal to the covariance between, say, x_{1980} and x_{1984}. In fact, very few time series found in economics are stationary; however, nonstationary series can usually be made stationary by first or second differencing.

As an example, suppose that a time series is stationary and estimated to be the ARMA(1, 1) process:

$$x_t = 0.6 x_{t-1} + \varepsilon_t + 0.2 \varepsilon_{t-1}.$$

Forecasting can be carried out as is done for any time series model. A one-step forecast would be

$$f_{T,1} = 0.6 x_T + 0.2 e_T,$$

while the two-step forecast would be

$$f_{T,2} = 0.6 x_{T+1},$$

because $E(e_{T+1}) = 0$.

We still do not know how to pick between models, much less determine the order of the selected model. The technique for doing so is the subject to which we now turn.

9.3

BOX-JENKINS ANALYSIS

The most popular method of time series forecasting, Box-Jenkins analysis, involves three steps: identification, estimation, and diagnostic checking. However, before taking these steps, the series must be checked for stationarity. To illustrate Box-Jenkins analysis, we will attempt to forecast the monthly 90-day treasury bill rate. Monthly data for the period 1980:10 through 1988:2 are plotted on Fig. 9.5 and shown in Data Set 14 of Appendix I.

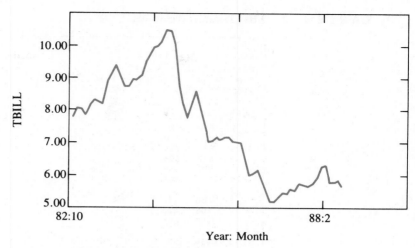

FIGURE 9.5   TBILL, 1982: 10–1988: 2

9.3.1 Stationarity

The TBILL series exhibits what appears to be a generally downward trend, but the data are too erratic to allow forecasting with simple linear extrapolation. Estimation may be possible with Box-Jenkins analysis but only if the series is stationary. As mentioned above, a series is stationary if the covariance between terms depends only on the time interval between the terms, not on time itself. Stationarity can be checked by looking at the *correlogram*. The correlogram will also be used later to identify the structure of the model.

THE CORRELOGRAM   The correlogram or *autocorrelation function* (ACF) is a plot of the autocorrelations between the data points in the series. The first entry in the correlogram is the correlation between x_t and x_{t-1}; the second term is the correlation between x_t and x_{t-2}, etc. If the correlogram declines very slowly, terms in the series are correlated several periods in the past. This in an indication that the series is nonstationary and that it must be transformed. If the correlogram appears random, or if the correlations clearly "cut off" at some point, the series is probably stationary. Table 9.2 presents the autocorrelations for monthly TBILL data. Note the very high correlation between x_t and x_{t-1} (0.968), between x_t and x_{t-2} (0.920); later correlations are almost as high. This is an indication that the raw TBILL series is nonstationary. As a general rule, economic data presented in "levels" form as opposed to percentage change, logs, or differences is nonstationary.

Usually, a series can be made stationary by first or second differencing. A plot of the differenced data is shown in Fig. 9.6. No discernible trend is evident,

TABLE 9.2   **TBILL autocorrelations**

```
Plot of     TBILL
Number of cases =    65
Mean of series =        7.46
Standard deviation of series =        1.53

Lag  Corr   SE -1.0  -.8  -.6  -.4  -.2  .0  .2  .4  .6  .8  1.0
                     |----|----|----|----|----|----|----|----|----|
  1  .968  .124                         (    |•••••)••••••••••••••••
  2  .920  .210                     (        |••••••••)•••••••••••••
  3  .873  .265                  (           |•••••••••)•••••••••
  4  .833  .306               (              |••••••••••)•••••
  5  .802  .339              (               |•••••••••••••)•••
  6  .762  .367            (                 |•••••••••••••••)•
  7  .713  .391           (                  |••••••••••••••• )
  8  .660  .410         (                    |••••••••••••••   )
  9  .608  .426        (                     |•••••••••••••    )
 10  .557  .440       (                      |•••••••••••      )
 11  .506  .450      (                       |••••••••••       )
 12  .454  .459      (                       |•••••••••        )
```

a requirement for stationarity. Further evidence that the differenced TBILL series is stationary is provided in Table 9.3, which presents the autocorrelations of the differenced TBILL series.[9] As required, there appears to be a significant "cutoff." In this case, the cutoff occurs after the first lag when the autocorrelation falls from a strong 0.414 to an insignificant −0.055.

9.3.2 Identification

The ACF is also used in the identification stage of Box-Jenkins analysis.[10] Three rules help in the identification stage, but, in practice, identifying model structure is something of a trial-and-error process, so these rules should be considered only as rough guides. The three rules for identification are:

RULE 1:

If the correlogram "cuts off" at some point, $k = q$, the underlying model is probably MA(q).

----

[9]The "SE" columns in Tables 9.2, 9.3, and 9.4 represent the standard errors of the estimated autocorrelation coefficients. Some analysts form a t-ratio by dividing $\hat{\rho}$ by the SE to determine which lags are significant. However, the criteria for the rejection region are quite arbitrary. For a discussion of such t-tests, see Bruce L. Bowerman and Richard T. O'Connell, *Time Series Forecasting*, 2nd ed. (Boston: Duxbury Press, 1987), p. 35–37.
[10]Note that the term "identification" is used differently here than in the discussion of 2SLS in Chapter 8.

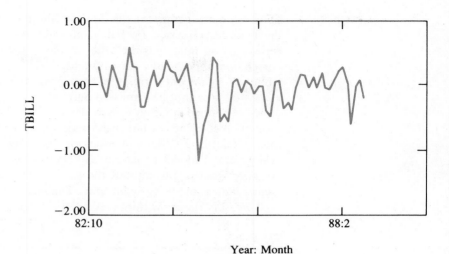

FIGURE 9.6   Differenced TBILL data

T A B L E   9 . 3   Differenced TBILL autocorrelations

```
Plot of     DiffTBILL
Number of cases =    64
Mean of series =        -0.03
Standard deviation of series =        0.32

Plot of Autocorrelations

Lag   Corr   SE -1.0  -.8  -.6  -.4  -.2  .0   .2   .4   .6   .8  1.0
                    |----|----|----|----|----|----|----|----|----|----|
  1   .414  .125                         (    |●●●●●)●●●●
  2  -.055  .145                         (   ●|     )
  3  -.185  .145                         ( ●●●●|     )
  4  -.047  .149                         (   ●|     )
  5   .152  .149                         (    |●●●  )
  6   .130  .151                         (    |●●●  )
  7   .006  .153                         (    |     )
  8  -.083  .153                         (  ●●|     )
  9  -.032  .154                         (    |     )
 10  -.023  .154                         (    |     )
 11  -.051  .154                         (   ●|     )
 12  -.035  .154                         (    |     )
```

To understand why this is true, recall that an MA(q) model is defined such that corr(x_t, x_{t-j}) = 0, $j > q$. In other words, the order of the model depends on how many periods the correlation lasts between terms. Recall from Eq. [9.13] that an MA(1) model is defined such that the correlation between x_t and x_{t-1} is given by:

$$\rho = \frac{b}{1 + b^2} \qquad \rho_k = 0, \, k = 2, 3, 4, \ldots.$$

Does the correlogram for the differenced data cut off clearly enough to indicate an MA(1) series? Probably, but this is far from clear. In fact, where the series cuts off (and thus the order of the series) is rarely obvious. A strong correlation appears to exist between x_t and x_{t-1} ($r_1 = 0.414$), but the possibility of significant correlation coefficients at later periods ($r_3 = -0.18$ and $r_5 = +0.15$) cannot be dismissed outright.

As mentioned in footnote 9, we can use a t-test to check the significance of individual correlations but the criteria for acceptance and rejection regions are quite arbitrary. Many investigators use rules of thumb and examine several potential model structures. In this case, the coefficient on the first lag is approximately three times the size of its standard error (0.414/0.125), a clear indication of its significance. The second lag is probably insignificant ($-0.055/0.145$) but the third ($-0.185/0.145$) may be significant.

RULE 2:

> If the correlogram does not cut off, the model is probably not MA(q) and the partial correlogram should be examined. If the partial correlogram cuts off at $k = p$, the underlying model is probably AR(p).

The partial correlogram or *partial autocorrelation function* (PACF), is a plot of the autocorrelations between x_t and x_{t-k} with the correlations between intervening correlations omitted. That is, the partial autocorrelation coefficient at lag three measures the extra or "partial" correlation accounted for by the third lag in a model explaining x_t, which already includes autocorrelation terms at lags one and two. If the partial correlation between x_t and x_{t-2} is significant while the partial correlation between x_t and x_{t-3} is not, the series is probably an AR(2) process.[11]

Because some of the values in the ACF for the differenced TBILL data were suspect, the partial correlogram was also estimated, and is shown in Table 9.4. The high partial correlation between x_t and x_{t-1} (0.414) indicates that the process is at least AR(1); however, the -0.273 correlation between x_t and x_{t-2} suggests that the process may be AR(2). Both terms also have t-scores greater than two.

RULE 3:

> If neither the correlogram nor the partial correlogram cuts off, the underlying model is probably an ARMA(p, q) process.

---

[11] We can also determine the order of an AR process by looking at the significance of the regression coefficients in the lagged model of Eq. [9.19]. If a_2 is statistically significant but a_3 is not, the model is probably AR(2). However, unless the sample size is very large, multicollinearity will make interpretation of these ratios difficult.

TABLE 9.4   **Partial autocorrelations, DiffTBILL**

```
Plot of     DiffTBILL
Number of cases =    64
Mean of series =        -0.03
Standard deviation of series =       0.32

Plot of Partial Autocorrelations

Lag   Corr   SE  -1.0  -.8  -.6  -.4  -.2  .0  .2  .4  .6  .8  1.0
                  |----|----|----|----|----|----|----|----|----|----|
  1   .414  .125                          (      |●●●●●)●●●●
  2  -.273  .125                          (●●●●●|      )
  3  -.056  .125                          (     ●|      )
  4   .074  .125                          (      |●      )
  5   .130  .125                          (      |●●●    )
  6  -.029  .125                          (      |       )
  7  -.015  .125                          (      |       )
  8  -.024  .125                          (      |       )
  9   .041  .125                          (      |●      )
 10  -.085  .125                          (    ●●|      )
 11  -.053  .125                          (     ●|      )
 12   .018  .125                          (      |       )
```

By convention, if it was first necessary to difference the data *d* times to render it stationary, the model is said to be an *integrated mixed autoregressive–moving average* or ARIMA(*p*, *d*, *q*) process for short. The ACF and PACF give us little reason to suspect that the TBILL series is an ARIMA process, but we will check that possibility during the diagnostic step.

While these three rules seem to make the identification process a rather mechanical procedure, we need to emphasize again that this is really not the case at all. In fact, it can be shown that an AR(1) process can always be represented as an MA(∞) process, and that an MA(1) process can be expressed as an equivalent AR(∞) process.[12] Further, if the observed series is measured with error, the identification process becomes even more muddled. For practical purposes, however, the only goal in time series forecasting is to find a model that forecasts well. Most investigators feel that it is important to examine several potential models in the identification stage, but practicality requires that the search be limited to models of relatively low order.

Fortunately, most economic time series can be estimated as low-order systems—rarely is the system more complex than ARIMA(2, 2, 2)—and it is considered sound econometric methodology to look for a low-order model. Box and Jenkins called the practice of searching for low-order

---

[12]For proofs of these statements, see C. W. J. Granger and Paul Newbold, *Forecasting Economic Time Series*, 2nd ed. (New York, Academic Press, 1986), p. 15–28.

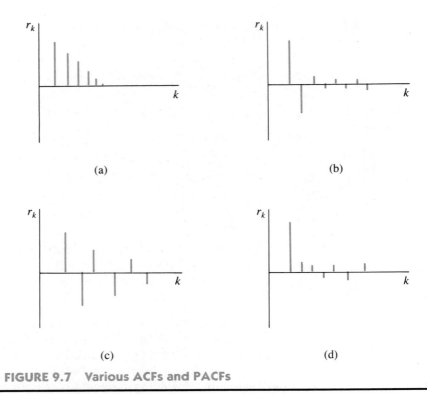

FIGURE 9.7   Various ACFs and PACFs

Inspection of the ACF and PACF is the crucial step in the identification stage of Box-Jenkins analysis. If the ACF appears as in (a) the series is nonstationary and differencing is necessary. Figure (b) suggests that the series is an MA(2) process because the ACF "cuts off" after the second lag, while (c) is typical of an AR process: The ACF declines slowly, and there are both positive and negative correlations. Figure (c) indicates that the PACF must be examined. Figure (d), a PACF, indicates that the series is probably an AR(1) process because it "cuts off" after the first lag. If the PACF declines slowly or does not have a clear pattern, the series is probably ARIMA.

models *parsimonious parameterization*. Note too that there is often very little difference between forecasts made with alternative models.[13] Figure 9.7 presents typical ACFs and PACFs used in the identification process.

❖ ❖ ❖

---

[13] In the present case, for example, the difference in one-step forecasts for the (0, 1, 1), (1, 1, 0), (2, 1, 0), and (2, 1, 1) models was less than 0.1 percentage points of interest. This is illustrated in Appendix 9.B.

9.3.3 Estimation

Our tentative conclusion is that the differenced TBILL series is either an MA(1) or an AR process of either the first or second order. Estimation is accomplished by working backward from the ACF and PACF. For the MA(1) model, take the general form of an estimated MA(1) process,

$$y_t = e_t + be_{t-1},$$ [9.27]

and note that b can be found from the formula for the estimated correlation between y_t and y_{t-1}:

$$r_1 = \frac{b}{1 + b^2}.$$ [9.28]

The first entry in Table 9.3 (0.414) is r_1 and can be used to solve for b by substituting into the quadratic formula:

$$b = \frac{-1 \pm \sqrt{1 - 4r^2}}{2r}.$$ [9.29]

Because there are two solutions to quadratic equations,[14] we are left to choose between two equations:

$$y_t = e_t - 0.53e_{t-1},$$

$$y_t = e_t - 1.88e_{t-1}.$$

Only the first equation is acceptable because the second would imply that past errors had more affect on current values than current errors.[15] The forecast equation to be tested in the diagnostic stage is:

$$y_{t+1} = e_{t+1} - 0.53e_t = -0.53e_t.$$

Once the e_t are estimated, forecasting is possible with the MA(1) model.

A similar technique is used to fit the AR models. Values from the partial correlogram are used directly as estimates of the a_i in AR models. The generic AR(2) model is:

$$x_t = a_1 x_{t-1} + a_2 x_{t-2} + e_t,$$

where a_1 and a_2 are the partial correlation coefficients between x_t and x_{t-1} and x_t and x_{t-2}, respectively. Taking these estimates from the partial correlogram gives our AR(2) equation as:

$$x_t = 0.41x_{t-1} - 0.27x_{t-2} + e_t,$$

[14] Note that $r = \hat{\rho} \le 0.5$ is necessary for real valued b.
[15] Technically speaking, only the first equation is said to be *invertible*.

while the corresponding forecast equation is:

$$x_{t+1} = 0.41x_t - 0.27x_{t-1},$$

because $E(e_t) = 0$.

Inspection of the correlograms leads us to doubt whether the series is ARMA,[16] but it would be a good idea to check whether it is ARMA(2, 1). If so, the fitted model would be

$$x_t = 0.42x_{t-1} - 0.27x_{t-2} + e_t - 0.53e_{t-1},$$

while the ARMA forecasting equation would be

$$x_{t+1} = 0.42x_t - 0.27x_{t-1} - 0.53e_t.$$

In practice, we rarely go through these computations because serious time series analysis will normally be done with a computer package that fits ARIMA models. However, some programs are only capable of computing the ACF and PACF, so it is necessary to calculate the coefficients by hand. Finally, we should note that the computer routines commonly used to estimate ARIMA models involve nonlinear techniques and will typically result in coefficients that differ somewhat from those that would be calculated by hand. This is especially true when the number of observations is small, say, less than 100, the number often considered the minimum for serious ARIMA modeling.

9.3.4 Diagnostic Checking

The validity of estimated models can be checked in several ways. The ideal way would be to find a later set of data and see how well the estimated model fits the new data. For example, the data used to estimate our TBILL model was from 1982:10 to 1988:2. The model that most closely forecasts actual interest rates for the rest of 1988 would be the preferred model. However, we rarely have the luxury of so much data that we can omit some of it in the estimation stage, so diagnostic checking is usually done with the same data that are used in the estimation process. The most common method is to estimate fitted values for the models and see which model tracks most closely with the actual data. For this example, fitted values for the last 20 observations were estimated with the MA(1), AR(2), and ARMA(2, 1) models.[17] The results are shown in Fig. 9.8.

---

[16] Actually, because the series was first differenced to make it stationary, we are trying to fit an ARIMA(2, 1, 1) process to the raw TBILL data. This is the same thing as fitting an ARMA(2, 1) process to the differenced data.

[17] The errors of the MA(1) model were estimated as: $e_t = y_t - 0.53y_{t-1} + 0.28y_{t-2} - 0.15y_{t-3} + 0.08y_{t-4}$. The AR(2) model was estimated as $x_t = 0.41x_{t-1} - 0.27x_{t-1} + e_t$.

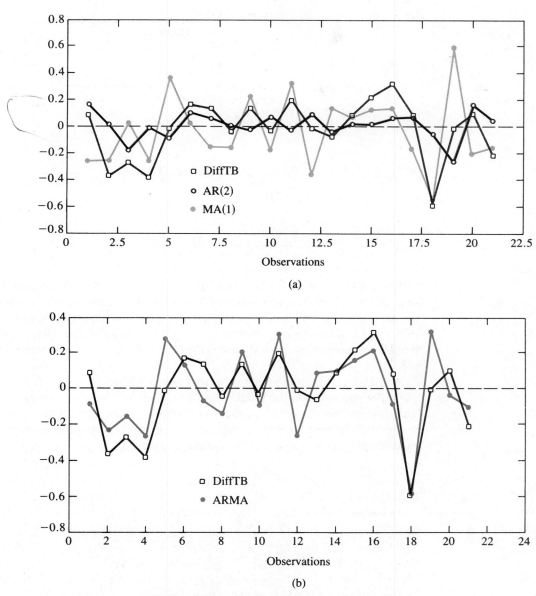

(a)

(b)

FIGURE 9.8   Estimation of fitted values

(a) MA(1) and AR(2) versus DiffTB and (b) ARMA versus DiffTB.

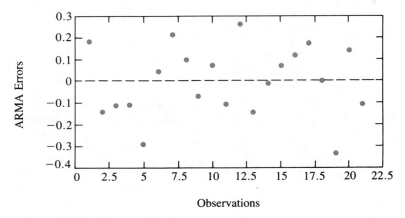

FIGURE 9.9   Random forecast errors

The ARMA model seems to fit the data most closely, but all three of the models track DiffTB quite well. When there is little difference between alternative models, it is best to practice the principle of parsimony and select the simplest model. In this case, most analysts would select the AR(2) model because autoregressive models are typically easier to work with than MA models.

A further check on model fit is to determine whether the forecast errors— the difference between the fitted values and the actual values—are random. This is done for the ARMA model in Figure 9.9. The apparently random distribution of the errors is an indication of a good fit. A statistical test for randomness, the *Q-statistic*, is discussed in Appendix 9B.

9.3.5   Forecasting

The ultimate test of a time series model, of course, is its forecasting accuracy. The actual value for DiffTB one period in the future was zero because the three-month TBILL rate did not change between February and March of 1988. The AR(2) model generated a one-step forecast that was slightly more accurate than the ARMA model. Over a longer period, the ARMA model might be slightly superior given that it seems to fit past data a bit more closely, but this is a matter of conjecture. Exercise 9.5 involves comparison of the forecast errors between the three models. Appendix 9.2B compares forecasts from different models estimated with the ARIMA module of Minitab™.

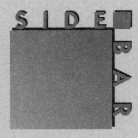

VECTOR AUTOREGRESSION

ONE OF the most widely used forecasting techniques in contemporary macroeconomics is *vector autoregression.* Vector autoregression (VAR) is a method used to estimate systems of time series equations. As with other types of time series analysis, it is atheoretical. In fact, this was the chief attribute that first attracted the attention of Robert Lucas, Thomas Sargent, Christopher Sims, and other macroeconomists. In addition to macroeconomics, VAR models are used in many areas of forecasting including regional models and policy stimulations. This sidebar discusses some of the philosophical issues that led to VAR models and presents a very simple illustration.

Structural Models and the Identification Problem   Recall from Chapter 8 that systems of simultaneous equations are identified by the presence of exogenous or predetermined variables that appear in some equations but not in others. For example, the system:

$$q^s = a_0 + a_1 p + a_2 w + e,$$
$$q^d = b_0 + b_1 p + b_2 y + u, \tag{1'}$$

is identified because the variables w and y are in one equation but not the other.

In the simple supply and demand system described in equation system [1'], identification is straightforward. However, identification is not nearly as easy in large macroeconometric models. In these models, which typically contain *hundreds* of variables and equations, it may not be possible to find enough variables that are truly exogenous. A few variables can correctly be considered exogenous—weather, war, and population growth are obvious examples—but most economic variables are endogenous to large equation systems. For example, policy variables are often treated as being exogenous, but if policy authorities enact changes in response to macroeconomic conditions, even policy is endogenous. In fact, if the aphorism "everything depends on everything else" is true, it may be impossible to find *any* truly exogenous variables in large macroeconomic models.

Other questions have been raised with structural models, including even single-equation models. For example, standard practice would include a lagged endogenous variable on the right side of the equation in order to improve the fit, even though there is rarely theoretical justification for doing so. The treatment of expectations is particularly ad hoc. Because expectations cannot be observed, many investigators include a term that weights lagged values of the current variable— something like $\sum w_j p_{t-j}$—even though no economic rationale exists to explain why such a variable should reflect inflationary expectations. Methodologists argue that such ad hoc specifications amount to little more than "data mining."

Identification problems and ad hoc constructions forced many econometricians to begin to question the value of structural models— something that would have been more difficult to do if these models had more successful forecasting records than they did. The *Lucas critique*, named after Robert Lucas, may have captured the problem with structural models most succinctly: Structural models cannot be used for successful forecasting because of shifting parameters. Once a forecast is made, economic agents will change their behavior if they believe the forecast to be reputable. This change in behavior shifts the parameters—the propensity to consume, inflationary expectations, etc.—that were used in the structural model and render the forecast obsolete. If the Lucas critique is correct, all economic variables are potentially endogenous, and econometric identification is theoretically impossible.

A Simple VAR Model   One result of these debates was the development of vector autoregression.[18] VAR models do not even attempt to capture the underlying structure of the economy, and no distinction between endogenous and exogenous variables is made.

---

[18] Another result was the rise of a radically new school of macroeconomics, the new classical school. See Christopher Sims, "Macroeconomics and Reality," *Econometrica*, Vol. 48, No. 1, January 1980, p. 1–48, for a technical discussion of the econometric implications of the new classical approach. A more accessible discussion is found in Robert E. Lucas and Thomas J. Sargent, "After Keynesian Economics," *Quarterly Review*, Federal Reserve Bank of Minnesota, Summer 1979, p. 1–7.

S I D E

■ B A R

Webb (1984) provided the following as an illustration of a simple VAR model for forecasting the commercial paper rate (R) and percentage change in the monetary base (M):

$$R = b_1 M_{t-1} + c_1 R_{t-1} + e_1,$$

$$M = b_2 M_{t-1} + c_2 R_{t-1} + e_2. \qquad [2']$$

The key attribute of the system in [2'] is that the variables are treated symmetrically; both variables appear on both sides of the equation.

Real VAR models have longer lags and more variables; the actual model Webb tested included five variables: capacity utilization (C), the GNP deflator (P), and real GNP (X) in addition to R and M. However, VAR models generally have fewer variables and less stringent data requirements than structural models, which makes them especially useful where there are likely data problems—simulation studies and regional models are but two examples.

VAR advocates contend that their models are atheoretical, but a certain amount of economic theory must go into the initial selection of variables. Decisions also need to be made as to the length of lag, the proper filtering techniques, etc. Still, the consensus view is that VAR models are potentially much simpler than structural models. Unfortunately, the computational demands of estimating VAR models are extensive and only a few computer packages are currently capable of estimating VAR systems.

The Accuracy of VAR Forecasts   If VAR models have less demanding data requirements and are simpler to develop than structural models, the only question is whether VAR forecasts are as good as those derived from other models. Several investigators have looked at this issue. Webb compared forecasts made with his five-equation VAR model to forecasts made by a major consulting service and a survey of professional forecasters. He could not conclude that VAR forecasts were superior, but he noted that a more sophisticated VAR model— something other than a model developed to describe the technique— might improve the results. Other investigators have reached similar conclusions. The VAR regional forecasting model developed by Kinal and Ratner (1986) was found to be slightly inferior to an ARIMA model, but a modified VAR model was superior. How was the model modified? By specifying some variables as "driving" variables and others as "responding" variables. What are "driving" and "responding" variables? You guessed it: exogenous and endogenous variables.

THE PHILOSOPHY OF TIME SERIES FORECASTING

If you are beginning to think that time series analysis is rather ad hoc, you're probably right. Because there is little economic theory behind the analysis, the goal is *to find a forecasting technique that works*. Our discussion may have made time series analysis seem more chaotic than it really is because we have tried to condense what should be an entire course into a single chapter. We have said nothing about Box-Jenkins forecasts of seasonal data, multiple equation time series models, or transfer function models—time series models that combine regression analysis with ARIMA modeling.

Modern time series analysts are forever trying new lag structures and new filtering techniques to improve their forecasts, and no one has ever accused them of being afraid to dirty their hands with data. Though it has a long history, time series analysis is still experiencing significant advances, as the preceding Vector Autoregression sidebar illustrates. Still, time series analysis will always have a glaring weakness: Even complicated models can do nothing more than capture the inertia of the data series under investigation. In the event of a policy change or exogenous shock, time series models will fail miserably. This is a telling criticism given that such a long data series is necessary to generate accurate ARMA estimates.

CONCEPTS FOR REVIEW

The goal of time series analysis is to generate accurate forecasts by fitting data to functional forms. In classical analysis, this is accomplished by smoothing the data and trying to fit it to a mathematical model. With Box-Jenkins analysis, a set of rules is used to fit the series as an MA, AR, or ARMA process, but model identification is rarely definitive. To guide your study, you should:

- know the steps to classical time series analysis: plot data, smooth, fit to mathematical models
- be able to illustrate various mathematical forms used in classical trend fitting
- define and distinguish between MA and AR processes
- know the steps to Box-Jenkins analysis: identification, estimation, diagnostic checking
- be able to interpret the correlogram and partial correlogram
- be able to define and use the following terms in context.

KEY TERMS

ARIMA	identification
ARMA	moving average
correlogram, ACF	partial correlogram, PACF
diagnostic checking	seasonal adjustment
difference equation	stationary
filter, smoothing	VAR
forecast error	white noise

EXERCISES

9.1 A common filter is the *exponential weighted average* defined as:

$$y_t = \alpha x_t + (1 - \alpha)x_{t-1}; 0 < \alpha < 1.$$

a. Smooth the last nine observations in Table 9.1 assuming $\alpha = 0.5$ and $\alpha = 0.9$. Which value makes the series smoother?

b. Show that y_t is a function of x_{t-2}.

c. Why might this filter be preferred to the moving average?

9.2 Given the time series:

t	1	2	3	4	5	6	7	8	9	10
x_t	-6	2	1	4	5	3	6	7	7	9

a. Plot the data above.

b. Use a three-period moving average to smooth the series. Plot it.

c. Smooth the series using the filter $z_t = 0.6y_{t-1} + 0.4x_t$, where $y_t = x_t - x_{t-1}$. What is the logic behind this filter?

d. Fit a straight line to both of the smoothed series.

9.3 Suppose you have reason to believe that production defects follow an AR(1) process of the form $x_t = 20 + 0.5x_{t-1} + \varepsilon_t$, where ε_t is white noise. If $x_{10} = 10$, $x_{11} = 11$, and $x_{12} = 12$:

a. Forecast x_{13} and x_{14} at time x_{12}.

b. Would you expect your forecasts to be more or less accurate if the process were $x_t = 20 + 0.9x_{t-1} + \varepsilon_t$. Why or why not?

9.4 Show that the model $y_t = \exp[\alpha + \beta(t) + \varepsilon_t]$ is not stationary. How can it be converted into a stationary model?

9.5 Compute the one- and two-step forecasts for the linear and exponential models developed in Sec. 9.1. How do these forecasts compare with the real data? With the forecast from the parabolic model?

9.6 The last five observations in the DiffTB series were $\{-0.21, 0.10, -0.01, -0.59, 0.08\}$, where -0.21 was the last observation. Calculate the one-step forecasts for the AR(2) and MA(1) models developed in Sec. 9.3. Compute the forecast errors and compare them to the forecast error for the ARMA model.

9.7 Suppose that you calculate the correlogram for x_t and find the following:

k	0	1	2	3	4	5	6
r_k	1	0.44	0.003	0.001	0	0	0

  a. What model would fit to x_t?

  b. Now suppose the one-step forecast error at $t = 8$ is 0.2, and $x_9 = 1.3$. Estimate x_8.

9.8 Another model for trend fitting is the *Gompertz curve*, which is given by the equation $\ln(y_t) = a + br^t$, with $0 < r < 1$ and $b > 0$. The graph of the Gompertz curve is illustrated below:

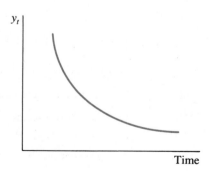

  a. To what other trend model is the Gompertz curve similar?

  b. Sketch how the Gompertz curve would appear if $b < 0$.

  c. List three business or economic scenarios that could be captured with a Gompertz curve model.

9.9 In an attempt to forecast the DOW Jones Index, one year of weekly data was collected and the following ACFs and PACF were calculated. The raw data are contained in Data Set 15 of Appendix I.

```
                                    DOW ACF
                 -1.0  -.8  -.6  -.4  -.2   .0   .2   .4   .6   .8  1.0
Lag  Corr   SE    |----|----|----|----|----|----|----|----|----|----|
  1  .764  .139                              (    |•••••)•••••••••••••
  2  .614  .204                         (         |•••••••••••)••••••
  3  .475  .237                    (              |•••••••••••)
  4  .312  .255                         (         |•••••••    )
  5  .255  .262                    (              |•••••••        )
  6  .156  .267                    (              |•••            )
  7  .163  .268                    (              |••••           )
```

```
                              Differenced DOW ACF
                 -1.0  -.8  -.6  -.4  -.2   .0   .2   .4   .6   .8  1.0
Lag  Corr   SE    |----|----|----|----|----|----|----|----|----|----|
  1 -.603  .141          •••••••••(•••••••|                )
  2  .083  .186                         (       |••              )
  3  .132  .187                         (       |•••             )
  4 -.226  .188                         (   •••••|              )
  5  .236  .194                         (       |•••••          )
  6 -.192  .199                         (    ••••|              )
  7  .051  .203                         (       |•              )
```

```
                             Differenced DOW PACF
                 -1.0  -.8  -.6  -.4  -.2   .0   .2   .4   .6   .8  1.0
Lag  Corr   SE    |----|----|----|----|----|----|----|----|----|----|
  1 -.603  .141          ••••••••(•••••••|               )
  2 -.441  .141              ••••(•••••••|               )
  3 -.121  .141                         (   •••|              )
  4 -.262  .141                         (•••••••|              )
  5 -.035  .141                         (       |              )
  6 -.147  .141                         (   •••|               )
  7 -.175  .141                         (  ••••|               )
```

a. Use this information to identify the structure of the model.

b. What additional information would you need to perform the diagnostic stage of Box-Jenkins analysis?

c. Suppose you ran a simple regression model on the DOW using a lagged dependent variable as your only independent variable:

$$\mathrm{DOW}_t = \beta_0 + \beta_1 \mathrm{DOW}_{t-1} + \varepsilon_t.$$

Do you think you would get good results? Why?

9.10 A key macroeconomic indicator is the change in business inventories. Unfortunately, it is also very difficult to forecast. Use the information below to explain why it is so difficult to forecast the change in business inventories. The data are provided in Data Set 16 of Appendix I.

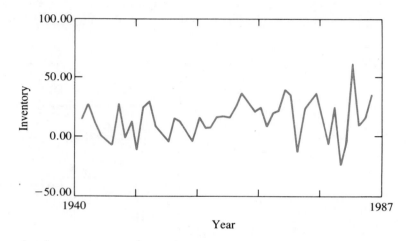

```
                              Inventory ACF
Lag   Corr    SE -1.0  -.8  -.6  -.4  -.2  .0   .2   .4   .6   .8  1.0
                   |----|----|----|----|----|----|----|----|----|----|
  1   .053   .144                      (        |•       )
  2  -.124   .145                      (     •••|        )
  3   .115   .147                      (        |••      )
  4  -.036   .149                      (        |        )
  5   .132   .149                      (    •   |•••     )
  6  -.001   .151                      (        |        )
  7   .072   .151                      (        |•       )


                              Inventory PACF
Lag   Corr    SE -1.0  -.8  -.6  -.4  -.2  .0   .2   .4   .6   .8  1.0
                   |----|----|----|----|----|----|----|----|----|----|
  1   .053   .144                      (        |•       )
  2  -.127   .144                      (     •••|        )
  3   .132   .144                      (        |•••     )
  4  -.071   .144                      (      • |        )
  5   .180   .144                      (        |••••    )
  6  -.064   .144                      (      • |        )
  7   .150   .144                      (        |•••     )
```

9.11 The first step in time series data is to plot the data to look for any special characteristics. Below are the plots of IBM and Apple stock prices, the weekly closing figures for the two-year period beginning October 1986. The actual data are shown in Data Set 17 of Appendix I. What can you determine from these plots? Are the series stationary? Is smoothing necessary? What steps would you take to answer these questions? Do you think times series models would be successful in forecasting these series?

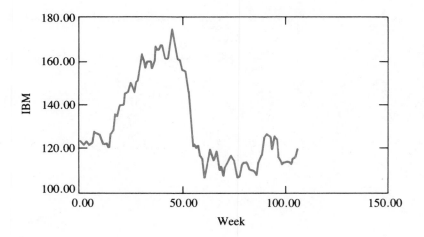

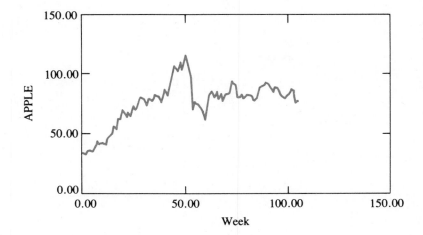

9.12 Like stock prices, corporate profits are extremely difficult to forecast. The graphs below plot the ratio of after-tax profits to stockholder's equity before and after smoothing with an MA(3) filter. The data are shown in Data Set 18 of Appendix I.

    a. Do you think the smoothed series provides as much information as the raw series?

    b. Outline the steps you would take to forecast these series.

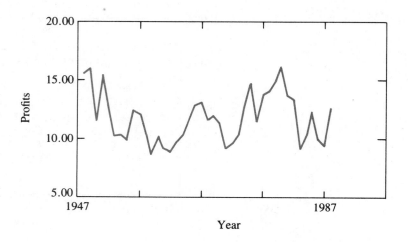

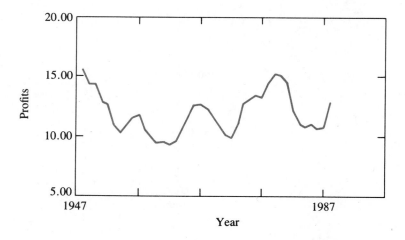

9.13 Use Box-Jenkins analysis to construct a forecasting equation for the monthly manufacturing inventory data in Data Set 19 of Appendix I.

    a. As always, plot the data before beginning the ARIMA estimation. Does the plot lead you to think that estimation will be successful? Why or why not? Does it look like differencing is necessary?

    b. Estimate the ACF and, if necessary, the PACF to identify the series.

    c. Write the forecast equation and construct one- and two-step forecasts.

9.14 Use Box-Jenkins analysis to construct a forecasting equation for the monthly, seasonally adjusted housing starts data in Data Set 19 of Appendix I.

    a. Plot the data before beginning the ARIMA estimation. Does the plot lead you to think that estimation will be successful? Why or why not? Does it look like differencing is necessary?

    b. Estimate the ACF and, if necessary, the PACF to identify the series.

    c. Write the forecast equation and construct one- and two-step forecasts.

APPENDIX 9.A

PROOFS

We skipped three important derivations in this chapter for the sake of continuity. We remedy these omissions now.

MA Coefficients

One of the essential results for MA models is that the correlation between terms is a function of β, or b when estimated. For an MA(1) model we have:

$$\rho(x_t, x_{t-1}) = \frac{\beta}{1 + \beta^2}. \qquad [A.1]$$

We will derive the result in Eq. [A.1] and refer the reader to Box and Jenkins (1976) or Granger and Newbold (1987) for the generalization.

Equation [A.1] can be derived with a simple extension of the techniques we used in Chapter 6 when we were dealing with autocorrelation. Recall that an MA(1) model is defined as:

$$x_t = \varepsilon_t + \beta\varepsilon_{t-1}, \qquad [A.2]$$

and that the correlation between x_t and x_{t-1} is:

$$\text{corr}(x_t, x_{t-1}) = \rho(x_t, x_{t-1}) = \frac{\text{cov}(x_t, x_{t-1})}{\text{var}(x_t)}. \qquad [A.3]$$

Substitute for x_t and x_{t-1} on the right side:

$$\rho(x_t, x_{t-1}) = \frac{\text{cov}[(\varepsilon_t + \beta\varepsilon_{t-1}), (\varepsilon_{t-1} + \beta\varepsilon_{t-2})]}{\text{var}(\varepsilon_t + \beta\varepsilon_{t-1})}. \qquad [A.4]$$

Because $E(\varepsilon_t) = 0$, and we assume homoscedastic errors, this can be written as:

$$\rho(x_t, x_{t-1}) = \frac{E[(\varepsilon_t + \beta\varepsilon_{t-1})(\varepsilon_{t-1} + \beta\varepsilon_{t-2})]}{E(\varepsilon_t + \beta\varepsilon_{t-1})^2}. \qquad [A.5]$$

Expanding terms yields:

$$\rho(x_t, x_{t-1}) = \frac{E(\varepsilon_t\varepsilon_{t-1} + \beta\varepsilon_{t-1}^2 + \beta\varepsilon_t\varepsilon_{t-2} + \beta^2\varepsilon_{t-1}\varepsilon_{t-2})}{E(\varepsilon_t^2 + 2\beta\varepsilon_t\varepsilon_{t-1} + \beta^2\varepsilon_{t-1}^2)}. \qquad [A.6]$$

Because $E(\varepsilon_t, \varepsilon_{t-j}) = 0$, $j > 0$, and $E(\varepsilon_t^2) = \text{var}(\varepsilon_t)$, we can simplify Eq. [A.6] considerably:

$$\rho(x_t, x_{t-1}) = \frac{\beta\,\text{var}(\varepsilon_t)}{\text{var}(\varepsilon_t) + \beta^2\text{var}(\varepsilon_t)} = \frac{\beta}{1 + \beta^2}, \qquad [A.7]$$

which is what we wanted to show.

AR Coefficients

For an AR(1) model, α represents the partial correlation between x_t and x_{t-j}. This can be demonstrated quite easily. Recall that an AR(1) process is defined as:

$$x_t = \alpha x_{t-1} + \varepsilon_t. \tag{A.8}$$

If $E(x_t) = 0$, the covariance between x_t and x_{t-1} is:

$$\mathrm{cov}(x_t, x_{t-1}) = E(x_t x_{t-1}). \tag{A.9}$$

Substituting for x_t gives:

$$\mathrm{cov}(x_t, x_{t-1}) = E[(\alpha x_{t-1} + \varepsilon_t)(x_{t-1})]. \tag{A.10}$$

Expanding the right side reveals:

$$E[(\alpha x_{t-1} + \varepsilon_t)(x_{t-1})] = E(\alpha x_{t-1}^2 + \varepsilon_t x_{t-1}). \tag{A.11}$$

After distributing the expectations operator, this becomes:

$$\mathrm{cov}(x_t, x_{t-1}) = \alpha E(x_{t-1}^2) + E(\varepsilon_t x_{t-1}). \tag{A.12}$$

Now, the second term goes to zero so we are left with:

$$\mathrm{cov}(x_t, x_{t-1}) = \alpha \, \mathrm{var}(x_t). \tag{A.13}$$

Finally, note that correlation between x_t and x_{t-1} is the ratio of covariance to variance. Using Eq. [A.13] for the covariance, this becomes:

$$\mathrm{corr}(x_t, x_{t-1}) = \frac{\alpha \, \mathrm{var}(x_t)}{\mathrm{var}(x_t)} = \alpha, \tag{A.14}$$

which is what we wanted to show. The generalization for an AR(q) model is:

$$\mathrm{corr}(x_t, x_{t-k}) = \alpha^k \; \forall \; k. \tag{A.15}$$

The proof of Eq. [A.15] can be found in Granger and Newbold (1987).

MA Errors

In Sec. 9.2.1 we used what may have appeared to be an arbitrary method to estimate the error terms in an MA(1) model. We now show why this works. The recommended estimation equation was:

$$\varepsilon_t = y_t - \beta y_{t-1} + \beta^2 y_{t-2} - \beta^3 y_{t-3} + \cdots + (-\beta)^k y_{t-k} + \cdots. \tag{A.16}$$

Equation [A.16] is a legitimate means for estimating the errors only if it can be shown to be equivalent to the MA(1) model expressed as:

$$y_t = \varepsilon_t + \beta \varepsilon_{t-1}. \tag{A.17}$$

Substitute the right side of Eq. [A.16] for ε_t and a lagged version for ε_{t-1} into Eq. [A.17] to give:

$$\begin{aligned} y_t = y_t - \beta y_{t-1} + \beta^2 y_{t-2} - \beta^3 y_{t-3} + \cdots + (-\beta)^k y_{t-k} + \cdots \\ + \beta[y_{t-1} - \beta y_{t-2} + \beta^2 y_{t-3} - \beta^3 y_{t-4} + \cdots + (-\beta)^k y_{t-k-1}]. \end{aligned} \tag{A.18}$$

Expanding the term in brackets yields:

$$\begin{aligned} y_t = y_t - \beta y_{t-1} + \beta^2 y_{t-2} - \beta^3 y_{t-3} + \cdots + (-\beta)^k y_{t-k} + \cdots \\ + \beta y_{t-1} - \beta^2 y_{t-2} + \beta^3 y_{t-3} - \beta^4 y_{t-4} + \cdots + (-\beta)^{k+1} y_{t-k-1}. \end{aligned} \tag{A.19}$$

We are able to cancel all but the last term, so we are left with:

$$y_t = y_t + (-\beta)^{k+1} y_{t-k-1}. \tag{A.20}$$

However, as long as $|\beta| < 1$, this term will be small enough to ignore safely.

APPENDIX 9.B

MORE ON BOX-JENKINS MODELING

The discussion in the text assumes that the computer program you have available does not have a specific ARIMA routine. As we just illustrated, it is possible to estimate the AR and MA coefficients using only the ACF and PACF. Then the procedure to construct a forecast is simple but tedious. As you might guess, it is *much* easier to let the computer estimate the MA and AR coefficients as well as compute the forecast. Additionally, most software programs will calculate confidence intervals around the forecasts, something that is not very easy to do by hand. Popular programs that do have ARIMA routines include Minitab™, SAS™, SPSS™, Systat™, TSP™, and RATS™. All of these programs are available in mainframe and MS-DOS versions; Minitab™, SPSS™, Systat™, and RATS™ are also available in Macintosh versions. This appendix takes you through the steps required to construct an ARIMA model using ARIMA software.

The initial steps are the same as those we discussed in the chapter. First, input the data and save it. Next, check to see if the series is stationary by looking at the ACF. If it is nonstationary, difference it and look at the ACF of the differenced data. Once the series has been made stationary, most programs require that you tentatively identify the series—pick the order (p, d, q) of the equation to be estimated.[19] It is then a simple matter of asking the computer to estimate an ARIMA model of the specified order.

In Minitab™, the command for an ARIMA $(2, 1, 1)$ model of the data in column 1 is:

```
MTB>  arima 2 1 1 c1;   <CR>
```

To get a ten-step forecast beginning at observation 60, use a subcommand:

```
SUBC>  forecast 60 10.   <CR>
```

Forecasts within the sample period are fitted values that can be used to see how well the model fits. Minitab™ and other programs capable of ARIMA modeling also can save the residuals in a separate column for later inspection for randomness.

The real advantage of using a computer to estimate an ARIMA model instead of doing it by hand is that several models can be estimated and compared. Recall that it is often somewhat of a judgment call as to the order of the model. In the TBILL example in the text, for example, we checked to see whether the model was $(2, 1, 0)$, $(1, 1, 0)$, or $(2, 1, 1)$. In fact, it could also be

---

[19] Some programs (i.e., EZ-RATS™) will estimate the best ARIMA model upon request, but most programs require that you designate the order of the equation.

(0, 1, 1) or (1, 1, 1). This is normal—the ACF and PACF rarely indicate a single model. Our model for selecting the (2, 1, 1) model—a visual inspection of a plot of the fitted and actual values—was rather naive. Most ARIMA programs provide at least two alternative methods for checking fit: t-ratios on the coefficients, and a χ^2-test on the residuals.[20] Also, the 95% confidence intervals around the forecast values can be used to see which model has the smallest forecast errors.

A Minitab™ ARIMA printout for a (2 1 0) model of the TBILL data used in the chapter is shown below.

```
Estimates at each iteration
Iteration      SSE    Parameters
       0    6.16015   0.100    0.100
       1    5.45647   0.250   -0.027
       2    5.03194   0.400   -0.154
       3    4.88891   0.539   -0.272
       4    4.88783   0.551   -0.283
       5    4.88782   0.552   -0.284
       6    4.88782   0.552   -0.284
Relative change in each estimate less than 0.0010

Final Estimates of Parameters
Type     Estimate  St. Dev.   t-ratio
AR   1     0.5517    0.1223      4.51
AR   2    -0.2837    0.1224     -2.32

Differencing: 1 regular difference
No. of obs.:  Original series 65, after differencing 64
Residuals:    SS = 4.86303 (backforecasts excluded)
              MS = 0.07844 DF = 62

Modified Box-Pierce chisquare statistic
Lag                  12          24          36          48
Chisquare   2.7(DF=10)  10.0(DF=22)  18.9(DF=34)  24.1(DF=46)
```

The first part of this printout, "Estimates at each iteration," presents the results from the computer's iterative search for the AR coefficients.[21] In this case, six iterations were needed to calculate the final estimates of 0.552 and -0.284, which are fairly close to the values of 0.41 and -0.27 that we cal-

---

[20] The χ^2-test is also called the *modified Box-Pierce statistic*, the *Ljung-Box Q-statistic*, or a *Portmanteau test*.

[21] Most programs use a nonlinear maximization technique to estimate ARIMA models. This technique involves a series of iterations and is computationally demanding so few low-level statistics programs have ARIMA routines.

culated manually from information in the PACF; they probably would have been closer had we used more observations.

The printout also contains t-ratios for the AR coefficients. There is quite a bit of debate over the reliability of t-ratios on the coefficients in ARIMA models. The standard errors are calculated somewhat differently than in regression analysis and they are only approximately normally distributed, so interpretation is not as clear cut as in regression analysis. Some people recommend a critical t-value of 1.0; others suggest ignoring them altogether.

The final statistical test provided by Minitab™ is the *modified Box-Pierce chi square statistic*, sometimes called the *Q-statistic*. The idea behind this test is that the residuals of the estimated model should be white noise; any nonrandom pattern in the residuals indicates that the model has been incorrectly identified. The Q-statistic tests to see whether groups of the residuals (the first 12, the first 24, etc.) are random. The null hypothesis of a Q-statistic test is that the residuals, as a group, are white noise; the alternate hypothesis is that the residuals are not white noise. If the calculated Q-statistic exceeds the critical χ^2 at the chosen level of significance (usually 5%), the null hypothesis is rejected. The hope, of course, is that the calculated Q-statistics will be *lower* than the critical value, an indication that the residuals are random and thus that the model has been adequately identified. Degrees of freedom are calculated as the number of lags (k) minus p. In this case, the estimated model is AR(2), therefore $p = 2$.

An inspection of the Q-statistic indicates that the residuals are random because calculated values are less the table value for every lag:

```
lag 12:   2.7 < 18.30 (df = 10, α = .05)
lag 24:  10.0 < 33.92 (df = 22, α = .05)
lag 36:  18.9 < 43.77 (df = 30, α = .05)
lag 48:  24.1 < 67.50 (df = 50, α = .05)
```

We should note, however, that the Q-test is not very powerful so most investigators interpret it cautiously,[22] and many people prefer to use a 10% significance level instead of the usual 5%.

As we have mentioned before, the only real test of a time series model is its forecasting ability. All ARIMA programs will generate a series of forecasts, and the best way to pick between alternative models is by comparing forecast

---

[22] On this point, see Walter Vandale, *Applied Time Series and Box-Jenkins Models* (New York: Academic Press, 1983), p. 108–109. Also, note that many statistics packages (among them Systat™) do not include the Q-statistic as part of their standard output for ARIMA models.

errors. The fitted values from periods 60–64, and forecasts of periods 65–70 for the (2 1 0) and (2 1 1) models are shown below. Notice that the one-step forecasts differ by only 0.02; 6.35 versus 6.33. Likewise, the 95% confidence intervals around x_{65} are virtually identical. Thus, because we have little reason to pick either model based on its forecasting ability, the simpler model (2 1 0) is preferred. Similar analysis of the (1 1 0) and (0 1 1) models would show that their forecasts of x_{65} are less accurate and have wider 95% confidence intervals.

```
ARIMA (2 1 0) Forecasts from period 60
             95 Percent Limits
Period      Forecast        Lower         Upper        Actual
  61        6.43414        5.88510       6.98317       6.40000
  62        6.40633        5.39281       7.41986       5.81000
  63        6.35862        5.02726       7.68998       5.80000
  64        6.34018        4.79531       7.88506       5.90000
  65        6.34355        4.63209       8.05500       5.69000

  66        6.35063        4.48879       8.21247
  67        6.35358        4.34839       8.35878
  68        6.35320        4.21169       8.49472
  69        6.35216        4.08223       8.62208
  70        6.35169        3.96076       8.74261
```

```
ARIMA (2 1 1) Forecasts from period 60
             95 Percent Limits
Period      Forecast        Lower         Upper        Actual
  61        6.43279        5.87956       6.98602       6.40000
  62        6.40218        5.38384       7.42053       5.81000
  63        6.34719        5.00840       7.68599       5.80000
  64        6.32236        4.77175       7.87296       5.90000
  65        6.32419        4.61318       8.03519       5.69000

  66        6.33321        4.47930       8.18713
  67        6.33830        4.34713       8.32947
  68        6.33864        4.21528       8.46199
  69        6.33723        4.08851       8.58596
  70        6.33625        3.96930       8.70319
```

Some final comments are in order before closing. None of these models is especially good, as evidenced by the relatively wide confidence intervals. More sophisticated analyses would consider seasonal effects and use a much longer data series. Finally, we selected the TBILL series because interest rates are a topic most economics and business students are familiar with, not because they are easy to forecast. They are, in fact, one of the most difficult series to forecast.

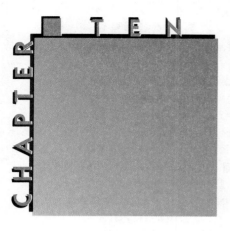

CHAPTER TEN

QUALITATIVE CHOICE MODELS

Why do you decide to rent or buy a home? Do economic issues determine whether you vote Democratic or Republican? How can you tell if your loan application will be approved? Until recently, at least two problems arose when trying to answer these questions with econometrics. First, very little of the data were available. The decisions to buy a home, vote, or grant a loan are personal decisions made to maximize the utility of the decision-maker. To study them requires micro data, the product of extensive—and often costly—surveys. Survey data are just now becoming available. Even if the data were available, however, constructing models to test such hypotheses is complicated because it requires the use of *qualitative*—as opposed to *quantitative*—dependent variables. Rent/buy, Democrat/ Republican, and approve/disapprove are all examples of qualitative dependent variables. Because qualitative variables are nonnumerical, they must be assigned values—usually 1 for a "success" and 0 for a "failure"—before analysis is possible.

Unfortunately, the analysis of qualitative dependent variables creates several problems. Among other things, the errors are nonnormal and heteroscedastic, and R^2 is an unreliable measure of goodness of fit. Despite these problems, the models of qualitative choice have received a great deal of attention in recent years. They have been applied successfully to automobile demand, labor force participation, and several other areas. In fact, some economists contend that individual choice models are crucial for understanding the causal relationships underlying demand and supply, the basis for most economic and econometric analysis.[1]

10.1

THE LINEAR PROBABILITY MODEL

The simplest way to estimate models with qualitative dependent variables is the *linear probability model*. The linear probability model has somewhat limited applicability but it is a good introduction to the logit model, the most popular model of qualitative choice.

10.1.1   An Example

One of the important changes in the economy over the past 30 years has been the increase in the labor force participation rate of women. There are several possible ways to study this phenomenon econometrically. An aggregate model could be constructed with the labor force participation rate on the left side and a host of plausible independent variables (education, husband's income, college costs, number of children, etc.) on the right side. Such a model could be analyzed with the techniques we have already covered in the text.

Alternatively, suppose the issue of concern is whether the woman's decision to work depends on her education. To answer this question econometrically would require survey data. The survey would consist of (at least) two questions: (1) Have you held a job outside of the home in the past x months?

---

[1] This point is made by Kenneth Train in *Qualitative Choice Analysis: Theory, Econometrics, and an Application to Automobile Demand* (Cambridge, Mass.: MIT Press, 1986).

(2) How many years of formal education have you completed? The woman would be required to answer "yes" or "no" to the first question and give a numerical response to the second question. Once these data were collected, the regression model could be specified as:

$$Y_i = \beta_0 + \beta_1 X_{1i} + \varepsilon_i,$$ [10.1]

where

> $X_{1i} =$ years of education, a continuous, quantitative independent variable
> $Y_i =$ dichotomous dependent variable assigned values of 0 for a "no" response and 1 for a "yes" response
> $\varepsilon_i =$ random error, $E(\varepsilon_i) = 0$, $\rho_{ij} = 0$, $\forall\, i \neq j$.

Equation [10.1] looks just like any other simple regression equation, but there are actually several important differences. In particular, notice how we have defined the error term: It is assumed to obey only some of the classical OLS assumptions; it is not assumed to be normal or homoscedastic for reasons we will discuss shortly. This leads to several problems and is the reason why we need to treat models involving qualitative dependent variables in a separate chapter.

10.1.2 Consequences of a Dichotomous Dependent Variable

To see the consequences of using qualitative dependent variables, we need to first define the concept of *conditional probability*. The conditional probability of Y_i given X_i is the expected value of Y_i given a particular X_i. The common notation for conditional probability is $E(Y_i | X_i)$. In regression analysis, the conditional probability of Y_i is the regression line:

$$E(Y_i | X_i) = \hat{Y}_i = \beta_0 + \beta_1 X_i,$$ [10.2]

because $E(\varepsilon_i) = 0$.

Now, because Y_i can have only two values, zero or one, in the linear probability model, the conditional probability of Y_i is equal to P_i, the probability that $Y = 1$; that is:

$$E(Y_i | X_i) \equiv \sum_{i=1}^{2} P_i Y_i = P(Y = 1) \times 1 + P(Y = 0) \times 0$$

$$= P(Y = 1) = P_i.$$ [10.3]

From the definition of a probability density function, we know that $\sum P_i = 1$, so it follows that:

$$P(Y = 0) = 1 - P_i.$$ [10.4]

Substituting Eq. [10.3] into [10.2], we have a result that helps in interpretation of the linear probability model;

$$E(Y_i \mid X_i) = P_i = \beta_0 + \beta_1 X_i. \qquad [10.5]$$

Equation [10.5] explains why this model is called a linear probability model. It is a linear equation and it fulfills the two requirements of a probability density function.[2] Intuitively, its name derives from the fact that the fitted values of the regression equation represent the probability that $Y_i = 1$ given the values of X_i; that is, $\hat{Y}_i = P_i = E(Y_i \mid X_i)$.

The error term of the linear probability model has two characteristics that cause problems when using and interpreting OLS. The less serious problem is that the error is *binomially* distributed instead of normally distributed. This follows directly from the constraints on Y:

If $Y_i = 0$,   then $0 = \beta_0 + \beta_1 X_{1i} + \varepsilon_i$ so $\varepsilon_i = -\beta_0 - \beta_1 X_{1i}$.

If $Y_i = 1$,   then $1 = \beta_0 + \beta_1 X_{1i} + \varepsilon_i$ so $\varepsilon_i = 1 - \beta_0 - \beta_1 X_{1i}$.

Because the error term is nonnormal, hypothesis tests on the parameter estimates cannot be trusted, at least not with a small sample. With a large sample, the error approaches the normal distribution, as a consequence of the central limit theorem, so standard hypothesis tests are appropriate.

The more serious problem is that errors of the linear probability model are heteroscedastic. To understand this, recall that the error variance is defined as:

$$\text{var}(\varepsilon_i) = E[\varepsilon_i - E(\varepsilon_i)]^2 = \sum P_i [\varepsilon_i - E(\varepsilon_i)]^2, \qquad [10.6]$$

and because $E(\varepsilon_i) = 0$, this is simply:

$$E(\varepsilon_i^2) = \sum P_i \varepsilon_i^2 = P_i (1 - \beta_0 - \beta_1 X_{1i})^2 + (1 - P_i)(-\beta_0 - \beta_1 X_{1i})^2. \qquad [10.7]$$

Equations [10.4] and [10.5] let us substitute for P_i and $(1 - P_i)$:

$$E(\varepsilon_i^2) = (\beta_0 + \beta_1 X_{1i})(1 - \beta_0 - \beta_1 X_{1i})^2$$
$$+ (1 - \beta_0 - \beta_1 X_{1i})(-\beta_0 - \beta_1 X_{1i})^2. \qquad [10.8]$$

After some manipulation, we find:

$$\text{var}(\varepsilon_i) = (\beta_0 + \beta_1 X_{1i})(1 - \beta_0 - \beta_1 X_{1i}), \qquad [10.9]$$

which is what we wanted to show. The error term is heteroscedastic because $\text{var}(\varepsilon_i)$ is a function of X_i—which can obviously vary.

---

[2] The requirements are $0 \le p_i \le 1$ and $\sum p_i = 1$.

10.1.3 Weighted Least Squares

Heteroscedastic errors do not bias parameter estimates, but they do result in inefficiency. Fortunately, we developed a method in Chapter 7 for dealing with heteroscedasticity, weighted least squares (WLS). In the case of the linear probability model, a very simple method can calculate the weights to use in WLS.

First, recall that if the heteroscedastic error was defined as:

$$\sigma_i^2 = \sigma^2 X_i^2, \tag{10.10}$$

the correct WLS procedure is to transform the data by dividing by X_i; that is,

$$Y_i^* = \frac{Y_i}{X_{1i}}; \qquad X_{0i}^* = \frac{X_{0i}}{X_{1i}}; \qquad X_{1i}^* = \frac{X_{1i}}{X_{1i}} = 1; \qquad \varepsilon_i^* = \frac{\varepsilon_i}{X_{1i}}. \tag{10.11}$$

OLS is then performed on the transformed data.[3] The problem, of course, is in finding the correct weighting procedure. In Chapter 7, we used the Park test — regression of the log of the squared residuals on the log of the X_{ji} thought to be the source of the heteroscedasticity — but also noted that it is far from infallible. The Park test is unnecessary with the linear probability model because an OLS regression can provide the correct weights. Note that Eq. [10.2] allows us to write Eq. [10.9] as:

$$\text{var}(\varepsilon_i) = P_i(1 - P_i). \tag{10.12}$$

From Eq. [10.5], we know that the P_i are the fitted values from the OLS regression. The procedure for WLS correction of the linear probability model follows immediately:

1. Run OLS on the linear probability model disregarding heteroscedasticity. Collect the fitted values, $\hat{Y}_i = P_i$.

2. Let $w_i = [P_i(1 - P_i)]^{1/2}$ be the weights and transform the data:

$$Y_i^* = \frac{Y_i}{w_i}; \qquad X_{0i}^* = \frac{X_{0i}}{w_i}; \qquad X_{1i}^* = \frac{X_{1i}}{w_i}; \qquad \varepsilon_i^* = \frac{\varepsilon_i}{w_i}. \tag{10.13}$$

3. Run OLS on the transformed model:

$$Y_i^* = \beta_0 \frac{1}{w_i} + \beta_1 X_{1i}^* + \varepsilon_i^*. \tag{10.14}$$

---

[3] Remember that we defined $X_{0i} = 1$ to simplify the transformation of the intercept.

Note that the intercept must be suppressed because of inclusion of the $(1/w_i)$ term. The resulting parameter estimates will be unbiased and efficient. Example 10.1 uses this method for estimating the linear probability model. Exercise 10.4 asks you to show that this transformation results in homoscedastic errors.

10.1.4   Complications: R^2 and Unacceptable Values for $\hat{Y}_i$

The procedure just outlined will establish efficient parameter estimates, but there are still two problems with the linear probability model. First, R^2 is not an accurate representation of goodness of fit, and the fitted values of the WLS regression can fall outside the permissible (0, 1) range.

A glance at Fig. 10.1 shows why R^2 cannot be relied on in the linear probability model. Because the data points can fall only at $Y = 1$ or $Y = 0$, only a few will be close to the fitted line. The result: Explained variation will be "small" relative to unexplained variation.[4] An R^2 between 0.2 and 0.6

FIGURE 10.1   Low R^2 and the linear probability model

A linear probability model will generally have a low R^2, regardless of how well the model fits, because the observations on Y will be on the horizontal axis or the $\hat{Y}_i = 1$ line, and the fitted line will be close to only a few of the data points. If the data points happen to be concentrated very closely to the fitted line, R^2 will be higher than if they are scattered more widely. Constraining the linear probability model (Fig. 10.2) to eliminate the values of $\hat{Y}_i$ that are greater than one or less than zero will increase the value of R^2.

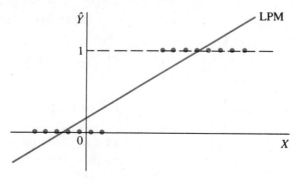

---

[4]Recall that R^2 equals the explained variation in Y divided by the total variation in Y.

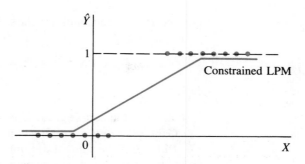

FIGURE 10.2   Constrained linear probability model

> To eliminate the problem of fitted values of the linear probability
> model falling outside the (0, 1) range, the linear probability model
> can be constrained. All values $\hat{Y}_i > 1$ are assigned an arbitrary value
> close to 1.0 (say, 0.999), and all values $\hat{Y}_i < 0$ are assigned an
> arbitrary value close to 0.0 (say, 0.001). This technique is satisfactory
> if there are only a few values that need to be constrained.

is usually considered quite good for a linear probability model, but most investigators dismiss R^2 entirely in models with qualitative dependent variables.

The second difficulty with the linear probability model is that some values of $\hat{Y}_i$ are likely to fall outside of the required (0, 1) range. Given that the fitted values represent the probabilities that $Y_i = 1$ for given values of X_i, such values make no sense. If only a few $\hat{Y}_i$ fall outside the region, the linear probability model can be constrained by setting negative values very close to zero (say, 0.001) and setting values greater than one very close to one (say, 0.999) before carrying out the WLS transformation. The *constrained linear probability model* is illustrated in Fig. 10.2. Other things equal, a constrained linear probability model will have a higher R^2 than an unconstrained linear probability model with the same data. However, if very many points fall outside the (0, 1) region, the appropriateness of the linear probability model specification must be questioned.

■ EXAMPLE 10.1

THE CONSTRAINED LINEAR PROBABILITY MODEL:
The Effect of Personalized Instruction on Macroeconomics Grades

In "Probit Analysis and Economic Instruction," L. Spector and M. Mazzeo[5] used qualitative dependent variables to test whether a system of personalized instruction (PSI) improved exam performance in an

---

[5] *Journal of Economic Education*, Vol. 11, 1980, p. 37–44. Data used with permission. This example is also used in Aldrich and Nelson.

intermediate macroeconomics class. The model they used to test their hypothesis was:

$$Y_i = \beta_0 + \beta_1 GPA_i + \beta_2 PSI_i + \beta_3 TUCE_i + \varepsilon_i,$$

where

> $Y_i = 0$ if the course grade is B or C; $= 1$ if the course grade is A
> GPA = student's entering cumulative GPA
> PSI = 0 if the student did not receive personalized instruction; $= 1$ if the student did receive personalized instruction.

TUCE is the score on a standardized test taken at the beginning of the course. The data were collected from a class of 32 students, 14 of whom received PSI.

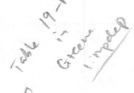

OBS	GPA	TUCE	PSI	GRADE	OBS	GPA	TUCE	PSI	GRADE
1	2.66	20	0	0	17	2.75	25	0	0
2	2.89	22	0	0	18	2.83	19	0	0
3	3.28	24	0	0	19	3.12	23	1	0
4	2.92	12	0	0	20	3.16	25	1	1
5	4.00	21	0	1	21	2.06	22	1	0
6	2.86	17	0	0	22	3.62	28	1	1
7	2.76	17	0	0	23	2.89	14	1	0
8	2.87	21	0	0	24	3.51	26	1	0
9	3.03	25	0	0	25	3.54	24	1	1
10	3.92	29	0	1	26	2.83	27	1	1
11	2.63	20	0	0	27	3.39	17	1	1
12	3.32	23	0	0	28	2.67	24	1	0
13	3.57	23	0	0	29	3.65	21	1	1
14	3.26	25	0	1	30	4.00	23	1	1
15	3.53	26	0	0	31	3.10	21	1	0
16	2.74	19	0	0	32	2.39	19	1	1

The first step in estimating the model is to perform OLS on the data in order to collect the $\hat{Y}_i$ to be used in the weights. For comparison, the results of the initial OLS regressions are shown on the following page.

These results seem reasonable, though they do appear to indicate that TUCE has no effect on the student's course grade. However, this was only a preliminary regression performed to collect the fitted values, $\hat{Y}_i$. Inspection of the $\hat{Y}_i$ showed five observations less than 0. These were assigned values of 0.001 before the weights were constructed: $w_i = [\hat{Y}_i(1 - \hat{Y}_i)]^{1/2}$. The data

```
Dep var: GRADE   N: 32  R-sq: .416  Adj  R-sq: .353  SER: 0.39

Variable  Coefficient  Std Error     T     P(2 tail)

CONSTANT        -1.50       0.52   -2.86      0.01
     GPA         0.46       0.16    2.86      0.01
     PSI         0.38       0.14    2.72      0.01
    TUCE         0.01       0.02    0.54      0.59
```

were transformed as in Eq. [10.13] and OLS was run again. The results are shown below.

```
Dep var: GRADE*  N: 32  R-sq: .765  Adj  R-sq: .740  SER: 0.901

Variable  Coefficient  Std Error     T    P(2 tail)

   1/W          -1.30       0.28   -4.53     0.00
  GPA*           0.40       0.09    4.52     0.00
  PSI*           0.39       0.11    3.68     0.00
 TUCE*           0.01       0.01    2.66     0.01
```

Several things are worth mentioning before we interpret this second regression. First, the intercept has been suppressed because the weighting scheme necessitates using the reciprocal of the weights $(1/W)$ as a regressor and, as we found out in Chapter 7, the coefficient on this term is actually the intercept. Second, we need to be careful before concluding that R^2 has improved between the two runs. The dependent variable used in the calculation of R^2 in WLS is different than the dependent variable used in OLS. We could construct an R^2 from the WLS regression that can be compared with the OLS R^2 by using the efficient WLS parameter estimates and the untransformed data, but because little meaning can be attached to R^2 in the linear probability model, we will omit this step.

What can we make of these results? Because all of the $\hat{\beta}_j$ are significant at the 1% level, the fitted regression equation is:

$$GRADE = -1.30 + 0.40GPA + 0.39PSI + 0.01TUCE.$$

Apparently, personalized instruction does affect the probability of getting an A in an intermediate macroeconomics class, and as expected, the positive signs on TUCE and GPA indicates that students who scored well on the TUCE exam and had a higher GPA coming into the class tended to earn higher grades.

Finally, we must qualify all of these results. The data set had only 32 observations—far too few to generate anything reliable. We should note too that the model actually selected by the authors was a probit model (discussed below), which eliminated the need to constrain the data, and improved the fit.

THE LINEAR PROBABILITY MODEL

1. The linear probability model is used when the dependent variable can take on only discrete values, usually designated 0 and 1.

2. Fitted values from the linear probability model represent the probability that $Y_i = 1$ given X_i.

3. Using regression analysis to estimate linear probability models is complicated because:

   a. the errors are nonnormal so standard hypothesis tests are appropriate only for large samples

   b. the errors are heteroscedastic

   c. R^2 is an unreliable measure of goodness of fit.

4. The most serious problem associated with the linear probability model is that fitted values often fall outside the required (0, 1) region. This can be corrected with a constrained linear probability model or a nonlinear model such as logit.

10.2

NONLINEAR MODELS

We can usually correct for heteroscedasticity, and a large sample size permits reliable hypothesis tests, so the main problem with the linear probability model is that the fitted values often fall outside of the required (0, 1) range. The solution we just suggested—the constrained linear probability model—is ad hoc, at best. A much better solution is to find a model that does not generate unacceptable fitted values. This requires the use of a nonlinear model.

A nonlinear model may also solve another problem associated with the linear probability model. Linear models assume that the effect of X on Y is constant over the entire range of observations. This is very unlikely in a model where the $\hat{Y}_i$ are interpreted as probabilities. For example, suppose that a linear model is used to test whether a student's chance of going to college is

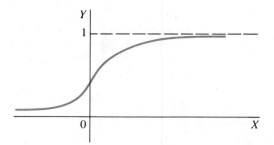

FIGURE 10.3   The logistic function, a nonlinear model

Most econometric work with qualitative dependent variables is specified somewhat like this graph. Notice that Y_i is confined to the (0, 1) region while X_i can assume any real value. Note too the nonlinear shape. The change in Y associated with a one-unit change in X depends on the beginning level of X, not just the change in X.

affected by his or her parents' income. Let $Y = 1$ if the student does attend college and $Y = 0$ if not. If income is measured in \$10,000's, the estimated regression equation might be something like $\hat{Y}_i = 0.2 + 0.1X_i$. Then, if parents' income = \$20,000 (so that $X_i = 2$), the chance of attending college would be 0.4; if the parents' income rises to \$30,000, the chance would be 0.5. Notice that a 50% increase in income resulted in a ten percentage point increase in the chance of going to college. Notice what happens, however, if income rises from \$60,000 to \$70,000, a 17% increase: There is still a ten percentage point increase in the chance of attending college. This is unreasonable. Once the parents' income reaches \$60,000, the chance that the child will go to college is virtually unaffected by an additional \$10,000 income. In general, we need a model that allows for the *level* as well as the *change* in X to affect $P_i(Y = 1)$.

The graph in Fig. 10.3 solves both of these problems. The nonlinear shape indicates a variable relationship between X and Y, and means that the response of Y to a change in X depends on the initial value of X as well as the amount of change in X. This function also eliminates the possibility of $\hat{Y}_i$ assuming values inconsistent with probability theory.

Several mathematical functions can generate graphs such as the one in Fig. 10.3, but only two are used with much frequency in econometrics: the logit and the probit. The two models are quite similar; so similar that it is usually difficult to discern between the two in practice.[6] The probit model

[6]On this point, see Takeshi Amemiya, "Qualitative Response Models: A Survey, "*Journal of Economic Literature*, Vol. XIX, December 1981, p. 1483–1536. With a very large data set, or with multiple response dependent variables, the two models differ more significantly.

also has more demanding computational requirements and is included on fewer statistics programs, so we will cover only the logit model in this chapter.[7]

10.3
THE LOGIT MODEL

The most popular model of qualitative choice is the logit model. The name "logit" is derived from the fact that the graph in Fig. 10.3 is derived from the *logistic function*, a cumulative probability distribution.[8] The computer routines involved in the estimation of logit models require nonlinear iterative techniques, techniques that are beyond the capability of many microcomputer statistics packages.[9] However, under certain instances, logit models can be estimated with WLS methods, as is done in Sec. 10.3.2. Section 10.4 provides some background on maximum likelihood estimation, the methodology used most often to estimate logit models, and an example that includes a sample printout from Systat™.[10]

10.3.1   The Mathematics of the Logit Model

At first glance, it may appear that the S-shaped graph in Fig. 10.3 cannot be estimated with linear methods, but it can be, as we will show presently. Graphs such as the one in Fig. 10.3 can be described by several functions, but the logistic distribution function is the easiest one to work with. The logistic distribution is:

$$P_i = E(Y_i = 1 \mid X_i) = [1 + e^{-(\beta_0 + \beta_1 X_i)}]^{-1}, \qquad [10.15]$$

---

[7]The probit model is sometimes called the *normit* model because it is a graph of a cumulative normal distribution. The advantage of the normal distribution is that it readily lends itself to analysis of utility theory and rational choice. See Duncan McFadden, "Conditional Logit Analysis of Qualitative Behavior," in Paul Zarembka, *Frontiers in Econometrics* (New York: Academic Press, 1973).

[8]The cumulative density distribution of the random variable is the probability that X is less than or equal to a given x_i. That is, if the cumulative density distribution is denoted $G(X)$, then $G(X = x_i) = \Pr(X \leq x_i)$.

[9]Microcomputer packages that do have logit routines include SAS™, SPSS™, Systat™, RATS™, and others.

[10]As discussed in Appendix 9.B, MLE methods are also used to estimate ARIMA models.

where e ($\cong 2.718$) is the base of natural logarithms. We need to manipulate Eq. [10.15] a little, so it will help to rewrite it as:

$$P_i = (1 + e^{-Z_i})^{-1}, \qquad\qquad\qquad [10.16]$$

where $Z_i = \beta_0 + \beta_1 X_i$. It is easy to show that $0 < P_i < 1$ as $-\infty < Z_i < +\infty$. This is a requirement because P is a probability density function. The second requirement for a probability density function, $\sum P_i = 1$, also holds.

As shown in Appendix 10.A, Eq. [10.16] implies that:

$$1 - P_i = (1 + e^{+Z_i})^{-1}. \qquad\qquad\qquad [10.17]$$

Now, we define the *odds ratio* as:

$$\frac{P_i}{1 - P_i} = \frac{1 + e^{+Z_i}}{1 + e^{-Z_i}} = e^{Z_i}. \qquad\qquad\qquad [10.18]$$

(The steps required to get from Eq. [10.17] to [10.18] are also shown in Appendix 10.A.) The odds ratio is the ratio of the probability of "success" ($Y_i = 1$) to the probability of "failure" ($Y_i = 0$).

We have just two more steps before the model is in a form we can use for linear regression analysis. Take the natural log of each side of Eq. [10.18] to get the *logits*:

$$L_i = \ln\left(\frac{P_i}{1 - P_i}\right) = \ln(e^{Z_i}) = Z_i, \qquad\qquad\qquad [10.19]$$

and substitute for Z_i to get:

$$L_i = \beta_0 + \beta_1 X_i, \qquad\qquad\qquad [10.20]$$

which should look familiar.

Unfortunately, we still have a problem in trying to estimate Eq. [10.20]. When we plug in values for P_i and $1 - P_i$, we have:

$$L_i = \ln\left(\frac{1}{0}\right) \qquad\qquad\qquad [10.21]$$

and

$$L_i = \ln\left(\frac{0}{1}\right), \qquad\qquad\qquad [10.22]$$

neither of which is defined.[11] The solution to this problem is to arrange the data in groups and calculate the *relative frequency* for each group, which are

---

[11] Equation [10.21] is undefined because ($1/0$) approaches ∞. Equation [10.22] is undefined because logs are undefined for 0.

defined as:

$$\hat{P}_i = \frac{n_i}{N_i},$$ [10.23]

where N_i is the size of the group and n_i is the number of "successes" that fall into the group. The use of grouped data and estimated odds ratios will yield efficient and consistent parameter estimates as long as the sample size is large.

For example, in the college attendance illustration, if the sample has $50 = N_i$ families with incomes between 19,000 and 20,999 of which $18 = n_i$ were able to send their children to college, the relative frequency would be:

$$\hat{P}_i = \frac{n_i}{N_i} = \frac{18}{50} = 0.36,$$

and the corresponding data entry into the regression package would be:

$$\hat{L}_i = \ln\left(\frac{\hat{P}_i}{1 - \hat{P}_i}\right) = \ln\left(\frac{0.36}{1 - 0.36}\right) = \beta_0 + \beta_1 X_i + \varepsilon_i.$$

Like the linear probability model, the logit model is heteroscedastic, so WLS is needed to assure efficient parameter estimates.[12]

10.3.2   WLS Estimation of the Logit Model

As mentioned, logit models are usually estimated with nonlinear methods, but if the data can be grouped, estimation is possible with standard regression techniques. A logit model with grouped data can be estimated in five steps:

1.   Compute the relative probabilities, $\hat{P}_i = n_i/N_i$, for each X_i.

2.   Estimate the logits as:

$$\hat{L}_i = \ln\left(\frac{\hat{P}_i}{1 - \hat{P}_i}\right).$$ [10.24]

3.   The errors are heteroscedastic, so it is necessary to transform the model with WLS. The appropriate weights are[13]:

$$w_i = [N_i \hat{P}_i(1 - \hat{P}_i)]^{1/2}.$$ [10.25]

---

[12] Heteroscedasticity occurs because of the binomial nature of the relative frequencies used as group probabilities. The demonstration follows along the same lines as in Eqs. [10.6] through [10.9].

[13] Notice that we are multiplying, not dividing, by the weights. The reason for this derives from the statistical properties of the binomial distribution. See Henry Theil, "On the Relationships Involving Qualitative Variables," *American Journal of Sociology*, Vol. 76, July 1970, p. 103–154.

4. Finally, perform OLS on the transformed model:

$$\hat{L}_i^* = \beta_0 w_i + \beta_1 X_i^* + \varepsilon_i^*, \qquad\qquad [10.26]$$

where $\hat{L}_i^* = w_i \hat{L}_i$; $X_i^* = w_i X_i$; and $\varepsilon_i^* = w_i \varepsilon_i$.

5. After estimating Eq. [10.26], estimated probabilities ($\hat{P}_i$) can be calculated by taking the antilog of the estimated logits ($\hat{L}_i^*$).

These steps are simple enough, but we need to keep two things in mind: First, because Eq. [10.26] has no intercept, the regression in step 4 must be through the origin. Most — but not all — statistics programs have routines that do this. Second, the logit model offers a significant improvement over the linear probability model, but it still does not have normally distributed errors. Thus, any hypothesis tests are valid only for a large sample. Example 10.2 illustrates logit estimation of a model with grouped data.

■ EXAMPLE 10.2

COLLEGE OPPORTUNITIES

As an illustration of the logit model, we continue our example of college attendance. To test the hypothesis that the parents' decision to send their children to college depends solely on family income, (hypothetical) data on income and college attendance were created.

The table below illustrates how the data must be manipulated before the logit model can be estimated with regression analysis. The raw data are

Hypothetical College Attendance/Family Income Data

(1) n_i	(2) N_i	(3) X_i	(4) P_i	(5) $1-P_i$	(6) $P_i(1-P_i)$	(7) $P_i/(1-P_i)$	(8) $N_i P_i(1-P_i)$	(9) W_i	(10) $\hat{L}_i$	(11) X_i^*	(12) $\hat{L}_i^*$
2	30	0.8	0.067	0.933	0.062	0.071	1.867	1.366	−2.639	1.093	−3.606
5	40	1.0	0.125	0.875	0.109	0.143	4.375	2.092	−1.946	2.092	−4.070
7	40	1.2	0.175	0.825	0.144	0.212	5.775	2.403	−1.551	2.884	−3.726
9	50	1.4	0.180	0.82	0.148	0.220	7.380	2.717	−1.516	3.803	−4.119
30	80	1.6	0.375	0.625	0.234	0.600	18.750	4.330	−0.511	6.928	−2.212
41	90	1.8	0.456	0.544	0.248	0.837	22.322	4.725	−0.178	8.504	−0.842
62	100	2.0	0.620	0.380	0.236	1.632	23.560	4.854	0.490	9.708	2.376
70	100	2.2	0.700	0.300	0.210	2.333	21.000	4.583	0.847	10.082	3.883
62	80	2.4	0.775	0.225	0.174	3.444	13.950	3.735	1.237	8.964	4.619
48	60	2.6	0.800	0.200	0.160	4.000	9.600	3.098	1.386	8.056	4.295
35	40	2.8	0.875	0.125	0.109	7.000	4.375	2.092	1.946	5.857	4.070
28	30	3.0	0.933	0.067	0.062	14.000	1.867	1.366	2.639	4.099	3.606

KEY: n_i = number of families within group able to send children to college; N_i = number of families within income group; X_i = income bracket; $P_i = n_i/N_i$; $w_i = [N_i \hat{P}_i(1 - \hat{P}_i)]^{1/2}$; $\hat{L}_i = \ln[\hat{P}_i/(1 - \hat{P}_i)]$; $X_i^* = w_i X_i$ and $\hat{L}_i^* = \hat{L}_i w_i$.

shown in columns 1, 2, and 3. The relative probabilities are calculated in columns 4, 5, and 6. The odds ratios, weights, estimated logits, and WLS transformed data are shown in the remaining columns.

INTERPRETATION   The table below presents the regression results on the transformed model. As expected, weighted family income (X^*) appears to have a positive effect on college attendance, but we must be careful about drawing too strong an inference from these results because the sample is far too small for us to be sure that the residuals are normally distributed. Likewise, R^2 means little in models with qualitative dependent variables, so it must be interpreted cautiously. Finally, notice that the WLS procedure required that the intercept be suppressed.

```
Model contains no constant.

Dep var: L*  N: 12  R-sq: .976  SER: 0.608

Variable  Coefficient  Std Error    T      P(2 tail)

   W        -4.265      0.229     -18.585    0.000
   X*        2.287      0.115      19.958    0.000
```

CALCULATING PROBABILITIES   Assuming that these results are reliable, the procedure to calculate the probabilities of college attendance for different family income levels is simple: Substitute the income level into the estimated equation to find the fitted value of $\hat{L}_i^*$, take the antilog, and then use algebra to find $\hat{P}_i$. For family income of $20,000 (i.e., $X_i = 2.0$), the calculations would be:

$$\hat{L}_i^* = \hat{\beta}_0 w_i + \hat{\beta}_1 X_i^*,$$

$$\hat{L}_i^* = -4.265 w_i + 2.287 X_i^*$$

$$\hat{L}_i^* = -4.265(4.854) + 2.287(9.708) = 1.500.$$

Because $\hat{L}_i^*$ is the log of the odds ratio, we need to take the antilog of 1.5. With most hand calculators, this can be done by taking the exponential (e^x) of the number 1.5:

antilog(1.5) = 4.48.

Finally, $\hat{L}_i^* = \ln[P_i/(1 - P_i)]$, so write:

$$4.48 = \frac{P_i}{1 - P_i} \quad \therefore P_i \cong 0.82.$$

Our conclusion: The chance that parents with $20,000 of family income will send their children to college is 82%. The figure below plots the probabilities of college attendance for various family income levels. As expected, it resembles the logistic curve: It is nonlinear and approaches $P_i = 1$ and $P_i = 0$ asymptotically.

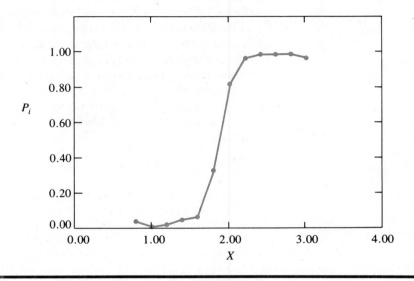

10.4

MAXIMUM LIKELIHOOD ESTIMATION OF THE LOGIT MODEL

The method used in Example 10.2 is appropriate only if the data can be conveniently grouped. If not, regression analysis cannot be used to estimate a logit model. The preferred method for estimating a logit model—even when the data can be grouped—is to use a statistics package designed specifically for logit estimation. These packages are available only for relatively powerful computers because nonlinear estimation requires an iterative process that is computationally demanding.[14]

---

[14] MS-DOS microcomputer logit packages usually require at least an 80286 (AT-compatible) microprocessor and at least 640k of RAM; Macintosh packages require at least 1 megabyte of RAM.

10.4.1   Maximum Likelihood Estimation

The nonlinear estimation technique used in most logit packages is *maximum likelihood estimation* (MLE). An in-depth discussion of MLE techniques would be inappropriate for an introductory-level book. However, a basic understanding of MLE is necessary for interpreting a logit printout because different information is provided than with a standard regression printout.

Like least squares, MLE is an approach for finding estimators. Under most circumstances, and with a large sample, MLE estimates will be identical to OLS estimates. The MLE of a sample is the hypothetical population value that maximizes the likelihood of observing the particular sample. For example, suppose that $X_1, X_2, \ldots, X_n$ make up a sample, that each X_i has a distribution $p(x_i)$, and that $p(x_i)$ depends on only one parameter, θ. Because X_i's are assumed to be independent, the joint probability distribution of the sample is:

$$
\begin{aligned}
P(X_1 = x_1, X_2 = x_2, \ldots, X_n = x_n) &= p(x_1, x_2, \ldots, x_n) \\
&= p(x_1)p(x_2)\cdots p(x_n).
\end{aligned}
\qquad [10.27]
$$

Now, each probability depends on θ, so we can make inferences about θ from the sample:

$$
p(x_1, x_2, \ldots, x_n \mid \theta) = p(x_1 \mid \theta)p(x_2 \mid \theta)\cdots p(x_n \mid \theta).
\qquad [10.28]
$$

This is known as a *likelihood function*. As such, it is usually denoted as:

$$
L(x_1, x_2, \ldots, x_n \mid \theta) = p(x_1 \mid \theta)p(x_2 \mid \theta)\cdots p(x_n \mid \theta).
\qquad [10.29]
$$

This is how MLE got its name: It attempts to find the θ that makes the probability of observing the sample the most likely. This is accomplished by maximizing the likelihood function—a procedure that requires the use of nonlinear methods.

In the case of the logit model, the task is to find the $\hat{\beta}_j$ that maximizes the likelihood of observing the (X, Y) pairs in an equation such as Eq. [10.20]. This is accomplished by differentiating the log likelihood function[15] with respect to the $\hat{\beta}_j$. The resulting equations, called the likelihood equations, are nonlinear in the $\hat{\beta}_j$ and thus require a nonlinear solution technique. The resulting MLE estimates, the $\hat{\beta}_j$'s, are identical to OLS estimates, and, as long

---

[15]Specification of the log likelihood function and likelihood equations need not detain us here, but interested students can study how to get from Eq. [10.18] to the likelihood equations in David W. Hosmer and Stanley Lemeshow, *Applied Logistic Regression* (Wiley: New York, 1989) p. 6–10. Though written primarily for biologists, this book serves as good introduction for business and economics students as well.

as the sample is large, their standard errors can be used to construct t-ratios and conduct hypothesis tests.

10.4.2   The Likelihood Ratio

Logit packages do not compute an R^2 because it has little meaning. An alternative measure of goodness of fit, the *likelihood ratio test* is used instead. The likelihood ratio test is a χ^2-statistic that tests the null hypothesis that a model that includes only the intercept "explains" the dependent variable better than the fitted model—a test very similar to the F-test used in multiple regression. In essence, the likelihood ratio compares the observed values of the dependent variable to fitted values from models with and without the independent variables.

The likelihood ratio test is calculated as:

$$D \equiv -2LLR = -2\ln\left(\frac{L0}{L1}\right) = -2(\ln L0 - \ln L1), \qquad \text{[10.30]}$$

where

  $L1 =$ value of the likelihood function for the fitted model
  $L0 =$ maximum value of the likelihood function if all coefficients are
    zero except the constant
  $LLR =$ log likelihood ratio.

This statistic follows a χ^2-distribution with k degrees of freedom, where k is the number of independent variables in the model. If D exceeds the table value at the chosen level of significance, the null hypothesis is rejected in favor of the alternate. We will use the likelihood ratio test to evaluate the model in Example 10.3.

The t-ratios on individual independent variables are reliable only with a very large sample, so inferences drawn from relatively small samples are suspect. Fortunately, a variation of the likelihood ratio test can be used to determine the statistical significance of individual independent variables. The steps for conducting this test are as follows:

1. Run the logit model with all variables to get the log likelihood, $\ln L1$.

2. Omit the variable in question and run a restricted logit model to get its log likelihood, $\ln L2$.

3. Compute the statistic: $d = -2[\ln L2 - \ln L1]$. This statistic will follow a χ^2-distribution with one degree of freedom. If d exceeds the critical value from the χ^2-table, the omitted variable is statistically significant.

10.4.3   Other Measures of Goodness of Fit

There is little standardization as to how different computer programs assess goodness of fit. For example, SPSS™ provides the *Pearson chi square test* instead of the likelihood ratio test. The null hypothesis of the Pearson chi square test is that a "saturated model"—a model with as many independent variables as observations—fits the data significantly better than the estimated model. If the calculated value exceeds the critical χ^2-value with $n - k - 1$ degrees of freedom, the null hypothesis is rejected. The Pearson chi square test is asymptotically equivalent to the likelihood ratio test; however, it should not be used for a small sample.

There are several ways to calculate statistics that resemble the R^2 from standard regression analysis. A measure recommended by Aldrich and Nelson[16] is *pseudo R^2*, which is defined as:

$$\text{pseudo } R^2 = \frac{D}{n + D}, \qquad \text{[10.31]}$$

where $D = -2LLR$ from Eq. [10.30] and n is the number of observations. McFadden[17] recommends a different measure:

$$\text{McFadden's } R^2 = 1 - \frac{\text{LL}f}{\text{LL}c}, \qquad \text{[10.32]}$$

where LLf is the log likelihood from the fitted model and LLc is the log likelihood from a model containing only the constant.

These and similar measures[18] are easy to calculate and have ranges between 0 and 1, but they cannot be easily adjusted for degrees of freedom. More importantly perhaps is the fact that, strictly speaking, they are not the "ratio of explained variation to total variation"—the intuitive and quite useful definition of R^2 used in regression analysis. Most analysts continue to rely on the likelihood ratio test for assessing goodness of fit.

Finally, most logit programs present a table that compares the actual choice probabilities to the predicted choice probabilities using the mean values of the independent variables. A good fit exists when actual and predicted probabilities are close; if the probabilities are far apart, the model could stand improvement. For example, in the final version of the spousal maintenance example below, the observed probability of receiving main-

---

[16]John H. Aldrich and Forest D. Nelson, *Linear Probability, Logic and Probit Models* (Newbury Park, Calif.: Sage University Paper 45, 1984), p. 57. This is an excellent introduction to the logit and probit model.
[17]Daniel McFadden, "Conditional Logit Analysis of Qualitative Choice Behavior," in Paul Zarembka, Ed., *Frontiers in Econometrics* (New York: Academic Press, 1974), p. 105–142.
[18]See Aldrich and Nelson, p. 57–61 for other suggestions.

tenance was 0.401, the predicted probability was 0.396. This indicates a reasonable model.

■ EXAMPLE 10.3

SPOUSAL MAINTENANCE

A topic that has been in the news recently is the large number of divorced mothers who do not receive the maintenance to which they are entitled. Why do divorced fathers refuse to pay? Is it simply that they cannot afford to; i.e., is income a determinant of the decision to pay spousal maintenance? Does the number of children affect the father's decision to make the maintenance payments? Does the wife's earning power as evidenced by income earned during marriage affect their maintenance? In an attempt to answer these questions, a logit model was constructed and tested using data from the University of Michigan's *Panel on Income Dynamics* survey data. The model was specified as:

$$L_i = \beta_0 + \beta_1 \text{HINC} + \beta_2 \text{WINC} + \beta_3 \text{NCH} + \varepsilon_i,$$

where

> L_i = 1 if the wife received maintenance in the second full year after divorce; = 0 if no maintenance was received[19]
> HINC = husband's annual income earned during the last year of marriage, thousands of 1981 dollars
> WINC = wife's annual income earned during the last year of marriage, thousands of 1981 dollars
> NCH = number of dependent children under age 17.

The logit module of SYSTAT™ was used and 197 data points were input. The data are contained in Data Set 20 of Appendix I. The estimated equation was:

$$\hat{L}_i = -1.734 + 0.012\text{HINC} - 0.046\text{WINC} + 0.308\text{NCH},$$
$$(0.454) \quad (0.004) \quad\quad (0.077) \quad\quad\quad (0.111)$$

$$LL = -122.13 \quad\quad -2LLR = 21.08, \quad\quad \text{d.f.} = 3,$$

standard errors in parentheses.

---

[19]A note for SYSTAT™ v. 3.2 users: To make the logit module consistent with the other modules of SYSTAT™, SYSTAT™ requires that the dependent variable be coded as (1, 2) instead of the more common (0, 1) coding. The only result is that the estimated logits are now interpreted as the log of the "failure odds ratio." In this case, the log is of the odds of not receiving maintenance. Multiplying the $\hat{\beta}_j$ by -1 is all that is necessary to convert the estimated equation into the more common (0, 1) logit model.

Interpretation of the t-ratios for a logit model is exactly the same as in regression analysis. The signs and t-ratios on HINC and NCH indicate that they have positive and significant effects on the odds of receiving maintenance, but the low t-ratio for the WINC variable ($= 0.597$) indicates that it may be insignificant, something we did not suspect when the model was specified. This inference is probably correct because of the large sample, but we should use a likelihood test to be sure.

To check whether the WINC variable is statistically significant, the model was run with WINC omitted. The results were:

$$L_i = -1.871 + 0.012\text{HINC} + 0.329\text{NCH},$$
$$\quad (0.394) \quad (0.004) \quad\quad (0.105)$$

$$\text{LL} = -122.30 \quad -2\text{LLR} = 20.72, \quad \text{d.f.} = 2,$$

standard errors in parentheses. To test whether the omitted variable was significant, compute the statistic $d = -2(L2 - L1)$ where $L1$ is the log likelihood of the original model and $L2$ is the log likelihood of the constrained model. This gives:

$$d = -2[-122.30 - (-122.13)] = 0.34.$$

Because 0.34 is less than the critical value, $\chi^2_{0.05}(\text{d.f.} = 1) = 3.84$, we conclude that WINC is not a statistically significant explanatory variable. There is one degree of freedom (d.f.) in this test because we have omitted one independent variable.

We cannot be confident of the model until we have assessed goodness of fit with the likelihood ratio test. There were two independent variables in the model, so there are two degrees of freedom in the likelihood ratio test. Because $-2\text{LLR} = 20.72$ is greater than critical value, $\chi^2_{0.05}(\text{d.f.} = 2) = 5.99$, we conclude that the fitted model explains the observed data better than a model that included only a constant.

The equation can be trusted, so we can use it to calculate the fitted logits and then convert these into the probabilities of receiving spousal maintenance. As an example, suppose NCH $= 3$ and HINC $= 10,000$, the calculations would be:

$$\hat{L}_i = -1.871 + 0.012(10) + 0.329(3) = -0.764.$$

Taking the antilog gives:

$$\text{antilog}(0.764) = 0.466.$$

Finally, because $\hat{L}_i^* = \ln[P_i/(1 - P_i)]$, we have:

$$0.466 = \frac{P_i}{1 - P_i},$$

$$P_i = 0.32.$$

Thus, the chance of a woman receiving maintenance if she has three dependent children and her former husband made $10,000 in the year before the divorce is about 32%.

If you have access to a computer program that does logit analysis, you might be tempted to run all sorts of logit models. Logit analysis is being used more often in econometric analysis, and if you have access to qualitative data the logit model is an obvious choice. Be careful, however, before trying to convert quantitative data into qualitative data just so you can fit a logit model. Such conversions often result in the loss of information. If the data are quantitative, regression analysis is almost always preferable to the logit or a similar model.   ◆ ◆ ◆

10.5

SUMMARY

Qualitative choice models are used when the dependent variable can take on only discrete values, usually assigned 1's and 0's. Simple versions of qualitative choice models—the linear probability model and relative probability logit models—can be estimated with standard regression techniques. However, serious qualitative choice modeling involves nonlinear estimation techniques, the logit and similar models. With a large sample, logit model parameter estimates can be evaluated with t-tests, but a likelihood ratio test is preferred with a small sample. Nothing in a logit model corresponds precisely to R^2, but a χ^2-test can be used to determine whether the fitted model explains the observed data better than a model consisting of only a constant.

Before closing, we need to emphasize that this chapter has been an extremely simplified introduction to the study of models of qualitative choice. Our focus was confined to the linear probability and logit model for two reasons. First, the mathematics of other qualitative choice models gets too complicated for an introductory course. Second, most econometricians now believe that the differences between the logit, probit, and other models of qualitative choice are insignificant except for *very* large samples. Students who wish to pursue these models further are encouraged to look at Aldrich and Nelson (1984) or Hosmer and Lemeshow (1989).

Finally, we need to reiterate that while the logit model is becoming more important to econometricians, it has not become standardized enough for various statistics packages to present the same information. Most programs provide information very similar to that presented in this chapter, but you will probably have to refer to the manual, sample printouts, and a text on logit analysis before embarking on any serious research.

CONCEPTS FOR REVIEW

The logit model represents a departure from most of the material in the book, so it may seem a bit daunting at first. However, it has become quite important in applied economic research and will only become more important in the future. To make sure you understand the problems encountered with qualitative dependent variables, make sure you:

- can list and discuss the econometric problems associated with qualitative dependent variables
- know when it is appropriate to use the linear probability model
- understand the need for MLE estimation of the logit model and can determine the statistical significance of the log likelihood ratio
- can derive odds ratios and probabilities from logit results
- can define and use the following terms in context.

KEY TERMS

binomial distribution	logistic function
conditional probability	maximum likelihood
constrained linear probability model	odds ratio
heteroscedasticity	qualitative variable
likelihood ratio test	quantitative variable
linear probability model	WLS

EXERCISES

10.1 Explain why constraining the linear probability model of Fig. 10.2 typically increases R^2.

10.2 The 1980s saw a record number of failures of savings and loan associations. Suggest how a logit model could be used to study the causes of saving and loans association failures.

10.3 We proved that the error term of the linear probability model is heteroscedastic. Is there reason to believe that the error variance always increases as X increases? Why or why not? Does your answer affect the suggested weighting scheme described in Eq. [10.13]?

10.4 Show that the WLS transformation in Eq. [10.13] results in homoscedastic errors.

10.5   Refer to Example 10.2.

   a. At what income level is the chance of college attendance 90%?

   b. At what income level is the chance of college attendance 50%?

10.6   In Example 10.1, we noted that the authors of the original study chose a probit model instead of the linear probability model. Is there anything about the analysis in Example 10.1 that would lead you to believe that the linear probability model was an incorrect model specification?

10.7   Show that Eq. [10.9] follows from Eq. [10.8].

10.8   Given $P_i = (1 + e^{-Z_i})^{-1}$, show that $0 < P_i < 1$ as $-\infty < Z_i < +\infty$.

10.9   **a.** Compute pseudo R^2 for the model run in Example 10.3.

   b. The logit model in Example 10.3 was run with just a constant. The log likelihood of that run was -132.66. Use this information to calculate McFadden's R^2.

10.10 OLS was performed on the data in Example 10.3. The results were:

```
DEP VAR: CS  N: 197  R-sq: .095  ADJ  R-sq: .086  SER: 0.470

VARIABLE  COEFFICIENT  STD ERROR    T      P(2 TAIL)

CONSTANT       1.117     0.071   15.679     0.000
    HINC       0.002     0.001    3.534     0.001
   YGCH2       0.069     0.022    3.119     0.002

                ANALYSIS OF VARIANCE

  SOURCE    SUM-OF-SQUARES   DF  MEAN-SQUARE  F-RATIO    P

REGRESSION      4.511        2     2.256     10.222   0.000
RESIDUAL       42.809      194     0.221
```

   a. Compare these results to those obtained in Example 10.3. Do you think they are significantly different?

   b. How would your interpretation of the fitted values from the OLS model differ from your interpretation of the fitted values from the logit model?

10.11 The model from Example 10.1 was estimated using logit analysis instead of WLS and the constrained linear probability model. The results are presented on the following page.

```
RESULTS OF ESTIMATION
********************

LOG LIKELIHOOD:          -12.8896

   PARAMETER        ESTIMATE        STANDARD ERROR  T-STATISTIC
==============================================================
   1  CONSTANT  |-13.0213           4.93044         -2.6410
   2     TUCE   |  0.951577E-01      .141542          .67229
   3      PSI   |  2.37869          1.06444          2.2347
   4      GPA   |  2.82611          1.26279          2.2380

-2 TIMES LOG LIKELIHOOD RATIO (CHI SQUARED) : 15.4042
             WITH      3 DEGREES OF FREEDOM
```

a. Compare these results to those obtained in Example 10.1. Do you think they are significantly different?

b. Would you be more inclined to rely on these results or those from Example 10.1? Why?

c. With a small sample, inferences based on asymptotic *t*-ratios are not reliable. To check the statistical significance of the individual regressors, four additional logit models were tested. The relevant results were:

Model 1: Grade = f(constant only);   LL = -20.59,

Model 2: Grade = f(constant, GPA, PSI);   LL = -13.13,
          -2LLR = 14.93,

Model 3: Grade = f(constant, GPA);   LL = -16.21, -2LLR = 8.77,

Model 4: Grade = f(constant, psi);   LL = -17.67, -2LLR = 5.84.

Use this information to determine the statistical significance of the individual regressors.

10.12 Refer to Example 10.3. What is the chance that a divorced mother with four children whose former husband made $20,000 the year before divorce will receive support? What if she had four children and income was only $8,000?

10.13 The yield curve spread—the difference between long-term and short-term interest rates—has long been used as an indicator of GNP turning points. Generally, an inversion of the yield curve (short rates are higher than long rates) is an indication of a pending recession, and recoveries are usually led by a reversion of the yield curve to its proper shape with long rates higher than short rates. Use the data in Data Set 21 of Appendix I to construct a logit model to predict the probability of recession. The yield curve was calculated as the difference between the three-year treasury bill rate and the three-month certificate of deposit where

$L2$ = yield curve lagged 2 quarters
$L3$ = yield curve lagged 3 quarters
Q = 1 if real GNP growth is positive; = 0 if real GNP growth is negative.

a. Construct two-quarter and three-quarter forecasting models and verify whether the coefficients are statistically significant.

b. Check to see how well these models predicted the recessions of 1974–75 and 1981–82.

c. Using current data (see Table A24 of the *Federal Reserve Bulletin*), predict the probability of a recession within two and three quarters from today.

10.14 Many economists and political scientists believe that economic issues are critical in determining individual voting preferences. Use the logit model to test whether the decision to vote Democrat or Republican in the 1984 presidential election (VOTE) depended on family income (INCOME), party identification (PARTY), and union membership (UNION). Fifty random observations from the 1984 American National Election Survey published by the Inter-University Consortium for Political and Social Research are presented in Data Set 22 of Appendix I. The variables are defined as

VOTE = 1 if the respondent voted Republican; = 0 if the respondent voted Democratic
UNION = 1 if there was a union member in the voting household; = 0 if no family members belonged to a union
PARTY = a discrete scale measuring party identification: = 1 if the respondent identified self as a strong Democrat; = 7 if the respondent identified self as a strong Republican
INCOME = a nonlinear scale measure of family income: = 1 if less than \$2,999; = 2 if \$3,000–\$4,999; = 21 if \$60,000–\$74,999; = 22 if \$75,000 or higher.

Before performing the logistic regression:

a. What signs do you expect to find on the regressors?

b. There are only 50 observations. How will this affect your interpretation of the results?

After performing the initial regression:

c. Are the results as you expected? Evaluate the individual t-statistics and the log likelihood ratio.

d. Conduct likelihood ratio tests to determine whether the individual explanatory variables are significant.

e. Calculate McFadden's R^2 for the final model. How helpful is this statistic?

APPENDIX 10.A

SOME DERIVATIONS

Show $1 - P_i = (e^{Z_i} + 1)^{-1}$

If you have not worked with exponents for a while, you may not have been able to follow the manipulations that got us from Eq. [10.16] to [10.18]. It is a bit tedious, but actually quite simple. Recall that Eq. [10.16] was:

$$P_i = (1 + e^{-Z_i})^{-1} = \frac{1}{1 + e^{-Z_i}}, \qquad [A.1]$$

where $Z_i = \beta_0 + \beta_1 X_i$. Hence,

$$1 - P_i = 1 - \frac{1}{1 + e^{-Z_i}}. \qquad [A.2]$$

When we find a common denominator and rewrite the first 1 on the right side as a fraction, we have:

$$1 - P_i = \left(\frac{1 + e^{-Z_i}}{1 + e^{-Z_i}}\right) - \left(\frac{1}{1 + e^{-Z_i}}\right). \qquad [A.3]$$

The 1's in the numerator cancel and we are left with:

$$1 - P_i = \frac{e^{-Z_i}}{1 + e^{-Z_i}}; \qquad [A.4]$$

rewriting the numerator gives:

$$\frac{e^{-Z_i}}{1 + e^{-Z_i}} = \frac{1}{e^{Z_i}}\left(\frac{1}{1 + e^{-Z_i}}\right). \qquad [A.5]$$

After expanding the denominator, we have:

$$1 - P_i = \frac{1}{e^{Z_i} + e^0} = \frac{1}{e^{Z_i} + 1} = (e^{Z_i} + 1)^{-1}, \qquad [A.6]$$

which is what we needed to show.

Show $\dfrac{P_i}{1 - P_i} = e^{Z_i}$

Equation [10.18] presented the odds ratio as:

$$\frac{P_i}{1 - P_i} = \frac{1 + e^{+Z_i}}{1 + e^{-Z_i}} = e^{Z_i}. \qquad (A.7)$$

This too can be shown quite easily. Substitute for e^{-Z_i} in the denominator:

$$\frac{P_i}{1 - P_i} = \frac{1 + e^{Z_i}}{1 + \dfrac{1}{e^{Z_i}}}. \qquad\qquad \text{[A.8]}$$

Multiply by e^{Z_i} to find a common denominator:

$$\frac{P_i}{1 - P_i} = \frac{1 + e^{Z_i}}{\dfrac{e^{Z_i} + 1}{e^{Z_i}}}. \qquad\qquad \text{[A.9]}$$

Then invert the denominator and multiply:

$$\frac{P_i}{1 - P_1} = (1 + e^{Z_i})\left(\frac{e^{Z_i}}{1 + e^{Z_i}}\right) = e^{Z_i}. \qquad\qquad \text{[A.10]}$$

Taking the log of the odds ratio gives the logits:

$$\ln\left(\frac{P_i}{1 - P_i}\right) = \ln(e^{Z_i}) = Z_i = \beta_0 + \beta_1 X_{1i}, \qquad\qquad \text{[A.11]}$$

which is what we estimate in the logit model.

CHAPTER ELEVEN

METHODOLOGICAL ISSUES

It's time to review what we have been doing for the last ten chapters. Except for chapter 9, the approach has been to use econometric methods to test given economic hypotheses. Think about that for a minute: We have been using econometrics to test *existing* theories. This is the opposite of how most scientists operate. Most scientists study data and *then* develop theories. Is there a reason why econometric methodology is reversed? Perhaps. Controlled experiments—experiments in which all factors are fixed except one in order to isolate the effects of one variable—are virtually impossible in the social sciences so econometric methodology must differ from physical science methodology. Unfortunately, econometric methodology can lead to several problems. For example, when we start with an *a priori* model specification, we must *assume* that causality runs from *X* to *Y*—an assumption that cannot be verified statistically. Also, too often, when preliminary regression results do not correspond to the initial hypothesis, econometricians are tempted to run different functional forms, add new variables, or do whatever is necessary to verify their initial hypothesis. Is this legitimate? Perhaps not, but the line between appropriate and inappropriate econometric methodology is far from precise. These and other issues are explored in this final chapter.

11.1

DATA GENERATING PROCESSES

We have been using econometric methods throughout the entire book, but really haven't stopped to look at econometric methodology *per se*. Doing so now will provide a starting place for a somewhat critical analysis of standard econometric practice—a necessary step to prevent you from concluding that econometrics is more developed than it really is.[1]

11.1.1   Model Specification

Econometric studies typically begin with a theory of economic "reality." This theory is then expressed as an equation before data are collected and the theory is tested. As we are about to find out, several problems can be introduced even before the data are input into the computer.

Suppose that we wanted to test a theory of consumer demand. Economic theory says that the quantity demanded will be inversely related to price and positively related to income. The general notation would be[2]:

$$q_d = f(p, y), \qquad f_p < 0, \qquad f_y > 0. \qquad [11.1]$$

Equation [11.1] cannot be estimated with econometrics, at least not as it is written. The econometrician must make additional assumptions to specify the model. A common specification is that quantity, price, and income have a

---

[1] This section is based on Chapters 1 and 26 of Aris Spanos, *Statistical Foundations of Econometric Modelling* (Cambridge, U.K.: Cambridge University Press, 1986).
[2] Recall that "$f_p < 0$" indicates that q and p are assumed to be inversely related while "$f_y > 0$" indicates that q and y are assumed to be directly related.

multiplicative relationship as in Eq. [11.2]:

$$q_d = \beta_0 p^{\beta_1} y^{\beta_2}.$$
[11.2]

We have little reason to suppose that consumer demand behaves this way, but such a specification is especially convenient mathematically. As we found out in Chapter 5, a log transformation gives:

$$\ln(q_t) = \ln(\beta_0) + \beta_1 \ln(p_t) + \beta_2 \ln(y_t),$$
[11.3]

which is linear, and the β_j can be interpreted as elasticities.

Equation [11.3] must be modified once more before econometric estimation is possible: An error term must be added to capture the effects of omitted variables, measurement errors, and other random factors:

$$\ln(q_t) = \ln(\beta_0) + \beta_1 \ln(p_t) + \beta_2 \ln(y_t) + \varepsilon_t.$$
[11.4]

At this stage, econometricians go about their business of estimation—collecting data, running regressions, revising hypotheses, etc.

Unfortunately, it is never clear whether the data used in the estimation process correspond precisely to the variables involved in the theory under investigation. For example, the theory of demand expressed in Eq. [11.1] relates to *intentions*—some sort of metaphysical utility maximization process—but the time series data most often used in the estimation process are actual *transactions*. Is it obvious that intentions and transactions are equivalent? Probably not; too many additional factors complicate the choice. If the econometric specification is inconsistent with the theoretical model, regression analysis is not a legitimate test of the theory. This is one reason—perhaps a major one—why so many regression studies have insignificant coefficients or coefficients with the wrong sign, at least until the model is respecified and reestimated. Proper econometric methodology, in fact, requires that the specified model correspond to the theory under investigation.

11.1.2 Estimable Equations

The theory of demand expressed in Eq. [11.1] may not be *estimable* because it is difficult or impossible to collect data on consumer intentions. With Eq. [11.4], we are testing a dynamic adjustment process—the process by which market transactions take place in response to price and income changes. This is an interesting phenomenon and certainly worthy of econometric investigation, but it is not a test of the theory of demand. Econometricians who do not recognize this problem are likely to use whatever methods necessary to fit their data to their theory—adding lagged endogenous variables, different function forms, etc. Such actions would cause physical scientists to cringe.

David Hendry,[3] Aris Spanos, and others feel that the link between estimable equations and economic theory is the most important issue in econometric modeling.[4] The key aim of the econometrician should be to make inferences about the *data generating process* that gives rise to the observable data. The data generating process is the underlying behavioral function that actually produces the data that are being analyzed. In the case of Eq. [11.1], the data generating process is the behavior of the market, not the utility maximization process of demand theory. Any equation that can be estimated— an *estimable model*—is an approximation of some data generating process. This approach broadens the scope of econometrics significantly. The traditional role of econometrics has been to test given economic theories, which themselves were developed to aid economic understanding. Restricting econometrics to filling in numbers for theoretical constructs is far too limiting.

A much better role for econometrics—and the one advocated by members of the Hendry school—is to use econometrics as a scientific tool to help us discover novel facts about the economy. This doesn't mean analyzing data without theory; it does mean that the data and regression results must be interpreted very carefully in the context of a data generating process. An initial theoretical construct—the estimable model—is required as are the statistical techniques that were developed in the first ten chapters. You must be careful, however, before assuming that the estimable model is consistent with economic theory. Many economic theories may not be testable with econometrics.

One additional difference between the Hendry approach and classical econometrics must be mentioned before leaving this very brief introduction to the Hendry approach: Autocorrelation and other "problems" with the error terms are usually not signals that GLS transformations are necessary. Instead, Hendry believes that autocorrelation is most often an indication of model misspecification.[5] Too often, the use of GLS methods designed to correct for the "problem" of autocorrelation results in hiding the data generating process behind transformed data.

---

[3] The British economist David Hendry was the pioneer in this line of reasoning and has written extensively on econometric methodology, but much of his work is a bit technical for beginning students. A good place to start is Christopher Gilbert, "Professor Hendry's Econometric Methodology," *Oxford Bulletin of Economics and Statistics* Special Issue, Vol. 48, No. 3, August 1986, p. 283–307.

[4] Spanos (p. 11) notes that Haavelmo (1944) and Stigler (1962) were aware of this issue as well.

[5] See footnote 14 in Chapter 6.

11.2

DATA MINING

One of the consequences of the failure to distinguish between the theoretical model and the estimable model is that investigators are apt to try different functional forms, lag structures, and so on until they get the desired results— or at least results that are interesting enough to warrant publication. This practice, often called *data mining*, is probably quite common, even though econometricians consider it unethical.

11.2.1 The Ethics of Data Mining

While data mining undoubtedly exists in the physical sciences, it is much less common for two reasons: controlled experiments and experimental replication. Controlled experiments allow the investigator to impose *ceteris paribus* on causal factors in order to isolate the effect of one independent variable on the dependent variable. This is sometimes possible in the laboratory, but rarely, if ever, in the social real world.[6] Because it is so difficult to conduct controlled experiments, economists are forced to look for ways to extract information from the data—including, too often, processes that would be classified as data mining.[7]

Experimental replication—performance of the same experiment by independent scientists—is also common in the hard sciences, but has only recently been practiced with any regularity in economics. Following the lead of the *Journal of Money, Credit and Banking*,[8] many economics journals now request

---

[6] Actually, controlled experiments are being used in economics today. Economists at Texas A&M, the University of Arizona, and a few other schools have been using laboratory experiments to test basic propositions of economic theory. This research has received mixed reviews from the economics profession. Two papers that deal with experimental economics are: David S. Brookshire et al., "The External Validity of Experimental Economics Techniques: Analysis of Demand Behavior," *Economic Inquiry*, Vol. 25, No. 2, April 1987, p. 239–250, and Alvin E. Roth, "Laboratory Experimentation in Economics," *Economic Journal*, Vol. 98, No. 393, December 1988, p. 975–1031.

[7] We should note that the partial regression coefficients in a correctly specified multiple regression model with zero multicollinearity could be considered the results of a controlled experiment because all independent variables except one are treated as fixed. Unfortunately, model specification is *rarely* sufficient to accept this as a definition of a controlled experiment.

[8] See William G. Dewald, Jerry G. Thursby, and Richard G. Anderson, "Replication in Empirical Economics: The *Journal of Money, Credit and Banking* Project," *American Economic Review*, Vol. 76, No. 4, September 1986, p. 587–603.

that authors of empirical papers include their data with their submissions. This will certainly reduce the incidence of "fraudulent" regressions, but these are probably very rare. What it may not eliminate is the econometrician who runs *hundreds* of regressions before hitting on one that works. The reviewers would see only the data and the final model specification.

We need to emphasize that what often appears to be data mining is not necessarily improper. Econometrics is a search for information, and it usually does require running a model several times with alternative specifications. Such "data mining" is only unwarranted when the investigator consciously manipulates the model in an attempt to get the desired results. Still, at least two potential problems arise whenever the econometrician starts manipulating the model or data: fewer degrees of freedom and systematic specification bias.

FEWER DEGREES OF FREEDOM   Some econometricians believe that every model specification and every regression run should be counted as a lost degree of freedom because each rejection imposes a restriction on acceptable parameter values. In the extreme case, it is possible to run the model more often than there are data points and use up all of the degrees of freedom. In reality, regression analysis is never completed after just one run, and if new specifications are based on alternative theoretical models, not enough degrees of freedom will be lost to make a difference. With today's desktop computers, however, the temptation is to run the model dozens—or even hundreds—of times and report only the few most "successful" runs. Ethical econometricians resist this temptation. As long as you can provide a reasonable theoretical justification for every model specification, you will be on safe ground.

SPECIFICATION BIAS   The process of model specification often proceeds as a *sequential search*; that is, the investigator specifies an initial model that includes several independent variables, some of which, according to economic theory, "have" to be included and some of which "might" be included. A sequence of regressions is then run and the variables with low t-ratios are dropped from subsequent runs. Unfortunately, there is no precise way to determine which variables really should be dropped in the search process, and we know from Chapter 5 that dropping the wrong variable can bias parameter estimates.[9] Is a 95% confidence region always appropriate even for the "have to" variables?

In fact, sequential searches are the norm in econometrics and, as long as the search process is based on theory, should not be abandoned entirely. However, two things should be kept in mind when doing a sequential search. First, run only as many regressions as theory allows. Second, the final report should include a discussion of the search procedure and a list of the preliminary regressions.

---

[9]The F-test developed in Appendix 4.A is one way to help determine whether variables should be included or excluded. The Granger causality test developed in the next section is quite similar.

11.2.2   Robust Results

Because "investigators" are usually capable of torturing the data until they get the results they want, it is important to know how to tell reliable from unreliable results. Unfortunately, there is no simple way. The best thing that can be said is this: *Be wary of any econometric result until different investigators have reached similar results using different model specifications.* Results that hold up under this criteria are said to be *robust*. Results that fail to meet these criteria are called *fragile*.[10] This is one reason why it is so important to conduct a literature search as part of the econometric process.

Finally, we need to reiterate a point that was made in Chapter 3 and elsewhere: Econometrics is more than the game of maximizing R^2. So many economic data series have a strong trend component that it is possible to *randomly* combine time series into models and generate acceptable R^2's.[11] However, R^2 means something *only* in the context of economic theory and, even then, it is not always clear that the model with the highest R^2 is correctly specified.[12] Careful analysis of the t- and F-scores and the residual and outlier plots is just as important as looking at the R^2, but none can substitute for a sound theoretical underpinning to the model under investigation.[13]

11.2.3   Stepwise Regression

A rather dubious regression technique that verges on data mining is *stepwise regression*. This technique allows the computer to search through a list of potential explanatory variables to come up with the model specification that maximizes R^2. In the first "step," the computer finds the single explanatory variable that results in the highest R^2. In the next step, the explanatory variable that adds the next highest increment to R^2 is added. The search continues until successive variables do not increase R^2 by the amount prespecified by the researcher.

---

[10] The term *fragile* comes from a classic article by Edward E. Leamer, "Let's Take the 'Con' Out of Econometrics," *American Economic Review*, March 1973, p. 31–43.

[11] In fact, this is just what Peach and Webb did in their paper, "Randomly Specified Macroeconomic Models: Some Implications for Model Selection," *Journal of Economic Issues*, Vol. XVII, No. 3, September 1983, p. 697–720.

[12] On this point, see James B. Ramsey, "Classical Model Selection Through Specification Error Tests," from Paul Zarembka, ed., *Frontiers in Econometrics* (New York: Academic Press, 1974), p. 13–47.

[13] Some programs have procedures that attempt to look at the robustness issue. For example, SAS® has a procedure, *Proc Jackreg*, which runs repetitive regressions leaving out each data point in order. It then presents the regression coefficients and summary statistics for each subset. A wide variation in results indicates a fragile model.

So many problems are associated with this technique that few econometricians use it anymore, but many popular statistics programs do have stepwise regression modules. The two main problems with stepwise regression
are: (1) Variable selection is based on economic theory only to the extent that
the list of potential explanatory variables was consciously chosen. This creates
all of the specification problems discussed in Sec. 5.3. (2) Multicollinearity
can make it difficult to choose between different variables. The result is that
whether a variable is included or excluded depends on its place in the selection queue.

■ EXAMPLE 11.1

DATA MINING:
The Relationship Between Deficits and Interest Rates

One of the most hotly debated economic issues of the early 1980s was the
relationship between interest rates and the federal deficit. The traditional
view held that higher federal deficits would raise interest rates, while the
then-radical new classical approach held that no relationship existed
between interest rates and deficits. The issue was important to the Reagan
administration, which was running the largest fiscal deficits in history. Few
observers were surprised when the Republican party—long known as the
party of fiscal conservatism—quickly converted to the new classical view
while the usually spendthrift Democrats began to preach traditional
economics.

The issue may have reached a head when Treasury Secretary Don Regan
announced that there was *no* empirical evidence linking interest rates to
deficits. Regan was stretching the point a bit; perhaps he should have said
that there was no *definitive* evidence. Regardless, the deficit/interest rate
issue is useful for demonstrating how easy it is to find what you are looking
for in econometrics. For example, the Democrats might have used a simple
regression model to show that the interest rate on Aaa bonds (AAA) is
positively affected by the deficit (DEF). One such run, using annual data for
the 1960–88 period, is shown as Regression 1 in the printout below. (The
data are in Data Set 23 of Appendix I.) The positive sign on the deficit
coefficient (0.028) indicates that when the deficit increases (i.e., becomes
more negative) the AAA bond rate also increases. Regression 2 shows that
the deficit coefficient can be reversed by simply adding a lagged endogenous
(LAAA) variable. Republicans might have relied on a similar model to
"prove" that deficits *lower* interest rates, if anything.[14]

---

[14] A paper by Paul Evans ["Do Large Deficits Produce High Interest Rates?"
American Economic Review, Vol. 75, No. 1, March 1985, p. 68–87] reached that
conclusion. His theoretical justification was that even though lower tax rates may
increase the deficit, they also increase the real after-tax return on saving. The
increase in private saving may lower aggregate demand enough to reduce interest
rates.

```
Regression 1: Dep var: AAA   N: 29   R-sq: .496   SER: 2.141

Variable  Coefficient   Std Error   T        P(2 tail)

CONSTANT       6.442       0.518   12.425      0.000
     DEF       0.028       0.005    5.151      0.000


Regression 2: Dep var: AAA   N: 28   R-sq: .920   Adj  R-sq: .914
              SER: 0.858

Variable  Coefficient   Std Error   T        P(2 tail)

CONSTANT      -0.461       0.637   -0.724      0.476
     DEF      -0.012       0.004   -3.053      0.005
    LAAA       1.176       0.100   11.723      0.000
```

Of course, *we* know that there are several problems associated with both regressions: Both are subject to specification error and simultaneous equation bias, multicollinearity is a problem in the second run, and so on, but the voting public and policy makers are less well versed in econometrics. Furthermore, most economists would say that the important issue is the effect of the deficit on the real interest rate, not the nominal rate that was used in this example. At any rate, the fact that it is this easy to "prove" your point econometrically means that politicians—and some econometricians—are likely to continue to find the results for which they are looking.

11.3

CAUSALITY IN ECONOMETRICS

We have said over and over that statistics cannot prove causality, but that causality must be assumed in regression analysis. The issue of causality is much more complex than that.[15] For example, when we say "*A* causes *B*," do we mean that *A* is a necessary and sufficient condition for *B*? That if *A* can be controlled, then *B* can be controlled as well? Does the phrase "*A* causes *B*" also

---

[15] It is also quite interesting. The reader is encouraged to look at the largely nontechnical piece by Arnold Zellner, "Causality and Econometrics," from *Basic Issues in Econometrics* (Chicago: The University of Chicago Press, 1984, 1987), p. 35–74. A short book by J. R. Hicks, *Causality in Economics* (New York: Basic Books, 1979) points out how the issue of causality in economics differs from what most philosophers mean by causality.

imply that *A* is the complete set of conditions required for *B*? If *A* and *B* are economic variables, the answer probably would have to be "no" to all of these questions.[16] Then what do we mean by causality? Economic methodologists will be debating that question forever; econometricians have begun to develop their own concepts of causality out of necessity.

11.3.1   Defining Causality

A working definition of causality might be: Causality is predictability according to a law or set of laws.[17] Methodologists would quibble about whether this definition suggests deterministic or probabilistic causality,[18] but this definition highlights the two key aspects of econometric causality: the link to time and the basis in theory.

ECONOMETRIC CAUSALITY IS LINKED TO TIME   Most econometricians have argued that if *A* "causes" *B*, then *A* must come before *B* in calendar time.[19] However, with annual or even quarterly data, the cause and the effect may take place within the same data period, meaning that *A* may be contemporaneous with *B*. The link to time is one way the econometrician's definition differs from the philosopher's definition: Many philosophers recognize that causality can be contemporaneous. However, the key to understanding causality is not that *A* precedes *B* but that the relationship between *A* and *B* is asymmetrical; i.e., *A* causes *B*, not vice versa. One reason econometricians are forced to tie their concept of causality to time is that there are so many two-way causal relationships in economics. For example, price "causes" the quantity demanded, but the quantity demanded also "causes" price.

---

[16] This statement is probably true for any set of economic variables. As an example, suppose *A* is money growth and *B* is the inflation rate. If inflation is ever caused by external factors, *A* is not necessary and sufficient. Controlling money growth doesn't always halt inflation, at least not immediately; and all but the most rigid monetarists would contend that factors other than money growth affect the inflation rate.

[17] This definition, credited to H. Feigel, "Notes on Causality," from H. Feigel and M. Brodbeck, Eds., *Readings in the Philosophy of Science* (New York: Appleton-Century-Crofts, 1953) is quoted in A. Zellner (1987), p. 38.

[18] Deterministic causality is a philosophical concept of causality; if causality is deterministic, all of the rhetorical questions asked in the previous sections would be answered in the affirmative. Probabilistic causality is more appropriate for econometric inquiry. It refers to stochastic relationships of the type generally assumed in econometrics.

[19] These and other questions regarding the nature of causality are raised by Kevin D. Hoover, "The Logic of Causal Inference: Econometrics and the Conditional Analysis of Causation," presented at the History of Economics Society Meeting, 1989.

ECONOMETRIC CAUSALITY MUST BE TIED TO THEORY   The time dimension requirement also means that econometric causality must be based on theory because, quite literally, there are an infinite number of events that follow each other in time. Suppose we "know" that event B is caused by the antecedent causal conditions A. In the real world, what can be observed is only a, a subset of A. Econometricians must restrict the causal field to the a that can be observed and are of the most interest. The only way to isolate the conditions to study is with the framework of economic theory. Because the structure of the model is assumed *a priori* and only the subset a of the A causal factors is under study, causality will depend on the specific model.

The link to theory removes causality from the realm of metaphysical final causation. To most modern scientists, "causal orderings. . . are. . . just logical properties of the model. . . ."[20] For example, in a simple model of inflation using wage growth as the independent variable, econometric analysis might reach the conclusion that wage growth "causes" inflation. However, an alternative model using money growth as the independent variable might reach the conclusion that money growth "causes" inflation. Can both conclusions be correct? Possibly. "Econometric causality" usually means little more than the predictable, temporal association between the a and B. Because both models have a theoretical basis, the practical issue is which model best explains the path of inflation and reduces inflation forecast errors.

11.3.2   Redefining Exogeneity

One key to the causality question is the differentiation between exogenous and endogenous variables. Several people have offered alternative definitions of exogeneity in an attempt to resolve this issue.[21] As the following definitions illustrate, the correct way to define exogeneity depends on how the model is being used.

---

[20] Arnold Zellner paraphrases Herbert Simon in "Causality and Econometrics," from Karl Brunner and Alan Meltzer, Eds., *Three Aspects of Policy and Policymaking: Knowledge, Data, and Institutions*, [Carnegie-Rochester Conference Series on Public Policy (a supplementary series to the *Journal of Monetary Economics*), Vol. 10; Amsterdam: North-Holland Publishing Company, 1979], p. 9–54. Reprinted in *Basic Issues in Econometrics* (Chicago: The University of Chicago Press, 1984), p. 47.

[21] Important work in this area has been done by E. E. Leamer, "Vector Autoregressions for Causal Influence," in Karl Brunner and Alan Meltzer, Eds., *Understanding Monetary Regimes* (supplement to the *Journal of Monetary Economics*), 1985, p. 255–304., and R. F. Engle, D. F. Hendry, and J. F. Richard, "Exogeneity," *Econometrica*, Vol. 51, 1983, p. 277–304, and Gilbert (1986). This discussion follows Gilbert (1986), p. 289–291.

WEAK EXOGENEITY   This is what we normally mean by an exogenous variable. If X is weakly exogenous, it is possible to "explain" Y in terms of X but it is *not* possible to "explain" X in terms of Y. Weak exogeneity fulfills the asymmetry requirement of causality. If X is not weakly exogenous, it is necessary to find a joint explanation for X and Y—and regression analysis is an inappropriate methodology. Regression models must have regressors that are at least weakly exogenous before estimation makes any sense.

STRONG EXOGENEITY   Weak exogeneity is not always sufficient, especially when the model is to be used for forecasting. Consider the equations:

$$Y_t = \beta_0 + \beta_1 X_{t-1} + \varepsilon_{1t}, \tag{11.5}$$

$$X_t = \alpha_0 + \alpha_1 Y_{t-1} + \varepsilon_{2t}, \tag{11.6}$$

where ε_{1t} and ε_{2t} obey the standard assumptions and are independent of each other. The interesting attribute of this system is the lagged *feedback* relationship between X and Y: X_{t-1} affects Y_t in Eq. [11.5], but Y_{t-1} feeds back on X_t in Eq. [11.6]. Strong exogeneity is defined as weak exogeneity without this kind of feedback relationship.

To understand why strong exogeneity is necessary for forecasting, note that Eq. [11.5] could be used to generate a reasonable one-step forecast of Y_t. However, if a two-step or longer forecast is needed, you must know Eq. [11.6], because the one-step forecast from Eq. [11.5] will show up as an explanatory variable on the right side of Eq. [11.6]. The feedback relationship means that X_t and Y_t are not completely exogenous over time; that is, X_t is only weakly exogenous with respect to Y_t. We'll see momentarily that strong exogeneity is closely linked to Granger causality.

SUPER EXOGENEITY   Policy analysis may require an even stronger concept of exogeneity: super exogeneity. Suppose we have the regression model in Eq. [11.7]:

$$Y_t = \beta_0 + \beta_1 X_{1t} + \beta_2 X_{2t} + \varepsilon_t, \tag{11.7}$$

where

     Y_t = target variable, say, the inflation rate
     X_{1t} = lagged growth rate of the money supply
     X_{2t} = expected growth rate of the money supply
     ε_t = well-behaved error term.

Now, suppose that the monetary authorities try to reduce the inflation rate by reducing monetary growth, X_{1t}. It is entirely possible—some economists would say very likely[22]—that people would change their expectations of the

---

[22] This is the now well-known *Lucas critique*, an idea we mentioned briefly in the Vector Autoregression sidebar in Chapter 9.

future growth rate of the money supply. This would result in a change in X_{2t}, which, if not recognized, would lead to policy errors. Note, however, that as long as the X_{jt} are strongly exogenous, Eq. [11.7] may generate adequate forecasts—as long as there are no policy changes.

11.3.3 Granger Causality

The most celebrated test for causality in time series models is based on the work of C. W. J. Granger.[23] Granger begins with the point that it is often difficult to determine the direction of causality in time series regressions because of the inherent autocorrelation of the variables. In most cases, regression of Y_t on X_t will yield summary statistics that are just as good as those from regression of X_t on Y_t. The methods he has developed are used to determine whether variables are "temporally related" and whether inclusion of a particular variable in the model specification reduces the "forecasting variance with respect to a given information set."[24] Philosophers would question whether these criteria constitute causality. They probably do not, but Granger causality may be as close to causality as is possible with statistical information.

The basic idea behind Granger causality testing is that the future cannot cause the past. This involves testing whether lagged values of X_t play a significant role in explaining Y_t in a model with several lagged values of Y_t on the right side. If so, then X is said to "Granger-cause" Y. For example, consider the two equations below:

$$Y_t = \alpha_1 Y_{t-1} + \alpha_2 Y_{t-2} + \alpha_3 Y_{t-3} + \cdots + \beta_1 X_{t-1} + \beta_2 X_{t-2}$$
$$+ \beta_3 X_{t-3} + \cdots + \varepsilon_{1t}, \qquad [11.8]$$

$$X_t = \theta_1 Y_{t-1} + \theta_2 Y_{t-2} + \theta_3 Y_{t-3} + \cdots + \delta_1 X_{t-1} + \delta_2 X_{t-2}$$
$$+ \delta_3 X_{t-3} + \cdots + \varepsilon_{2t}. \qquad [11.9]$$

If the $X_{t-\tau}$ terms in Eq. [11.8] play a significant role in explaining Y_t (as determined by an F-test discussed below), X is said to "Granger-cause" Y. Ideally, when X is shown to Granger-cause Y, a similar test on Eq. [11.9] would show that Y does not Granger-cause X. This is an indication of *unidirectional causality*. It is also possible to find *bidirectional causality* or *independence* between X and Y.

---

[23] C. W. J. Granger, "Investigating Causal Relations by Econometric Models and Cross-Spectral Methods," *Econometrica*, Vol. 34, 1969, p. 424–438.

[24] Quotes are from Granger and C. F. Ansley and were cited by Arnold Zellner, "Causality and Econometrics," p. 36–37, from *Basic Issues in Econometrics*, Chicago: The University of Chicago Press, 1984, 1987.

Testing for Granger causality is quite simple but somewhat tedious. To check whether X Granger-causes Y or whether Y Granger-causes X for the model in Eqs. [11.8] and [11.9], the steps are as follows:

1. Run an *unrestricted regression*, Eq. [11.8], using an arbitrary lag length. Collect ESS_u, the error sum of squares from the unrestricted regression.

2. Omit all of the $X_{t-\tau}$ terms from Eq. [11.8] and run a regression on this equation. This is the *restricted regression*. Collect ESS_r, the error sum of squares from the restricted regression.

3. An F-statistic is used to test the null hypothesis that X does not Granger-cause Y versus the alternate that it does. The F-statistic is computed as:

$$F_{r,n-k-1} = \frac{(ESS_r - ESS_u)/r}{ESS_u/n - k - 1},$$ [11.10]

where r is the number of restrictions (the number of $X_{t-\tau}$ terms omitted) and $n - k - 1$ is the number of degrees of freedom in the unrestricted regression. If the calculated value from Eq. [11.10] exceeds the table value at the chosen level of significance (usually 0.05), the null hypothesis is rejected, and we conclude that X does Granger-cause Y.

4. To test whether Y Granger-causes X, repeat steps 1 through 3 using Eq. [11.9] and dropping the $Y_{t-\tau}$ variables in the restricted regression.

PROBLEMS WITH GRANGER CAUSALITY   When Granger first developed this method, it immediately attracted a great deal of attention and is still being used today. However, there are several problems, so many that some econometricians have begun to question its usefulness. Among the potentially most serious problems are:

1. There is no good way to select the lag length and, unfortunately, the lag length can be critical to the outcome of the test.

2. With small samples, choice of a bivariate (one X and one Y) or multivariate (several X's and one Y) will affect the results.

3. The errors between the two equations are likely to be correlated. If so, an additional step is required in the test.[25]

---

[25]This is the case of *seemingly unrelated regressions* (SUR) and requires estimation methods based on work done by Arnold Zellner. For a discussion of these techniques, see Chapter 11 of R. S. Pindyck and D. L. Rubenfeld, *Econometric Models and Economic Forecasts*, 2nd ed. (New York: McGraw-Hill, 1981).

4. Finally, as Example 11.2 illustrates, economists have been able to use Granger tests to generate conflicting results—not exactly what we want in a test for causality.

■ EXAMPLE 11.2

MONEY/INCOME CAUSALITY:
An Example of Granger Causality

One of the theoretical debates that has raged between the Keynesians and monetarists has been the question of whether money causes changes in nominal income, or whether changes in nominal income affect the money supply. Because good arguments can be made in support of either position,[26] econometricians have attempted to determine the direction of causality with Granger tests. The Granger test is necessary because money and income are so highly trended that regression of money on income, or income on money, both yield extremely good summary statistics—high R^2, good t-ratios, etc. Unfortunately, as this example will show, simple Granger tests do not yield very definitive results either.

To test the money/income causality question, quarterly data on nominal GNP (Q) and M2 (M) were collected for the period 1966:1–1986:2. (The data are in Data Set 24 of Appendix I.) Four lags on each variable were used in the initial test. The unrestricted equations were:

$$M_t = \alpha_0 + \alpha_1 Q_{t-1} + \cdots + \alpha_4 Q_{t-4} + \beta_1 M_{t-1} + \cdots + \beta_4 M_{t-4} + \varepsilon_{1t}, \tag{1'}$$

$$Q_t = \theta_0 + \theta_1 Q_{t-1} + \cdots + \theta_4 Q_{t-4} + \delta_1 M_{t-1} + \cdots + \delta_4 M_{t-4} + \varepsilon_{2t}, \tag{2'}$$

while the restricted equations were:

$$M_t = \beta_0 + \beta_1 M_{t-1} + \cdots + \beta_4 M_{t-4} + v_{1t}, \tag{3'}$$

$$Q_t = \theta_0 + \theta_1 Q_{t-1} + \cdots + \theta_4 Q_{t-4} + v_{2t}. \tag{4'}$$

The relevant results from the four regressions are shown below. The null hypothesis of the Granger test is that the variables excluded in the restricted regression ($Q_{t-\tau}$ from Eq. [1'], $M_{t-\tau}$ from Eq. [2']) do not "cause" the dependent variable; the alternate hypothesis is that the excluded variables do "cause" the dependent variable. If the calculated F-ratio is greater than the table entry at the chosen level of significance, the null

---

[26] For a nontechnical discussion of these arguments, see Basil Moore, "The Endogenous Money Stock," *Journal of Post Keynesian Economics*, Vol II, No. 1, Fall 1979, p. 49–70; or Chapter 8 of William S. Brown, *Macroeconomics* (Englewood Cliffs, N.J.: Prentice-Hall, 1988).

hypothesis is rejected in favor of the alternate. The conclusion we must reach from these tests is that M2 does Granger-cause nominal GNP, and that nominal GNP does not Granger-cause M2.

Regression 1: M = f(Q, M), unrestricted

n = 78   AdjR-sq = .999   ESSu = 7822.62

Regression 3: M = f(M), restricted

n = 78   AdjR-sq = .998   ESSr = 8286.73

$$F = \frac{(8286.73 - 7822.62)/4}{7822.62/69} = 1.02 < 2.53$$

Regression 2: Q = f(Q, M), unrestricted

n = 78   AdjR-sq = .998   ESSu = 37711.46

Regression 4: Q = f(Q), restricted

n = 78   AdjR-sq = .998   ESSr = 44587.93

$$F = \frac{(44587.93 - 37711.46)/4}{37711.46/69} = 3.14 > 2.53$$

These results are consistent with those obtained by Christopher Sims,[27] Robert Hafer,[28] and others, but they are inconsistent with studies done by Basil Moore (1979) and some other Keynesians. Of course, those tests were more sophisticated than the one presented here—more independent variables are used, the data are smoothed, etc.—but even a model this simple can show the basic problem with Granger causality: The results depend crucially on the number of lags that is used. For example, if

---

[27] The most widely cited reference is probably Christopher Sims, "Money, Income, and Causality," *American Economic Review*, September 1972, p. 540–552.

[28] R. W. Hafer, "The Role of Fiscal Policy in the St. Louis Equation." *Review of the Federal Reserve Bank of St. Louis*, January 1982, p. 17–22.

Eqs. [1′] through [4′] are tested using eight one-quarter lags, we would be forced to conclude that money and nominal GNP are independent because both of the *F*-statistics are lower than the table entries. Do you really believe that M2 and nominal GNP are independent over a two-year period? Few economists would answer in the affirmative—and *very* few would rely on a Granger causality study similar to this one without an accompanying theoretical explanation.

Regression 1': M = f(Q, M), unrestricted

n = 74   AdjR-sq = .999   ESSu = 6299.96

Regression 3': M = f(M), restricted

n = 74   AdjR-sq = .998   ESSr = 7367.77

$$F = \frac{(7367.77 - 6299.96)/8}{6299.96/57} = 1.21 < 2.10$$

Regression 2': Q = f(Q, M), unrestricted

n = 74   AdjR-sq = .999   ESSu = 35344.95

Regression 4': M = f(M), restricted

n = 74   AdjR-sq = .998   ESSr = 43020.33

$$F = \frac{(43020.33 - 35344.95)/8}{35344.95/57} = 1.55 < 2.10$$

11.4

SUMMARY

Econometricians have only recently begun to look carefully at the link between their theories and their econometrics. This review has been prompted for several reasons. The forecasting and policy failures of the 1970s and 1980s were certainly reasons, but the growing role of econometrics in business and academia has been just as important: With more people doing econometrics, more people began to wonder just what they were doing. The widespread availability of friendly and powerful econometrics packages for personal computers is also significant. For the first time, it is easy to sit in a comfortable chair at home and mine the data—a practice universally agreed to be improper, but also something that is practiced frequently.

If we can reach a conclusion from this chapter, it is this: There is no "right" way to do econometrics—but there are many wrong ways. Economic scientists trying to test theories or understand data may make mistakes, but they are rarely unscrupulous. If you remember that negative results are still results and that all econometric studies represent ongoing research, your econometrics will be OK.

CONCEPTS FOR REVIEW

This chapter has been the least technical in the book, but it may be the most important. It should help you design and interpret econometric models well enough to trust your results. Make sure you can:

- describe the relationship between the data generating process, estimable equations, and economic theory
- distinguish between proper econometrics and improper data mining
- know what is meant by econometric causality and how to check for Granger causality
- define and use the following terms in context.

KEY TERMS

causality	fragile
controlled experiment	robust
data generating process	sequential search
data mining	stepwise regression
degrees of freedom	strong exogeneity
estimable equation	systematic specification bias
experimental replication	weak exogeneity

EXERCISES

11.1 Is a match the cause of an explosion in a house with a gas leak? In a gas plant?

11.2 The new field of experimental economics often uses laboratory animals to test economic theories. Do you think that there is much of a future for this kind of science? Why or why not?

11.3 The regressions in Example 11.2 reported the R^2's but not the t-scores or individual parameter estimates.

a. Do you think t-scores or individual parameter estimates would be useful? What values would you expect to get?

b. Are you surprised by the $0.99+$ values for all of the R^2's?

11.4 In Example 11.1, multicollinearity was suggested as a possible problem in the second regression. What evidence is there to suggest that multicollinearity is present?

11.5 A Granger causality test was performed on annual M2 and nominal GNP (Y) data using a one-period lag. The results were:

Regression 1: $M2 = \beta_0 + \beta_1 M2_{t-1} + \beta_2 Y_{t-1}$ for $n = 27$;
$$ESS_U = 25446.21; \qquad ESS_R = 34690.49.$$

Regression 2: $Y = \alpha_0 + \alpha_1 M2_{t-1} + \alpha_2 Y_{t-1}$ for $n = 27$;
$$ESS_U = 76917.34; \qquad ESS_R = 78346.97.$$

a. Use this information to determine the direction of causality.

b. Would you be more confident with these results or with those using quarterly data from Example 11.2? Why?

11.6 Some econometricians believe that plotting the data before specifying the model is good practice. Can you think of any problems that might be associated with this methodology? Is it preferable to using *a priori* theory to suggest a model specification? Why or why not?

11.7 Some economists say that the only role of economic theory is prediction; others say that good economics must explain as well as predict. Does Granger causality "explain" causality?

11.8 We pointed out in Chapter 9 that time series models are atheoretical; i.e., that they have no underlying economic theory. What is the economic justification for including lagged values of X and Y on the right side in a Granger test?

11.9 The policy of deeming no econometric result credible "until different investigators have reached similar results using different model specifications" is widely accepted in the economic profession. Why then are there so many disagreements among econometricians?

11.10 Suppose you conducted a Granger test to determine the causality between price and quantity demanded, and price and quantity supplied. Would you expect to find causality to be uni- or bidirectional? Why?

11.11 Some economists say that econometrics can be used only to verify existing economic theory, not to generate new theories. Comment.

11.12 The Hendry school's focus on estimable models and data generating processes seems to be at odds with Box-Jenkins analysis. Is it?

11.13 Most economists believe that the rate of money growth affects the interest rate. However, it is often argued that the Federal Reserve sets monetary policy in response to interest rates, specifically, the federal funds rate (FFR). Test these propositions with the data in Data Set 25 of Appendix I. You will need to convert the nominal money supply (M2) into the rate of growth of the money supply.

11.14 The Phillips curves estimated in Chapter 5 were based on the Keynesian assertion that inflation is "caused" by unemployment; that is, that a decline in unemployment represents a tight labor market, which tends to cause wage growth and inflation. New classical economists have argued the opposite; they believe that an acceleration in inflation can lower unemployment as long as expected inflation lags behind actual inflation. Use the data in Data Set 26 of Appendix I to test the direction of causality between inflation and unemployment with a Granger causality test. You will need to convert the producer price index (PPI) into the inflation.

DATA SETS

DATA SET 1 ■ **Consumption Function Data***

Year	CONS	DPI	AAA	TBILL	Year	CONS	DPI	AAA	TBILL
1960	1005	1091	4.41	2.93	1974	1674	1897	8.57	7.89
1961	1025	1123	4.35	2.38	1975	1712	1932	8.83	5.84
1962	1069	1170	4.33	2.78	1976	1804	2001	8.43	4.99
1963	1108	1207	4.26	3.16	1977	1884	2067	8.02	5.26
1964	1171	1291	4.40	3.55	1978	1961	2167	8.73	7.22
1965	1236	1366	4.49	3.95	1979	2004	2213	9.63	10.04
1966	1299	1431	5.13	4.88	1980	2000	2214	11.94	11.51
1967	1338	1493	5.51	4.32	1981	2024	2249	14.17	14.03
1968	1406	1551	6.18	5.34	1982	2051	2262	13.79	10.69
1969	1457	1600	7.03	6.68	1983	2146	2332	12.04	8.63
1970	1492	1668	8.04	6.46	1984	2249	2470	12.71	9.58
1971	1539	1728	7.39	4.35	1985	2353	2542	11.37	7.48
1972	1622	1797	7.21	4.07	1986	2451	2645	9.02	5.98
1973	1690	1916	7.44	7.04	1987	2495	2676	9.38	5.82

*For Tables 3.1, 3.2, 4.1, 4.2, 4.3, Exercise 4.4, Examples 5.5, 6.1.

SOURCE: *1989 Economic Report of the President*, Tables B-15 (CONS), B-27 (DPI), B-71 (AAA and TB3).

DATA SET 2 ■ Consumer durables, consumer confidence data*

Date	CD	CN	CCI	CD6	ICS	Date	CD	CN	CCI	CD6	ICS
1981.1	91.300	109.200	74.900	15.900	71.400	1983.7	99.700	114.300	87.800	9.900	93.900
1981.2	91.500	109.000	69.300	16.000	66.900	1983.8	102.600	115.700	89.900	10.200	90.900
1981.3	91.300	109.600	80.200	14.500	66.500	1983.9	104.300	116.700	92.200	9.600	89.900
1981.4	91.400	109.100	82.400	15.100	72.400	1983.10	106.500	116.200	93.500	9.300	89.300
1981.5	93.200	109.700	86.100	17.700	76.300	1983.11	106.700	116.100	96.700	9.500	91.100
1981.6	92.600	109.000	84.800	16.100	73.100	1983.12	109.700	116.100	104.900	9.800	94.200
1981.7	92.400	109.600	84.100	17.400	74.100	1984.1	113.000	117.300	105.000	9.600	100.100
1981.8	91.200	109.800	84.700	18.000	77.200	1984.2	113.000	118.300	102.000	9.700	97.400
1981.9	88.000	108.800	77.000	17.200	73.100	1984.3	112.800	118.900	102.900	10.400	101.000
1981.10	87.800	108.900	73.900	15.700	70.300	1984.4	113.000	120.300	103.800	10.700	96.100
1981.11	84.400	109.400	66.200	12.700	62.500	1984.5	111.800	119.900	102.000	11.600	98.100
1981.12	79.800	109.600	66.500	13.100	64.300	1984.6	111.700	120.900	103.700	12.000	95.500
1982.1	78.400	108.900	66.000	14.200	71.000	1984.7	113.800	120.900	98.500	12.100	96.600
1982.2	81.400	109.500	63.300	15.100	66.500	1984.8	113.300	120.200	101.600	11.700	99.100
1982.3	82.000	109.000	59.100	14.200	62.000	1984.9	111.500	120.700	102.400	11.500	100.900
1982.4	83.500	107.800	56.200	14.400	65.500	1984.10	111.400	121.000	101.700	10.600	96.300
1982.5	84.000	107.800	59.400	13.800	67.500	1984.11	113.300	121.800	106.100	9.400	95.700
1982.6	85.900	107.800	56.900	14.700	65.700	1984.12	113.100	122.100	98.700	8.800	92.900
1982.7	86.200	107.500	62.400	13.800	65.400	1985.1	112.800	121.100	103.000	8.400	96.000
1982.8	86.200	107.900	55.900	11.500	65.400	1985.2	112.800	121.400	104.000	9.000	93.700
1982.9	83.000	107.700	58.600	11.500	69.300	1985.3	113.500	122.100	98.000	9.600	93.700
1982.10	81.000	108.300	54.800	9.700	73.400	1985.4	111.500	122.500	101.000	8.800	94.600
1982.11	81.200	108.700	57.500	9.100	72.100	1985.5	111.800	123.100	96.600	8.100	91.800
1982.12	81.400	108.400	59.700	8.800	71.900	1985.6	112.000	123.500	100.000	7.600	96.500
1983.1	86.300	109.200	59.800	8.500	70.400	1985.7	111.300	123.400	101.200	7.800	94.000
1983.2	89.400	109.000	70.100	8.800	74.600	1985.8	114.000	124.200	99.600	8.000	92.400
1983.3	91.600	109.200	81.200	8.800	80.800	1985.9	112.900	125.100	98.900	8.100	92.100
1983.4	93.200	111.000	81.800	8.800	89.100	1985.10	111.400	124.300	99.300	8.000	88.400
1983.5	95.600	112.300	85.900	8.600	93.300	1985.11	115.500	125.400	98.700	7.800	90.900
1983.6	97.500	112.900	87.000	9.400	92.200	1985.12	116.800	127.000	99.800	7.800	93.900

*For Exercises 3.22, 4.11, A.4.3, 6.12.
SOURCE: CitiBase.

DATA SET 3 ■ Auto theft model*

State	AUTOTHEF	POPDEN	INCOME	State	AUTOTHEF	POPDEN	INCOME
ME	146.0	32.0	3054.0	WV	92.0	71.0	2603.0
NH	172.0	80.0	3471.0	NC	169.0	101.0	2888.0
VT	124.0	47.0	3247.0	SC	256.0	83.0	2607.0
MA	878.0	719.0	4156.0	GA	309.0	77.0	3071.0
RI	859.0	879.0	3858.0	FL	397.0	123.0	3525.0
CT	484.0	613.0	4595.0	KY	346.0	79.0	2847.0
NY	682.0	376.0	4442.0	TN	289.0	93.0	2808.0
NJ	557.0	941.0	4241.0	AL	223.0	66.0	2582.0
PA	340.0	259.0	3659.0	MS	78.0	46.0	2218.0
OH	493.0	257.0	3738.0	AR	109.0	36.0	2488.0
IN	429.0	142.0	3687.0	LA	385.0	79.0	2781.0
IL	518.0	196.0	4285.0	OK	280.0	36.0	3047.0
MI	464.0	154.0	3994.0	TX	394.0	42.0	3259.0
WI	218.0	80.0	3632.0	MT	222.0	5.0	3130.0
MN	346.0	48.0	3635.0	ID	144.0	8.0	2953.0
IA	175.0	50.0	3549.0	WY	165.0	3.0	3353.0
MO	538.0	67.0	3458.0	CO	588.0	21.0	3604.0
ND	91.0	9.0	3012.0	NM	392.0	8.0	2897.0
SD	94.0	9.0	3027.0	AZ	501.0	15.0	3372.0
NE	292.0	19.0	3609.0	UT	316.0	13.0	2997.0
KS	257.0	27.0	3488.0	NV	661.0	4.0	4458.0
DE	559.0	273.0	4107.0	WA	362.0	50.0	3848.0
MD	548.0	392.0	4073.0	OR	333.0	21.0	3573.0
VA	297.0	114.0	3307.0	CA	689.0	126.0	4290.0

*For Exercise 4.9.

SOURCE: *Statistical Abstract of the United States, 1987*, Tables 279 (AUTOTHEF), 22 (POPDEN), and 699 (INCOME).

DATA SET 4 ■ Stock index data*

Date	DJ	FFR	M2	DDJ	Date	DJ	FFR	M2	DDJ
1980:01	860.7	13.82	−0.854	•	1983:01	1064.3	8.68	2.452	31.21
1980:02	878.2	14.13	−0.273	17.48	1983:02	1087.4	8.51	1.868	23.14
1980:03	803.6	17.19	−1.079	−74.66	1983:03	1129.6	8.77	0.751	42.15
1980:04	786.3	17.61	−1.296	−17.23	1983:04	1168.4	8.80	0.125	38.85
1980:05	828.2	10.98	−0.306	41.86	1983:05	1212.9	8.63	0.407	44.43
1980:06	869.9	9.47	0.305	41.67	1983:06	1221.5	8.98	0.349	8.61
1980:07	909.8	9.03	1.181	39.93	1983:07	1213.9	9.37	0.214	−7.54
1980:08	947.3	9.61	0.388	37.54	1983:08	1189.2	9.56	0.101	−24.72
1980:09	946.7	10.87	0.000	−0.660	1983:09	1237.0	9.45	0.224	47.83
1980:10	949.2	12.81	−0.201	2.50	1983:10	1252.2	9.48	0.602	15.16
1980:11	971.1	15.85	−0.226	21.91	1983:11	1250.0	9.34	0.267	−2.19
1980:12	946.0	18.90	−0.836	−25.12	1983:12	1257.6	9.47	0.155	7.63
1981:01	962.1	19.08	−0.318	16.17	1984:01	1258.9	9.56	0.022	1.25
1981:02	945.5	15.93	−0.217	−16.63	1984:02	1164.5	9.59	0.354	−94.43
1981:03	987.2	14.70	0.381	41.68	1984:03	1162.0	9.91	0.254	−2.49
1981:04	1004.9	15.72	0.693	17.68	1984:04	1152.7	10.29	0.297	−9.26
1981:05	979.5	18.52	−0.354	−25.34	1984:05	1143.4	10.32	0.449	−9.29
1981:06	996.3	19.10	−0.279	16.75	1984:06	1121.1	11.06	0.273	−22.28
1981:07	947.9	19.04	−0.433	−48.33	1984:07	1113.3	11.23	0.076	−7.87
1981:08	926.2	17.82	0.165	−21.69	1984:08	1212.8	11.64	0.207	99.55
1981:09	853.4	15.87	−0.306	−72.87	1984:09	1213.5	11.30	0.434	0.69
1981:10	853.2	15.08	0.482	−0.13	1984:10	1199.3	9.99	0.281	−14.21
1981:11	860.4	13.31	0.493	7.19	1984:11	1211.3	9.43	0.857	12.00
1981:12	878.3	12.37	0.640	17.84	1984:12	1189.0	8.38	0.829	−22.34
1982:01	853.4	13.22	0.648	−24.87	1985:01	1238.2	8.35	0.895	49.20
1982:02	833.1	14.78	−0.062	−20.26	1985:02	1283.2	8.50	0.597	45.07
1982:03	812.3	14.68	0.669	−20.82	1985:03	1268.8	8.58	−0.168	−14.40
1982:04	845.0	14.94	0.358	32.63	1985:04	1266.4	8.27	−0.137	−2.47
1982:05	846.7	14.45	−0.235	1.76	1985:05	1279.4	7.97	0.502	13.04
1982:06	804.4	14.15	−0.548	−42.35	1985:06	1314.0	7.53	0.849	34.60
1982:07	818.4	12.59	0.124	14.04	1985:07	1343.2	7.88	0.495	29.17
1982:08	832.1	10.12	0.752	13.70	1985:08	1326.2	7.90	0.554	−16.99
1982:09	917.3	10.31	0.783	85.16	1985:09	1318.0	7.92	0.368	−8.23
1982:10	988.7	9.71	0.402	71.44	1985:10	1351.6	7.99	−0.020	33.63
1982:11	1027.8	9.20	0.726	39.05	1985:11	1432.9	8.05	−0.061	81.30
1982:12	1033.1	9.85	1.065	5.32	1985:12	1517.0	8.27	0.214	84.14

*For Exercise 4.12.
SOURCE: CitiBase.

DATA SET 5 ■ The Phillips curve model*

Year	U	P	NATU	Year	U	P	NATU
1960	5.5	1.6	5.2	1973	4.9	6.5	5.8
1961	6.7	1.0	5.2	1974	5.6	9.1	5.9
1962	5.5	2.2	5.3	1975	8.5	9.8	6.0
1963	5.7	1.6	5.4	1976	7.7	6.4	5.9
1964	5.2	1.5	5.5	1977	7.1	6.7	6.0
1965	4.5	2.7	5.6	1978	6.1	7.3	5.9
1966	3.8	3.6	5.6	1979	5.8	8.9	5.9
1967	3.8	2.6	5.6	1980	7.1	9.0	5.9
1968	3.6	5.0	5.6	1981	7.6	9.7	6.0
1969	3.5	5.6	5.6	1982	9.7	6.4	6.0
1970	4.9	5.5	5.6	1983	9.6	3.9	6.0
1971	5.9	5.7	5.8	1984	7.5	3.7	6.0
1972	5.6	4.7	5.8	1985	7.2	3.0	6.0

*For Example 5.2, Exercise 5.17.

SOURCE: NATU estimates are from Robert J. Gordon, *Macroeconimics*, 4th ed. (Boston: Little-Brown, 1987), Appendix A. P and U data are from the 1989 *Economic Report of the President*, Tables B-3 and B-34, respectively.

DATA SET 6 ■ Interest rate turning points*

Year	TB3	INF	M1	Year	TB3	INF	M1
1959.000	3.405	2.400	140.000	1974.000	7.886	9.100	274.400
1960.000	2.928	1.600	140.700	1975.000	5.838	9.800	287.400
1961.000	2.378	1.000	145.200	1976.000	4.989	6.400	306.500
1962.000	2.778	2.200	147.900	1977.000	5.265	6.700	331.400
1963.000	3.157	1.600	153.400	1978.000	7.221	7.300	358.700
1964.000	3.549	1.500	160.400	1979.000	10.041	8.900	386.100
1965.000	3.954	2.700	167.900	1980.000	11.506	9.000	412.200
1966.000	4.881	3.600	172.100	1981.000	14.029	9.700	439.100
1967.000	4.321	2.600	183.300	1982.000	10.686	6.400	476.400
1968.000	5.339	5.000	197.500	1983.000	8.630	3.900	522.100
1969.000	6.677	5.600	204.000	1984.000	9.580	3.700	551.900
1970.000	6.458	5.500	214.500	1985.000	7.480	3.000	620.100
1971.000	4.348	5.700	228.400	1986.000	5.980	2.700	725.400
1972.000	4.071	4.700	249.400	1987.000	5.820	3.300	750.800
1973.000	7.041	6.500	263.000				

*For Example 6.2.

SOURCE: 1989 *Economic Report of the President*, Tables B-71, B-67, and B-3.

DATA SET 7 ■ Exchange rates/balance of trade*

Month	BT	XR	Month	BT	XR
1982:01	− 5014.6	106.96	1984:01	− 9508.3	135.07
1982:02	− 1785.0	110.36	1984:02	− 10379.4	131.71
1982:03	− 2427.3	112.45	1984:03	− 10272.1	128.07
1982:04	− 503.2	114.07	1984:04	− 11880.3	130.01
1982:05	− 3297.4	111.03	1984:05	− 9284.2	133.99
1082:06	− 3305.9	116.97	1984:06	− 8755.2	134.31
1982:07	− 2696.7	118.91	1984:07	− 13771.1	139.30
1982:08	− 6529.1	119.63	1984:08	− 10089.8	140.21
1982:09	− 4197.9	120.93	1984:09	− 11543.1	145.70
1982:10	− 5261.0	123.16	1984:10	− 9652.9	147.56
1982:11	− 3885.1	124.27	1984:11	− 10221.9	144.92
1982:12	− 3655.2	119.22	1984:12	− 8033.3	149.24
1983:01	− 3843.1	117.73	1985:01	− 10285.4	152.83
1983:02	− 3370.5	119.70	1985:02	− 11445.6	158.43
1983:03	− 3696.4	120.71	1985:03	− 11045.8	158.14
1983:04	− 4726.4	121.82	1985:04	− 11850.0	149.56
1983:05	− 6751.0	122.05	1985:05	− 12665.6	149.92
1983:06	− 4893.4	125.16	1985:06	− 13415.4	147.71
1983:07	− 6371.2	126.62	1985:07	− 10508.7	140.94
1983:08	− 7163.7	129.77	1985:08	− 9903.5	137.55
1983:09	− 6220.6	129.74	1985:09	− 15549.8	139.14
1983:10	− 8432.1	127.50	1985:10	− 11453.0	130.71
1983:11	− 7121.8	130.26	1985:11	− 13681.9	128.08
1983:12	− 6735.2	132.84	1985:12	− 17373.5	125.80

*For Exercise 6.11.

SOURCE: CitiBase. XR = Weighted average exchange value of U.S. dollar, March 1973 = 100; BT = U.S. merchandise trade balance: exports minus imports, millions of current dollars, seasonally adjusted.

D A T A   S E T   8 ■ **Life expectancy in less-developed countries***

Country	PCGNP	Life	Food	Country	PCGNP	Life	Food
Ethiopia	97.0	45.0	110.0	India	120.0	56.0	270.0
Bangladesh	110.0	51.0	150.0	Rwanda	106.0	48.0	280.0
Burkino Faso	114.0	45.0	150.0	Somalia	102.0	46.0	280.0
Mali	114.0	46.0	160.0	Kenya	99.0	54.0	290.0
Bhutan	110.0	44.0	160.0	Tanzania	108.0	52.0	290.0
Mozambique	98.0	47.0	160.0	Sudan	103.0	48.0	300.0
Nepal	116.0	47.0	160.0	China	125.0	69.0	310.0
Malawi	105.0	45.0	170.0	Haiti	104.0	54.0	310.0
Zaire	113.0	51.0	170.0	Guinea	102.0	40.0	320.0
Burma	129.0	59.0	190.0	Sierra Leone	108.0	40.0	350.0
Burundi	106.0	48.0	230.0	Senegal	105.0	47.0	370.0
Togo	103.0	51.0	230.0	Ghana	118.0	53.0	380.0
Madagascar	112.0	52.0	240.0	Pakistan	114.0	51.0	380.0
Niger	96.0	44.0	250.0	Sri Lanka	98.0	70.0	380.0
Benin	121.0	49.0	260.0	Zambia	107.0	52.0	390.0
Cent. Africa	105.0	49.0	260.0				

*For Exercise 7.11.

SOURCE: *World Bank World Development Report*, 1987, Tables 1 and 6.

D ATA S E T 9 ■ **Keynesian macroeconomic model***

Year	Y	I	G	X	R	C	M	T	Dy
1960	1665.3	260.5	403.7	−4.0	4.41	1005.1	369.291	242.8	1422.5
1961	1708.7	259.1	427.1	−2.7	4.35	1025.2	378.125	245.8	1462.9
1962	1799.4	288.6	449.4	−7.5	4.33	1069.0	382.171	257.6	1541.8
1963	1873.3	307.1	459.8	−1.9	4.26	1108.4	392.327	272.6	1600.7
1964	1973.3	325.9	470.8	5.9	4.4	1170.6	405.051	284.3	1689.0
1965	2087.6	367.0	487.0	−2.7	4.49	1236.4	418.703	291.3	1796.3
1966	2208.3	390.5	532.6	−13.7	5.13	1298.9	418.735	318.2	1890.1
1967	2271.4	374.4	576.2	−16.9	5.51	1337.7	435.392	353.4	1918.0
1968	2365.6	391.8	597.6	−29.7	6.18	1405.9	451.945	350.1	2015.5
1969	2423.3	410.3	591.2	−34.9	7.03	1456.7	447.368	409.9	2013.4
1970	2416.2	381.5	572.6	−30.0	8.04	1492.0	454.449	408.5	2007.7
1971	2484.8	419.3	566.5	−39.8	7.39	1538.8	468.033	383.4	2101.4
1972	2608.5	465.4	570.7	−49.4	7.21	1621.9	495.825	412.1	2196.4
1973	2744.1	520.8	565.3	−31.5	7.44	1689.6	495.292	434.7	2309.4
1974	2729.3	481.3	573.2	0.8	8.57	1674.0	479.720	460.1	2269.2
1975	2695.0	383.3	580.9	18.9	8.83	1711.9	465.372	451.6	2243.4
1976	2826.7	453.5	580.3	−11.0	8.43	1803.9	470.814	457.9	2368.8
1977	2958.6	521.3	589.1	−35.5	8.02	1883.9	484.503	519.9	2438.7
1978	3115.2	576.9	604.1	−26.8	8.73	1961.0	493.398	549.7	2565.5
1979	3192.4	575.2	609.1	3.6	9.63	2004.4	489.975	587.9	2604.5
1980	3187.1	509.2	620.5	57.0	11.94	2000.4	478.746	600.6	2586.5
1981	3248.8	545.5	629.7	49.4	14.17	2024.2	466.631	636.9	2611.9
1982	3166.0	447.3	641.7	26.3	13.79	2050.7	476.400	617.8	2548.2
1983	3279.1	504.0	649.0	−19.9	12.04	2146.0	501.537	576.9	2702.2
1984	3501.4	658.4	677.7	−84.0	12.71	2249.3	509.603	615.4	2886.0
1985	3618.7	637.0	731.2	−104.3	11.37	2354.8	554.155	656.0	2962.7
1986	3721.7	643.5	760.5	−137.5	9.02	2455.2	630.783	668.8	3052.9
1987	3847.0	674.8	780.2	−128.9	9.38	2521.0	630.395	717.1	3129.9

*For Sec. 8.3.1.
SOURCE: 1989 *Economic Report of the President.*

DATA SET 10 ■ **Cost-push inflation data***

Year	CPH	OPH	IPD	U	Year	CPH	OPH	IPD	U
1948	8.5	5.0	7.2	3.8	1968	7.9	2.7	4.6	3.6
1949	1.7	1.1	−0.6	5.9	1969	7.0	0.1	5.1	3.5
1950	7.3	8.3	1.5	5.3	1970	7.3	0.7	4.7	4.9
1951	9.8	4.0	6.3	3.3	1971	6.4	3.2	4.9	5.9
1952	6.3	3.1	1.3	3.0	1972	6.4	3.0	4.0	5.6
1953	6.7	3.6	0.7	2.9	1973	8.3	2.0	6.4	4.9
1954	3.2	1.6	1.2	5.5	1974	9.5	−2.1	9.6	5.6
1955	2.5	3.0	2.6	4.4	1975	9.7	2.0	10.3	8.5
1956	6.7	1.3	3.2	4.1	1976	8.9	2.8	5.9	7.7
1957	6.5	2.6	3.5	4.3	1977	7.8	1.7	6.4	7.1
1958	4.6	3.0	1.6	6.8	1978	8.5	0.8	7.3	6.1
1959	4.4	3.3	2.0	5.5	1979	9.7	−1.2	9.0	5.8
1960	4.3	1.7	1.4	5.5	1980	10.5	−0.3	9.0	7.1
1961	3.9	3.5	0.5	6.7	1981	9.2	1.4	9.6	7.6
1962	4.7	3.6	1.9	5.5	1982	7.8	−.4	5.9	9.7
1963	3.8	4.0	0.9	5.7	1983	4.2	2.7	3.3	9.6
1964	5.2	4.3	1.0	5.2	1984	4.1	2.5	3.3	7.5
1965	3.8	3.0	2.3	4.5	1985	4.5	2.1	2.5	7.2
1966	6.9	2.8	3.3	3.8	1986	4.3	2.2	2.3	7.0
1967	5.4	2.7	2.5	3.8	1987	4.0	0.8	2.8	6.2

*For Example 8.1.

SOURCE: 1989 *Economic Report of the President*, Tables B-47 (CPH, OPH and IPD) and B-39 (U).

DATA SET 11 ■ **Simple Keynesian macromodel***

Quarter	CONS	GPDI	GNP	DEF	Quarter	CONS	GPDI	GNP	DEF
1968.1	1378.1	368.6	2327.3	−30.9	1977.1	1863.7	467.8	2896.0	−61.5
1968.2	1396.7	365.8	2366.9	−37.6	1977.2	1869.0	493.1	2942.7	−64.6
1968.3	1421.5	368.8	2385.3	−8.0	1977.3	1888.0	502.2	3001.8	−80.0
1968.4	1427.1	379.7	2383.0	0.9	1977.4	1914.2	505.5	2994.1	−76.0
1969.1	1442.9	385.4	2416.5	34.3	1978.1	1923.0	512.4	3020.5	−70.1
1969.2	1451.7	386.2	2419.8	34.6	1978.2	1960.8	543.5	3115.9	−37.1
1969.3	1459.9	390.3	2433.2	19.0	1978.3	1970.3	550.2	3142.6	−34.9
1969.4	1472.0	378.6	2423.5	12.4	1978.4	1989.7	554.6	3181.6	−28.6
1970.1	1481.5	374.1	2408.6	−3.6	1979.1	1997.5	558.3	3181.7	−13.5
1970.2	1488.1	366.5	2406.5	−35.7	1979.2	1994.1	557.3	3178.7	−8.1
1970.3	1501.3	374.5	2435.8	−40.4	1979.3	2007.9	564.9	3207.4	−26.6
1970.4	1497.2	378.2	2413.8	−54.0	1979.4	2018.0	560.5	3201.3	−36.2
1971.1	1520.9	383.8	2478.6	−47.7	1980.1	2015.4	552.6	3233.4	−46.7
1971.2	1533.0	397.8	2478.4	−59.7	1980.2	1974.1	496.9	3157.0	−77.7
1971.3	1541.0	405.4	2491.1	−59.5	1980.3	1996.3	497.2	3159.1	−89.8
1971.4	1560.1	411.7	2491.0	−54.0	1980.4	2015.6	518.1	3199.2	−75.8
1972.1	1581.8	431.5	2545.6	−30.4	1981.1	2022.9	524.9	3261.1	−52.1
1972.2	1607.9	436.7	2595.1	−48.4	1981.2	2022.4	529.4	3250.2	−53.8
1972.3	1629.9	441.4	2622.1	−23.6	1981.3	2031.5	525.0	3264.6	−66.9
1972.4	1667.8	465.0	2671.3	−53.4	1981.4	2020.0	507.4	3219.0	−98.7
1973.1	1689.9	481.7	2734.0	−19.8	1982.1	2031.2	488.2	3170.4	−110.9
1973.2	1687.2	482.1	2741.0	−19.6	1982.2	2041.0	473.0	3179.9	−113.4
1973.3	1694.5	481.3	2738.3	−6.2	1982.3	2051.8	458.1	3154.5	−158.0
1973.4	1686.8	477.9	2762.8	−3.7	1982.4	2078.7	468.1	3159.3	−200.0
1974.1	1667.5	465.8	2747.4	−9.0	1983.1	2094.2	469.4	3186.6	−181.5
1974.2	1677.2	459.0	2755.2	−21.5	1983.2	2135.1	496.2	3258.3	−165.9
1974.3	1686.7	446.7	2719.3	−15.1	1983.3	2163.0	525.8	3306.4	−172.8
1974.4	1664.7	420.6	2695.4	−42.9	1983.4	2191.9	550.3	3365.1	−163.0
1975.1	1677.1	392.4	2642.7	−84.7	1984.1	2213.8	564.1	3444.7	−147.4
1975.2	1706.0	388.4	2669.6	−177.5	1984.2	2246.3	592.7	3487.1	−154.0
1975.3	1723.9	397.8	2714.9	−112.7	1984.3	2253.3	598.3	3507.4	−160.2
1975.4	1740.4	405.7	2752.7	−111.5	1984.4	2271.7	615.9	3520.4	−175.5
1976.1	1777.5	420.3	2804.4	−90.3	1985.1	2292.3	615.0	3547.0	−148.7
1976.2	1790.4	425.9	2816.9	−80.5	1985.2	2311.9	638.1	3567.6	−196.2
1976.3	1809.9	429.1	2828.6	−90.0	1985.3	2342.0	643.1	3603.8	−180.5
1976.4	1837.8	450.3	2856.8	−91.3	1985.4	2351.7	658.4	3622.3	−198.4

*For Exercise 8.11.
SOURCE: CitiBase.

DATA SET 12 ■ CPI inflation, MA(5), MA(3)*

Year	CPI	MA(5)	MA(3)	Year	CPI	MA(5)	MA(3)
1950	5.8	•	•	1969	6.1	4.5	5.4
1951	5.9	•	4.2	1970	5.5	4.6	5.0
1952	0.9	2.5	2.5	1971	3.4	5.4	4.1
1953	0.6	1.5	0.3	1972	3.4	6.7	5.2
1954	−0.5	0.9	0.2	1973	8.8	7.0	8.1
1955	0.4	1.3	0.9	1974	12.2	7.2	9.3
1956	2.9	1.5	2.1	1975	7.0	7.9	8.0
1957	3.0	1.9	2.6	1976	4.8	8.0	6.2
1958	1.8	2.1	2.1	1977	6.8	8.2	6.9
1959	1.5	1.7	1.6	1978	9.0	9.3	9.7
1960	1.5	1.3	1.2	1979	13.3	10.1	11.6
1961	0.7	1.3	1.1	1980	12.4	9.5	11.5
1962	1.2	1.2	1.2	1981	8.9	8.5	8.4
1963	1.6	1.3	1.3	1982	3.9	6.6	5.5
1964	1.2	1.9	1.6	1983	3.8	4.9	3.9
1965	1.9	2.2	2.2	1984	4.0	3.3	3.9
1966	3.4	2.8	2.8	1985	3.8	3.4	3.0
1967	3.0	3.8	3.7	1986	1.1	•	3.1
1968	4.7	4.5	4.6	1987	4.4	•	•

*For Table 9.1 and Fig. 9.1.

SOURCE: 1989 *Economic Report of the President*, Table B-61.

DATA SET 13 ■ Unemployment trend*

Year	U	DU	Year	U	DU
1950	5.3	•	1968	3.6	−0.2
1951	3.3	−2.0	1969	3.5	−0.1
1952	3.0	−0.3	1970	4.9	1.4
1953	2.9	−0.1	1971	5.9	1.0
1954	5.5	2.6	1972	5.6	−0.3
1955	4.4	−1.1	1973	4.9	−0.7
1956	4.1	−0.3	1974	5.6	0.7
1957	4.3	0.2	1975	8.5	2.9
1958	6.8	2.5	1976	7.7	−0.8
1959	5.5	−1.3	1977	7.1	−0.6
1960	5.5	0.0	1978	6.1	−1.0
1961	6.7	1.2	1979	5.8	−0.3
1962	5.5	−1.2	1980	7.1	1.3
1963	5.7	0.2	1981	7.6	0.5
1964	5.2	−0.5	1982	9.7	2.1
1965	4.5	−0.7	1983	9.6	−0.1
1966	3.8	−0.7	1984	7.5	−2.1
1967	3.8	0.0	1985	7.2	−0.3

*For Fig. 9.4.
SOURCE: 1989 *Economic Report of the President*, Table B-39.

DATA SET 14 ■ TBILL rates*

Month	TBILL	DTBILL	Month	TBILL	DTBILL
1982:10	7.75	•	1986:01	7.04	−0.03
1982:11	8.04	0.29	1986:02	7.03	−0.01
1982:12	8.01	−0.03	1986:03	6.59	−0.44
1983:01	7.81	−0.20	1986:04	6.06	−0.53
1983:02	8.13	0.32	1986:05	6.12	0.06
1983:03	8.30	0.17	1986:06	6.21	0.09
1983:04	8.25	−0.05	1986:07	5.84	−0.37
1983:05	8.19	−0.06	1986:08	5.57	−0.27
1983:06	8.82	0.63	1986:09	5.19	−0.38
1983:07	9.12	0.30	1986:10	5.18	−0.01
1983:08	9.39	0.27	1986:11	5.35	0.17
1983:09	9.05	−0.34	1986:12	5.49	0.14
1983:10	8.71	−0.34	1987:01	5.45	−0.04
1983:11	8.71	0.00	1987:02	5.59	0.14
1983:12	8.96	0.25	1987:03	5.56	−0.03
1984:01	8.93	−0.03	1987:04	5.76	0.20
1984:02	9.03	0.10	1987:05	5.75	−0.01
1984:03	9.44	0.41	1987:06	5.69	−0.06
1984:04	9.69	0.25	1987:07	5.78	0.09
1984:05	9.90	0.21	1987:08	6.00	0.22
1984:06	9.94	0.04	1987:09	6.32	0.32
1984:07	10.13	0.19	1987:10	6.40	0.08
1984:08	10.49	0.36	1987:11	5.81	−0.59
1984:09	10.43	−0.06	1987:12	5.80	−0.01
1984:10	9.97	−0.46	1988:01	5.90	0.10
1984:11	8.79	−1.18	1988:02	5.69	−0.21
1984:12	8.16	−0.63		•	•
1985:01	7.76	−0.40		•	•
1985:02	8.22	0.46		•	•
1985:03	8.57	0.35		•	•
1985:04	8.00	−0.57		•	•
1985:05	7.56	−0.44		•	•
1985:06	7.01	−0.55		•	•
1985:07	7.05	0.04		•	•
1985:08	7.18	0.13		•	•
1985:09	7.08	−0.10		•	•
1985:10	7.17	0.09		•	•
1985:11	7.20	0.03		•	•
1985:12	7.07	−0.13		•	•

*For Figs. 9.5, 9.6, Tables 9.2, 9.3, 9.4.

SOURCE: *Federal Reserve Bulletin*, various issues, Table A-24.

DATA SET 15 ■ Dow-Jones index*

Week	DOW	DiffDOW	Week	DOW	DiffDOW
1	1938.83	•	27	2131.58	−11.38
2	1911.31	−27.52	28	2106.15	−25.43
3	1956.07	44.76	29	2129.45	23.30
4	1903.51	−52.56	30	2060.99	−68.46
5	1958.22	54.71	31	2128.50	67.51
6	1910.48	−47.74	32	2119.13	−9.37
7	1983.26	72.78	33	2037.52	−81.61
8	2014.59	31.33	34	2016.00	−21.52
9	2023.21	8.62	35	2017.43	1.43
10	2057.86	34.65	36	2054.59	37.16
11	2034.98	−22.88	37	2068.81	14.22
12	2087.37	52.39	38	2094.15	25.34
13	1978.95	−108.42	39	2090.68	−3.47
14	1988.06	9.11	40	2112.91	22.23
15	2090.19	102.13	41	2150.25	37.34
16	2013.93	−76.26	42	2133.18	−17.07
17	2015.09	1.16	43	2183.50	50.32
18	2032.33	17.24	44	2149.89	−33.61
19	2007.46	−24.87	45	2145.80	−4.09
20	1990.05	−17.41	46	2067.03	−78.77
21	1952.59	−37.46	47	2062.41	−4.62
22	1956.44	3.85	48	2074.68	12.27
23	2071.30	114.86	49	2092.28	17.60
24	2101.71	30.41	50	2143.49	51.21
25	2104.02	2.31	51	2150.71	7.22
26	2142.96	38.94	52	2168.93	18.22

*For Exercise 9.9.

SOURCE: *Wall Street Journal*, various issues, October 1986–87.

DATA SET 16 ▧ **Business inventory change***

Year	ΔINV	Year	ΔINV
1940	14.4	1964	15.7
1941	27.8	1965	25.2
1942	12.0	1966	36.9
1943	0.7	1967	28.8
1944	−5.2	1968	21.0
1945	−8.4	1969	25.1
1946	27.9	1970	8.2
1947	−1.0	1971	19.6
1948	12.3	1972	21.8
1949	−9.7	1973	40.0
1950	24.2	1974	33.3
1951	30.8	1975	−12.8
1952	10.0	1976	22.1
1953	2.8	1977	29.1
1954	−4.8	1978	36.8
1955	16.3	1979	15.0
1956	12.9	1980	−6.9
1957	3.0	1981	23.9
1958	−3.4	1982	−24.5
1959	16.5	1983	−6.4
1960	7.7	1984	62.3
1961	7.3	1985	9.1
1962	16.2	1986	15.4
1963	16.6	1987	34.4

*For Exercise 9.10.

DATA SET 17 ■ IBM and Apple computer stock prices*

IBM	APPLE	IBM	APPLE	IBM	APPLE
121.83	33.63	160.38	82.00	113.38	83.50
121.38	33.00	166.50	81.00	115.75	83.50
123.63	34.63	164.25	81.25	116.78	93.75
121.50	35.50	167.00	76.00	115.50	91.50
121.83	35.25	167.00	86.50	114.25	89.50
123.25	35.75	161.25	85.00	107.00	80.25
127.83	40.00	161.00	82.50	107.63	80.00
126.63	43.75	164.38	93.00	111.63	82.00
126.50	41.25	173.25	98.00	114.13	79.00
125.13	42.13	174.75	106.00	113.75	80.25
122.00	41.00	166.50	104.00	113.38	82.00
122.00	40.83	160.75	101.00	110.50	82.50
122.25	45.83	161.13	109.00	110.38	81.00
120.00	48.38	155.63	103.50	109.50	77.50
126.25	50.25	156.00	115.00	108.00	79.50
128.75	55.50	155.25	117.00	113.25	86.00
135.75	54.00	147.38	108.25	116.00	89.00
134.50	62.13	135.00	96.50	117.50	89.50
139.63	61.25	120.75	71.00	125.13	90.00
139.50	70.00	122.50	77.25	126.63	93.00
139.63	67.25	119.50	75.50	126.38	90.50
144.83	63.50	121.63	74.50	125.50	90.00
145.63	68.25	117.75	71.00	120.13	85.00
150.75	65.00	114.83	70.00	125.75	88.75
149.50	71.75	107.25	61.50	123.83	88.50
145.00	70.25	110.13	68.00	116.00	85.00
150.00	71.50	117.25	81.00	112.75	81.50
151.75	74.75	119.83	85.25	112.50	80.50
160.63	80.00	115.50	84.00	114.00	79.50
163.75	79.00	114.83	80.00	114.38	81.00
160.63	78.25	119.00	85.75	114.25	84.50
156.63	74.13	110.50	78.50	112.83	87.50
160.00	79.00	112.38	83.00	115.38	86.50
160.00	77.75	108.00	77.25	116.00	75.50
156.63	79.00	112.00	82.00		

*For Exercise 9.11.

SOURCE: *Wall Street Journal*, various issues, October 1986–88.

DATA SET 18 ■ **Profit/equity ratios***

Year	Pr/Eq	Year	Pr/Eq
1947	15.6	1968	12.1
1948	16.0	1969	11.5
1949	11.6	1970	9.3
1950	15.4	1971	9.7
1951	12.1	1972	10.6
1952	10.3	1973	12.8
1953	10.5	1974	14.9
1954	9.9	1975	11.6
1955	12.6	1976	13.9
1956	12.3	1977	14.2
1957	10.9	1978	15.0
1958	8.6	1979	16.4
1959	10.4	1980	13.9
1960	9.2	1981	13.6
1961	8.9	1982	9.2
1962	9.8	1983	10.6
1963	10.3	1984	12.5
1964	11.6	1985	10.1
1965	13.0	1986	9.5
1966	13.4	1987	12.8
1967	11.7	●	●

*For Exercise 9.12.

SOURCE: 1989 *Economic Report of the President*, Table B-91.

D A T A S E T 19 ▪ **Housing starts and manufacturing inventories***

Starts	Inventories	Starts	Inventories	Starts	Inventories	Starts	Inventories
1367.000	160.571	2092.000	200.303	1547.000	267.528	1785.000	257.605
1538.000	161.132	1996.000	202.338	1246.000	269.523	1910.000	258.547
1421.000	162.513	1970.000	203.905	1306.000	271.708	1710.000	258.710
1395.000	163.205	1981.000	205.491	1360.000	272.684	1715.000	258.998
1459.000	164.380	2094.000	208.104	1140.000	274.638	1785.000	259.727
1495.000	166.446	2044.000	210.509	1045.000	275.226	1688.000	260.682
1401.000	167.760	1630.000	213.147	1041.000	276.939	1892.000	261.494
1550.000	168.804	1520.000	215.648	940.000	278.179	2213.000	264.315
1720.000	171.002	1847.000	217.611	911.000	281.065	1671.000	268.234
1629.000	172.940	1748.000	220.579	873.000	282.360	1880.000	270.640
1641.000	174.024	1876.000	222.321	837.000	283.760	1786.000	274.268
1804.000	175.193	1913.000	225.511	910.000	282.645	1853.000	277.207
1527.000	176.051	1760.000	227.799	843.000	281.375	1733.000	279.774
1943.000	177.320	1778.000	230.694	866.000	281.362	1589.000	282.774
2063.000	178.255	1832.000	233.074	931.000	280.352	1702.000	284.531
1892.000	179.699	1681.000	235.798	917.000	279.181	1582.000	285.597
1971.000	181.566	1524.000	238.190	1025.000	276.451	1649.000	285.668
1893.000	182.442	1498.000	241.100	902.000	275.127	1607.000	285.709
2058.000	183.499	1341.000	245.318	1166.000	274.401	1804.000	285.785
2020.000	184.639	1350.000	247.898	1046.000	272.714	1632.000	286.146
1949.000	186.237	1047.000	251.820	1144.000	270.688	1849.000	286.171
2042.000	187.262	1051.000	255.910	1173.000	269.390	1851.000	286.049
2042.000	188.359	927.000	257.762	1372.000	266.887	1684.000	284.900
2142.000	189.214	1196.000	258.652	1303.000	264.909	1693.000	285.678
1718.000	190.240	1269.000	259.520	1586.000	262.667	1673.000	285.036
1738.000	191.683	1436.000	259.423	1699.000	261.391	1737.000	284.688
2032.000	193.026	1471.000	259.705	1606.000	258.439	1653.000	284.030
2197.000	194.691	1523.000	259.403	1472.000	258.041	1784.000	282.444
2075.000	196.572	1510.000	260.798	1776.000	258.079	1654.000	281.993
2070.000	198.591	1482.000	264.281	1733.000	257.513	1882.000	281.884

*For Exercises 9.13, 9.14.

SOURCE: *CitiBase*. Data are monthly, 1976–85. "Starts" is new private housing units, in thousands, seasonally adjusted. "Inventories" is manufacturing inventories, billions of dollars, seasonally adjusted.

DATA SET 20 ■ Spousal support*

DEP	HINC	WINC	NCH	DEP	HINC	WINC	NCH	DEP	HINC	WINC	NCH
1.000	147.926	0.000	4.000	0.000	64.890	4.523	0.000	1.000	55.650	0.000	2.000
1.000	115.142	2.156	1.000	0.000	38.280	2.667	3.000	1.000	138.360	0.587	1.000
1.000	132.713	0.000	2.000	0.000	17.890	0.184	7.000	0.000	237.050	1.804	0.000
0.000	34.789	3.138	3.000	1.000	48.250	0.000	2.000	0.000	74.290	5.734	3.000
0.000	33.786	3.078	0.000	0.000	19.830	0.825	5.000	0.000	61.550	1.706	0.000
1,000	89.013	0.000	4.000	0.000	225.090	1.360	1.000	1.000	114.600	5.911	1.000
1.000	124.372	0.018	2.000	0.000	54.660	4.174	0.000	1.000	104.810	0.201	2.000
0.000	70.028	3.217	0.000	0.000	72.660	0.059	2.000	1.000	104.600	0.736	5.000
1.000	96.415	0.631	2.000	1.000	0.010	5.201	0.000	1.000	134.740	0.000	2.000
0.000	0.000	2.728	0.000	0.000	0.960	0.000	0.000	1.000	74.600	0.000	3.000
1.000	99.930	0.055	1.000	1.000	82.820	4.286	1.000	0.000	117.820	0.000	1.000
0.000	75.250	3.245	0.000	1.000	83.780	6.708	2.000	0.000	54.360	2.434	1.000
1.000	56.090	0.000	4.000	0.000	84.400	2.713	0.000	0.000	19.920	0.684	2.000
1.000	97.870	4.016	3.000	0.000	83.660	3.902	0.000	1.000	84.610	0.861	2.000
0.000	47.360	1.844	0.000	1.000	29.150	3.170	2.000	0.000	64.750	2.543	2.000
0.000	42.560	1.242	3.000	0.000	78.632	5.229	0.000	0.000	80.760	3.045	0.000
1.000	98.730	2.758	1.000	1.000	76.711	0.258	3.000	1.000	45.550	0.000	2.000
1.000	98.500	0.000	0.000	0.000	110.777	1.888	1.000	1.000	69.150	0.000	4.000
0.000	182.890	2.108	0.000	1.000	90.988	0.000	1.000	0.000	68.310	3.395	0.000
0.000	70.100	0.614	1.000	1.000	42.468	7.071	1.000	1.000	92.370	1.239	1.000
0.000	70.510	5.672	2.000	0.000	42.053	2.690	0.000	0.000	54.920	0.000	3.000
0.000	45.060	1.113	4.000	0.000	30.092	0.000	1.000	1.000	41.090	1.039	3.000
0.000	221.630	0.000	0.000	1.000	54.580	1.314	2.000	1.000	31.410	0.176	2.000
1.000	52.310	2.063	1.000	0.000	48.240	1.511	2.000	0.000	76.120	0.491	2.000
1.000	107.890	4.341	1.000	0.000	47.450	3.493	1.000	0.000	84.610	1.942	0.000
0.000	36.720	0.644	2.000	1.000	70.430	2.379	1.000	1.000	36.200	4.641	2.000
1.000	84.640	0.012	3.000	0.000	0.000	0.000	0.000	1.000	140.630	0.168	3.000
0.000	55.130	2.494	0.000	1.000	65.970	0.000	4.000	0.000	49.620	0.000	4.000
0.000	0.000	0.000	0.000	1.000	149.380	0.643	2.000	0.000	68.140	0.000	1.000
0.000	65.330	0.114	2.000	0.000	76.800	0.385	2.000	0.000	72.920	0.573	1.000
1.000	39.180	3.090	4.000	1.000	137.490	3.369	0.000	0.000	5.590	0.705	5.000
1.000	147.270	0.000	2.000	0.000	34.300	0.617	0.000	1.000	45.070	2.672	2.000
1.000	59.750	0.000	4.000	1.000	60.690	0.000	3.000	0.000	24.460	0.000	4.000
0.000	51.010	2.679	1.000	0.000	0.000	3.132	0.000	0.000	95.950	2.837	3.000
1.000	67.070	6.554	1.000	0.000	55.260	2.876	0.000	1.000	141.060	0.856	1.000
0.000	108.120	0.654	4.000	0.000	44.720	5.507	0.000	0.000	57.830	4.827	0.000
0.000	65.020	8.391	0.000	0.000	38.880	3.842	0.000	1.000	75.470	5.856	3.000
1.000	57.620	.689	2.000	1.000	73.290	2.893	2.000	0.000	84.020	5.112	1.000
0.000	93.500	4.497	0.000	0.000	61.780	4.472	2.000	0.000	121.140	4.565	0.000
0.000	77.280	2.799	0.000	0.000	56.180	6.168	0.000	0.000	164.050	0.125	0.000
0.000	76.440	0.160	0.000	1.000	31.840	1.214	4.000	0.000	55.090	0.000	4.000
0.000	93.360	1.148	2.000	0.000	47.650	0.414	3.000	0.000	17.340	0.297	1.000
0.000	49.520	3.961	0.000	0.000	49.930	8.917	0.000	0.000	54.240	2.636	3.000
0.000	73.570	4.131	1.000	0.000	62.920	5.794	1.000	0.000	77.040	0.239	2.000

(continued on next page)

DATA SET 20 ■ Spousal support* (*continued*)

DEP	HINC	WINC	NCH	DEP	HINC	WINC	NCH	DEP	HINC	WINC	NCH
0.000	86.550	0.152	0.000	1.000	460.140	0.000	4.000	0.000	185.570	7.973	0.000
1.000	137.950	0.582	5.000	0.000	62.460	4.956	3.000	0.000	57.380	0.490	4.000
0.000	40.540	0.062	3.000	0.000	28.350	0.953	2.000	1.000	78.580	0.020	2.000
1.000	83.730	0.000	1.000	1.000	66.690	3.577	1.000	0.000	39.130	1.295	2.000
0.000	77.910	2.898	1.000	1.000	75.790	1.883	2.000	0.000	81.150	0.326	0.000
0.000	40.630	2.873	1.000	0.000	61.390	0.000	0.000	0.000	47.900	3.674	0.000
1.000	61.870	0.673	1.000	0.000	47.160	1.516	7.000	0.000	41.380	2.671	1.000
0.000	31.640	2.525	0.000	0.000	0.000	2.853	2.000	1.000	123.550	0.196	2.000
1.000	64.220	0.000	1.000	0.000	73.530	2.794	1.000	1.000	72.290	0.464	5.000
1.000	65.110	1.088	2.000	0.000	26.170	7.541	2.000	1.000	222.970	0.137	2.000
0.000	59.150	0.000	2.000	1.000	101.980	3.583	3.000	0.000	81.010	2.357	0.000
0.000	92.320	0.000	4.000	0.000	15.190	3.809	5.000	0.000	45.620	3.021	2.000
0.000	46.470	0.227	3.000	0.000	168.850	2.654	0.000	1.000	37.670	2.932	2.000
1.000	105.000	0.266	2.000	1.000	89.310	9.720	3.000	1.000	83.060	2.079	1.000
1.000	50.570	0.625	2.000	1.000	81.610	1.319	2.000	0.000	66.930	0.000	3.000
0.000	32.490	0.260	4.000	0.000	45.350	0.970	1.000	0.000	74.390	2.948	4.000
0.000	71.460	0.221	0.000	1.000	39.960	0.035	1.000	1.000	0.680	0.000	2.000
1.000	65.080	4.035	1.000	1.000	65.850	3.941	2.000	0.000	89.780	3.626	3.000
1.000	197.130	1.889	1.000	0.000	41.870	0.266	5.000	0.000	14.180	0.000	3.000
0.000	22.610	0.858	2.000	0.000	32.880	0.000	5.000	0.000	30.110	1.165	1.000
0.000	115.810	6.680	0.000	0.000	32.340	5.424	0.000	0.000	275.110	0.154	1.000
1.000	45.460	0.367	2.000	1.000	239.880	5.686	0.000				

*For Example 10.3, Exercise 10.10.

SOURCE: University of Michigan Panel on Income Dynamics. Data are from 1982.

DATA SET 21 ■ **Yield curve***

L2	L3	DEP	Quarter	L2	L3	DEP	Quarter	L2	L3	DEP	Quarter
0.31	•	1	1964.1	1.42	1.47	1	1973.1	−5.81	0.22	0	1981.2
0.33	0.31	1	1965.4	0.93	1.42	1	1973.2	−1.31	−5.81	1	1981.3
0.04	0.33	1	1965.2	−0.34	0.93	0	1973.3	−3.43	−1.31	0	1981.4
−0.06	0.04	1	1965.3	−1.26	−0.34	1	1973.4	−1.52	−3.43	0	1982.1
−0.10	−0.06	1	1965.4	−3.50	−1.26	0	1974.1	1.23	−1.52	1	1982.2
−0.05	−0.10	1	1966.1	−2.53	−3.50	1	1974.2	−0.35	1.23	0	1982.3
−0.13	−0.05	1	1966.2	−1.63	−2.53	0	1974.3	−0.16	−0.35	1	1982.4
−0.32	−0.13	1	1966.3	−3.84	−1.63	0	1974.4	1.68	−0.16	1	1983.1
−0.69	−0.32	1	1966.4	−3.56	−3.84	0	1975.1	1.88	1.68	1	1983.2
−0.68	−0.69	1	1967.1	−1.80	−3.56	1	1975.2	1.82	1.88	1	1983.3
−0.81	−0.68	1	1967.2	1.55	−1.80	1	1975.3	1.65	1.82	1	1983.4
−0.47	−0.81	1	1967.3	2.04	1.55	1	1975.4	2.26	1.65	1	1984.1
0.30	−0.47	1	1967.4	1.40	2.04	1	1976.1	2.14	2.26	1	1984.2
0.39	0.36	1	1968.1	1.97	1.40	1	1976.2	2.24	2.14	1	1984.3
0.08	0.39	1	1968.2	2.39	1.97	1	1976.3	2.22	2.24	1	1984.4
0.16	0.08	1	1968.3	2.02	2.39	1	1976.4	1.23	2.22	1	1985.1
−0.40	0.16	0	1968.4	2.26	2.02	1	1977.1	2.90	1.23	1	1985.2
−0.32	−0.40	1	1969.1	2.20	2.26	1	1977.2	2.84	2.90	1	1985.3
−0.24	−0.32	1	1969.2	2.62	2.20	1	1977.3	2.72	2.84	1	1985.4
−0.35	−0.24	1	1969.3	1.86	2.62	0	1977.4	2.44	2.72	1	1986.1
−1.44	−0.35	0	1969.4	1.15	1.86	1	1978.1	1.46	2.44	0	1986.2
−1.31	−1.44	0	1970.1	0.98	1.15	1	1978.2	0.54	1.46	1	1986.3
−1.12	−1.31	0	1970.2	1.18	0.98	1	1978.3	1.07	0.54	1	1986.4
−1.01	−1.12	1	1970.3	0.63	1.18	1	1978.4	1.74	1.07	1	1987.1
−0.23	−1.01	0	1970.4	−0.22	0.63	1	1979.1	1.07	1.74	1	1987.2
0.09	−0.23	1	1971.1	−1.71	−0.22	0	1979.2	1.08	1.07	1	1987.3
0.72	0.09	0	1971.2	−1.01	−1.71	1	1979.3	1.46	1.08	1	1987.4
1.85	0.72	1	1971.3	−1.04	−1.01	0	1979.4	2.05	1.46	1	1988.1
1.12	1.85	0	1971.4	−2.56	−1.04	1	1980.1	1.33	2.05	1	1988.2
0.51	1.12	1	1972.1	−3.04	−2.56	0	1980.2	1.74	1.33	1	1988.3
1.28	0.51	1	1972.2	−4.82	−3.04	1	1980.3	1.41	1.74	1	1988.4
1.99	1.28	1	1972.3	1.29	−4.82	1	1980.4	0.66	1.41	1	1989.1
1.47	1.99	1	1972.4	0.22	1.29	1	1981.1	−0.14	0.66	1	1989.2

*For Exercise 10.13.

SOURCE: *Federal Reserve Bulletin*, various issues, Table A-24 (interest rates) and A-51 (GNP). The L2, L3, and DEP columns are as defined in Exercise 10.13.

D A T A   S E T 22 ■ **Voting behavior***

Vote	Union	Party	Income	Vote	Union	Party	Income
0	0	2	2	0	0	0	12
1	0	5	22	0	1	1	13
0	0	0	15	1	0	6	8
1	0	4	17	0	1	0	11
1	1	2	19	1	0	4	22
0	1	0	16	1	0	6	22
1	0	6	6	1	0	4	14
1	0	4	16	1	0	5	16
1	1	3	21	1	0	4	17
0	0	0	15	0	0	1	6
1	1	5	16	0	0	0	6
1	0	4	19	1	0	3	16
1	1	6	8	1	0	5	14
0	0	0	8	1	0	3	22
0	1	1	7	0	1	3	12
1	0	5	4	1	0	6	20
1	0	5	6	1	0	5	15
0	1	2	18	0	0	3	6
1	0	4	19	1	1	6	14
0	1	1	14	1	0	4	15
1	0	5	19	0	0	0	12
1	1	3	2	1	0	4	15
1	1	2	4	1	0	0	10
0	0	0	13	1	0	0	16
0	1	1	15	1	0	15	11

*For Exercise 10.14.

SOURCE: Sample from the American National Election Survey, 1984. Inter-University Consortium for Political and Social Research.

DATA SET 23 ■ Deficits and interest rates*

Year	AAA	LAAA	DEF	Year	AAA	LAAA	DEF
1960	4.41	•	−0.3	1975	8.83	8.57	53.2
1961	4.35	4.41	3.3	1976	8.43	8.83	73.7
1962	4.35	4.35	7.1	1977	8.02	8.43	53.6
1963	4.26	4.33	4.8	1978	8.73	8.02	5.9
1964	4.40	4.26	5.9	1979	9.63	8.73	40.2
1965	4.49	4.40	1.4	1980	11.94	9.63	73.8
1966	5.13	4.49	3.7	1981	14.17	11.94	78.9
1967	5.51	5.13	8.6	1982	13.79	14.17	127.9
1968	6.18	5.51	25.2	1983	12.04	13.79	207.8
1969	7.03	6.18	−3.2	1984	12.71	12.04	185.3
1970	8.04	7.03	2.8	1985	11.37	12.71	212.3
1971	7.39	8.04	23.0	1986	9.02	11.37	221.2
1972	7.21	7.39	23.4	1987	9.38	9.02	149.7
1973	7.44	7.21	14.9	1988	9.71	9.38	155.1
1974	8.57	7.44	6.1				

*For Example 11.1

SOURCE: 1989 *Economic Report of the President*, Tables B-76 (DEF) and B-71 (AAA).

DATA SET 24 ■ Money/income test*

Quarter	GNP	M2	Quarter	GNP	M2	Quarter	GNP	M2
66.1	754.8	464.7	73.1	1311.6	816.8	79.4	2591.5	1491.6
66.2	764.6	470.2	73.2	1342.9	830.5	80.1	2673.0	1518.1
66.3	777.7	473.0	73.3	1369.4	843.1	80.2	2672.2	1535.4
66.4	790.9	477.9	73.4	1413.3	854.6	80.3	2734.0	1588.3
67.1	799.7	485.4	74.1	1426.2	870.8	80.4	2848.6	1625.1
67.2	805.9	497.1	74.2	1459.1	881.8	81.1	2978.8	1653.5
67.3	822.9	510.8	74.3	1489.1	891.5	81.2	3017.7	1697.3
67.4	837.1	521.4	74.4	1516.8	904.7	81.3	3099.6	1731.9
68.1	862.9	530.2	75.1	1524.6	921.3	81.4	3114.4	1775.8
68.2	886.7	539.2	75.2	1563.5	955.1	82.1	3112.2	1817.9
68.3	903.6	549.9	75.3	1627.4	989.8	82.2	3159.5	1850.3
68.4	917.4	562.2	75.4	1678.2	1014.2	82.3	3179.4	1891.9
69.1	943.8	571.7	76.1	1730.9	1046.2	82.4	3212.5	1938.0
69.2	957.6	577.1	76.2	1761.8	1078.9	83.1	3265.8	2037.8
69.3	976.4	580.9	76.3	1794.7	1108.3	83.2	3367.4	2093.6
69.4	978.0	586.8	76.4	1843.7	1149.3	83.3	3443.9	2130.8
70.1	994.2	589.7	77.1	1899.1	1188.2	83.4	3545.8	2175.1
70.2	1008.9	594.1	77.2	1968.9	1221.1	84.1	3670.9	2214.2
70.3	1027.9	606.3	77.3	2031.6	1250.3	84.2	3743.8	2255.9
70.4	1030.9	622.7	77.4	2062.4	1278.0	84.3	3799.7	2293.0
71.1	1075.2	642.7	78.1	2111.4	1302.0	84.4	3845.6	2348.6
71.2	1094.3	668.4	78.2	2230.3	1325.4	85.1	3909.3	2417.0
71.3	1113.9	687.8	78.3	2289.5	1351.2	85.2	3966.0	2455.1
71.4	1127.3	706.7	78.4	2367.6	1379.8	85.3	4030.5	2513.7
72.1	1166.5	727.9	79.1	2420.5	1403.0	85.4	4067.7	2551.5
72.2	1197.2	747.0	79.2	2474.5	1435.8	86.1	4149.2	2578.7
72.3	1223.9	771.7	79.3	2546.1	1470.6	86.2	4182.3	2645.0
72.4	1263.5	797.1						

*For Example 11.2, Exercise 11.5.
SOURCE: *Federal Reserve Bulletin*, various issues, Tables A-13 (M2) and A-51 (Q)

DATA SET 25 ■ Money/interest causality*

Date	FFR	M2	Date	FFR	M2	Date	FFR	M2
1976:01	4.87	1034.0	1979:05	10.24	1433.6	1982:09	10.31	1908.7
1976:02	4.77	1047.8	1979:06	10.29	1448.3	1982:10	9.71	1923.7
1976:03	4.84	1056.8	1979:07	10.47	1460.5	1982:11	9.20	1937.7
1976:04	4.82	1068.3	1979:08	10.94	1469.8	1982:12	8.95	1952.6
1976:05	5.29	1082.0	1979:09	11.43	1481.5	1983:01	8.68	2007.1
1976:06	5.48	1086.3	1979:10	13.77	1487.1	1983:02	8.51	2044.7
1976:07	5.31	1095.5	1979:11	13.18	1490.1	1983:03	8.77	2061.5
1976:08	5.29	1108.8	1979:12	13.78	1497.5	1983:04	8.80	2078.2
1976:09	5.25	1120.6	1980:01	13.82	1507.2	1983:05	8.63	2094.5
1976:10	5.03	1135.8	1980:02	14.13	1520.5	1983:06	8.98	2108.1
1976:11	4.95	1148.5	1980:03	17.19	1526.5	1983:07	9.37	2120.4
1976:12	4.65	1163.6	1980:04	17.61	1522.1	1983:08	9.56	2129.7
1977:01	4.61	1177.1	1980:05	10.98	1531.9	1983:09	9.45	2142.2
1977:02	4.68	1188.3	1980:06	9.47	1552.2	1983:10	9.48	2163.2
1977:03	4.69	1199.3	1980:07	9.03	1572.8	1983:11	9.34	2176.1
1977:04	4.73	1211.2	1980:08	9.61	1589.0	1983:12	9.47	2186.0
1977:05	5.35	1221.7	1980:09	10.87	1603.1	1984:01	9.56	2199.5
1977:06	5.39	1230.3	1980:10	12.81	1615.8	1984:02	9.59	2215.8
1977:07	5.42	1241.2	1980:11	15.85	1629.2	1984:03	9.91	2227.4
1977:08	5.90	1249.9	1980:12	18.90	1630.3	1984:04	10.29	2242.6
1977:09	6.14	1259.7	1981:01	19.08	1639.6	1984:05	10.32	2256.5
1977:10	6.47	1269.5	1981:02	15.93	1651.6	1984:06	11.06	2268.5
1977:11	6.51	1277.9	1981:03	14.70	1669.3	1984:07	11.23	2277.5
1977:12	6.56	1286.6	1981:04	15.72	1689.9	1984:08	11.64	2291.8
1978:01	6.70	1296.2	1981:05	18.52	1696.4	1984:09	11.30	2309.8
1978:02	6.78	1301.2	1981:06	19.10	1705.6	1984:10	9.99	2323.6
1978:03	6.79	1308.5	1981:07	19.04	1717.6	1984:11	9.43	2348.3
1978:04	6.89	1316.8	1981:08	17.82	1733.6	1984:12	8.38	2373.8
1978:05	7.36	1325.9	1981:09	15.87	1744.6	1985:01	8.35	2399.9
1978:06	7.60	1333.4	1981:10	15.08	1758.8	1985:02	8.50	2421.8
1978:07	7.81	1341.9	1981:11	13.31	1775.8	1985:03	8.58	2429.4
1978:08	8.04	1349.3	1981:12	12.37	1792.8	1985:04	8.27	2434.4
1978:09	8.45	1362.4	1982:01	13.22	1812.2	1985:05	7.97	2452.0
1978:10	8.96	1371.6	1982:02	14.78	1815.6	1985:06	7.53	2479.0
1978:11	9.76	1379.0	1982:03	14.68	1826.0	1985:07	7.88	2496.1
1978:12	10.03	1388.9	1982:04	14.94	1838.2	1985:08	7.90	2515.4
1979:01	10.07	1395.1	1982:05	14.45	1850.8	1985:09	7.92	2529.5
1979:02	10.06	1401.9	1982:06	14.15	1861.8	1985:10	7.99	2538.4
1979:03	10.09	1411.9	1982:07	12.59	1874.4	1985:11	8.05	2550.8
1979:04	10.01	1425.4	1982:08	10.12	1892.6	1985:12	8.27	2565.8

*For Exercise 11.13.

SOURCE: *Federal Reserve Bulletin*, various issues, Tables A-24 (FFR) and A-13 (M2, seasonally adjusted).

DATA SET 26 ■ Unemployment/inflation causality*

Month	U	PPI	Month	U	PPI	Month	U	PPI
1976:01	7.9	179.4	1979:05	5.6	232.0	1982:09	10.1	229.3
1976:02	7.7	179.4	1979:06	5.7	233.5	1982:10	10.4	299.8
1976:03	7.6	179.7	1979:07	5.7	236.9	1982:11	10.7	300.3
1976:04	7.7	181.3	1979:08	6.0	238.3	1982:12	10.7	330.7
1976:05	7.4	181.9	1979:09	5.9	242.0	1983:01	10.4	299.9
1976:06	7.6	183.2	1979:10	6.0	245.6	1983:02	10.4	300.9
1976:07	7.8	184.4	1979:11	5.9	247.2	1983:03	10.3	300.6
1976:08	7.8	183.8	1979:12	6.0	249.7	1983:04	10.2	300.6
1976:09	7.6	184.8	1980:01	6.3	254.9	1983:05	10.2	301.5
1976:10	7.7	185.3	1980:02	6.3	260.2	1983:06	10.1	302.4
1976:11	7.8	185.6	1980:03	6.3	261.9	1983:07	9.4	303.2
1976:12	7.8	187.1	1980:04	6.9	262.8	1983:08	9.5	304.7
1977:01	7.5	188.1	1980:05	7.5	264.2	1983:09	9.2	305.3
1977:02	7.6	190.2	1980:06	7.6	265.6	1983:10	8.8	306.0
1977:03	7.4	192.0	1980:07	7.8	270.4	1983:11	8.5	305.5
1977:04	7.2	194.3	1980:08	7.7	273.8	1983:12	8.2	306.1
1977:05	7.0	195.2	1980:09	7.5	274.6	1984:01	8.0	308.0
1977:06	7.2	194.5	1980:10	7.5	277.8	1984:02	7.8	308.9
1977:07	6.9	194.8	1980:11	7.5	279.1	1984:03	7.8	311.0
1977:08	7.0	194.6	1980:12	7.2	280.8	1984:04	7.8	311.3
1977:09	6.8	195.3	1981:01	7.5	284.8	1984:05	7.5	311.5
1977:10	6.8	196.3	1981:02	7.4	287.6	1984:06	7.2	311.3
1977:11	6.8	197.1	1981:03	7.4	290.3	1984:07	7.4	311.9
1977:12	6.4	198.2	1981:04	7.2	293.4	1984:08	7.5	310.7
1978:01	6.4	200.1	1981:05	7.5	294.1	1984:09	7.4	309.3
1978:02	6.3	202.1	1981:06	7.5	294.8	1984:10	7.3	309.4
1978:03	6.3	203.7	1981:07	7.2	296.2	1984:11	7.2	310.3
1978:04	6.1	206.5	1981:08	7.4	296.4	1984:12	7.2	309.8
1978:05	6.0	208.0	1981:09	7.6	295.7	1985:01	7.4	309.5
1978:06	5.9	209.6	1981:10	7.9	296.1	1985:02	7.3	309.1
1978:07	6.2	210.7	1981:11	8.3	295.5	1985:03	7.3	308.6
1978:08	5.9	210.6	1981:12	8.5	295.8	1985:04	7.3	309.3
1978:09	6.0	212.4	1982:01	8.6	298.3	1985:05	7.3	309.8
1978:10	5.8	214.9	1982:02	8.9	298.6	1985:06	7.3	309.2
1978:11	5.9	215.7	1982:03	9.0	298.0	1985:07	7.3	309.0
1978:12	6.0	217.5	1982:04	9.3	298.0	1985:08	7.1	307.3
1979:01	5.9	220.8	1982:05	9.4	298.6	1985:09	7.1	305.9
1979:02	5.9	224.1	1982:06	9.6	299.3	1985:10	7.1	307.9
1979:03	5.8	226.7	1982:07	9.8	300.4	1985:11	7.0	309.5
1979:04	5.8	230.0	1982:08	9.9	300.2	1985:12	6.9	310.2

*For Exercise 11.14.

SOURCE: *Federal Reserve Bulletin*, various issues, Tables A-45 (U) and A-50 (PPI).

APPENDIX II

WRITING AN ECONOMETRICS PAPER

The best way to learn econometrics is by doing it, and most beginning econometrics students are required to complete a research paper. Econometrics papers, even more than other term papers, are not something you can put off to the last minute. If you make a schedule and follow the steps below, you'll find that the paper isn't nearly the chore you might have expected it to be. Also, if you pick a topic you are actually interested in, you may even *enjoy* writing your econometrics paper!

STEP 1: PRELIMINARY DECISIONS

Before you begin your computer work or writing, you need to make several decisions and do some background work.

MODEL FORMULATION   You will be better off if you choose an area you know something about. For example, if you are a finance major, think about estimating a beta from the CAPM model; if you have had no course work in international economics, don't try to do a study on exchange rates or the trade deficit. Most important, select an area that you find *interesting*! Spending the time necessary to write a good paper on a subject that bores you wouldn't be very much fun.

LITERATURE REVIEW   Once you have an idea for your project, do a literature review. The best place to start is the *Journal of Economic Literature*. The *JEL* is published quarterly by the American Economics Association. Each issue contains: (1) the contents of current economics journals, (2) book reviews, (3) journal article abstracts, and (4) one or two survey articles. The *JEL* lists articles by journal and subject. You will almost certainly come up with a long list of references by just taking a quick look at the last few issues of the *JEL*. Unfortunately, although the *JEL* lists hundreds of economics journals (as well as a few from finance, accounting, and other areas), many of the references are too technical for most undergraduates, so the list will be narrowed a bit. Few undergraduates or first-year graduate students are ready to tackle anything from *Econometrica, Journal of Mathematical Economics*, or *Journal of Economic Theory*, but most other journals have occasional articles that can be read by typical undergraduates. Remember also that articles do not have to be quantitative or technical to be useful. Even largely literary economics journals such as *Challenge Magazine, Journal of Economic Issues*, and *Review of Social Economy* can provide information that will help you formulate the model, interpret your results, etc. A few of the most widely read journals that often have articles useful to beginning researchers include:

• *American Economic Review:* The most widely circulated and respected economics journal in the world. Some articles are too technical, but the "Papers and Proceedings" issue (May) contains largely nontechnical, invited papers on current topics.

• *Brookings Papers on Economic Activity:* Published three times a year, it devotes two issues to macroeconomics, one to microeconomics. Largely policy oriented. The editor's summary contains an elaborate abstract of each article.

• *Challenge Magazine:* The "magazine of economic affairs," is an extremely well-written journal aimed at the educated layperson as much as the professional economist. Very rarely uses regression analysis, but does offer timely articles written by well-known economists and suggestions for further reading.

• *Federal Reserve Bank Reviews:* The 12 Federal Reserve banks each have monthly or quarterly publications with journal-quality articles. Many use regression analysis and most are written at a level understandable by people who have studied this book.

• *Federal Reserve Bulletin:* Monthly. Each issue has one or two articles on the current economy as well as monthly and quarterly macroeconomic data.

• *Survey of Current Business:* Monthly. Like the *Federal Reserve Bulletin*, the *SCB* contains one or two articles as well as monthly and quarterly macroeconomic data.

STEP 2: DATA COLLECTION

It is impossible to do an econometrics project without data, so make sure the data are available before you commit to a particular project.

MACROECONOMICS DATA SOURCES   You will probably find macroeconomic data easier to collect than other kinds. All college and university libraries have several government sources that contain sources for macroeconomic data, and most have an on-line database as well. Annual data are available in the *Economic Report of the President*, quarterly and monthly data are in the *Federal Reserve Bulletin* (monthly) and the *Survey of Current Business* (monthly, with annual supplement). *Employment and Earnings* (monthly) has all the information you would ever need about labor. The annual *U.S. Statistical Abstract* has enormous amounts of aggregate U.S. data as well as quite a bit of data broken down by state and SMSA (Standard Metropolitan Statistical Area). If you will be working with macroeconomic data, you will find it useful to look at Norman Frumkin's book, *Guide to Economic Indicators* (Armonk, NY: M. E. Sharpe, 1990). This invaluable reference defines more than 50 of the most important macroeconomic data series and lists where they can be found, how they are compiled, and even how accurate they are.

MICROECONOMICS DATA SOURCES   There are fewer general sources for microeconomic data. You may find what you need in industry-specific publications. For example, *Ward's Automotive Reports* contains several data series related to the automobile industry. However, it is often best to simply make an appointment to talk to a professor whose research centers on your general area of interest. You may also be able to find data sources cited in the reference articles you read in preparation for the study. The *Census of Manufacturing* provides data by industry often broken down by *Standard Industrial Classification* (SIC) codes. Many financial data series for individual firms can be found in *Value Line*.

INTERNATIONAL DATA SOURCES   Again a wealth of information exists in this area. The monthly (with annual supplement) publication of the *International Financial Statistics* provides series on imports, exports, exchange rates, and other series for hundreds of countries. The World Bank publishes *Economic Development* annually. This lists important data — per capita GNP, doctors per capita, infant mortality rates, etc. — for developed as well as underdeveloped nations. Similar information can be found in the *United Nations Yearbook*.

OTHER DATA SOURCES   It is impossible to list all useful sources, but two additional comments are necessary. First, the Congressional Information

Service publishes the *Statistical Reference Index*, which lists most data sources that you really want to know about—as well as the one you need—probably. Second, most university libraries have reference librarians who should be able to point you in the right direction.

Once you find the data sources, make sure enough data are available: With less than about 40 observations, you will probably run into a degrees-of-freedom problem. Remember that *t*-statistics cannot be trusted unless the errors are approximately normal, and that with time series data correction for autocorrelation is going to be difficult without quite a bit of data. Think about whether you need to use annual, quarterly, monthly, or cross-sectional data. If you use data that are collected more often than annually, you may have a seasonality problem.

REAL VERSUS NOMINAL VALUES   For most models, it is best to work with data that have been adjusted for inflation. If possible, collect data that have already been adjusted. In most U.S. government publications, nominal data are indicated as simply "billions of dollars," while real data are denoted as "billions of 1982 dollars," where 1982 is the base year of the price index. If real data are not available, nominal data can be converted to real data. Nominal data in levels form—GNP, the money supply, etc.—can be converted to real by dividing by the relevant price index; that is:

$$\frac{\text{nominal GNP}}{\text{GNP deflator}} = \text{real GNP}. \qquad \text{[II.1]}$$

This technique does *not* work when data are in percentage change form. In particular, the real interest rate is *not* the nominal interest rate divided by a price index. A *very* rough approximation of the real interest rate (r) can be found by subtracting the inflation rate (p) from the nominal interest rate (i):

$$r = i - p. \qquad \text{[II.2]}$$

The approximation is so rough that it may be best to just use nominal rates or a real interest rate series that has been compiled in a previous study.

BASE YEAR CONVERSION   A common problem encountered when using real data is a change in the base year. The solution is actually quite simple. Pick a price index that was calculated for both base years and take the ratio, then multiply this number by all of the data in the older set to convert it to the new base year. The GNP deflator for 1980 using 1972 as the base year was 212.9; using 1982 as a base year, the GNP deflator for 1980 was 90.2. Prices obviously did not fall by more than half; the dramatic change is due to the change in base years. To use the GNP deflator in any analysis requires adjustment for the different base years. First, take the ratio of the two indices:

$$\frac{90.2}{212.9} = 0.42.$$

Then multiply 212.9 by 0.42 to get 89.42. This is the GNP deflator for 1980 with 1982 as the base year. (The actual value published in the 1989 *Economic Report of the President* was 90.2.) All of the data using a 1972 base year can be converted by multiplying by 0.42.

STEP 3: COMPUTER WORK

The particular methods you can use will depend on the software available in the computer lab. You will be thankful later if you spend some time in the lab "playing" with the software before you have to begin actually working on the project. Most modern software is very easy to use, but you cannot just sit down and expect to run your regression project. Spending a couple of hours investigating before you actually begin inputting your data is usually enough time to find out how to crash and lose files. If you work on a mainframe with a time-sharing system, don't wait until the last minute to get an account number.

INITIAL PRECAUTIONS   Back up your program disk and put the master away. Back up your data frequently. Then back it up again.

ENTERING DATA   How you enter data will again depend on the particular system you are working with, but keep a couple things in mind regardless of what system you use. First, unless you are able to use an on-line database, be sure to keep photocopies of all of the data you use. This will allow you to check for typos and save you from having to run back to the library (or wherever) if you lose your file. Save your work frequently, and be sure to keep a backup copy of your data set.

SCALING AND UNITS OF MEASUREMENT   Save yourself some work: When you input the data, use 350 instead of 350,000,000,000 for three hundred and fifty billion. As long as you remember to interpret the resulting regression coefficients accordingly, you won't have problems with this time-saving shortcut. But haven't you lost something? If the number is actually 350,000,000,250, the computer will have lost some of the variation and the calculation of the $\hat{\beta}_j$ will be off by a *tiny* amount; but the gains will almost certainly outweigh the losses. Computers use different levels of precision when carrying out calculations. Entering the data as 450,682,243 will result in a huge sum of squares and would require rounding; you will probably get more accurate results by entering 450.682 and remembering that you have changed the scale of your variables.

Once you have entered your data, it is often a good idea to plot it against time or observation for two reasons. First, it is an easy way to check for typos—leaving out a decimal or digit will usually show up immediately. Second, plotting the data can be informative. You might be able to detect a trend, etc.

REGRESSION ANALYSIS Now you're ready to run. Assign variables as specified in your theoretical model, and see what the regression looks like. Be sure to look at a plot of the residuals. Don't be frustrated if the results are not quite what you expected; they almost certainly won't be. Keep a copy of the run regardless of the results and use it to rethink your model. Remember that all regression results are considered ongoing research, and that additional analysis will be necessary—always. However, don't fall into the temptation of massaging the data until they yield the results for which you are looking. Not only is it unethical econometrics, but it will certainly affect your grade.

STEP 4: WRITING THE PAPER

Be forewarned: The purpose of your project is not to push back the frontiers of knowledge, but to demonstrate that you can design, perform, and report an econometric study. The final paper, then, should be much more than a stack of printouts. It should include a discussion of the theory behind your model and any implications of your research. The results *per se* are less important that your interpretation of them. Remember, too, that your professor will grade the writing style as well as your research methods.

The following is a generic outline that, with a little modification, should suffice for most undegraduate term papers.

A Generic Econometrics Paper Outline

I. Introduction
   a. State the problem you are studying. You may want to include a plot of the dependent variable.
   b. Include a brief literature review.

II. The Model
   a. Why did you construct the model as you did? Why did you select the functional form?
   b. What signs do you expect on the individual regressors? If you had to construct any variables—calculate ratios, take logs, etc.—explain why you did so.

III. The Data
   a. Why did you select the variables you did?
   b. Where did the data come from? Cite data sources and/or include an appendix with the data you used. If you smoothed the data or found it necessary to drop outliers, be sure to mention this.

     c. Are you comfortable with the data? That is, do you believe they are reliable? Do you suspect errors in variables?

IV. Reporting Results

     a. Don't include every regression, only the important ones. Include data and residual plots that are especially interesting.

     b. Unless required to do so, do not go into the details of how you corrected for autocorrelation, etc. Stating something such as "Cochran-Orcutt was used to estimate $\hat{\rho} = 0.677$, and generalized differencing was performed to eliminate autocorrelation" should be adequate. The *exams* are when you get the chance to show the instructor you know how to perform Cochran-Orcutt processes.

     c. *Interpret* and *use* your results. Simply stating that the t-ratios are significant is of little use. For example, if the model uses time series data, make a one-step forecast. Is the forecast reasonable?

     d. Remember, "negative" results—results that are inconsistent with your initial hypothesis—are results nevertheless. If your hypothesis is not verified by the data, do not try to hide it. Do try to explain what happened. Was there a specification error? A structural shift you could not isolate? Multicollinearity that could not be eliminated?

V. Summary and Conclusions

Don't even *pretend* that your study is the final word. If your hypothesis appears to be verified and your summary statistics are good, fine, but more sophisticated methods might shed doubt on your study. Econometric analysis is never finished. Even practicing econometricians invariably call their studies "preliminary" and mention that research is continuing. Conclude your paper with a section discussing further work.

GLOSSARY

Almon lag Very general distributed lag structure. See also *Koyck lag*.

Alternative hypothesis In hypothesis testing, the hypothesis the investigator usually hopes to accept by rejecting the *null hypothesis*. The most common alternate hypotheses in regression analyses are $H_a: \beta_j \neq 0$ (two-tailed test) and $H_a: \beta_j < 0$ or > 0 (one-tailed test).

ANOVA Acronym for analysis of variance, the techniques used to assess the overall statistical significance of the regression equation. See also *F-test, Coefficient of determination.*

ARIMA Acronym for integrated autoregressive moving average, an ARMA model that has been differenced to render it stationary. All stationary time series can be fitted with an ARIMA model. The basic method for fitting time series models. See *Box-Jenkins analysis, stationary.*

ARMA A time series model composed of autoregressive and moving average components; i.e., an ARMA(2, 1) has a two-period autoregressive stem and a one-period moving average error and would be indicated as:

$$x_t = \alpha_1 x_{t-1} + \alpha_2 x_{t-2} + \beta_1 \varepsilon_{t-1} + \varepsilon_t.$$

Autocorrelation Also called *serial correlation*, a violation of the assumption that consecutive errors are independent. Extremely common in models using time series data. Autocorrelation biases R^2 and t-ratios upward and makes parameter estimates inefficient. It does not result in biased parameter estimates. See also *Durbin-Watson statistic.*

Autocorrelation function (ACF)   Plot of correlations between different observations in a time series. The autocorrelation at lag one gives the correlation between X_t and X_{t-1} for the entire series; the autocorrelation at lag two gives the correlation between X_t and X_{t-2} for the entire series, etc. Used in the identification stage of Box-Jenkins analysis. See also *Stationary, Partial autocorrelation function.*

Best estimate   Minimum variance. OLS estimates are best.

Biased estimate   An estimate is biased if $E(\hat{\theta}) \neq \theta$. OLS estimates are unbiased.

Binomial distribution   Statistical distribution that can take on only two values. The error terms in the logit and linear probability models are binomially distributed. The binomial distribution approaches the normal distribution for a large sample.

BLUE   Acronym for <u>B</u>est <u>L</u>inear <u>U</u>nbiased <u>E</u>stimate. OLS estimates are BLUE.

Box-Jenkins analysis   The most popular method for forecasting stationary time series. The three steps in Box-Jenkins analysis are identification, estimation, and diagnostic checking. See also *ARIMA,* stationary.

Breusch-Pagan test   Test for detecting heteroscedasticity. Can determine whether heteroscedasticity is caused by more than one independent variable. See also *Goldfeld-Quandt test, Park test.*

Causality   Philosophical concept that should be *carefully* applied to econometrics. Generally, X "causes" Y if control of X allows control of Y, but the concept is much more complex. Statistics cannot prove causality. See *Granger causality; Weak, Strong, and Super exogeneity.*

Central Limit Theorem   One of the most powerful theorems in statistics and crucial for conducting hypothesis tests. Its simplest version states that $\bar{X} \sim N(\mu_x, \sigma_n^2/n)$, regardless of the distribution of the parent population.

Chi-square test   The sum of the squares of n independent standard normal distributions follows a chi-square (χ^2)-distribution with n degrees of freedom. Several tests involving the χ^2-distribution are important, including tests for the significance of omitted variables in regression and logit models and time series model specification.

Chow test F-test used to check for structural change; can sometimes be used instead of a dummy variable.

Cobb-Douglas production function $(Y_t = \beta_0 X_{1t}^{\beta_1} X_{2t}^{\beta_2} \varepsilon_t)$ Production function model used in microeconomic and macroeconomic studies. Estimation with linear regression analysis requires a log transformation.

Cochran-Orcutt   Most common method for calculating $\hat{\rho}$ in models with first-order autocorrelation. Built into many computer packages.

Coefficient of determination   Most often called R^2. The most common measure of goodness of fit for a regression model. Calculated as the ratio of the variation explained by the regression model (RSS) to total variation in the dependent variable (TSS). See also *Corrected R-Squared*.

Conditional forecast   A forecast that is conditional on a forecast of the independent variables. Forecast error will thus depend on the stochastic nature of the parameter estimates as well as any error made in the forecast of X_{t+1}. See also *Unconditional forecast*.

Conditional Probability   The probability of A occurring given a particular value of B, indicated $P(A \mid B)$, where $P(A) = P(A \mid B)$ if A and B are statistically independent.

Confidence interval   Interval around the point estimate of a parameter. With a large sample, two standard deviations on either side of the sample mean is a 95% confidence interval.

Consistency   Large sample unbiasedness. A parameter estimate is consistent if $E(\hat{\theta}) = \theta$ as the sample size gets large. 2SLS estimates are consistent but biased in small samples.

Constrained linear probability model   A problem with the linear probability model is that fitted values can fall outside the required (0, 1) region. This is prevented by constraining the model such that all values greater than 1 are arbitrarily assigned a value very close to 1, say, 0.99 and all values less than 0 are assigned very low values, say, 0.01. Nonlinear methods are usually preferred estimation techniques.

Controlled experiment   Used in the hard sciences but only rarely in economics and the other social sciences. Involves fixing all factors except one in order to determine causality. One reason why there are conflicting econometric results.

Corrected R-squared ($\bar{R}^2$)   The coefficient of determination adjusted for degrees of freedom. If $\bar{R}^2$ and R^2 are far apart, there are probably extraneous variables in the model. See also *F-test*.

Correlation [corr(X, Y), $\rho_{x,y}$]   A measure of the linear association between two variables. Mathematically,

$$\rho_{x,y} = \frac{\operatorname{cov}(x, y)}{\sigma_x \sigma_y}.$$

Correlation matrix   Matrix showing the correlation between Y and one or several X's. Used to determine whether multicollinearity is significant enough to be a problem. If $\rho_{X2, X1} > \rho_{Y, X1}$ or $\rho_{Y, X2}$, multicollinearity is significant.

Correlogram   Plot of the autocorrelation function.

Covariance   A measure of the linear association between X and Y. Defined as $\text{cov}(X, Y) = E[X - E(X)][Y - E(Y)]$. See also *Correlation*.

Cubic cost function   Standard assumption regarding cost in neoclassical economics: $\text{TC} \equiv C = \beta_0 + \beta_1 Q + \beta_2 Q^2 + \beta_3 Q^3$. Estimated with a polynomial model.

Data generating process   According to the Hendry school of econometrics, the main aim of econometric inquiry should be to make inferences about the underlying process that generates the data to be observed. Any equation that can be estimated—an estimable model—is an approximation of the data generating process. Many econometricians do not realize that the estimable model is not consistent with their *a priori* theory.

Data mining   Unethical econometric practice of massaging and manipulating the data to obtain the desired results.

Degrees of freedom (d.f.)   The number of pieces of data used in the estimation of a parameter minus the number of constraints placed on the data.

Dependent variable   In regression analysis, the variable on the left side of the equation, usually indicated as Y_i, which is assumed to be caused by the independent variables, the X_{ji}.

Deviation form   The difference between the actual data and their means; $x_i = X_i - \bar{X}$, $y_i = Y_i - \bar{Y}$. Estimation of the regression model in deviation form forces the intercept to zero.

Difference equation   An equation with data expressed in period to period differences; i.e.,

$$Y_t - Y_{t-1} = \beta_1(X_{1t} - X_{1t-1}) + \beta_2(X_{2t} - X_{2t-1}) + \cdots,$$
$$\Delta Y_t = \beta_1 \Delta X_{1t} + \beta_2 \Delta X_{2t} + \cdots.$$

Quasi-differencing is used to eliminate autocorrelation; first or second differencing can be used to make a time series stationary.

Distributed lag   A model of the form:

$$Y_t = \beta_0 + \beta_1 X_t + \beta_2 X_{t-1} + \beta_3 X_{t-2} + \cdots.$$

See also *Koyck lag*.

Dummy variable   Qualitative independent variable assigned values of 0 and 1 to check for structural change. See also *Dummy variable trap, Intercept dummy, Logit model, slope dummy*.

Dummy variable trap   When using dummy vaziables, use one less dummy than the number of structural shifts; i.e., for peace/war, use only one dummy. Otherwise, perfect multicollinearity between the dummies and the intercept will result. Suppression of the intercept will avoid the dummy variable trap.

Durbin *h*-test　　Test for autocorrelation in models that include lagged endogenous variables.

Durbin method　　Method used to estimate models with autocorrelation. Involves running the model with current and lagged values of all independent variables and a lagged dependent variable on the right side. Good for very large samples.

Durbin–Watson statistic (d)　　Primary statistic used to check for the presence of first-order autocorrelation. If d is "close" to 2, autocorrelation is probably not present; if it is close to 0, there is probably positive autocorrelation; if it is close to 4.0, there is negative autocorrelation.

Econometrics　　Collection of statistical techniques used by economists to test economic theories and make forecasts. Most important statistical method is regression analysis.

Efficiency　　An efficient parameter estimate has a small variance relative to other estimates. See also *Best estimate*.

Elasticity　　In economics, the percentage change in the dependent variable divided by the percentage change in the independent variable. For the linear regression model, elasticity can be calculated as $\eta = \hat{\beta}_j \bar{X} / \bar{Y}$.

Endogenous variable　　In regression analysis, it is assumed that the endogenous variables are caused by the *exogenous variables*. In single-equation models, the variable on the left side, Y. In simultaneous-equation models, any variable whose value is determined by the equation system.

Error term　　A random element present in all regression models, usually indicated with the symbol ε. The error term is attributed to omitted variables and measurement errors.

ESS (error sum of squares)　　The unexplained portion of the variation in the dependent variable, $\text{ESS} = \sum (Y_i - \hat{Y}_i)^2$.

Estimable model　　Any model that can be estimated is an approximation of some data generating process. However, it is not always clear that the estimable model is a good approximation of the theory that the econometrician intends to test.

Estimation　　The key task of econometrics is to approximate populations with a small sample of the data. This is known as *estimation*.

Exogenous variable　　The assumed causal variables in regression analysis. In single-equation models, the variables on the right side, usually indicated as X_j. In simultaneous models, any variables whose values are determined separately from the model.

Expected value $[E(\bullet)]$ The most likely outcome from a probability distribution. The expected value of the random variable X is a weighted average of each observation times its probability.

Extraneous variable   In multiple regression analysis, inclusion of a variable that does not offer significant explanatory power on the dependent variable. Will result in inefficient parameter estimates.

F-test   Several F-tests are used in econometrics, the most common is a test of the overall significance of the regression equation and reliability of R^2. Tests hypothesis H_0: all $\beta_j = 0$ versus H_a: at least one $\beta_j \neq 0$. See also *Chow test, Granger causality.*

Filter   Differencing, moving average, and other techniques used to *smooth* data. Filtering is done to eliminate the random and/or cyclical elements in time series data.

First differences   See *Difference equation.*

Forecast error   The error associated with forecasts made from regression or time series models. For a regression model, the forecast error is given by Eq. [3.34]. A main criteria in the selection of alternative time series models is forecast error.

Fragile   The opposite of *robust*. An econometric model is fragile if a slight change in specification or sample results in a significant change in parameter estimates and/or summary statistics.

Gauss-Markov theorem   The basic theorem of regression analysis. If Assumptions 1 through 6 hold, the Gauss-Markov theorem establishes that OLS parameter estimates will be BLUE.

Generalized least squares   A set of techniques including weighted least squares and quasi-differencing that is used to modify models so that they conform to the OLS assumptions.

Goldfeld-Quandt test   A standard test for heteroscedasticity. To perform, sort data by the X variable thought to be the source of heteroscedasticity, omit $d = 0.2$ middle observations, run OLS on the two data sets, and form an F-ratio of the ESS.

Granger causality   A test for econometric causality or, more properly, temporal association. Granger causal tests involve checking whether lagged values of X_t play a significant role in explaining Y_t in a model with several lagged values of Y_t on the right side. If so, X_t is said to Granger-cause Y_t.

Heteroscedasticity   A violation of Assumption 4, which requires that error variance be constant. Heteroscedasticity results in inefficient but unbiased parameter estimates. It is most common in cross-sectional data.

Hildreth-Lu test   A method to estimate $\hat{\rho}$, the autocorrelation coefficient. To perform, form grid of possible $\hat{\rho}$'s, i.e., $\hat{\rho} \in \{0.1, 0.2, \ldots, 0.9\}$, and run OLS with quasi-differences for each $\hat{\rho}$. Select the run with the lowest ESS and form a grid about it; i.e., $\hat{\rho} \in \{0.41, 0.42, \ldots, 0.54\}$, and again run quasi-differenced OLS. Continue until successive iterations have $\hat{\rho}$'s that are close.

Homoscedasticity   The opposite of heteroscedasticity. A requirement for BLUE parameter estimates.

Identification problem   From 2SLS. Structural equations are identified only if the rank and order conditions are met. Under-identified equations cannot be estimated. Most equations in large econometric models are over identified.

Independent variable   The X- or exogenous variables assumed to cause Y in regression analysis.

Instrument   A substitute variable. The fitted values from the first-stage regressions are used as instruments in the second stage of 2SLS to eliminate correlation between the errors and endogenous variables that appear on the right side of the structural equations. Instrumental variables are also used when there are errors in variables.

Interaction effects   When the effect of one variable on the model depends on the level of another variable, an interaction term is included in the model specification. This often takes the form of the product between the two variables; i.e.,

$$Y_i = \beta_0 + \beta_1 X_{1i} + \beta_2 X_{2i} + \beta_3 X_{1i} X_{2i} + \varepsilon_i.$$

Intercept   The Y-intercept of the regression equation, β_0. The intercept rarely has meaning in econometric analysis. It is often interpreted as the average effect of all omitted variables.

Intercept dummy   A dummy variable used to determine if a structural change has shifted the intercept. In the model $Y_t = \beta_0 + \beta_1 X_t + \beta_2 D_t + \varepsilon_t$, the dummy variable D_t is assigned a value of 1 or 0 to indicate structural shift. The sign and statistical significance on $\hat{\beta}_2$ is evaluated to determine whether a shift has taken place.

Joint Distribution   A probability distribution involving two or more random variables.

Just identified   The minimum conditions for estimation of equations in simultaneous systems. By the order condition, an equation is just identified when there is exactly one exogenous variable omitted.

Koyck lag   A common distributed lag model. To avoid multicollinearity and lost degrees of freedom, a lagged endogenous variable can be used instead of several lags on the exogenous variable; i.e.,

$$Y_t = \beta_0^* + \beta_1 X_t + \lambda Y_{t-1} + \varepsilon_t^*.$$

Least-squares analysis   Another name for regression analysis. This name derives from the fact that parameter estimates are found by minimizing the sum of squared residuals.

Log transformation   Taking logs of a multiplicative relationship converts a nonlinear model into a model that is linear in the logs. Additionally, regression coefficients are now interpreted as elasticities.

Logistic function   A cumulative probability density function and the basis for the logit model: $P_i = [1 + e^{-(\beta_0 + \beta_1 X_i)}]^{-1}$. The logistic function is used because it overcomes most of the problems of the linear probability model.

Logit model   The most common nonlinear model of qualitative choice, usually estimated with maximum likelihood techniques.

Linear probability model   A simplistic model used to estimate relationships involving qualitative dependent variables. Because fitted values often fall outside of the required (0, 1) region, it is often necessary to constrain the linear probability model or use a nonlinear model such as the logit.

Marginal Distribution [$m(x)$]   The sum of probabilities along the margin of a joint distribution; i.e., the marginal distribution of X consists of the probabilities that X will take on particular values regardless of the value of Y. The marginal distribution can be used to simplify calculation of the mean and variance.

Mathematical economics   Compared to econometrics, mathematical economics is usually more concerned with abstract relationships and theory; econometrics attempts to test these relationships with actual data.

Mean (μ_x)   The arithmetic average or expected value, $\mu_x = \sum X_i / n$.

Mean squared error (MSE)   A criteria used for selecting estimators when it is impossible to obtain an unbiased estimate. The MSE weights both the bias and the variance, $\text{MSE}(\theta) = \text{bias}(\theta)^2 + \text{var}(\theta)$. A good estimator will minimize MSE.

Moving average   (1) A smoothing technique used in the initial stages of time series analysis. A five-period moving average, MA(5), is given by:

$$y_t = \frac{1}{2(2) + 1} \sum_{j=-2}^{+2} x_{t-j}.$$

(2) A common pattern followed by the error term in an ARIMA model. A

one-period moving average model is written: $y_{t+2} = x_{t+2} - x_{t+1} = \varepsilon_{t+2} + \beta\varepsilon_{t+1}$. An MA($q$) model is identified by looking at the ACF. If the ACF cuts of at period k, the model is probably MA(k).

Multicollinearity   Significant correlation between regressors. The classic symptoms of multicollinearity are low t-ratios and a high R^2. See also *Correlation matrix*.

Multiple regression   Regression analysis using one dependent variable and two or more independent variables. Estimation is possible only if there is no perfect correlation between X variables.

Nonstochastic   Nonrandom. The X variables are usually assumed to be nonstochastic.

Normal distribution   Bell-shaped curve that can be completely described by its mean and variance. Many probability distributions can be approximated with the normal distribution.

Null hypothesis   In hypothesis testing, the hypothesis the investigator usually hopes to refute so that the alternative hypothesis can be accepted. The most common null hypothesis in regression analysis is $H_0: \beta_j = 0$.

Odds ratio   In the logit model, the ratio of "success" to "failure." The log of the odds ratio is the logit, the dependent variable in the logit model.

Omitted variable   A specification error occurs when a statistically significant independent variable is omitted from the model. This will result in biased parameter estimates. See *Extraneous variable*.

Order condition   A necessary, but not sufficient, condition for determining whether an equation is identified well enough for estimation with 2SLS. Involves counting equations and exogenous and endogenous variables.

Ordinary least squares (OLS)   The name given to regression analysis when it is applied to a model that fulfills all of the six classical assumptions.

Over identified   A structural equation is over identified if more than one exogenous variable from the simultaneous system is omitted from it. Most equations in large econometric models are over identified. See also *Just identified, Order condition, Rank condition, Under identified*.

Parameter   Measures that describe a population or model. For example, the mean and variance are parameters that describe the normal distribution. The main goal of econometrics is to estimate population parameters from the sample data.

Park test   Common test for heteroscedasticity that involves collecting OLS residuals, squaring and taking their logs, and regressing them on the X variable thought to be the source of heteroscedasticity. If $\hat{\beta}_1$ is statistically significant, heteroscedasticity is present and X is the source. The Park test can also be used to estimate the weights for WLS.

Parsimonious parameterization   In Box-Jenkins analysis, the philosophy that a simple low-order model is usually preferred to a higher order model.

Partial autocorrelation function (PACF)   Function that plots the correlation between x_t and x_{t-s} while omitting the intervening lags. If the correlation between x_t and x_{t-s} is significant, but the correlation between x_t and x_{t-s+1} is not, the series is probably an AR(p) series. See also *Autocorrelation function*.

Partial regression coefficients   In multiple regression, the $\hat{\beta}_j$ are called partial because they are interpreted as the effect of a small change in an individual X_j on Y, assuming all other X_j are held constant.

Phillips curve   A macroeconomic relationship between inflation and unemployment; used as an illustration of the reciprocal model. A typical Phillips curve is

$$P_t = \beta_0 + \beta_1 U_t^{-1} + \varepsilon_t.$$

Piecewise linear model   Model specification that uses one dummy to check for simultaneous shifts in the intercept and slope; i.e.,

$$Y_t = \beta_0 + \beta_1 X_t + \beta_2 (X_t - X_{t0}) D_t + \varepsilon_t.$$

Also called jackknife model or spline function. See also *Slope dummy, Intercept dummy*.

Polynomial Model   Model specification involving multiple X-terms raised to different powers; i.e., $Y = \beta_0 + \beta_1 X + \beta_2 X^2 + \beta_3 X^3$. Used to model nonlinear relationships.

Population regression function   A regression equation estimated with the entire data set. The main task of regression analysis is the estimation of the population regression function from the sample data:

$$Y_i = \beta_0 + \beta_1 X_i + \varepsilon_i.$$

See also *Sample regression function*.

Probability density function   The process that generates a random variable. To be a probability density function two requirements must be fulfilled: $0 \leq p_i \leq 1$, and $\sum p_i = 1$.

Qualitative variable   A nonquantitative variable usually assigned values of 1 and 0. See also *Dummy variable, Logit model*.

Quantitative variable   A variable that can take on continuous numerical values; most variables used in econometrics are quantitative. See also *Dummy variable, Logit model*.

Quasi-differencing   A GLS techniques used to correct for autocorrelation.

Lag the equation, multiply by $\hat{\rho}$, and subtract from the original equation; i.e.,

$$Y_t - \rho Y_{t-1} = \beta_0 - \rho\beta_0 + \beta_1 X_t - \beta_1 \rho X_{t-1} + \varepsilon_t - \rho\varepsilon_{t-1}$$
$$Y_t^* = \beta_0(1 - \rho) + \beta_1 X_t^* + v_t.$$

R-squared (R^2) The basic measure of goodness of fit used in regression analysis; defined as the ratio of explained variation (RSS) in Y to total variation (TSS) in Y. See also *F-test, Corrected R^2*.

Random variable Variable that takes on values by chance. See also *Stochastic*.

Rank condition Sufficient condition for determining the identification of structural conditions in 2SLS models. See also *Order condition*.

Reciprocal model Model specification that permits linear estimation of certain nonlinear functions:

$$Y_t = \beta_0 + \beta_1 X_t^{-1} + \varepsilon_t.$$

See also *Phillips curve*.

Reduced form equations In 2SLS, the reduced form equations are constructed from the structural equations and used to estimate instruments for use in the second-stage regressions. There is one reduced form equation for each endogenous variable in the system, and each reduced form equation has one endogenous variable on the left side and all exogenous variables from the entire system on the right side.

Regressand The dependent variable in regression analysis; usually indicated as Y_i.

Regression analysis The fundamental statistical method of econometrics. Also called *least-squares analysis*.

Regressor An independent variable in regression analysis; usually indicated as X_{ji}.

Residual The difference between the actual Y values (Y_i) and the fitted Y values ($\hat{Y}_i$): $e_i = Y_i - \hat{Y}_i$. Regression residuals are used as approximations of the true errors.

Robust Econometric results that stand up to different model specifications and data sets are called robust. Compare to *Fragile*.

RSS (Regression sum of squares) The amount of "explained" variation in the regression model, RSS $= \sum(\hat{Y}_i - \bar{Y})^2$. A good model usually has a large RSS relative to TSS and ESS.

Sample regression function A regression function estimated using sample data. If the sample is random and large, the sample regression function will be a good approximation of the population regression function:

$$Y_i = \hat{\beta}_0 + \hat{\beta}_1 X_i + e_i.$$

Sequential search   A common methodology used to search for the best model specification; involves running a sequence of regressions and selecting regressors based on t-ratios. Can lead to biased parameter estimates. See also *Data mining, Stepwise regression*.

Serial correlation   A common name for autocorrelation.

Simple regression   Regression analysis with one independent variable.

Slope   The ratio of "rise to run." In (X, Y)-space, the amount that Y changes in response to a one-unit change in X. In regression analysis, the $\hat{\beta}_j$ are slope estimates in (X_j, Y)-space.

Slope dummy   A dummy variable used to check whether there has been a structural shift that affected the slope. In the model

$$Y_t = \beta_0 + \beta_1 X_t + \beta_2 X_t D_t + \varepsilon_t,$$

the dummy variable D_t is assigned a value of 1 or 0 to indicate structural shift. The sign and statistical significance on $\hat{\beta}_2$ is evaluated to determine whether a structural shift in the slope has taken place. See also *Intercept dummy, Piecewise linear model*.

Smoothing   Methods used to eliminate or reduce the influence of the random elements in time series data; also called *filtering*. See also *Moving average*.

Specification error   Error that occurs when a model uses the wrong functional form, or has extraneous or omitted variables. Specification error can lead to biased parameter estimates.

Standard error of the regression (SER, s)   The square root of the sum that is minimized by least-squares analysis; a small SER indicates a model that fits well. For the two-variable model:

$$s = \sqrt{s^2} = \left(\frac{\sum e_i^2}{n-2} \right)^{1/2} = \left[\frac{\sum(Y_i - \beta_0 - \beta_1 X_i)^2}{n-2} \right]^{1/2}.$$

As a simple rule of thumb, SER should be 15% or less of $\bar{Y}$ for the model to be useful for forecasting.

Standard deviation   The square root of the variance. Used in hypothesis tests and the construction of confidence intervals. The t-ratio on regression coefficients is formed by dividing $\hat{\beta}_j$ by their standard errors.

Standard normal distribution (Z)   Normal distribution used in normal tables. Any normal distribution can be standardized by transforming it with $Z = (X - \mu_x)/\sigma_x$.

Stationary   A series is stationary if the covariance between terms depends only on the time interval between the terms, not on time itself. Stationarity is checked by looking at the ACF. If the ACF cuts off abruptly, the series is probably stationary; if it declines slowly, it is not. Box-Jenkins analysis can be applied only to stationary series.

Statistical independence   The random variables X and Y are statistically independent (i.e., $X \perp Y$) if the outcome on X has no influence on the outcome on Y. Also, $\text{cov}(X, Y) = 0$ and $p(X_i Y_i) = p(X_i)p(Y_i)$, $\forall\ X, Y$.

Stepwise regression   Regression technique that instructs the computer to search through a list of potential explanatory variables to come up with the model specification that maximizes R^2. Rarely used in econometric analysis; considered a form of data mining.

Stochastic random   The regression error term is assumed to be stochastic.

Strong exogeneity   Weak exogeneity without any feedback effects. Necessary for Granger causality. See also *Super exogeneity*.

Structural equations   Equations based on economic theory. In 2SLS, the reduced form equations are derived from the structural equations. Instruments from the first stage are then substituted into the structural equations for second-stage estimation.

Super exogeneity   A concept of exogeneity necessary for policy analysis. Equivalent to strong exogeneity and no unexpected parameter shifts in response to policy changes.

t-ratio   Key statistical test used to evaluate the significance of individual $\hat{\beta}_j$. Formed by taking the ratio of $\hat{\beta}_j$ to its standard error, $\text{se}(\hat{\beta}_j)$. For a large sample (d.f. > 30), a *t*-ratio equal to 2.0 indicates that the coefficient is statistically significant at the 95% level.

-test   Same as *t*-ratio.

Total sum of squares (TSS)   The total variation in the dependent variable, $\sum(Y_i - \bar{Y})^2$. Used in the denominator of R^2 and many F-tests. See also *Error sum of squares, Regression sum of squares*.

Type I error   The probability of incorrectly rejecting a true null hypothesis; equal to the area in the tails of the normal or *t*-distribution used in the hypothesis test.

Type II error   The probability of incorrectly accepting a false null hypothesis. The chance of making a Type II error is high when the hypothesized parameter is very close to the true parameter.

Unconditional forecast   A forecast that is made without having to estimate the independent variable(s). For example, the model $Y_t = \beta_0 + \beta_1 X_{t-1} + \varepsilon_t$ can be used for an unconditional one-step forecast, the model $Y_t = \beta_0 + \beta_1 X_t + \varepsilon_t$ cannot.

Under identified   In 2SLS, an equation that is under identified cannot be estimated. The order condition for under identification occurs when there are no exogenous variables from the system omitted from the equation.

Variance   The most important measure of disperson of a random variable:

$$\text{var}(X) = \sum p_i(X - \mu_x)^2 = E[X - E(X)]^2.$$

Weak exogeneity   The standard definition of exogeneity used in regression analysis. If X is weakly exogenous, it is possible to "explain" Y in terms of X but it is not possible to "explain" X in terms of Y; i.e., there is an asymmetry between X and Y. Regressors must be weakly exogenous before regression analysis can be conducted. See also *Strong exogeneity, Super exogeneity, Independent variable.*

Weighted least squares (WLS)   The method most often used to correct for heteroscedasticity. WLS is performed by dividing the model by a weighting factor, usually a function of the independent variable thought to be the source of heteroscedasticity. See also *Park test, Goldfeld-Quandt test, Breusch-Pagan test.*

White noise   Term used in time series analysis to indicate a random element, often the error term.

APPENDIX IV

ANSWERS, HINTS, AND SOLUTIONS TO SELECTED EXERCISES

CHAPTER 1

1.1 Note that this problem asks you to omit the last observation before estimation.

(a) $P_t = 7.64 - 0.05\text{M2}$ (b) $P_{t+1} = 7.21$
(c) Very poor fit ($R^2 = 0.002$)

1.2 Let $\bar{X} = \bar{Y} = 0$ and the proof follows directly.

1.4 Regression analysis cannot prove causality.

1.5 Because the regression line is linear, several values for $\hat{\beta}_0$ and $\hat{\beta}_1$ will minimize $\sum e_i$. Squaring the residuals results in a parabola with a unique minimum.

1.6 R^2 is higher, but the fact that less data were used suggests that these results are less reliable. As noted in Chapter 11, a good model should be *robust* in the sense that small changes in model specification or the sample do not have appreciable affects on the regression results. This model is not robust.

1.7 (a) A one percentage point rise in the GNP gap raises unemployment by 0.36 percentage points. The model apparently explains 87% of the variation in unemployment.

APPENDIX 1.A

A1 Expand $\sum y_i = \sum (Y_i - \dot{\bar{Y}})$.

A2 Expand the term in brackets and distribute the summation sign.

A3 93.75.

A4 One counter example is enough to prove this result. Define X as $\{1, 2, 3\}$ and compute both sums: $\sum X_i = 1 + 2 + 3 = 6$; so $(\sum X_i)^2 = 36$. Because $\sum X_i^2 = 1^2 + 2^2 + 3^2 = 14$, $(\sum X_i)^2 \neq \sum X_i^2$.

A5 Let X be $\{1, 2, 3\}$ so that $\bar{X} = 2$. Then $x_i = \{-1, 0, 1\}$ and $\sum x_i^2 = 1 + 4 + 1 = 6$. This is interesting because $\sum x_i = 0$.

CHAPTER 2

2.1 Apply the two criteria for a probability density function: $0 \leq p_i \leq 1$ and $\sum p_i = 1$.

2.2 Because $Y = a + bX$, it follows that $\mu_Y = E(a + bX) = a + b\mu_X$.

2.3 Write $\text{var}(a + bX) = E[(a + bX) - E(a + bX)]^2$ and expand the square.

2.4 Because each X observation appears only once, $p_i = 1/n$.

2.5 $\text{var}(\bar{X}) = \text{var}\left(\dfrac{\sum X}{n}\right) = \dfrac{1}{n^2}\text{var}(\sum X) = \dfrac{1}{n^2}\text{var}(X_1 + X_2 + \cdots + X_n) = \dfrac{1}{n^2}n\,\text{var}(X) = \dfrac{1}{n}\text{var}(X)$.

2.6 Expand $(X_i - \bar{X})(Y_i - \bar{Y})$. To show that it is unbiased, take the expected value of $\dfrac{1}{n-1}\sum\limits_{i=1}^{n} X_i Y_i - n\bar{X}\bar{Y}$.

2.7 Let $\bar{\bar{\theta}}$ be the expected value of $\hat{\theta}$ where $\hat{\theta}$ is the estimate of q. Then write:
$$E(\hat{\theta} - \theta)^2 = E[(\hat{\theta} - \bar{\bar{\theta}}) + (\bar{\bar{\theta}} - \theta)]^2.$$
Expand the term in brackets and distribute the expected value operator.

2.8 Apply the rules in Eqs. [2.8] and [2.9].

2.9 For both questions, the calculations are:
$$\frac{12 - 10}{3/7} = \frac{14}{3} = 4.67.$$

The null hypothesis in part **(a)** is rejected; the null hypothesis in part **(b)** cannot be rejected.

2.10 **(a)** $\bar{X} = 25.5$ **(b)** $s_x^2 = 311.73$; $s_x = 19.48$
(c) cannot reject null hypothesis.

2.12 **(a)** The data are nonlinearly related, $X = Y^2$.

(b) cov $= 0$. This implies that the data are *linearly* independent, not that they are independent.

2.13 There is only one constraint on the data, the value of $\sum \bar{X}\bar{Y}$.

2.14 Write variance in terms of expected values; i.e., $\text{var}(X - Y) = E(X - Y)^2 - [E(X - Y)]^2$ and expand.

2.15 Use the definition of correlation to solve for covariance.
(a) $\text{var}(X + Y) = 13.46$ **(b)** $\text{cov}(X, Y) = 1.23$
(c) 9.23. Note that $\text{cov}(X, X + Y) = E(X^2 + XY) - E(X)E(X + Y)$, which reduces to $\text{var}(X) + \text{cov}(X, Y)$.

2.16 **(a)** 0.045 **(b)** 0.274 **(c)** 0. Remember the 2 is the variance, not the standard deviation.

CHAPTER 3

3.1 They would be the same because $\sigma_x = \sigma_y$.

3.2 t-ratio on intercept $= 18.04$. t-ratio on slope $= 2.12$. Reject both.

3.3 **(a)** $\hat{\beta}_0 = 0.154$, $\hat{\beta}_1 = 0.873$. **(b)** $s^2 = 7.996$ **(c)** $\text{se}(\hat{\beta}_1) = 0.006$
(d) $R^2 = 0.98$.

3.4 The intercept will be biased by the amount the expected value of the error differs from zero. To prove this, find $E(\hat{\beta}_0)$ given that $E(e_i) \neq 0$.

3.5 This follows directly from the first proof in Appendix 3.A.

3.6 $H_0: \beta_1 = 0$, $H_a: \beta_1 > 0$. This would change the critical t-value and rejection region. The critical t-value for 26 d.f. at the 5% significance level is 1.706.

3.7 More confident if $\text{var}(X)$ is large. A large X variance increases the precision of the parameter estimate. The formula for $\text{se}(\hat{\beta}_1)$ has $\text{var}(X)$ in the denominator; thus, a large $\text{var}(X)$ reduces $\text{se}(\hat{\beta}_1)$.

3.10 Substitute the formulae for $\hat{\beta}_0$ and $\hat{\beta}_1$ into Eq. [2.51], expand, and note that, for any particular sample, the mean of ε_i is not necessarily zero.

3.11 $\eta = 0.24$; inelastic.

3.14 It would change the $\hat{\beta}_1$ to 247.0. The summary statistics, t-ratios, and intercept would not be affected.

3.15 As long as the errors are independent, the probability that $e_4 < 0$ will be 0.5.

3.16 Cannot reject the null hypothesis of a zero intercept at either significance level. To reject the null hypothesis would require an estimate of $\hat{\beta}_0$ that exceeded 1.706, the critical t-value for 26 d.f. at a 5% significance level.

3.18 Write $R^2 = \sum \hat{y}_i^2 / \sum y_i^2$ and substitute for $\hat{y}_i^2$.

3.19 Note that RSS $= \sum \hat{y}_i^2 = \sum \hat{\beta}_1^2 x_i^2 = \hat{\beta}_1^2 \sum x_i^2$, then substitute for $\hat{\beta}_1$.

3.20 Begin by substituting for R^2:

$$R^2 = \frac{\text{RSS}}{\text{TSS}} = \frac{\sum \hat{y}_i^2}{\sum y_i^2} = \frac{\text{var}(\hat{Y})}{\text{var}(Y)},$$

and note that the square of the correlation coefficient can be defined as:

$$[\rho(Y, \hat{Y})]^2 = \frac{[\text{cov}(Y, \hat{Y})]^2}{\text{var}(Y)\text{var}(\hat{Y})}.$$

3.21 $\hat{D} = -0.05 + 2.47U; R^2 = 0.784, \text{SER} = 1.38, F = 32.70.$
     (2.06) (0.43)

CHAPTER 4

4.1 Perfect multicollinearity implies that $\text{corr}(X_1, X_2) = 1$.

4.2 Calculate the correlation between X_1 and X_2 and their standard errors. Use this in the formula $\text{cov}(X_1, X_2) = \rho(X_1, X_2)/\sigma_{x1}\sigma_{x2}$.

4.3 Tough call. Many people would drop the variable with the lowest correlation with the dependent variable; however, because there is so little difference between the two interest rate variables, a better solution would be to use economic theory to determine which interest rate should be included, the long rate (AAA) or the short rate (TBILL).

4.5 Multicollinearity has probably been eliminated, but it is now difficult to assign meaning to the artificial variable FACTOR. Because FACTOR is composed of a long and a short interest rate, it might be interpreted as the mythical "the" interest rate so often discussed in elementary macroeconomics courses.

4.6 **(a)** Good t's, R^2's, and F-statistics. A plot of the residuals would indicate autocorrelation which would make any forecast based on this model suspect. **(b)** No classic signs of multicollinearity. However, if BFI and DRGNP are correlated, there is a chance that LBFI and DRGNP are correlated as well. Further testing for multicollinearity is probably warranted. **(c)** No.

4.7 **(a)** AAA seems to be the most likely source of multicollinearity. Yes. **(b)** This method might be better if multicollinearity is associated with a group of variables. **(c)** Essentially the same.

4.8 A larger sample may increase variance of X. Note that $\sum x_{ji}^2$ is in the denominator of the expressions for $\hat{\beta}_j$.

4.9 **(a)** The sign on POPDEN is as expected; it is not clear what the sign on INCOME should be. A better specification would include other variables—number of auto alarms, police per capita, etc. **(b)** Coefficients, R^2, and F-statistics good. **(c)** Plot of the residuals to check for possible heteroscedasticity.

4.10 TSS = RSS + ESS. TSS has $n - 1$ d.f.; ESS has $n - k - 1$ d.f.; RSS has k d.f.

APPENDIX 4.A

A4.1 $ESS_u = 13458.71$, d.f. $= 24$; $ESS_r = 17285.16$, d.f. $= 26$; $F_{2,24} = 3.41$. The critical value at the 5% significance level is 3.40. Thus, reject the null hypothesis that both interest rate variables are insignificant.

A4.3 Running the model with the three regressors CCI, CD6 and ICS gives an $ESS_u = 657.33$. Omitting CD6 and ICS gives $ESS_r = 906.75$. This gives an F-statistic of $[(906.75 - 657.33)/2]/657.33/56 = 10.62$. This is greater than the critical F-value so the combined effect of the two regressors is significant. Omitting just the ICS variable gives $ESS_r = 662.58$ and an F-statistic of $[(662.58 - 657.33)/2]/657.33/56 = 0.45$. ICS does not add significant explanatory power.

CHAPTER 5

5.2 Multicollinearity measures the *linear* relationship between the regressors; a polynomial relationship is nonlinear. However, for any particular sample, an apparent linear relationship may exist between terms in the polynomial.

5.3 Multicollinearity lowers t-ratios and may result in incorrectly dropping a variable. This will lead to specification bias.

5.4 Use one dummy instead of three.

5.5 (a) Nonlinear. Shape depends on values of slope and intercept.
(b) Take the reciprocal of both sides; i.e., $1/Y_t = \beta_0 + \beta_{1t} X_{1t} + \varepsilon_i$.

5.7 (a) $Y_t = \beta_0 + \beta_1 X_t + \beta_2 (X_t - X_{t0}) D_t + \varepsilon_t$. $D_t = 0$ before the shift, $D_t = 1$ after the shift. *A priori*, β_2 should be greater than zero.
(b) $Y_t = \beta_0 + \beta_1 X_t + \beta_2 D_{1t} + \beta_3 D_{2t} X_t + \varepsilon_t$.

5.8 Neither the tolerance coefficient nor the correlation matrix is presented, so there is no clear evidence. The classic symptoms—high R^2 and low t-ratios—are absent. NATU and RECIPU may be nonlinearly related.

5.9 Several things can bias R^2 upward—autocorrelation is the most common culprit with time series data. Remember the usual interpretation of the intercept: It is often thought of as the average value of omitted variables, just the sort of thing for which Denison was looking.

5.11 One way would be to add a dummy variable such that $D_t = 0$ if LAGP < 2.5 and $D_t = 1$ if LAGP > 2.5. Alternatively, a piecewise linear model could be constructed letting $LAGP_{t0} = 2.5$.

5.12 Use an interaction term: $G = \beta_0 + \beta_1 T + \beta_2 P + \beta_3 TP + \varepsilon$.

5.13 There is still a reasonable chance that X_t and Y_{t-1} are collinear because X_t affects Y_t.

5.15 **(a)** $\ln(P_t) = \ln(\beta_0) + t\ln(1 + g) + \varepsilon_t$
(b) From inspection of log transformation.

5.16 Reciprocal model: $Y_t = \beta_0 + \beta_1 X_t^{-1} + \varepsilon_t.\ dY_t/dX_t = \beta_1 X_t^{-2}$
$\eta = -\beta_1 X_t^{-2}(\bar{X}/\bar{Y})$.
Semi-log model: $Y_t = \beta_0 + \beta_1\ln(X_t) + \varepsilon_t.\ dY_t/dX_t = \beta_1 X_t^{-1}$
$\eta = \beta_1 X_t^{-1}(\bar{X}/\bar{Y})$.

CHAPTER 6

6.1 Positive: upward sloping line in (e_t, e_{t-1})-space. Negative: downward sloping line in (e_t, e_{t-1})-space.

6.2 See the discussion of multicollinearity in Chapter 4.

6.3 If all coefficients are positive, then X_1 and X_2 are probably positively correlated as well. The residual captures the omitted positive relationship between X_2 and Y.

6.4 $d = \dfrac{\sum\limits_{t=2}^{T} e_t^2 + \sum\limits_{t=2}^{T} e_{t-1}^2 - 2\sum\limits_{t=2}^{T} e_t e_{t-1}}{\sum\limits_{t=1}^{T} e_t^2} \cong 1 + 1 - 2\rho = 2(1 - \rho)$ because

$\sum\limits_{t=2}^{T} e_t e_{t-1} \cong \rho(e_t e_{t-1})$.

6.6 **(a)** $Y_t - Y_{t-1} = (\beta_0 + \beta_1 X_t + \varepsilon_t) - (\beta_0 + \beta_1 X_{t-1} + \varepsilon_{t-1}) =$
$\Delta Y_t = \beta_1 \Delta X_t + \varepsilon_t - \varepsilon_{t-1}$.
(b) The intercept must be capturing the combined effects of omitted variables.
(c) $Y_t - Y_{t-1} = (\beta_0 + \beta_1 X_t + \beta_2 t + \varepsilon_t) -$
$[\beta_0 + \beta_1 X_{t-1} + \beta_2(t-1) + \varepsilon_{t-1}] = \Delta Y_t = \beta_1 \Delta X_t + \beta_2 + \varepsilon_t - \varepsilon_{t-1}$.

6.7 **(a)** $n = 27$, d.f. $= 24$. One-tailed test: $t_c = 1.711$.
Two-tailed test: $t_c = 2.064$. **(b)** $\hat{\beta}_0 = -74.34$
(c) It would be nice if $d = 2.00$ and $\rho = 0$ after correction, but these values are quite close, especially for such a small sample.

6.9 Because autocorrection is often associated with inertia, it is less likely with annual than monthly data because the inertia will die out over time.

CHAPTER 7

7.3 City population would be one possibility since this series would exhibit a large variation.

7.4 Any data series that shows a wide variation is suspect of being the source of heteroscedasticity. **(a)** firm size **(b)** Perhaps labor because there is a wide variation in skill level. **(c)** Advertising, because it has a wide variation of success. **(d)** Perhaps population density because very dense areas have both high rents (Manhattan) and low rents (Harlem).

7.6 **(a)** All points would be above the X axis. **(b)** If $\hat{Y}_i$ is on the horizontal axis and ε_i is on the vertical axis, the graph would be upward sloping if ε_i increases with Y. The slope would increase if ε_i^2 is on the vertical axis.

7.8 Not necessarily. The error should be essentially random. An R^2 of 0.177 still indicates a significant heteroscedastic component in the relationship between LNRESID and LNINCOME.

7.9 Calculate ESS by summing and squaring the regression residuals, and compute R^2 as $1 - \text{ESS}/\text{TSS}$. Note that the technique in the text was shown to be correct in Exercise 3.21.

7.10 **(a)** Suppressing the intercept is necessary when weighting by σ_i eliminates the intercept in the transformed regression. **(b)** The slope appears to be the intercept when weighting by one of the X_{ji}.

7.12 **(a)** Division by either will reduce the larger residuals more than smaller residuals; i.e., will reduce the tendency for heteroscedasticity. **(b)** The same reasoning applies. Weighting by $\hat{Y}_i$ or $\sqrt{Y_i}$ will reduce the error variance because larger weights will be used for larger X_{ji} and ε_i.

7.13 **(a)** Logs reduce the variation of the data. **(b)** Interpretation is changed somewhat. Coefficients are now percentages.

7.14 Given that the error terms are homoscedastic in Eqs. [7.8] and [7.14], the proof follows immediately. For the case where the weights are $1/\sigma_i$, the proof is as follows:

$$\hat{\beta}_1^* = \frac{\sum x_i^* y_i^*}{\sum x_i^{*2}} = \frac{\sum x_i^* (\beta_1^* x_i^* + \varepsilon_i^*)}{\sum x_i^{*2}} = \frac{\sum \frac{x_i}{\sigma_i} \left(\beta_1 \frac{x_i}{\sigma_i} + \frac{\varepsilon_i}{\sigma_i} \right)}{\sum \left(\frac{x_i}{\sigma_i} \right)^2}$$

$$= \beta_1 \frac{\sum \left(\frac{x_i}{\sigma_i} \right)^2}{\sum \left(\frac{x_i}{\sigma_i} \right)^2} + \frac{\sum \left(\frac{x_i}{\sigma_i} \right) \left(\frac{\varepsilon_i}{\sigma_i} \right)}{\sum \left(\frac{x_i}{\sigma_i} \right)^2} = \beta_1$$

because x_i and ε_i are independent.

7.16 The results are: $\widehat{\text{OR}/\sqrt{\text{INC}}} = -1.78\sqrt{\text{INC}} + 2.7\text{E-4INC}/\sqrt{\text{INC}}$; $R^2 = 0.85$, $\bar{R}^2 = 0.85$, SER $= 8.9\text{E-3}$, $F_{2,57} = 161.23$. Both t's were significant at the 1% level.

CHAPTER 8

8.1 Perhaps, but the real problem is that the equation is under identified.

8.2 **(a)** First, solve the consumption equation to find $\hat{\beta}_1$:

$$\hat{\beta}_1 = \frac{\sum c_t y_t}{\sum y_t^2} = \frac{\sum y_t(\beta_1 y_t + \varepsilon_t)}{\sum y_t^2} = \beta_1 + \frac{\sum y_t \varepsilon_t}{\sum y_t^2}.$$

This is unbiased only if the expected value of the last term is zero. It is not. To show this, substitute for c_t in the income equation and rearrange to get:

$$y_t = \frac{1}{1 - \beta_1} i_t + \frac{1}{1 - \beta_1} g_t + \frac{\varepsilon_t}{1 - \beta_1}.$$

To show $\hat{\beta}_1$ is biased, take the expected value and note that:

$$E(\sum y_t \varepsilon_t) = \frac{1}{1 - \beta_1} [E(\sum i_t \varepsilon_t) + E(\sum g_t \varepsilon_t) + E(\sum \varepsilon_t^2)]$$

$$= \frac{T}{1 - \beta_1} \text{var}(\varepsilon_t) \neq 0.$$

(b) $E(\hat{\beta}_1) > \beta_1$.

8.3 **(a)** $Y_t = \pi_{10} + \pi_{11} M_t^s + \pi_{12} I_t + \pi_{13} G_t + v_{1t}$;
$R_t = \pi_{20} + \pi_{21} M_t^s + \pi_{22} I_t + \pi_{23} G_t + v_{2t}$.
(b) According to the order condition, the money market is over identified and the goods market is just identified. The rank condition is satisfied for both equations as well. Money market: $2 > G - 1 = 1$, goods market: $1 = G - 1 = 1$.

8.4 **(a)** Let the equation system be:

$$y_1 = \beta_1 x_1 + \beta_2 x_2 + \varepsilon_1,$$
$$y_2 = \alpha_1 x_1 + \varepsilon_2,$$

where the y_i are endogenous and x_i are exogenous. Because there are two equations in the system, $M = 2$. The y_1 equation is under identified; the y_2 equation is just identified. **(b)** $M = 2$ because Eq. [8.3] is an identity. The supply equation is just identified because it excludes exactly one ($= M - 1$) variable. The demand equation is over identified because it excludes two variables ($> M - 1$).

8.6 Not if policy-makers enact policy changes in response to changes in economic activity. This is a main criticism of structural models. See the Vector Autoregression sidebar in Chapter 9.

8.7 $G = 5, H = 6$. **(a)** Order conditions. Consumption equation: $6 - 0 > 3 - 1$, over identified. Interest rate equation: $6 - 1 > 2 - 1$, over identified. Investment equation: $6 - 2 > 1 - 1$, over identified. All equations satisfy the rank condition. **(b)** The investment equation could be estimated with OLS because it has only exogenous variables on the right side. **(c)** Substitute the interest rate and disposable income equations into the consumption function, then substitute the consumption function and interest rate equations into the income identity.

8.8 No. The R^2 on the reduced form equations would be very low.

8.9 **(a)** Using the expression $d = 2(1 - \rho)$, the coefficients are: consumption, $\hat{\rho} = 0.589$; interest rate, $\hat{\rho} = 0.677$; investment, $\hat{\rho} = +0.07$. **(b)** Autocorrelation is usually present with data that are in levels form; IPD is in percent change form. Also, CPH and OPH do not have an obvious trend.

APPENDIX 8.A

A8.1 $\hat{\beta}_1^* = \dfrac{\sum y_i z_i}{\sum x_i^* z_i} = \dfrac{\sum z_i(\beta_1 x_i^* + \varepsilon_i)}{\sum x_i^* z_i} = \dfrac{\beta_1 \sum x_i^* z_i}{\sum x_i^* z_i} + \dfrac{\sum \varepsilon_i z_i}{\sum x_i^* z_i}$. Taking expected values gives: $E(\hat{\beta}_1^*) = \beta_1$ because z_i is independent of ε_i.

A8.2 The first term on the right side does not reduce to β_1.

A8.4 From Eqs. [8.15] and [8.16], we have:
$$p_t = \pi_{11} r_t + u_{1t} \text{ and } q_t = \pi_{21} r_t + u_{2t},$$
$$\hat{\alpha}_2^* = \frac{\hat{\pi}_{11}}{\hat{\pi}_{21}} = \frac{\sum r_t p_t / \sum r_t^2}{\sum r_t q_t / \sum r_t^2} = \frac{\sum r_t p_t}{\sum r_t q_t}.$$

A8.5 This can be demonstrated with the system in Eqs. [8.11] and [8.12].

CHAPTER 9

9.1 **(a)** $\alpha = 0.5$: $y_t = \{\bullet, 12.9, 10.7, 6.4, 3.9, 3.9, 3.9, 2.5, 2.8\}$
$\alpha = 0.9$: $y_t = \{\bullet, 12.5, 9.3, 4.4, 3.8, 4.0, 3.8, 1.4, 4.1\}$. $\alpha = 0.5$ is smoother.

(b) $y_t = \alpha x_t + (1 - \alpha)x_{t-1} = \alpha x_t + [y_{t-1} + (1 - \alpha)x_{t-2}]\left(\dfrac{1-\alpha}{\alpha}\right)$

(c) Forming the moving average based on past and future values complicates the issue of causality. Why should future values affect the present?

9.2 **(b)** MA(3): -1, 2.2, 3.3, 4, 4.7, 5.3, 6.7, 7.7 **(c)** y_t is the first difference of the data, so z_t consists of the first differences of the data plus 40% of the current value of x_t.

9.3 **(a)** $x_{13} = 20 + 0.5(12) = 26$; $x_{14} = 20 + 0.5(26) = 33$.

9.4 Take logs to get $\ln(y_t) = a + b(t) + \varepsilon_t$. Because t is present in the expression, there is a time trend: the model is nonstationary. Taking first differences gives:
$\ln(y_t) - \ln(y_{t-1}) = [a + b(t) + \varepsilon_t] - [a + b(t - 1) + \varepsilon_{t-1}] = b + \varepsilon_t - \varepsilon_{t-1}$, which is stationary.

9.5 Linear: $\hat{y}_{t+1} = 11.02 - 1.35(8) = 0.22$,
$\hat{y}_{t+2} = 11.02 - 1.35(9) = -1.13$.

Exponential: $\ln(y_{t+1}) = 2.51 - 0.23(8) = 0.67$; antilog$(0.67) = 1.95$; $\ln(\hat{y}_{t+2}) = 2.51 - 0.23(9) \doteq 0.44$; anti-log$(0.44) = 1.55$. Parabolic: $\hat{y}_{t+1} = 15.21 - 4.15(8) + 0.35(8^2) = 4.41$; $\hat{y}_{t+2} = 15.21 - 4.15(9) + 0.35(9^2) = 6.21$. Actual data at $t = 8$ was 1.1; at $t = 9$, it was 4.4.

9.6 The MA(1) model is $y_t = e_t - 0.53e_{t-1}$ so the forecast equation is $y_{t+1} = 0.53e_t$. Using the formula in footnote 17, e_t was estimated as -0.171. This gives a one-step forecast of 0.091. The AR(2) model is $y_t = 0.414y_{t-1} - 0.273y_{y-2} + \varepsilon_t$ and the forecast equation is $y_{t+1} = 0.414y_t - 0.273y_{y-1}$. This gives a one-step forecast of -0.114. Both forecasts are quite close to the actual value of 0.0.

9.7 **(a)** There appears to be a clear cutoff at $k = 1$ so the series is probably an MA(1) process.   **(b)** The MA(1) process is designated $x_t = e_t + b_1e_{t-1}$ and $e_t = x_t - f_{t1,1}$. Because $x_9 = 1.3$ and $e_9 = 0.2$, it follows that $0.2 = 1.3 - f_{8,1}$ so $x_8 = f_{8,1} = 1.1$.

9.8 **(a)** Parabolic with $b < 0$ and $c > 0$.   **(b)** The curve would be concave to the origin.   **(c)** Factory defects, unit costs, agricultural employment.

9.10 The data appear to be stationary; however, none of the lags in the ACF or PACF are significant. Thus, the series is essentially white noise.

9.12 **(a)** Smoothing *always* removes some of the information from the data series. In this case, the smoothing process may have eliminated too many of the prominent spikes.   **(b)** Check for stationarity, then the three steps of Box-Jenkins analysis. However, a better technique might be to study the specific firm.

CHAPTER 10

10.2 Let $Y_i = 1$ if the savings and loan remains solvent; $Y_i = 0$ if it goes bankrupt. As always in econometrics, the X_j variables would be selected based on economic theory: The percentage of loans to the oil industry and less-developed countries have been cited as possible reasons.

10.3 Not ncessarily; it may decrease with X. Note that the error is defined as:

$$\text{var}(\varepsilon_i) = (\beta_0 + \beta_1X_{1i})(1 - \beta_0 - \beta_1X_{1i})$$
$$= \beta_0 - \beta_0^2 - \beta_0\beta_1X_{1i} + \beta_1X_{1i} - \beta_0\beta_1X_{1i} - \beta_1^2X_{1i}^2.$$

Because the relationship between X and e depends on X as well as X^2, it is possible for the error to increase or decrease as X increases. The same weighting scheme would work.

10.4 $\text{var}(\varepsilon_i^*) = \text{var}\left(\dfrac{\varepsilon_i}{w_i}\right)$ where $w_i = [P_i(1 - P_i)]^{1/2}$. The P_i are constants, so this can be written as $[P_i(1 - P_i)]\text{var}(\varepsilon_i)$ and because $\text{var}(\varepsilon_i) = P_i(1 - P_i)$, the transformed error is a constant.

10.5 **(a)** If $X = \$24,000$ $\hat{L}_i = -4.265(3.735) + 2.287(8.964) = 4.57$, so $P_i = 99\%$. Thus an income level between \$22,000 and \$24,000 would result in a probability of attendance of 90%.   **(b)** Between \$18,000 and \$20,000.

10.6 There were a significant number of fitted values that fell outside of the required (0, 1) region.

10.7 Expand Eq. [10.8] and simplify.

10.8 Simply rewrite and substitute for Z_i:

$$P_i = \frac{1}{1 + e^{-\infty}} = \frac{1}{1 + \dfrac{1}{e^{\infty}}} \Rightarrow 1 \quad \text{and} \quad P_i = \frac{1}{1 + e^{\infty}} = \frac{1}{\infty} \Rightarrow 0.$$

10.9 **(a)** Pseudo $- R^2 = 0.095$.   **(b)** McFadden's $R^2 = 0.078$.

10.10 **(a)** The parameter estimates are comparable and the same coefficients are statistically significant. Even R^2 is in line with the answers from the previous exercise. However, the OLS residuals are heteroscedastic so the parameter estimates are inefficient.   **(b)** The fitted values from OLS represent $E(Y|X)$, which is not quite the same thing as $\Pr(Y = 1|X)$. Also, it is possible that a number of the fitted values fall outside the required (0, 1) range. This is unlikely, however, because the logit and OLS results are so similar.

10.12 For four children and \$20,000, the calculations are: $\hat{L}_i = -1.871 + 0.012(20) + 0.329(4) = -0.315$. Taking the antilog gives 0.730. Because $0.73 = P_i/(1 - P_i)$, $P_i = 0.42$. For four children and \$8,000: $\hat{L}_i = -1.871 + 0.012(8) + 0.329(4) = -0.459$. The antilog is 0.63. This gives $P_i = 0.39$.

CHAPTER 11

11.1 A gas leak is abnormal in a house; therefore, it may be regarded as the cause. Use of matches is prohibited in most gas plants; therefore, the match would be regarded as the causal factor.

11.2 Can rat studies be used to help understand liquidity preference? Risk aversion?

11.3 **(a)** Severe multicollinearity would make t-scores unreliable. **(b)** Not at all; there is a strong trend component in most time series.

11.4 The classic signs of multicollinearity—low t's and high R^2—are not present. However, the results from the first regression indicate that

AAA and LDEF may be correlated. A correlation matrix or other check for multicollinearity is warranted.

11.5 **(a)** Regression 1:

$$F_{r,n-k-1} = \frac{(34690.49 - 25446.21)/1}{25446.21/27 - 2 - 1} = 8.72.$$

Regression 2:

$$F_{r,n-k-1} = \frac{(78346.97 - 76917.34)/1}{76917.34/27 - 2 - 1} = 0.45.$$

Because the critical value at the 5% significance level is $F[1, 26] = 4.23$, the conclusion is that Y does cause M but that M does not cause Y.

(b) Quarterly data would probably be superior because most studies show that M affects Y within two to four quarters.

11.6 Plotting the data initially is useful for determining whether there have been any input errors. However, if the data plot influences the *a priori* model selection, hypothesis tests regarding individual parameters and model selection are, strictly speaking, inappropriate. Note, however, that this point does *not* apply to time series models in which the only purpose is development of a model that forecasts well.

11.8 There may be economic justification for the particular model under investigation. In general, however, the justification is simply the temporal association concept of causality underlying the Granger test.

11.10 Probably bidirectional, at least in many markets. Price affects quantity demanded, but quantity demanded affects price, the quantity supplied, etc. The length of the lag will affect the results because the responsiveness of price to demand (and vice versa) is rarely instantaneous.

11.12 Yes and no. Box-Jenkins analysis attempts to discover the process that gives rise to observed data. No attempts are made in Box-Jenkins analysis to attach "meaning" to the process. Hendry would probably want to show how the data generating process he discovered fit into economic theory.

11.14 The results depend on lag length. Using six lags and defining inflation as $12\Delta PPI/PPI$, the conclusion is that P causes U, but not the reverse. The results of the unemployment regression are: $ESS_u = 3.457$, d.f. $= 100$; $ESS_r = 4.105$. Substitution into Eq. [11.10] gives an F-value of 3.12, which is significant at the 5% level. The results of the inflation regression are: $ESS_u = 2353.924$, d.f. $= 100$; $ESS_r = 2492.48$. Substitution into Eq. [11.10] gives an F-value of 0.98, which is insignificant at the 5% level. The same conclusion is reached with a four-period lag, but the opposite conclusion is reached with a twelve-period lag.

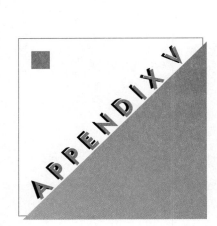

APPENDIX V

STATISTICAL TABLES

TABLE 1 ▪ The normal distribution

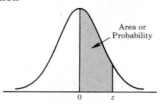

Area or Probability

Entries in the table give the area in the upper tail of the standard normal distribution. For example, the entry corresponding to $z = 1.96$ indicates that the probability of $Z > z$ is 0.0250 or 2.5%.

z	.00	.01	.02	.03	.04	.05	.06	.07	.08	.09
0.0	.5000	.4960	.4920	.4880	.4840	.4801	.4761	.4721	.4681	.4641
0.1	.4602	.4562	.4522	.4483	.4443	.4404	.4364	.4325	.4686	.4247
0.2	.4207	.4168	.4129	.4090	.4052	.4013	.3974	.3936	.3897	.3859
0.3	.3821	.3873	.3745	.3707	.3669	.3632	.3594	.3557	.3520	.3483
0.4	.3446	.3409	.3372	.3336	.3300	.3264	.3228	.3192	.3156	.3121
0.5	.3085	.3050	.3015	.2981	.2946	.2912	.2877	.2843	.2810	.2776
0.6	.2743	.2709	.2676	.2643	.2611	.2578	.2546	.2514	.2483	.2451
0.7	.2420	.2389	.2358	.2327	.2296	.2266	.2236	.2206	.2217	.2148
0.8	.2119	.2090	.2061	.2033	.2005	.1977	.1949	.1922	.1894	.1867
0.9	.1841	.1814	.1788	.1762	.1736	.1711	.1685	.1660	.1635	.1611
1.0	.1587	.1562	.1539	.1515	.1492	.1469	.1446	.1423	.1401	.1379
1.1	.1357	.1335	.1314	.1292	.1271	.1251	.1230	.1210	.1190	.1170
1.2	.1151	.1131	.1112	.1093	.1075	.1056	.1038	.1020	.1003	.0985
1.3	.0968	.0951	.0934	.0918	.0901	.0885	.0869	.0853	.0838	.0823
1.4	.0808	.0793	.0778	.0764	.0749	.0735	.0721	.0708	.0694	.0681
1.5	.0668	.0655	.0643	.0630	.0618	.0606	.0594	.0582	.0571	.0559
1.6	.0548	.0537	.0526	.0516	.0505	.0495	.0485	.0475	.0465	.0455
1.7	.0446	.0436	.0427	.0418	.0409	.0401	.0392	.0384	.0375	.0367
1.8	.0359	.0351	.0344	.0366	.0329	.0322	.0314	.0307	.0301	.0294
1.9	.0287	.0281	.0274	.0268	.0262	.0256	.0250	.0244	.0239	.0233
2.0	.0228	.0222	.0217	.0212	.0207	.0202	.0197	.0192	.0188	.0183
2.1	.0179	.0174	.0170	.0166	.0162	.0158	.0154	.0150	.0146	.0143
2.2	.0139	.0136	.0132	.0129	.0125	.0122	.0119	.0116	.0113	.0110
2.3	.0107	.0104	.0102	.0099	.0096	.0094	.0091	.0089	.0087	.0084
2.4	.0082	.0080	.0078	.0075	.0073	.0071	.0069	.0068	.0066	.0064
2.5	.0062	.0060	.0059	.0057	.0055	.0054	.0052	.0051	.0049	.0048
2.6	.0047	.0045	.0044	.0043	.0041	.0040	.0039	.0038	.0037	.0036
2.7	.0035	.0034	.0033	.0032	.0031	.0030	.0029	.0028	.0027	.0026
2.8	.0026	.0025	.0024	.0023	.0023	.0022	.0021	.0020	.0020	.0019
2.9	.0019	.0018	.0018	.0017	.0016	.0016	.0015	.0015	.0014	.0014
3.0	.0013	.0013	.0013	.0012	.0012	.0011	.0011	.0010	.0011	.0010

The table plots the cumulative probability $Z \geq z$.

TABLE 2 ■ The *t*-distribution

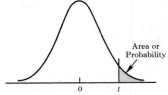

Entries in the table give *t* values for an area or probability in the upper tail of the *t* distribution. For example, with 10 degrees of freedom and a .05 area in the upper tail, $t_{0.5} = 1.812$

Degrees of freedom	Area in upper tail				
	.10	.05	.025	.01	.005
1	3.078	6.314	12.706	31.821	63.657
2	1.886	2.920	4.303	6.965	9.925
3	1.638	2.353	3.182	4.541	5.841
4	1.533	2.132	2.776	3.747	4.604
5	1.476	2.015	2.571	3.365	4.032
6	1.440	1.943	2.447	3.143	3.707
7	1.415	1.895	2.365	2.998	3.499
8	1.397	1.860	2.306	2.896	3.355
9	1.383	1.833	2.262	2.821	3.250
10	1.372	1.812	2.228	2.764	3.169
11	1.363	1.796	2.201	2.718	3.106
12	1.356	1.782	2.179	2.681	3.055
13	1.350	1.771	2.160	2.650	3.012
14	1.345	1.761	2.145	2.624	2.977
15	1.341	1.753	2.131	2.602	2.947
16	1.337	1.746	2.120	2.583	2.921
17	1.333	1.740	2.110	2.567	2.898
18	1.330	1.734	2.101	2.552	2.878
19	1.328	1.729	2.093	2.539	2.861
20	1.325	1.725	2.086	2.528	2.845
21	1.323	1.721	2.080	2.518	2.831
22	1.321	1.717	2.074	2.508	2.819
23	1.319	1.714	2.069	2.500	2.807
24	1.318	1.711	2.064	2.492	2.797
25	1.316	1.708	2.060	2.485	2.787
26	1.315	1.706	2.056	2.479	2.779
27	1.314	1.703	2.052	2.473	2.771
28	1.313	1.701	2.048	2.467	2.763
29	1.311	1.699	2.045	2.462	2.756
30	1.310	1.697	2.042	2.457	2.750
40	1.303	1.684	2.021	2.423	2.704
60	1.296	1.671	2.000	2.390	2.660
120	1.289	1.658	1.980	2.358	2.617
∞	1.282	1.645	1.960	2.326	2.576

TABLE 3 The F-distribution

Entries in the table give F_α values, where α is the area or probability in the upper tail of the F distribution. For example, with 12 numerator degrees of freedom, 15 denominator degrees of freedom, and a .05 area in the upper tail, $F_{.05} = 2.48$.

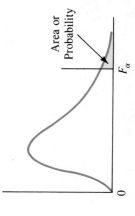

Area or Probability

F_α

Table of $F_{.05}$ values

Denominator degrees of freedom	Numerator degrees of freedom																		
	1	2	3	4	5	6	7	8	9	10	12	15	20	24	30	40	60	120	∞
1	161.4	199.5	215.7	224.6	230.2	234.0	236.8	238.9	240.5	241.9	243.9	245.9	248.0	249.1	250.1	251.1	252.2	253.3	254.3
2	18.51	19.00	19.16	19.25	19.30	19.33	19.35	19.37	19.38	19.40	19.41	19.43	19.45	19.45	19.46	19.47	19.48	19.49	19.50
3	10.13	9.55	9.28	9.12	9.01	8.94	8.89	8.85	8.81	8.79	8.74	8.70	8.66	8.64	8.62	8.59	8.57	8.55	8.53
4	7.71	6.94	6.59	6.39	6.26	6.16	6.09	6.04	6.00	5.96	5.91	5.86	5.80	5.77	5.75	5.72	5.69	5.66	5.63
5	6.61	5.79	5.41	5.19	5.05	4.95	4.88	4.82	4.77	4.74	4.68	4.62	4.56	4.53	4.50	4.46	4.43	4.40	4.36
6	5.99	5.14	4.76	4.53	4.39	4.28	4.21	4.15	4.10	4.06	4.00	3.94	3.87	3.84	3.81	3.77	3.74	3.70	3.67
7	5.59	4.74	4.35	4.12	3.97	3.87	3.79	3.73	3.68	3.64	3.57	3.51	3.44	3.41	3.38	3.34	3.30	3.27	3.23
8	5.32	4.46	4.07	3.84	3.69	3.58	3.50	3.44	3.39	3.35	3.28	3.22	3.15	3.12	3.08	3.04	3.01	2.97	2.93
9	5.12	4.26	3.86	3.63	3.48	3.37	3.29	3.23	3.18	3.14	3.07	3.01	2.94	2.90	2.86	2.83	2.79	2.75	2.71

10	4.96	4.10	3.71	3.48	3.33	3.22	3.14	3.07	3.02	2.98	2.91	2.85	2.77	2.74	2.70	2.66	2.62	2.58	2.54
11	4.84	3.98	3.59	3.36	3.20	3.09	3.01	2.95	2.90	2.85	2.79	2.72	2.65	2.61	2.57	2.53	2.49	2.45	2.40
12	4.75	3.89	3.49	3.26	3.11	3.00	2.91	2.85	2.80	2.75	2.69	2.62	2.54	2.51	2.47	2.43	2.38	2.34	2.30
13	4.67	3.81	3.41	3.18	3.03	2.92	2.83	2.77	2.71	2.67	2.60	2.53	2.46	2.42	2.38	2.34	2.30	2.25	2.21
14	4.60	3.74	3.34	3.11	2.96	2.85	2.76	2.70	2.65	2.60	2.53	2.46	2.39	2.35	2.31	2.27	2.22	2.18	2.13
15	4.54	3.68	3.29	3.06	2.90	2.79	2.71	2.64	2.59	2.54	2.48	2.40	2.33	2.29	2.25	2.20	2.16	2.11	2.07
16	4.49	3.63	3.24	3.01	2.85	2.74	2.66	2.59	2.54	2.49	2.42	2.35	2.28	2.24	2.19	2.15	2.11	2.06	2.01
17	4.45	3.59	3.20	2.96	2.81	2.70	2.61	2.55	2.49	2.45	2.38	2.31	2.23	2.19	2.15	2.10	2.06	2.01	1.96
18	4.41	3.55	3.16	2.93	2.77	2.66	2.58	2.51	2.46	2.41	2.34	2.27	2.19	2.15	2.11	2.06	2.02	1.97	1.92
19	4.38	3.52	3.13	2.90	2.74	2.63	2.54	2.48	2.42	2.38	2.31	2.23	2.16	2.11	2.07	2.03	1.98	1.93	1.88
20	4.35	3.49	3.10	2.87	2.71	2.60	2.51	2.45	2.39	2.35	2.28	2.20	2.12	2.08	2.04	1.99	1.95	1.90	1.84
21	4.32	3.47	3.07	2.84	2.68	2.57	2.49	2.42	2.37	2.32	2.25	2.18	2.10	2.05	2.01	1.96	1.92	1.87	1.81
22	4.30	3.44	3.05	2.82	2.66	2.55	2.46	2.40	2.34	2.30	2.23	2.15	2.07	2.03	1.98	1.94	1.89	1.84	1.78
23	4.28	3.42	3.03	2.80	2.64	2.53	2.44	2.37	2.32	2.27	2.20	2.13	2.05	2.01	1.96	1.91	1.86	1.81	1.76
24	4.26	3.40	3.01	2.78	2.62	2.51	2.42	2.36	2.30	2.25	2.18	2.11	2.03	1.98	1.94	1.89	1.84	1.79	1.73
25	4.24	3.39	2.99	2.76	2.60	2.49	2.40	2.34	2.28	2.24	2.16	2.09	2.01	1.96	1.92	1.87	1.82	1.77	1.71
26	4.23	3.37	2.98	2.74	2.59	2.47	2.39	2.32	2.27	2.22	2.15	2.07	1.99	1.95	1.90	1.85	1.80	1.75	1.69
27	4.21	3.35	2.96	2.73	2.57	2.46	2.37	2.31	2.25	2.20	2.13	2.06	1.97	1.93	1.88	1.84	1.79	1.73	1.67
28	4.20	3.34	2.95	2.71	2.56	2.45	2.36	2.29	2.24	2.19	2.12	2.04	1.96	1.91	1.87	1.82	1.77	1.71	1.65
29	4.18	3.33	2.93	2.70	2.55	2.43	2.35	2.28	2.22	2.18	2.10	2.03	1.94	1.90	1.85	1.81	1.75	1.70	1.64
30	4.17	3.32	2.92	2.69	2.53	2.42	2.33	2.27	2.21	2.16	2.09	2.01	1.93	1.89	1.84	1.79	1.74	1.68	1.62
40	4.08	3.23	2.84	2.61	2.45	2.34	2.25	2.18	2.12	2.08	2.00	1.92	1.84	1.79	1.74	1.69	1.64	1.58	1.51
60	4.00	3.15	2.76	2.53	2.37	2.25	2.17	2.10	2.04	1.99	1.92	1.84	1.75	1.70	1.65	1.59	1.53	1.47	1.39
120	3.92	3.07	2.68	2.45	2.29	2.17	2.09	2.02	1.96	1.91	1.83	1.75	1.66	1.61	1.55	1.50	1.43	1.35	1.25
∞	3.84	3.00	2.60	2.37	2.21	2.10	2.01	1.94	1.88	1.83	1.75	1.67	1.57	1.52	1.46	1.39	1.32	1.22	1.00

TABLE 4 ■ **The Durbin-Watson Statistic**

Entries in the table give the critical values for a one-tailed Durbin–Watson test for autocorrelation. For a two-tailed test, the level of significance is doubled.

	Significance points of d_L and d_U: $\alpha = .05$ Number of independent variables									
k	**1**		**2**		**3**		**4**		**5**	
n	d_L	d_U	d_L	d_U	d_L	d_U	d_L	d_U	d_L	d_U
15	1.08	1.36	0.95	1.54	0.82	1.75	0.69	1.97	0.56	2.21
16	1.10	1.37	0.98	1.54	0.86	1.73	0.74	1.93	0.62	2.15
17	1.13	1.38	1.02	1.54	0.90	1.71	0.78	1.90	0.67	2.10
18	1.16	1.39	1.05	1.53	0.93	1.69	0.82	1.87	0.71	2.06
19	1.18	1.40	1.08	1.53	0.97	1.68	0.86	1.85	0.75	2.02
20	1.20	1.41	1.10	1.54	1.00	1.68	0.90	1.83	0.79	1.99
21	1.22	1.42	1.13	1.54	1.03	1.67	0.93	1.81	0.83	1.96
22	1.24	1.43	1.15	1.54	1.05	1.66	0.96	1.80	0.86	1.94
23	1.26	1.44	1.17	1.54	1.08	1.66	0.99	1.79	0.90	1.92
24	1.27	1.45	1.19	1.55	1.10	1.66	1.01	1.78	0.93	1.90
25	1.29	1.45	1.21	1.55	1.12	1.66	1.04	1.77	0.95	1.89
26	1.30	1.46	1.22	1.55	1.14	1.65	1.06	1.76	0.98	1.88
27	1.32	1.47	1.24	1.56	1.16	1.65	1.08	1.76	1.01	1.86
28	1.33	1.48	1.26	1.56	1.18	1.65	1.10	1.75	1.03	1.85
29	1.34	1.48	1.27	1.56	1.20	1.65	1.12	1.74	1.05	1.84
30	1.35	1.49	1.28	1.57	1.21	1.65	1.14	1.74	1.07	1.83
31	1.36	1.50	1.30	1.57	1.23	1.65	1.16	1.74	1.09	1.83
32	1.37	1.50	1.31	1.57	1.24	1.65	1.18	1.73	1.11	1.82
33	1.38	1.51	1.32	1.58	1.26	1.65	1.19	1.73	1.13	1.81
34	1.39	1.51	1.33	1.58	1.27	1.65	1.21	1.73	1.15	1.81
35	1.40	1.52	1.34	1.58	1.28	1.65	1.22	1.73	1.16	1.80
36	1.41	1.52	1.35	1.59	1.29	1.65	1.24	1.73	1.18	1.80
37	1.42	1.53	1.36	1.59	1.31	1.66	1.25	1.72	1.19	1.80
38	1.43	1.54	1.37	1.59	1.32	1.66	1.26	1.72	1.21	1.79
39	1.43	1.54	1.38	1.60	1.33	1.66	1.27	1.72	1.22	1.79
40	1.44	1.54	1.39	1.60	1.34	1.66	1.29	1.72	1.23	1.79
45	1.48	1.57	1.43	1.62	1.38	1.67	1.34	1.72	1.29	1.78
50	1.50	1.59	1.46	1.63	1.42	1.67	1.38	1.72	1.34	1.77
55	1.53	1.60	1.49	1.64	1.45	1.68	1.41	1.72	1.38	1.77
60	1.55	1.62	1.51	1.65	1.48	1.69	1.44	1.73	1.41	1.77
65	1.57	1.63	1.54	1.66	1.50	1.70	1.47	1.73	1.44	1.77
70	1.58	1.64	1.55	1.67	1.52	1.70	1.49	1.74	1.46	1.77
75	1.60	1.65	1.57	1.68	1.54	1.71	1.51	1.74	1.49	1.77
80	1.61	1.66	1.59	1.69	1.56	1.72	1.53	1.74	1.51	1.77
85	1.62	1.67	1.60	1.70	1.57	1.72	1.55	1.75	1.52	1.77
90	1.63	1.68	1.61	1.70	1.59	1.73	1.57	1.75	1.54	1.78
95	1.64	1.69	1.62	1.71	1.60	1.73	1.58	1.75	1.56	1.78
100	1.65	1.69	1.63	1.72	1.61	1.74	1.59	1.76	1.57	1.78

Durbin, J. and Watson, G. S. "Testing for Serial Correlation in Least Squares Regression," *Biometrika*, Vol 38 (1951), pp. 159–177. Used with permission of the Biometrika Trustees.

TABLE 5 ■ The χ^2-distribution

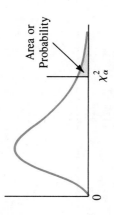

Area or Probability

χ^2_α

Entries in the table give χ^2_α values, where α is the area or probability in the upper tail of the chi-square distribution. For example, with 10 degrees of freedom and a .01 area in the upper tail, $\chi^2_{.01} = 23.2093$.

Degrees of freedom	.995	.99	.975	.95	.90	.10	.05	.025	.01	.005
					Area in upper tail					
1	$392{,}704 \times 10^{-10}$	$157{,}088 \times 10^{-9}$	$982{,}069 \times 10^{-9}$	$393{,}214 \times 10^{-8}$	0.157908	2.70554	3.84146	5.02389	6.63490	7.87944
2	.0100251	.0201007	.0506356	.102587	2.10720	4.60517	5.99147	7.37776	9.21034	10.5966
3	.0717212	.114832	.215795	.351846	.584375	6.25139	7.81473	9.34840	11.3449	12.8381
4	.206990	.297110	.484419	.710721	1.063623	7.77944	9.48773	11.1433	13.2767	14.8602
5	.411740	.554300	.831211	1.145476	1.61031	9.23635	11.0705	12.8325	15.0863	16.7496
6	.675727	.872085	1.237347	1.63539	2.20413	10.6446	12.5916	14.4494	16.8119	18.5476
7	.989265	1.239043	1.68987	2.16735	2.83311	12.0170	14.0671	16.0128	18.4753	20.2777
8	1.344419	1.646482	2.17973	2.73264	3.48954	13.3616	15.5073	17.5346	20.0902	21.9550
9	1.734926	2.087912	2.70039	3.32511	4.16816	14.6837	16.9190	19.0228	21.6660	23.5893
10	2.15585	2.55821	3.24697	3.94030	4.86518	15.9871	18.3070	20.4831	23.2093	25.1882
11	2.60321	3.05347	3.81575	4.57481	5.57779	17.2750	19.6751	21.9200	24.7250	26.7569
12	3.07382	3.57056	4.40379	5.22603	6.30380	18.5494	21.0261	23.3367	26.2170	28.2995
13	3.56503	4.10691	5.00874	5.89186	7.04150	19.8119	22.3621	24.7356	27.6883	29.8194
14	4.07468	4.66043	5.62872	6.57063	7.78953	21.0642	23.6848	26.1190	29.1413	31.3193
15	4.60094	5.22935	6.26214	7.26094	8.54675	22.3072	24.9958	27.4884	30.5779	32.8013
16	5.14224	5.81221	6.90766	7.96164	9.31223	23.5418	26.2962	28.8454	31.9999	34.2672
17	5.69724	6.40776	7.56418	8.67176	10.0852	24.7690	27.5871	30.1910	33.4087	35.7185
18	6.26481	7.01491	8.23075	9.39046	10.8649	25.9894	28.8693	31.5264	34.8053	37.1564
19	6.84398	7.63273	8.90655	10.1170	11.6509	27.2036	30.1435	32.8523	36.1908	38.5822

(continued on next page)

TABLE 5 ■ The χ^2-distribution (continued)

Degrees of freedom	.995	.99	.975	.95	.90	Area in upper tail .10	.05	.025	.01	.005
20	7.43386	8.26040	9.59083	10.8508	12.4426	28.4120	31.4104	34.1696	37.5662	39.9968
21	8.03366	8.89720	10.28293	11.5913	13.2396	29.6151	32.6705	35.4789	38.9321	41.4010
22	8.64272	9.54249	10.9823	12.3380	14.0415	30.8133	33.9244	36.7807	40.2894	42.7958
23	9.26042	10.19567	11.6885	13.0905	14.8479	32.0069	35.1725	38.0757	41.6384	44.1813
24	9.88623	10.8564	12.4011	13.8484	15.6587	33.1963	36.4151	39.3641	42.9798	45.5585
25	10.5197	11.5240	13.1197	14.6114	16.4734	34.3816	37.6525	40.6465	44.3141	46.9278
26	11.1603	12.1981	13.8439	15.3791	17.2919	35.5631	38.8852	41.9232	45.6417	48.2899
27	11.8076	12.8786	14.5733	16.1513	18.1138	36.7412	40.1133	43.1944	46.9630	49.6449
28	12.4613	13.5648	15.3079	16.9279	18.9392	37.9159	41.3372	44.4607	48.2782	50.9933
29	13.1211	14.2565	16.0471	17.7083	19.7677	39.0875	42.5569	45.7222	49.5879	52.3356
30	13.7867	14.9535	16.7908	18.4926	20.5992	40.2560	43.7729	46.9792	50.8922	53.6720
40	20.7065	22.1643	24.4331	26.5093	29.0505	51.8050	55.7585	59.3417	63.6907	66.7659
50	27.9907	29.7067	32.3574	34.7642	37.6886	63.1671	67.5048	71.4202	76.1539	79.4900
60	35.5346	37.4848	40.4817	43.1879	46.4589	74.3970	79.0819	83.2976	88.3794	91.9517
70	43.2752	45.4418	48.7576	51.7393	55.3290	85.5271	90.5312	95.0231	100.425	104.215
80	51.1720	53.5400	57.1532	60.3915	64.2778	96.5782	101.879	106.629	112.329	116.321
90	59.1963	61.7541	65.6466	69.1260	73.2912	107.565	113.145	118.136	124.116	128.299
100	67.3276	70.0648	74.2219	77.9295	82.3581	118.498	124.342	129.561	135.807	140.169

APPENDIX VI

BIBLIOGRAPHY

Aftalion, A. "Les Trois Notions de la Producitite et Revenus," *Revue d'Economie Politique*, 1911.

Aldrich, John H., and Charles F. Cnudde, "Probing the Bounds of Conventional Wisdom: A Comparison of Regression, Probit and Discriminant Analysis," *American Journal of Political Science*, Vol. XIX, No. 3, Auguest 1975, p. 571–608.

Aldrich, John H., and Forest D. Nelson, *Linear Probability, Logit and Probit Models* (Newbury Park, Calif.: Sage University Paper 45, 1984).

Almon, Shirley, "The Distributed Lag Between Capital Appropriations and Expenditures," *Econometrica*, Vol. 33, January 1965, p. 178–196.

Amemiya, Takeshi, "Qualitative Response Models: A Survey," *Journal of Economic Literature*, Vol. XIX, December 1981, p. 1483–1536.

Brookshire, David S., et al., "The External Validity of Experimental Economics Techniques: Analysis of Demand Behavior," *Economic Inquiry*, Vol. 25, No. 2, April 1987, p. 239–250.

Bowerman, Bruce L., and Richard T. O'Connell, *Time Series Forecasting*, 2nd ed. (Boston: Duxbury Press, 1987).

Bowles, Samuel, David Gordon, and Thomas E. Weisskopf, "Hearts and Minds: A Social Model of U.S. Productivity Growth," *Brookings Papers*, Vol. 2, 1983.

Breusch, T. S., and A. R. Pagan, "A Simple Test for Heteroscedasticity and Random Coefficient Variation," *Econometrica*, Vol. 47, 1979, p. 1287–1294.

Brown, William S., *Macroeconomics*. (Englewood Cliffs, N.J.: Prentice-Hall, 1988).

Chiang, Alpha C., *Fundamental Methods of Mathematical Economics*, 3rd ed. (New York: McGraw-Hill, 1984).

Chow, Gregory C., "Tests for Equality Between Sets of Coefficients in Two Linear Regressions," *Econometrica*, Vol. 28, No. 3, 1960, p. 591–605.

Christensen, L. R., and D. W. Jorgenson, "U.S. Real Product and Real Factor Input, 1929–67," *Review of Income and Wealth*, March 1970.

Clark, John M., "Business Acceleration and the Law of Demand," *Journal of Political Economy*, March 1917, p. 217–235.

Cochrane, D., and G. H. Orcutt, "Application of Least Squares Regressions to Relationships Contain Autocorrelated Error Terms," *Journal of the American Statistical Association*, Vol. 44, 1949, p. 32–61.

Denison, Edward, *Trends in American Economic Growth, 1929–1982* (Washington, D.C.: Brookings Institute 1985).

Dewald, William G., Jerry G. Thursby, and Richard G. Anderson, "Replication in Empirical Economics: *The Journal of Money, Credit and Banking* Project," *American Economic Review*, Vol. 76, No. 4, September 1986, p. 587–603.

Downs, George W., and David M. Rocke, "Interpreting Heteroscedasticity," *American Journal of Political Science*, Vol. 23, No. 4, November 1979, p. 816–828.

Durbin, J., "Estimation of Parameters in Time Series Regression Models," *Journal of the Royal Statistical Society*, Series B, Vol. 22, 1960, p. 139–153.

Durbin, J., and G. S. Watson, "Testing for Serial Correlation in Least Squares Regression," *Biometrika*, 1950, p. 409–428; 1951, p. 159–178.

Engle, R. F., D. F. Hendry, and J. F. Richard, "Exogeneity," *Econometrica*, Vol. 51, 1983, p. 277–304.

Epstein, Roy J., *A History of Econometrics* (Amsterdam: North-Holland, 1987).

Evans, Paul, "Do Large Deficits Produce High Interest Rates?" *American Economic Review*, Vol. 75, No. 1, March 1985, p. 68–87.

Feigel, H., "Notes on Causality," from H. Feigel and M. Brodbeck, Eds., *Readings in the Philosophy of Science* (New York: Appleton-Century-Crofts, 1953).

Friedman, Milton, *The Theory of the Consumption Function* (Cambridge, Mass.: NBER, 1957).

Frumkin, Norman, *Guide to Economic Indicators* (Armonk, NY: M. E. Sharpe, 1990).

Gilbert, Christopher, "Professor Hendry's Econometric Methodology," *Oxford Bulletin of Economics and Statistics*, special issue, Vol. 48, No. 3, August 1986, p. 283–307.

Glejser, H., "A New Test for Heteroscedasticity," *Journal of the American Statistical Association*, Vol. 64, 1969, p. 316–323.

Goldberger, Arthur, *Econometric Theory* (New York: John Wiley and Sons, 1964).

Goldfeld, S. M., and R. E. Quandt, *Nonlinear Methods in Econometrics* (Amsterdam: North-Holland, 1972).

Gordon, Robert J., *Macroeconomics*, 4th ed. (Boston: Little-Brown, 1987).

Gordon, Robert J., and S. R. King, "The Output Cost of Disinflation in Traditional and Vector Autoregression Models," *Brookings Papers on Economic Activity*, Vol. 1, 1982, p. 205–241.

Granger, C. W. J., "Investigating Causal Relations by Econometric Models and Cross-Spectral Methods," *Econometrica*, Vol. 34, 1969, p. 424–438.

Granger, C. W. J., *Forecasting in Business and Economics* (New York: Academic Press, 1980).

Granger, C. W. J., and Paul Newbold, *Forecasting Economics Time Series*, 2nd ed. (New York, Academic Press, 1986), p. 15–28.

Gujarati, Damodar N., *Basic Econometrics*, 2nd ed. (New York: McGraw-Hill, 1988).

Hafer, R. W., "The Role of Fiscal Policy in the St. Louis Equation." *Review of the Federal Reserve Bank of St. Louis*, January 1982, p. 17–22.

Hendry, David, "Econometric Modelling: The 'Consumption Function' in Retrospect," *Scottish Journal of Political Economy*, November 1982, p. 193–219.

Hicks, John R., *Causality in Economics* (New York: Basic Books, 1979).

Hildreth, G., and J. Y. Lu, "Demand Relations with Autocorrelated Disturbances," *Technical Bulletin 276*, Michigan State University, November 1960.

Hoover, Kevin D., "The Logic of Causal Inference: Econometrics and the Conditional Analysis of Causation," presented at the History of Economics Society Meeting, 1989.

Hosmer, David W., and Stanley Lemeshow, *Applied Logistic Regression* (New York: John Wiley and Sons, 1989).

Humphrey, Thomas M., *A History of the Phillips Curve*, Federal Reserve Bank of Richmond, October 1986.

Jevons, William S., *The Theory of Political Economy*, 5th ed. (New York: A. M. Kelley, 1965).

Johnston, Jack, *Econometric Methods* (New York: McGraw-Hill, 1963, 1984).

Judge, George G., et al., *The Theory and Practice of Econometrics*, 2nd ed. (New York: John Wiley and Sons, 1980).

Kelejian, Harry H., and Wallace E. Oates, *Introduction to Econometrics* (New York: Harper & Row, 1989).

Kinal, Terrence, and Jonathan Ratner, "A VAR Forecasting Model of a Regional Economy: Its Construction and Comparative Accuracy," *International Regional Science Review*, Vol. 10, No. 2, 1986, p. 113–126.

Kmenta, Jan, *Elements of Econometrics* (New York: Macmillan, 1986).

Koyck, L. M., *Distributed Lags and Investment Analysis* (Amsterdam: North-Holland, 1954).

Leamer, Edward E., "Let's Take the 'Con' Out of Econometrics," *American Economic Review*, March 1973, p. 31–43.

Leamer, Edward E., "Vector Autoregressions for Causal Influence," in Karl Brunner and Alan Meltzer, Eds., *Understanding Monetary Regimes* (supplement to the *Journal of Monetary Economics*), 1985, p. 255–304.

Lucas, Robert E., and Thomas J. Sargent, "After Keynesian Economics, *Quarterly Review*, Federal Reserve Bank of Minnesota, Summer 1979, p. 1–7.

Maddala, G. S., *Introduction to Econometrics* (New York: Macmillan, 1988).

McFadden, Daniel, "Conditional Logit Analysis of Qualitative Choice Behavior," in P. Zarembka, Ed., *Frontiers in Econometrics* (New York: Academic Press, 1974), p. 105–142.

Moore, Basil, "The Endogenous Money Stock," *Journal of Post Keynesian Economics*, Vol. II, No. 1, Fall 1979, p. 49–70.

Park, R. E., "Estimation with Heteroscedastic Error Terms," *Econometrica*, Vol. 34, No. 4, October 1966, p. 888.

Peach, James T., and James L. Webb, "Randomly Specified Macroeconomic Models: Some Implications for Model Selection," *Journal of Economic Issues*, Vol. XVII, No. 3, September 1983, p. 697–720.

Phillips, A. W., "The Relation Between Unemployment and the Rate of Change of Money Wages in the United Kingdom, 1861–1957," *Economica*, November 1958, p. 283–299.

Pindyck, Robert S., and Daniel L. Rubenfeld, *Econometric Models and Economic Forecasts*, 2nd ed., (New York: McGraw-Hill, 1981).

Ramsey, James B., "Classical Model Selection through Specification Error Tests," in P. Zarembka, Ed., *Frontiers in Econometrics* (New York: Academic Press, 1974), p. 13–47.

Roth, Alvin E., "Laboratory Experimentation in Economics," *Economic Journal*, Vol. 98, No. 393, December 1988, p. 975–1031.

Samuelson, Paul, *Foundations of Economic Analysis* Cambridge, Mass.: Harvard University Press, 1947).

Simon, Herbert, "Causality and Econometrics," in Karl Brunner and Alan Meltzer, Eds., *Three Aspects of Policy and Policymaking: Knowledge, Data, and Institutions*, Carnegie-Rochester Conference Series on Public Policy (a supplementary series to the *Journal of Monetary Economics*), Vol. 10 (Amsterdam: North-Holland, 1979).

Sims, Christopher, "Money, Income, and Causality," *American Economic Review*, September 1972, p. 540–552.

Sims, Christopher, "Macroeconomics and Reality," *Econometrica*, Vol. 48, No. 1, January 1980, p. 1–48.

Slemrod, Joel, "Post-War Capital Accumulation and the Threat of Nuclear War," *NBER Working Paper 887*, May 1982.

Spanos, Aris, *Statistical Foundations of Econometric Modelling* (Cambridge, U.K.: Cambridge University Press, 1986).

Spector, L., and M. Mazzeo, "Probit Analysis and Economic Instruction," *Journal of Economic Education*, Vol. 11, 1980, p. 37–44.

Studenmund, A. H., and Henry J. Cassidy, *Using Econometrics* (Boston: Little-Brown, 1987).

Theil, Henry, "On the Relationships Involving Qualitative Variables," *American Journal of Sociology*, Vol. 76, July 1970, p. 103–154.

Train, Kenneth, *Qualitative Choice Analysis: Theory, Econometrics, and an Application to Automobile Demand* (Cambridge, Mass.: MIT Press, 1986).

Valentine, Lloyd, *Business Cycles and Forecasting*, 7th ed. (Cincinnati, Ohio: Southwestern, 1987).

Vandale, Walter, *Applied Time Series and Box-Jenkins Models* (New York: Academic Press, 1983).

Webb, Roy H., "Vector Autoregressions as a Tool for Forecast Evaluation," *Economic Review*, Federal Reserve Bank of Richmond, Vol. 70, No. 1, January/February 1984, p. 3–11.

Zellner, Arnold, "Causality and Econometrics," in *Basic Issues in Econometrics* (Chicago: The University of Chicago Press, 1984, 1987), p. 36–37.

Software

Except where noted, all of the results reported in the text were done by the author on a Macintosh, primarily an SE/30 with 8 Mbytes of memory and an 80-Mbyte hard drive. Several programs were used. Because it is fast and easy to edit output, *Fastat*, v. 1.1, was used for most of the regression analysis. Much of the data came from the Macintosh version of Citibase, available from VAR Econometrics. Often the data were exported to *StatView 512+*, v. 1.2, and then exported to *Fastat*. Many of the diagrams sent to the artist were done in *StatView* as well. *Fastat* can compute ACFs and PACFs, but it is incapable of performing maximum likelihood estimation, and thus could not be used to estimate ARIMA models. The Macintosh version of *Minitab* was not out when the writing began, so the MS-DOS version of *Minitab*, v. 7.0, run under *SoftPC*, v. 1.3, on the Macintosh, *Systat*, v. 3.2, and *RATS*, v. 3.1, were all used in Chapter 9. The logit module of *Systat, LOGIT*, v. 1.0, was used in Chapter 10.

Finally, the manuscript for the text, instructor's manual, and study guide were done on a Macintosh as well. The main word processing program was *WriteNow*, v. 2.2. *WriteNow* is easy to use and extremely fast—something that was important given that the typical chapter weighted in at nearly 300k with all of the equations and PICT drawings. Drawings were done in *SuperPaint*, v. 2.0, with some final editing in *DeskDraw*, v. 1.3. The equations in the text and study guide were set with *Expressionist*, v. 2.07r.

Anderson, D. John, et al., *WriteNow for the Macintosh* (Mountain View, Calif.: T/Maker, 1988).

Bonadio, Allan, *Expressionist: The Personal Mathematical Equation Editor* (San Francisco, Calif.: Allan Bonadio Associates, 1988).

Bjerknes, Mark, and Leland Wilkerson, *Fastat, Fast Statistics for the Macintosh* (Evanston, Ill.: SYSTAT, 1989).

Doan, Thomas A., *MacRATS (Regression Analysis of Time Series)* (Evanston, Ill.: VAR Econometrics, 1988).

Gagnon, Jim, and Daniel S. Feldman, *StatView 512+, the Professional, Graphic, Statistics Utility* (Calabasas, Calif.: Brainpower, 1986).

Gay, Jonathan, et al., *SuperPaint. v. 2.0* (San Diego, Calif.: Silicon Beach Software, 1988).

Insignia Solutions, *SoftPC for the Macintosh* (Sunnyvale, Calif.: Insignia Solutions, 1988).

Krenek, Mark, *DeskDraw* (Tucson, Ariz.: Zedcor, 1988).

Ryan, Barbara F., Brian L. Joiner, and Thomas A. Ryan, *Minitab* (State College, Pa: Minitab, 1989).

Steinberg, Dan, *LOGIT: A Supplementary Module for SYSTAT.* (Evanston, Ill.: Systat, 1985).

Wilkerson, Leland, *SYSTAT, the System for Statistics* (Evanston, Ill.: SYSTAT, 1988).

INDEX